The Masculine Self
Third Edition

The Masculine Self

Third Edition

Christopher T. Kilmartin
The University of Mary Washington

2007
SLOAN PUBLISHING
Cornwall-on-Hudson, NY 12520

Library of Congress Control Number: 2006923377

Kilmartin, Christopher T.
  The Masculine Self / Christopher T. Kilmartin.
    p.   cm.
  Includes bibliographic references and index.
  ISBN 1-59738-005-9

Cover designer: Amy Rosen
Cover image: © Nathan Ben / Corbis

Printed in Canada
10 9 8 7 6 5 4 3 2 1

ISBN 1-59738-005-9

To my dad and my brother

Table of Contents

Preface

I have been interested in Men's Studies for nearly my entire professional career. It has been gratifying to see a burgeoning literature in this area of study produced over the last quarter century. The field has come of age and attracted impressive scholars from a wide variety of disciplines. It seems to me that, over the years, it has become increasingly important to introduce students to gender concepts. I would argue that, similar to helping students learn computer skills, helping students to come to an awareness of gender is only gong to become more important as time goes on and the world changes at a fast pace.

I have three broad objectives for this text, and these goals are reflected in the three parts of the book. First, I want to introduce the reader to contemporary concepts of gender and masculinity. Only recently have men begun to understand the difference between being male and being a "generic human being." As you shall see, the distinction is an important one.

Second, I want to bring male gender theory into the mainstream of psychology. I undertake this task in Chapters 3 through 7 by applying concepts of masculinity to major theoretical schools of thought. These chapters contribute perspectives on masculine development against the backgrounds provided by great thinkers such as Freud, Jung, Bem, Maccoby, Rogers, Lerner, Pleck, and O'Neil, to name only a few. You may disagree with some of their positions, but you will find the application of their theories to masculinity stimulating and enlightening. Only recently has social science begun to seriously consider the effects of age, race, sexual identities, and ethnicity on behavior, and Chapters 5 and 6 place masculinities into the context of culture and history.

Third, I want to organize and summarize the available research on men and masculinity. I do so by identifying themes or issues common to many men (emotion, health, work, sexuality, violence, relationships, mental health, and social change), and then reviewing the available scholarship in each area—a body of literature that is constantly changing and growing. This book is a snapshot in time—a map of a territory that continues to evolve.

As I wrote, I tried to keep in mind that my primary aim is to teach. This book is intended to introduce the student to the theoretical and scientific study of men without losing sight of the fact that we are talking about real human beings. I use examples, whenever possible, to move a concept from the abstract into the real world. I especially enjoyed writing the many box features that give the book a "face" and provide illustrations of various concepts in some depth. You may find that these boxes can serve as food for thought—"appetizers" to introduce you to a topic, or "desserts," enjoyable finishing touches. In many cases, I also included some questions for critical thinking in these features. You may find them useful for starting discussions, either in the classroom or in less formal settings.

I have been writing this edition of *The Masculine Self* ever since I finished the manuscript for the second edition in 1999. As new data and ideas emerged, I found myself sometimes reconsidering and even disagreeing with aspects of the first two editions, found many things that would further enhance the text, collecting feedback from colleagues and students, and continued to think critically about the book. I wished for another chance to correct mistakes, change emphases, and incorporate current events and new findings that relate to the topic at hand. With this new edition of *The Masculine Self*, I get my wish, and it is exciting to have the opportunity to add what I have learned in these past few years and bring it to the reader.

During the twelve years since the first edition of this work, there has been an explosion of publishing in the field of men's studies, and keeping up with all of the new material in my discipline, psychology, has been a daunting task. As if that were not enough, I have also come to a much greater awareness and appreciation of the contributions of history, sociology, anthropology, cultural studies, theatre, and other disciplines, each with its own impressive literature, to the understanding of men's issues. Each edition uses much broader strokes than the previous, as I continue to develop and incorporate a multi-disciplinary perspective.

This third edition of *The Masculine Self* is another attempt to cover the territory of men's studies in a comprehensive way. I have summarized and synthesized the latest research, integrating new information with the classic work that remains relevant to the topics under discussion. At the same time, I have not forgotten that we are telling stories about people. In fact, my work as a playwright (of the solo performance theatrical works *Crimes Against Nature* and *Guy Fi: The Fictions that Rule Men's Lives*) has highlighted the importance of story telling as a mode of understanding. Therefore, I have tried to integrate data and narrative.

I am grateful to a number of people who have helped in the formulation and realization of this work. Bill Webber did a wonderful job of overseeing the entire process of editing and production for Sloan Publishing. Colleagues such as Alan Berkowitz, Will Courtenay, Jim Mahalik, Don McCreary, Julie Allison, Jim O'Neil, Andrew Smiler, Michael Addis, Fred Rabinowitz, and all of the scholars in the Society for the Psychological Study of Men and Masculinity have helped me to sort out difficult theoretical and conceptual issues. I am especially indebted to my life partner, Dr. Allyson Poska, not only for her unwavering personal support, but also for the intellectual gifts she has shared with me as an impressive historian, most notably a broad awareness of the value of anthropology, sociology, history, and economics in the understanding of gender in its many contexts. Everyone should be so fortunate to have a partner that makes one smarter.

Of course, I am certain that I will now wish for a fourth chance to continue my exploration of this fascinating field in the false hope that I will eventually say all there is to say. But every area of study is a moving target, and so these snapshots-in-time are all that scholars can bring. I hope that you will find half the interest and enjoyment in this third freeze frame that I have found in producing it.

C. K.

1

Introduction

The biological categorization of sex is perhaps the most basic division among human beings and often the first characteristic we notice about others. There is evidence to suggest that even very young children are able to make this distinction (Maccoby, 1998), and a profound distinction it is. Every culture in the world prescribes norms for behavior that are assigned on the basis of sex. Obviously, reproductive roles (childbirth, impregnation, and lactation) are bound in biology, but the socially perceived division of behavior based on sex goes far beyond reproduction into areas of work, child care, and social convention. Cultures even ascribe personality characteristics such as aggressiveness or nurturance disproportionately to one sex or the other. Many people believe that males and females should and do wear different colors, drink different drinks, enjoy different activities, and desire different things in relationships.

Developmental psychology literature abounds with studies of differences in the socialization of males and females as well as speculations about the effects of these differences on the personalities of adult men and women (Lytton & Romney, 1991). Biological psychologists search for differences in brain structure and hormone levels and attempt to describe the influences of these differences on behavior. Social psychologists seek to specify the interpersonal conditions that give rise to gendered actions. And, of course, other social scientists, including sociologists, historians, anthropologists, linguists, economists, and philosophers, have long been interested in the study of male and female.

Beginning around the 1960s, modern feminist writers began to make strong critiques of mainstream social science theory and research methods. New ideas about female development and functioning gave rise to a new field, Women's Studies. Theorists and researchers in this area urged people to take seriously the idea that a person's sex and gender have important effects on his or her behavior and on the ways that others react to him or her. If we want to understand human behavior in all of its complexity, we would do well to take these effects into consideration when we construct our theories and research designs. Thus, Women's Studies created a stronger awareness of people as *gendered beings*.

In the early 1970s, scholars expanded this awareness into a new area, Men's Studies. They began to ask the question, "If the experience of being female has a profound effect on a woman's behavior and on others' reactions to her, does the experience of being male have similarly powerful implications for men?" The answer would seem to be an emphatic "yes."

The idea that men need their own area of intellectual inquiry was (and sometimes still is) greeted with skepticism. As a psychologist, I have frequently heard the argument that *all* Psychology is the Psychology of Men because mainstream psychological theory was constructed largely by males. In fact, many research studies were undertaken using only male participants, as if male behaviors generalized to the entire human race. It was said that, in psychology experiments, "even the rat was male." Therefore, the argument against the existence of such a field is that, because scholars have studied males as the *normative referent* for behavior, we do not need to identify a new area of inquiry to investigate male behavior and experience.

Joseph Pleck (1988) made a compelling counterargument in favor of distinguishing the study of men as a normative referent from the study of men from a *gender-aware perspective*. The literature is replete with models of men as "generic human beings," but (prior to the emergence of Men's Studies) it was difficult to find reference to men as *gendered beings*. Men are powerfully affected by the experiences of growing up male, having people respond to them as males, expecting and having others expect certain behaviors based on "masculine gender roles," and having feelings about their masculinities.

Brod (1987b) pointed out that traditional scholarship is "about men only by virtue of not being about women" (p. 264). Men's Studies move masculinity from the periphery of inquiry into its center. The subject of investigation is not, as in most traditional scholarship, about men as historical, political, and cultural actors, but rather about men *as men*.

There exists a good deal of confusion about Men's Studies. When I tell people that I am a psychologist specializing in the study of "Men's Issues," the typical reactions are:

1. "Why do we need to look at men's issues? Men have all the power and get to do whatever they want."

2. "Men are becoming a bunch of complainers who can't deal with women being strong."

3. "It's surprising that a psychologist would be antiwoman or antifeminist."

4. "What are 'men's issues'? I didn't know men had any issues."

These reactions come from both men and women, and they reveal misunderstandings about, and biases against, the study of men from a gender-aware perspective. I would respond to these reactions with the following:

1. Although it is true that men-as-a-group have enormous social power, and that many men often get to do what they want, there are also many men who feel quite power-

less and have been damaged by harsh masculine socialization. By virtue of their greater social power, men are also in a unique position to help shift this power into better balance. Men need an understanding of the effects of masculine privilege to do so, and only a gender-aware perspective can bring this understanding.

2. It is true that many men have trouble dealing with strong women, having been socialized to believe that men should be powerful and dominant. As a result, they may experience strong women as threats to masculinity. This is an issue that men must address, because women *are* powerful, and men must learn to accept and deal with them in constructive ways. Men's Studies can enlighten us to various aspects of relationships between the sexes and contribute to agendas for alliances between the sexes.

3. Although there are some Men's Studies scholars and "Men's Movement" leaders who might be considered antiwomen or antifeminist, there are others who can be characterized as just the opposite. The purpose of studying men from a gender aware perspective is not to further oppress women, but to address quality of life issues for men and women. Men's issues are often very compatible with women's issues. For instance, if we can understand the nature of the threat that many men feel when confronted with the power of women, we can perhaps take steps to decrease or prevent that threat. As a result, men would become both more comfortable with themselves *and* more respectful of women, which in turn would help to improve their relationships with women.

4 What are "men's issues?" Consider the following:
   - Most males are encouraged from an early age to suppress their feelings. (Levant, 1998; Pollack, 1998) Emotional constriction may lead to a variety of psychological, physical, and social problems.
   - Many men have problems establishing and maintaining intimacy in relationships (Lynch & Kilmartin, 1999). Many experts regard intimacy as a basic human need.
   - Men have more psychological difficulties than women adjusting to divorce and separation (Siegel & Kuykendall, 1990). It is doubtful that men are as emotionally independent as the social image of masculinity would have us believe.
   - Men commit most acts of violence (U.S. Department of Justice, 2003).
   - Males comprise the vast majority of incarcerated (U.S. Department of Justice, 2004) and homeless (Gugliotta, 1994) people.
   - The average lifespan of a man is significantly shorter than a woman's average lifespan (Arias, 2005).
   - Many men seem to have strong feelings of being disappointed with their fathers (Kupers, 1993).
   - The general quality of men's relationships with others is often impoverished (Bergman, 1995).
   - Definitions of masculinity are changing (Levant & Pollack, 1995).

This is a partial list. As you read on, you will come across many more men's issues. It should be clear from this list that all is not well with men. While there are many positive facets to traditional masculinity, there are also many destructive ones, both for individual men and for others around them.

DESCRIBING MASCULINITIES

"Snips and snails and puppy dog tails." This is the first description of masculinity I remember hearing as a child, the answer to the question, "What are little boys made of?" And what are little girls made of? "Sugar and spice and everything nice." These sayings are supposed to describe personality differences between the sexes. It is not too difficult to interpret the statement about girls. Sugar and spice are pleasant and palatable. A "sweet" person is someone who can evoke positive responses from others, someone who cares about people. The statement about boys is more cryptic, but it seems to create images of being dirty, scattered, and hyperactive (Puppy dog tails don't remain still for very long.).

From the earliest days of childhood, cultures bombard males with messages about what it means to be masculine. These messages serve to communicate expectations for their behavior. Some messages, like the one described above, are verbal. Others are more subtle, such as a parent's communication of silent approval for behaviors like refusing to cry when one is sad or hurt, or selecting toys that they consider appropriate for boys. Because a good deal of behavior is learned through imitation, boys receive many of these messages through merely observing the behaviors of men in their families, neighborhoods, and in the media.

These messages have powerful effects on boys, who often learn to act in culturally defined "masculine" ways and to avoid behaviors that are considered "feminine." The social settings in which adult men find themselves tend to reinforce these standards. For example, a man who displays aggression at a business meeting might gain the approval of his colleagues, whereas a woman might experience disapproval for exactly the same behavior.

What is masculinity? How does one define it? We see romanticized views of masculinity in Boxes 1.1 and 1.2. The stereotypical "Real Man" can be described as having certain personality traits:

strong   tough
independent   aggressive
achieving   unemotional
hardworking   physical
dominant   competitive
heterosexual   forceful

We could also describe him in terms of activities or behaviors, that is, what a man *does*:

earns money
initiates sex
solves problems

gets the job done
takes control
takes action
enjoys "masculine" activities (e.g., hunting, sports, drinking)
takes physical risks
supports his family financially

We can describe him in terms of prohibited activities, i.e., what a man *does not do* (see Box 1.1):

cry
express feelings other than anger
perform "women's work" (e.g., washing dishes, changing diapers)
back down from a confrontation
get emotionally close to other men
ask for help
behave in "feminine" ways

We can describe him in terms of stereotypical *roles*:

athlete
professional
working man
father
husband
buddy
playboy
leader

What do these varying definitions have in common? Robert Brannon's classic (1985) essay described four major themes of traditional masculinity in the United States:

1. Antifemininity: Males are encouraged from an early age to avoid behaviors, interests, and personality traits that are considered "feminine." Among these are expression of feeling, emotional vulnerability, sexual feelings for other men, and feminine professions (e.g., elementary school teacher, nurse, secretary). Brannon labeled this masculine norm *"No Sissy Stuff."*

2. Status and Achievement: Men gain status by being successful in all that they do, especially in sports, work, and heterosexual "conquest." Powerful men earn the respect and admiration of others. Brannon called this dimension *"The Big Wheel."*

3. Inexpressiveness and Independence: Men are expected to maintain emotional composure and self control even in the most difficult of situations, to solve problems without help, to keep their feelings to themselves, and to disdain any display of weakness. This dimension is *"The Sturdy Oak"* or *"The Male Machine."*

Box 1.1: A Negative Description of Masculinity

The following is a definition of "gentleman" from an old version of the handbook of the Virginia Military Institute:

Without a strict observance of the fundamental code of honor, no man, no matter how 'polished' can be considered a gentleman. The honor of a gentleman demands the inviolability of his word and the incorruptibility of his principles. He is the descendant of the knight, the crusader, he is the defender of the defenseless and the champion of justice—or he is not a gentleman.

A gentleman *does not* discuss his family affairs in public or with acquaintances.

Does not speak more than casually about his wife or girlfriend.

Does not go to a lady's house if he is affected by alcohol. He is temperate in the use of alcohol.

Does not lose his temper nor exhibit anger, fear, hate, embarrassment, ardor, or hilarity in public.

Does not hail a lady from a club window.

Never discusses the merits or demerits of a lady.

Does not borrow money from a friend, except in dire need. Money borrowed is a debt of honor and must be repaid as promptly as possible. Debts incurred by a deceased parent, brother, sister, or grown child are assumed by honorable men as a debt of honor.

Does not display his wealth, money, or possessions.

Does not put his manners on and off, whether in the club or in a ballroom. He treats people with courtesy, no matter what their social positions may be.

Does not slap strangers on the back nor so much as lay a finger on a lady.

Does not 'lick the boots of those above him' nor 'kick the face of those below him on the social ladder.'

Does not take advantage of another's helplessness or ignorance and assumes that no gentleman will take advantage of him.

A gentleman respects the reserves of others but demands that others respect those which are his.

A gentleman *can* become what he wills to be...

Notice that the positive parts of the description (what gentlemen *are* and what they *do*) are rather vague: defender of the defenseless, champion of justice, etc. These are high ideals that do not necessarily transfer easily into a prescription for any specific behavior. When the description turns to negative guidelines (what gentlemen *do not do*), however, there are very specific behaviors stated. You might notice the prohibitions against acknowledging a connection to another person ("never speaks more than casually about his wife or girlfriend"), expressing emotion ("does not exhibit fear, hate, ardor..."), and being vulnerable or in need of help ("does not borrow money from a friend..."). The last line reflects the masculine value on self-determination.

4. Adventurousness and Aggressiveness: Masculinity is characterized by a willingness to take physical risks and become violent if necessary. Brannon called this masculine norm *"Give 'Em Hell."*

Many theorists (Chodorow, 1978; O'Neil, 1981; Brannon, 1985; Hartley, 1959) consider *antifemininity* the central organizing principle from which all other masculine social demands derive. In other words, social expectations devalue and punish the open display of vulnerable emotions, orientations toward relationships, and physical self-protection for men because these characteristics are culturally defined as feminine. There is ample evidence that, beginning early in childhood, adults and peers punish males for acting in feminine ways (termed *cross-gender* or *out-role* behavior) more harshly than females who violate social gender expectations (Lytton & Romney, 1991; McCreary, 1994). Thus, antifemininity acts as a powerful enforcer of masculine gender behavior. For example, in mainstream U.S. culture, perhaps the worst insult for a boy is to suggest that he throws, looks, or acts like a girl. *Homophobia*—the hostility, fear, and intolerance of sexual attraction or behavior between persons of the same sex—is a construct closely related to antifemininity (I often refer to homophobia as "antifemininity's vicious little brother."). For males, acting like a stereotypical female is likely to result in social disapproval, and few things are socially defined as more feminine than loving or being sexually attracted to a man. Males who act in socially defined feminine ways are often suspected of being gay (McCreary, 1994; Blumenfeld, 1992). The term "sissy" can refer to either femininity or homosexuality, which are closely linked in many people's minds. The threats of being considered homosexual or feminine also act as a powerful enforcer of gender norms for males, who are much more likely than females to hold negative attitudes toward gay men and lesbians (Herek, 1991, 1994; Shea, 1995). Male peer groups use antifemininity and homophobia to police the boundaries of acceptable behavior (Plummer, 2001). If a boy or man behaves in ways associated with women or gay men, others may ridicule, shame, or even physically attack him. Not surprisingly, homophobic attitudes are strongly related to traditional gender role ideologies (Kerns & Fine, 1994).

There are variations in the cultural definitions and stereotypes of masculinity (see Chapter 6), which lead many theorists to describe masculine role expectations using the plural *masculinities* (Brod, 1987a; Connell, 2005; Harris, 1995, and others). For example, African-American men are considered more emotionally expressive than White American men (Basow, 1992). Jewish men are encouraged to incorporate a love of knowledge into their conception of masculinity, in contrast with some other groups of men (Brod, 1987a). Tahitian men do not tend to display aggressiveness or other traits that people from most other cultures would consider masculine; in fact they are hard to differentiate from Tahitian women in their average behavior (Gilmore, 1990). At the same time, there is a good deal of cross-cultural similarity in gender roles (see Adler, 1993). Williams and Best (1990) found that men were described as forceful, active, and strong across a variety of cultures.

Most cultures encourage men to be unemotional, task and achievement oriented, aggressive, fearless, and status seeking. Male gender roles are powerful influences on behavior partly because men who are seen as "masculine" receive many social rewards. For

Box 1.2: Thinking About Masculinity

Below is Rudyard Kipling's classic poem, "If-", which reflects a romanticized view of masculinity. As you read the poem, try to answer the following questions:

1. What kinds of masculine traits is Kipling describing?

2. Which of these traits are positive, negative, or neutral? Why?

3. Are there differences in what is judged to be positive or negative for the *individual* compared with *society*?

4. In what ways is modern masculinity different or similar to Kipling's description, which Gilmore (1990) refers to as "iffy" masculinity)?

If-
If you can keep your head when all about you
    Are losing theirs and blaming it on you,
If you can trust yourself when all men doubt you,
    But make allowance for their doubting too;
If you can wait and not be tired by waiting,
    Or being lied about, don't deal in lies,
Or being hated, don't give way to hating,
    And yet don't look too good, nor talk too wise:
If you can dream - and not make dreams your master;
    If you can think - and not make thoughts your aim;

Source: *Rudyard Kipling's Verse: Definitive Edition*. Garden City, NY: Doubleday.

If you can meet with Triumph and Disaster
    And treat those two imposters just the same;
If you can bear to hear the truth you've spoken
    Twisted by knaves to make a trap for fools,
Or watch the things you gave your life to, broken,
    And stoop and build 'em up with worn-out tools;
If you can make one heap of all your winnings
    And risk it on one turn of pitch-and-toss,
And lose, and start again at your beginnings
    And never breathe a word about your loss;
If you can force your heart and nerve and sinew
    To serve your turn long after they are gone,
And so hold on when there is nothing in you
    Except the Will which says to them: "Hold on!"
If you can talk with crowds and keep your virtue,
    Or walk with Kings - nor lose the common touch,
If neither foes nor loving friends can hurt you,
    If all men count with you, but none too much;
If you can fill the unforgiving minute
    With sixty seconds' worth of distance run,
Yours is the Earth and everything that's in it,
    And— which is more— you'll be a Man, my son!

instance, financially successful men gain the admiration of others and are seen as more sexually desirable than other men. As actress Zsa Zsa Gabor (quoted in James, 1984) said, "No rich man is ugly." Competitive and inexpressive men are seen as good candidates for promotion in many work environments. The man who shows a willingness to be "one of the boys" may enjoy the approval of others and have a large circle of supportive acquaintances.

On the other hand, men who are seen as "unmasculine" may experience a good deal of social and even physical punishment. Gay men are subject to abusive comments, stigmatization, and sometimes unprovoked violence. Men who are willing to talk about personal problems or admit weakness are judged to be unhealthy (Lewis & McCarthy, 1988). Male politicians who display out-role behaviors may damage their chances for election (Tobin, 1991).

In general, men who overemphasize the negative aspects of traditional masculinity risk losing their self-esteem, health, freedom, connectedness with others, and even their lives. Men commit suicide four times more often than women (Arias, 2005). There are nearly nine times more men in U. S. prisons than women (U.S. Department of Justice, 2004), and males comprise nearly 80% of the U.S. homeless population (Gugliotta, 1994).

STEREOTYPES AND REALITY

It is important to note that the above descriptions are stereotypes, and that there is a great deal of variation in the actual behaviors of individual men. I define gender as *a social pressure to behave and experience the self in ways that the culture considers appropriate for one's sex*. And so gender is, in a critical sense, "in the air." It is important to keep in mind that individual responses to gender pressure are highly variable. In defiance of masculine norms, some men are emotional, gentle, and interpersonally connected, just as some women fit masculine stereotypes. Many people possess characteristics of both masculine and feminine stereotypes (such people are termed *androgynous*). Thus, it is possible to be both gentle and strong, both independent and connected, and in parenting, both strict and nurturing.

All men do not display or even aspire to stereotypical masculinity. In fact, there is a great deal of variation in men's endorsements of masculine ideologies (Thompson & Pleck, 1995). Therefore, the description above does not apply to some unchangeable essence that all individual men share, but rather to the social influence that nearly all males experience. Although some men make masculine striving a major goal in their lives (these men are often referred to as *macho*), others reject masculine expectations, and most men find some middle ground between masculine conformity and individual personality expression. And, the level of stereotypical masculinity often varies even within an individual as a function of changes in his age, relationships, and social settings. For example, in my teaching or consultations, I often ask heterosexual women, "Are there ways in which your husband or boyfriend behaves *when he is just with you* that might surprise some of his buddies?" Most women respond with a resounding "yes," citing among other things, laughter, dancing, emotional tenderness, and playfulness. Thus, gender is not a once-and-forever, static entity, even for an individual person.

BEWARE THE "TURKEY THEORY"

When I was a graduate student at Virginia Commonwealth University, one of the members of the faculty was Dr. John P. Hill, a remarkable scholar and researcher who had a profound effect on my thinking about gender. At that time, I mainly concentrated on the gender *socialization* of males, that is, the ways in which boys are raised that lead to certain characteristics and behaviors when they become adult men. Dr. Hill pointed out to me that, although childhood socialization undoubtedly has a powerful effect on adults' behavior, an exclusive emphasis on these forces reflects an acceptance of the "turkey theory."

The "turkey theory" is the belief that the adult behavioral process is parallel to the preparation of a Thanksgiving turkey. As Dr. Hill explained, the socialization emphasis assumes that we get "stuffed" with characteristics when we are young, and then, as adults, we come out of the "oven" — a completed "turkey," tasting (behaving) on the basis of what we have been "stuffed" with.

His point was that, although the childhood "stuffing" undoubtedly shapes people's habits and senses of self, people respond to much more than what they learned as children. They are also strongly influenced by social forces that occur in the moment. Robert Brannon (1985) makes this point powerfully when he asks what the typical reaction would be if one man were to say to another, "Mike, I've been so upset since we had that argument. I could hardly sleep last night. Are you *sure* you're really not mad at me?" (p. 307). As defined by mainstream contemporary U.S. culture, this language is decidedly "feminine," and men who engage in this kind of behavior are often ostracized, attacked, or neglected by others. Therefore they tend to avoid such behaviors, not necessarily because their boyhood experiences have led them to be unconnected to others, but because the social pressure of the moment threatens these behaviors with negative social consequences. I ask young, stereotypically heterosexual men what would happen if, in a group of their friends, they initiated a conversation about how much they loved their girlfriends and how close they feel to them. Most respond that, at best, the introduction would meet with uncomfortable silence. At worst, it would meet with ridicule and shame.

Burn (1996) reviews a number of studies indicating that people behave more gender-stereotypically in public than in private, suggesting that they are, at least partially, responding to the perceived gender pressure of the social setting and not merely to internal forces. To carry the above examples further, I often ask audiences, "Is it possible that I *was* so upset about my conversation with Mike that I couldn't sleep?" Is it possible that these men *do* love their girlfriends and feel close to them?" Nearly everyone acknowledges that these are quite possible, perhaps even likely.

Therefore, we should be careful not to take behaviors, even stereotypical ones, at face value. Seeing a group of men behaving in similar ways, we are tempted to think that all men are alike. But within the group, there might be enormous variations in internal experiences such as the level of comfort with the behavior. To add a nongendered example, I often ask, "Have you ever laughed at a joke you didn't think was funny?" Nearly everyone acknowledges that he or she has. If I watched you laugh at the joke, I would think that you considered it funny unless you told me that your internal reaction was different from your external behavior. It is not only childhood socialization that keeps many boys and men behaving within narrow gender roles, it is also *ongoing* forces within their social environments.

Avoiding the "turkey theory" is important because, although we cannot change the events that adult men experienced as boys, we can change the social environments that support the stereotypical masculine behaviors that are destructive. A solid understanding of the interactions between masculine socialization and interpersonal pressure can lead to changes in the negative aspects of masculinity.

CONSEQUENCES OF MASCULINE GENDER ROLES

Cultural norms of masculinity are enforced and maintained through expectations, rewards, and social sanctions. Adhering to traditional masculine gender roles has positive and negative, long- and short-term effects on individual men and on societies.

Benefits

The man who is able to live up to gender role demands has the opportunity to reap many rewards. Chief among these are money, status, and privilege. Men who are "winners" are often able to live in the lap of luxury, enjoy the admiration of others, and do basically what they want to do. The traditional man bases his self-esteem in work, wealth, and achievement. Men who acquire large amounts of these things may feel quite good about themselves, and they are often viewed as desirable lovers, friends, and associates. As Farrell (1991) put it, financially successful men are comparable to beautiful women; they have "centerfold" status.

Work, wealth, and achievement are often very quantifiable. It is much easier for one to evaluate success by how much money one has made rather than, for example, by how good a parent one has been. The latter (which has been traditionally defined as "women's work") is a more difficult judgment because it is more qualitative. Thus, a traditional man can operate in somewhat of a closed system, with his worth as a person measured by a convenient and relatively unambiguous "yardstick." Such a man can be singular in his purpose and rarely has to deal with mixed feelings.

The traditional man is a "breadwinner," supporting his family financially by working hard. Whether or not he is a "big wheel," a man can take a great deal of pride in fulfilling this role. Working hard every day so that your family can have food, shelter, and other resources is a very loving thing to do. The contribution of the provider role to family is one of the most positive aspects of traditional masculinity. Men have also usually participated in other aspects of family life like physical work in and around the house, money management, protecting others, and everyday problem solving. Certain aspects of masculinity are well suited to these important activities.

The masculine achievement and problem-solving orientation has resulted in a great many positive contributions to society and the world. Men's achievements in engineering, literature, and the sciences, for example, should not be overlooked, nor should the contributions of working men who produce goods, build houses, and otherwise labor for the greater good. This is not to deny that women have made significant contributions (a fact which has historically been downplayed), but only to note that the traditional masculine ethic of "getting the job done" has had enormous positive implications for the quality of life and is one aspect of gender that deserves to be celebrated.

Costs

It is clear that being a so-called "real man" has many tangible rewards. However, there has also been a price to pay for some of traditional masculinity, both for society and for individual men. Living up to masculine gender demands is largely an impossible task that often exacts a heavy toll.

The expectations that men compete, achieve, be "on top," and always want more have left many men feeling driven, empty, disillusioned, and angry. No matter how talented and hard working one is, winning every time is impossible. There is always another man who has more money, higher status, a more attractive partner, or a bigger house. The traditional man can never get enough, and thus he can never really enjoy what he has. He must constantly work harder and faster. Such a lifestyle sometimes results in stress-related physical and psychological symptoms.

To strip a man of his emotional life is to take away one of the most basic aspects of human existence. The experience of positive emotion would seem to be profoundly important. When a man is made into a machine, he loses his humanity and is rendered less capable of having empathic, caring, intimate relationships with other people. Emotional intimacy requires one to share power, be vulnerable, and disclose oneself. Traditional masculine socialization is antithetical to these behaviors (Jourard, 1971). The damage that destructive masculinity does to the quality of connectedness to other people and to feelings about the self can hardly be overestimated. Many men feel alienated from their partners, children, and other men, and these feelings are often mutual.

The most serious result of being interpersonally unconnected to others is its influence on men's willingness to do physical and psychological harm to others. It is easier to hurt people when one can not identify or empathize with them. Many men are socialized away from understanding their own feelings or those of others, and this enables them to be cruel toward anyone who gets in their way. The disproportionate participation of men in war, violence, damage to the Earth, the oppression of marginalized social groups, and psychological cruelty must (at least partly) be laid at the doorstep of traditional masculinity.

CONTEXTS FOR THE STUDY OF MASCULINITY

Gender roles are embedded within several important historical, social, political, economic, and ideological contexts. Therefore, one can only achieve a thorough understanding of men and masculinity by learning about these various frames of reference. By way of introduction to these important issues, the following are brief sketches of some of the themes that will run throughout this book.

Definitions of *Sex* and *Gender*

Many people use the terms *sex* and *gender* interchangeably, and this linguistic convention can contribute to misunderstandings of the relative contributions of biology and social forces (a subject of heated debate which I will take up later). Rhoda Unger (1979) suggested that we reserve the term *sex* for referral to biological entities—genes, hormones, genitalia, etc.—and that we use the term *gender* when speaking of social forces such as socialization, stereotyping, social role behavior, and self-presentation. Thus, I use the terms *male* and *female* when referring to sex and the terms *masculine* and *feminine* when referring to gender. Although biological forces may have effects on social behaviors, the use of biological terms (e.g., *male aggression, maternal instinct*) to describe behaviors communicates the assumption that biological forces have been demonstrated to be the singular causes of those behaviors. The connection between biology and behavior is an empirical matter—one that researchers investigate through scientific methods. *Gender* is a broader and more inclusive term than *sex* as it refers to feminine and masculine behaviors, mental, and social processes that are determined by biology and/or social forces (Lips, 2005).

Patriarchy and Power

Patriarchy is a system in which a society confers greater levels of economic power, influence, and prestige on males than on females. According to historian Gerda Lerner (1986), patriarchy has existed in most parts of the world for over 5,000 years. It is expressed in the typical behaviors that people believe are appropriate for males and females, in the dominant values of the culture, in social customs and economic arrangements, and in what Lerner terms "leading metaphors, which become part of the cultural construct and explanatory system." (p. 212). For example, many theologies are constructed around male gods and female subservience, which, by extension, privileges male experience over female experience in the collective consciousness of the culture. In many places (including the United States well into the twentieth and twenty-first centuries), male-centered ideologies have been used to justify the exclusion of women from educational opportunities, owning property, voting, or having legal recourse when their husbands rape them. Although laws in many parts of the world prohibit discrimination against women (see Adler, 1993), the persistence of patriarchal ideologies and traditions continues to bestow on men a disproportionate amount of social power and privilege. Sexist language (see Box 1.3) and marked versus unmarked status (see Box 1.4) are two manifestations of patriarchal ideology.

Because of the long tradition of the men's dominance of women, *power*, the influence and access to resources that are provided by authority, force, strength, and control, is a word that occupies a central place in the world of gender studies. As Michael Kaufman

(1994) states, "In a world dominated by men, the world of men is, by definition, a world of power. That power is a structured part of the economies and systems of political and social organization; it forms part of the core of religion, family, forms of play, and intellectual life." (p. 142). Collectively, men have the vast majority of power in the forms of money, social influence, and control of the world.

And yet, as Kaufman points out, many individual men do not feel powerful. Poor men often feel little sense of control over their lives. Men of color and gay men are often systematically oppressed by a White and heterosexually dominated society. Even a man whom one might consider powerful, for example, a man of relative wealth, may feel powerless because others are more wealthy or because he is alienated and disliked by his friends and family.

Johnson (1997) provides an important perspective on the contrast between *feeling* powerful and *being* powerful:

> Men's misery *does* deserve sympathy, but not if it means we ignore where it comes from and what men get in exchange for it. It's all too easy to go from sympathy for men to forgetting that patriarchy and male privilege even exist. Part of what makes it so easy is misunderstanding what privilege is, where it comes from, and how it is distributed. Many men argue, for example that men *are* privileged only to the degree that they *feel* privileged. A key aspect of privilege, however, is to be unaware of it *as* privilege. In addition, even though men as a group are privileged in society, factors such as race and class affect how much gender each man gets to enjoy and how he experiences it." (p. 175, emphasis original).

One example of the invisibility of privilege is flying first class on an airplane. You have a great deal more room than people in the coach class in the rear of the aircraft and are served better food, but you do not know that others are cramped and hungry unless you turn around and look at them, and then try to imagine how they feel. Owning a private plane takes the invisibility of privilege one step further.

This seeming contradiction between collective power and individual senses of powerlessness comprises a core issue in Men's Studies. As we will see in the final chapter of this book, some theorists go so far as to describe women as more powerful than men, a proposition that many people find preposterous, arrogant, and offensive.

Many men find it very difficult to appreciate the relative privilege they have by virtue of being male. For example, as a (White) male, I can:

- expect that people will take me seriously,
- go out in public feeling rather certain that I will not be followed or harassed,
- have people of my sex disproportionately represented at the highest positions in government, business, education, and other institutional structures,
- see people who look like me widely and positively portrayed in media,
- take college courses that give attention to members of my sex as important historical actors,
- be paid better than most women for the same work,

Box 1.3: The Power of Language

Language can communicate gender expectations in subtle ways, and linguistic distinctions between the sexes have received a good deal of attention in recent years. Sexist terms like *chairman, mankind*, and the use of the generic masculine pronoun *he* (instead of *chairperson, humankind*, and constructions like *he/she*) communicate that males are the standard and females the exceptions. People frequently complain that using newer, nonsexist terms is awkward and overly "p.c." ("politically correct"). However, many researchers have discovered that the use of masculine-biased language results in readers and listeners predominantly perceiving males (Gastil, 1990; Hamilton, 1991). Therefore, the use of generic masculine language is poor communication when a speaker or writer intends to refer to people of both sexes.

The opposite sex and the *battle of the sexes* are two frequently used and pernicious terms. Both communicate the belief that males and females have little common ground. *Battle of the sexes* implies that men and women are natural enemies, yet the vast majority of heterosexual people are loving and having children with these enemies — a curious "battle" indeed!

The opposite sex communicates that male and female are not only different, they are contrary and antithetical to each other. This view of the sexes is analogous to acids and bases — adding acid to a base makes the substance more acidic, and vice versa. A more modern view would conceptualize the sexes as different but not opposite, like salt and pepper (adding salt to a food does not make it less peppery) or IBM-type and Macintosh personal computers. In this view, we would be more accurate to use the term *the other sex*. Humans have 46 chromosomes; only one is different between the sexes. Even reproductive roles are not opposite; they are complementary (We would not describe impregnation as the opposite of gestation, or, to use a basic parallel, a bolt as the opposite of a nut.).

Richardson (1997) describes a variety of ways in which the common use of the English language disparages women. For instance, it is quite common to refer to adult females as *girls*, implying that, like children, they are immature and relatively powerless. An adult man is rarely referred to as a *boy* except in a conscious attempt to disparage him. Richardson also notes the variant gender meanings of linguistically equivalent terms such as *master* (someone with power) and *mistress* (a sexual partner), governor (official) and governess (nanny), *lord* and *lady, sir,* and *mister* [are] titles of courtesy, but at some time, *madam, miss,* and *mistress* have come to designate, respectively, a brothelkeeper, a prostitute, and an unmarried sexual partner of a male." (p. 120, emphases original).

Martin (1991) provides an interesting perspective on the use of language to smuggle (albeit perhaps in a nonconscious way) gender stereotypes into scientific language. She notes that most human sexuality books describe conception as a set of events that involve active (male) sperm swimming to and penetrating passive (female) eggs. In reality, female reproductive anatomy is anything but passive. Within women's bodies, cilia direct sperm along the path to the egg, and the egg changes chemically to favor some sperm but not others. Zuk (2005) observed that several scholarly articles refer to young birds as "illegitimate" when they had been fathered by males that were not pair-bonded with the mother "as if their parents had tiny avian marriage licenses and chirped their vows." (p. 14). Another paper refers to "wife-sharing" among male birds. Cases in which more than one female are associated with a male are never referred to as "husband sharing." Zuk points out that this language casts the males as the active parties—"they 'share' the female, as if she were a six-pack of beer." (p. 14). The subtext of subjective gender stereotypes finds its way into language even in fields many people consider "objective."

- have my successes or failures attributed to my efforts and abilities, rather than to the fact that I am a man,

- go to work in a female-dominated profession and expect not to be harassed or paid a lower salary than others.

This is a partial list; you may be able to think of other social privileges for men-as-a-group. Because men have always lived in a world where their ways of being are privileged over those of most others, and because men are not encouraged to identify with women, it is easy for male privilege to be invisible in their experiences. As Kimmel (1994) puts it, "men's experience of powerlessness is *real*—the men actually feel it and certainly act on it—but it is not *true*, that is, it does not actually describe their condition." (p. 137). True gender awareness for men involves not only their understanding of the pressures of traditional masculinity role, but also the appreciation of their advantaged social positions.

Race and Class

As I stated above, the privilege of masculinity does not extend to all males in equal shares. Goffman (1963) explains that, in the United States, there is only one "complete, unblushing male…a young, married, white, urban, northern heterosexual, Protestant father of college education, fully employed, of good complexion, weight and height, and a recent record in sports. . . Any male who fails to qualify in any one of these ways is likely to view himself. . . as unworthy, incomplete, and inferior." (p. 128). Therefore, masculinity is somewhat of a "deficit model." The opportunity to reap all of the social benefits of being a so-called "real man" are available to relatively few men even though many (perhaps most) men accrue some of these benefits. Social conceptions of masculinity exert somewhat similar pressures on nearly all men to experience themselves and the world, and to behave in prescribed ways, but these demands interact in important ways with the oppression of racism, classism, and heterosexism.

Box 1.4: *On Entitlement and Being "Marked"*

Karen Rosenblum and Toni-Michelle Travis (2003) frame race, sex, class, and sexual orientation as having "master statuses." In mainstream U. S. culture, these statuses are White, male, wealthy, and heterosexual. They point out that "Two privileges in particular appear common among non-stigmatized statuses: the sense of entitlement and the privilege of being 'unmarked.' "(p. 182).

My student, Laura Ramsey (2005), provided an example of entitlement in an interview with a young heterosexual man, who said:

"Everybody on TV as far as I'm concerned is a homosexual nowadays. That's why I don't like to watch television, you know what I mean? It's like, you turn it on and you got *Queer Eye for the Straight Guy* and *Will and Grace*. It's like the media is almost trying to breed homosexuals as far as I'm concerned. Not that I have a problem with gays. It's just like, you turn it on and it's like gay gay gay gay gay, you know? I guess that's what they're pushing right now."

In fact, this person would have great difficulty citing other television programs that are dominated by gay characters. He has extrapolated to all of television from these two shows for several possible reasons. First, he has probably failed to notice the preponderance of heterosexual characters on television. Second, he may have strong feelings of revulsion to gay characters. Third, he has likely not engaged in much critical reflection on his reactions. His sexuality is displayed as the norm nearly everywhere but he does not notice it. There-

fore, when heterosexuality is not the norm, he raises his hand and says that he feels excluded. Ettinger (quoted in Rosenblum & Travis, 2003) notes that, if, as a marginalized person, "I wanted to raise my hand every time I felt excluded, I would have to glue my wrist to the top of my head." (p. 182).

With regard to gender, the unmarked status (e.g., "judge") presents men as the taken-for-granted norm and the marked status ("woman judge") presents women as the stigmatized exception. Bonvillain (2001) notes that many female names are derived from male names by adding endings like –a, -ette, and –ine (e.g., Alexandra, Bernadette, Josephine) as markers, and that the ending –ette is also used as a diminutive, which denotes smallness ("kitchenette," "booklet," "kittenette"). Women who advocated voting rights in the early twentieth century were termed "suffragettes." Modern feminist scholars now refer to them as "suffragists" to erase the diminutive implication.

One can see a good deal of marked an unmarked statuses in athletic teams. The men's team is the "Eagles," and the woman's team is the "*Lady* Eagles." In remarkable oxymoronic fashion, the Fairfield University (CT) women's teams are the "Lady Stags" and a number of teams (Johnson C. Smith College, NC; University of South Florida; Hereford High School, MD; an Arizona AAU team) are the "Lady Bulls." These titles convey a secondary status for girls' and women's athletics.

Rosenblum and Travis note that "those in marked statuses appear to be operating from an 'agenda' or 'special interest,' while those in unmarked statuses can appear to be agenda-free." (p. 182). Criticisms of people in unmarked statuses are more likely to refer to the individual ("He was incompetent as a mechanic."), conveying the assumption that the rest of the group are competent until proven otherwise. Conversely, criticism of people from marked statuses may include the assumption that the entire group is flawed ("I shouldn't have let a woman mechanic work on my car.").

Essentialism versus Social Constructionism

One major debate in gender studies is the distinction between essentialist and social constructionist models. *Essentialists* argue that the collections of attitudes, behaviors, and social conditions that we call masculinities are "hard-wired" into males through biology (see Barash and Lipton, 1997; Daly & Wilson, 1983; Thornhill & Palmer, 2000) and/or the heritability of human psyche (see Jung, 1959/1989; Bly, 1990). They view masculinity as static, trans-historical, cross-cultural, and cross-situational. From this perspective, gender change is either impossible, or it involves the use of powerful force to constrain what is seen as "naturally" male.

The opposing view of *social constructionism* is summarized by Michael Kimmel (1994), who views masculinity as…"a constantly changing collection of meanings that we construct through our relationships with ourselves, with each other, and with our world. Manhood is neither static nor timeless; it is historical. Manhood is not the manifestation of an inner essence; it is socially constructed. Manhood does not bubble up to consciousness from our biological makeup; it is created in culture. Manhood means different things at different times to different people." (p. 120). From this perspective, social definitions of masculinity are quite malleable — they have the potential to shift in response to changes in ideologies, values, social conditions, economic factors, and historical events.

Even the most extreme essentialists do not deny the influence of social forces in behavior, just as even the most extreme social constructionists do not deny the effect of biology. However, scholars show a strong tendency to position themselves within one camp or the other. Essentialist E.O. Wilson (1979) once remarked that biology holds behavior on a "leash" and that the debate is about the length and tightness of that leash. Essentialists like Wilson see it as very short and tight; social constructionists such as Steven J. Gould (1987) see the leash as "long and noncon- straining, though well worth our continued examination" (p. 115). These two theoretical positions provide very different sets of assumptions about gender as backdrops for very different views on what exists, why it exists, whether it can change, whether it should change, and how it can change. It is important to think critically about these assumptions in order to fully evaluate each of the many perspectives of Men's Studies scholars.

© Jennifer Berman

GOALS FOR STUDENTS

Gender is an area of intellectual inquiry, but it is also a very personal topic, since we all experience the social pressure to conform to cultural conventions based on whether we are male or female. One of the most rewarding aspects of taking on the study of gender is to integrate the intellectual and the personal. To that end, I suggest the following goals for students:

1. *To see the self as a gendered being.* You will be better able to understand the gender pressures in your own lives.

2. *To explore the range of possibilities in response to gender pressure.* Everyone has choices about how they respond to these forces. As you make progress toward the first goal of identifying gendered influences in your own life, you will be in better position to resist these influences when doing so is in concert with your values and life choices. People who cannot identify gender effects have a great deal of difficulty resisting them, as it is quite difficult to resist a pressure that one cannot name (see Box 1.5). Gender education moves gendered behavior from non-conscious into conscious ideologies and put the person into better position to make informed choices rather than just "going along with the program."

3. *To build intellectual skills by investigating the histories, cultures, psychologies, images, and mechanisms of gender.* Taking on this area of inquiry contributes to the more general skills of critical thinking.

4. *To facilitate empathy for men and women.* Understanding gendered forces allows the person to better take the perspectives of others.

5. *To explore the possibilities for social justice work.* Much of gendering involves social inequality, and an awareness of it may encourage the student to make efforts toward making the world a better place.

Box 1.5: Resetting the "Default Options"
The Importance of Men's Studies

Sandra Bem (1993) defined gender roles as the "default options" that a culture "programs" into its natives. The most common modern use of the term default options is in describing computer functions that are set at the factory and remain in place unless the computer user changes them. If we carry the computer analogy forward in examining gender roles, we find that changing a default option requires at least three conditions:

1 The person must *know that the option exists*.

On a standard personal computer, you can change the size of the icons that appear on the screen when you first boot the computer. If you do not know that you can, you surely will not change them, except by accident. By the same token, many people consciously and unconsciously accept gender arrangements as "the way things are" because they have no awareness that things could be different. Men's studies, with its examinations of cultural, individual, and social-environmental variations in men's behaviors, can illuminate these options. Gender studies are developing the language that we need in order to undertake an in-depth examination of the use of gender as a cultural organizing principle.

2. The person must be *motivated to change* from the default option.

Maybe you know that you can change the size of the icons on your screen, but you don't want to do so.

However, if your eyesight is not good, you might want them to be larger; if you have many icons you want to display, you might want them to be smaller. Or you may merely want your computer screen to look different from others; it's a fashion choice. You need a motivation to change—otherwise it is easiest to allow things to remain as they are.

So it is with gender roles. Even if men know that they could behave otherwise, they may feel no particular urge to do so. Men's studies can point out the important quality-of-life issues involved in adhering to rigid gender beliefs for both the individual and the society. People who see the disadvantages of rigid gendering through a process of formal and informal education may become more motivated to change individually and to work for social change.

3. The person must *know how to change* from the default option.

Perhaps you want to change the size of your computer icons, but you do not know the procedure for doing so. Obviously, you would need to find out in order to change the default option. Men's studies can inform in the service of investigating methods for individual and social change of the destructive aspects of traditional masculinity. Men's studies experts are investigating aspects of gender in individuals, social groups, public policy, and culture.

Judith Lorber (1986) articulated the direction of gender studies from a feminist perspective: "The long term goal of

> feminism must be no less than the eradication of gender as an organizing principle of postindustrial society" (p.568). Coltrane (1998) adds: "Paradoxically, one of the ways to work toward this long-term political goal of reducing the importance of gender is for scholars to call attention to it…ultimately to reduce its importance in everyday life" (p. 78).
>
> Gender is a set of social pressures, and it is quite difficult to resist a pressure that one cannot name. One goal of men's studies is to help men to articulate this pressure and make informed choices about their lives rather than merely conforming to the "default options."

6. *To understand the risks involved in uncritically accepting the dominant forms of masculinity, both for individuals and for groups.* Some aspects of masculinity, such as the valuing of aggression, emotional stoicism, and sexism toward women, have dire negative consequences for men and others around them. Men who wholly conform to gender pressures are at risk for reducing their quality of life as well as that of others.

7. *To gain an awareness of how gender affects one's daily life and experiences.* In teaching men's studies, I ask my students to keep journals in which they observe gendered arrangements in their everyday lives. Within a few weeks, they often state, "It's everywhere!"

8. *To join with the other sex in respectful ways to work toward common goals.* Contrary to what some people believe, men and women are not enemies, and gender study can lead to an appreciation of our commonalities.

THE ORGANIZATION OF THIS BOOK

The Masculine Self is oriented toward understanding masculinity in the contexts of social scientific theory. This first chapter is a description of masculine gender roles and the multiple contexts in which they are embedded. Chapter 2 will provide the necessary background for conceptualizing the many different facets of gender roles as well as reviewing the attempts to measure the varied components of gendered behaviors and beliefs.

Part II (Chapters 3 through 7) provides some theoretical viewpoints on men and masculinity as seen by scholars in major schools of social scientific thought (sociobiological, psychoanalytic, historical, anthropological, sociological, cross-cultural, and psychological). These chapters contain a wide variety of sometimes overlapping, sometimes competing perspectives.

Part III (Chapters 8 through 15) examines research findings and other scholarship related to various themes that have been identified as "Men's Issues" — emotion, physical health, work, sexuality, violence, relationships, and mental health. The final chapter is a description of various social movements that are concerned with the state of masculinities in the world.

SUMMARY

1. The distinction between the sexes is learned very early in life, and gender roles are culturally assigned based on this distinction. Only recently have researchers and theorists begun a serious investigation of the effect of gender on boys and men. This study has met with a good deal of resistance due to misunderstanding and mistrust. Nevertheless, there is a growing body of literature that suggests that masculinity is an important cultural construct highly worthy of investigation.

2. From very early in life, males receive messages about what it means to be a man. These messages are communicated through interpersonal relationships and the culture, and they are later reinforced in adult social settings. There is considerable similarity in gender role definitions across cultures but also great variation in the ways that individual males respond to gender pressures.

3. Traditional gender roles provide expectations that men be unemotional, independent, aggressive, competitive, achieving, and unfeminine. Living in these roles can have positive results, such as financial rewards, social status, and contribution to family and society. However, there can also be negative effects, including overattention to work, impoverished emotional life, poor relationships, and violence.

4. The terms *sex*, *male*, and *female* refer to biological essences such as hormones, genes, instincts, and anatomical structures. The terms *gender*, *masculine*, and *feminine* refer to behavioral aspects of social roles.

5. Masculinity is embedded in the historical context of patriarchy, a 5,000-year-old system by which men-as-a-group retain the vast majority of power in a society. However, there is a contradictory experience of men's aggregate power and individual men's feelings of powerlessness. Many men do not have an appreciation of male privilege and therefore fail to appreciate their social power.

6. Masculine demands interact strongly with race, class, sexual orientation, and other forms of social identity and status.

7. Essentialism is the belief that gender resides in a biological or psychical substrate that is unchangeable and/or very slow and difficult to change. Social constructionism is the view that gender is a product of highly malleable social forces. These two opposing perspectives form the assumptive background of most gender theorists.

8. Undertaking the study of gender entails a personal journey in addition to an intellectual pursuit.

2

Models for Understanding Masculinity

Masculinity can be understood as a set of role behaviors that cultures encourage most men to perform. In this chapter, we examine the nature of roles, the historical development of models for understanding gender roles, and various attempts to measure gender role characteristics.

ROLES AND GENDER ROLES

A *role* is a collection of behaviors expected of a person in a given situation. The most familiar use of this term is as a description of a person's prescribed behavior in a movie, play, or other acting situation. *Social roles* define a set of expected behaviors for a person in any given social position. For example, the social role of student includes the expectations that one will attend classes, take tests, and complete assignments. Note that the role comprises expectations but not necessarily performance. All students do not fulfill their assigned role.

A *gender role* is a generalized social role, one that cuts across many situations. A gender role is a set of expectations for behaving, thinking, and feeling that is based on a person's biological sex. Historically, the term *sex role* has been used throughout social science literature as an equivalent term. Its use decreased as scholars began to understand that it is problematic to uncritically combine a biological category (sex) with a set of social behaviors (role) (Sherif, 1982). For example, a writer who describes aggressiveness as a characteristic of the "male sex role" might lead a reader to assume that men are more aggressive than women because they have "aggressive genes" or "aggressive hormones." As we shall see in Chapter 13, explanations of aggression are much more complicated than those which appeal to a singular biological cause. When one is speaking about such behaviors without necessarily implicating biology, the term *gender role* is more accurate and inclusive than the term sex role.

Components of Gender Roles

There are several components to gender roles. *Stereotypes* are culturally based overgeneralizations about the characteristics of people who belong to the biological category of male or female. Gender stereotypes are a part of the social fabric (Bem, 1993) and take the form of seldom-questioned, socially shared beliefs and images of how men and women are (Pleck, 1981a). For instance, in mainstream U.S. culture, it is widely believed that men are competitive and that women are not.

Many people conceive of stereotypical masculine and feminine traits as opposites. For example, one may believe that women are romantic and men are unromantic. As noted in Chapter 1, the use of the term *opposite sex* rather than *other sex* reflects the tendency to think in this gender-polarized way. Although a good deal of research refutes this bias, people tend to characterize masculinity and femininity as antithetical to each other (Tavris, 1992).

Gender roles also include *norms*, which are prescriptive and proscriptive beliefs. That is, they are beliefs about how males and females should be (prescriptive) and about how they should *not* be (proscriptive). A norm within a social role is analogous to a script in an acting role. For example, one might believe that, although sexual fidelity is uncharacteristic of men (a stereotype), nevertheless men *should* be faithful (a norm).

It is quite possible for a gender role stereotype to conflict with a gender role norm. For instance, college students in one study (Street, Kimmel, & Kromrey, 1995) tended to describe *ideal* men as highly compassionate (a prescriptive norm), but also tended to believe that *most* men are not very compassionate (a gender stereotype). The term "real man" appears to have become shorthand for the description of male gender role norms, for example "real men" make a lot of money, don't cry, and don't ask for directions when they are lost. The use of this term provides a social shaming of men by unsexing them if they do not live up to socially defined masculine standards of behavior.

Discrepancies between gender role stereotypes and norms are rather commonplace. In one study, college students reported beliefs that males and females differed on over 50 characteristics (gender role stereotyping), but that they *should* differ only on 12 characteristics (gender role norms) (Ruble, 1983). Street, Kimmel, and Kromrey (1995) concluded that gender stereotypes held by college students had not changed very much over the 15 years prior to their study, and there is little reason to believe that they have changed radically in the time since the study.

Gender role norms and stereotypes are also applied to the self. A man may have a conception of "how men are" (*stereotype*) that is in conflict with "how I am" (*self-concept*). It would not be unusual for a man to view men in general as aggressive and at the same time view himself as not aggressive, even though he is a man.

Norm-based beliefs also apply to the individual. I have beliefs about "how I should be" (*ideal self-concept*) and these may conflict with the other components already mentioned. Thus, I may believe that men are dominant (stereotype); men should not be dominant (norm); I am not dominant (self-concept), but I should be more dominant (ideal self-concept). Martin (1987) found that a sample of college students reported the belief that males and females differ in 32 characteristics. When asked to rate themselves with regard to these characteristics, however, males and females differed significantly on only five of them. Discrepancies between self-concept and stereotype, then, are more the rule than the exception. Most people see themselves as significantly gender nonconforming, and most men (and probably most women as well) overestimate the gender conformity of same-sex peers (Kilmartin, Green, Heinzen, Kuchler, & Smith, 2004).

I have described these components of gender roles as beliefs, which are the *cognitive* (thinking) components of attitudes about the sexes. However, attitudes do not just occur in our heads. They also include *affective* (emotional), and *behavioral* aspects, and these can be discrepant from or in concert with one another (Myers, 2005). For example, a person might believe that men are aggressive (cognitive), feel uncomfortable about it (affective), and avoid men (behavioral).

In the above example, the three aspects go together logically and consistently, but it does not always work this way. For instance, I might think that men should be emotionally expressive (cognitive), but I feel anxiety in the presence of an emotionally expressive man (affective), and I cut conversations short with such men (behavioral). These different components of gender roles are summarized in Box 2.1.

To make matters more complicated, there are *conscious* and *unconscious* aspects to each component as well. People may feel and behave in consistent and distinctive ways toward men and women while, at the same time, they are not aware of their behaviors and attitudes. Most parents *state* that they treat their sons and daughters similarly (Antill, 1987). Nevertheless there is research evidence that most parents discourage their children (especially their sons) from engaging in behaviors associated with the other sex (Lytton & Romney, 1991), and that they react more positively when children select toys that are gender stereotypical (Caldera, Huston, & O'Brien, 1989). There is a large literature of parents' differential reactions to sons and daughters. For instance, parents punish boys more often than girls (Lips, 2005), respond to crying girls faster than to crying boys, assign different chores, and handle boys more roughly (Basow, 1992).

The Power of Roles

If you were to obtain a part in a stage play, you would have a script that told you what to say and how to behave while acting. On occasion, actors will improvise, saying or doing things that are not in the script. If you decided to improvise, the director of the play might or might not tolerate it, depending on his or her rigidity and on whether or not your improvisation was consistent with the role. However, if you were to improvise too extensively or in a way that was inconsistent with the role, the director would probably discipline you

Box 2.1: Components of Gender Roles

	SELF		OTHERS
Descriptive: *Self-Concept*	• "How I am as a man" • "I am independent" (cognitive	*Descriptive:* *Stereotypes*	• "How men are" • "Men are emotionally distant" (cognitive)
	• Feeling anxious when dependent feelings emerge (affective)		• Feeling frustrated in the company of distant men (affective)
	• Avoiding situations that highlight dependence (behavioral)		• Demanding that the man come closer emotionally (behavioral)
Prescriptive: *Ideal* *Self-Concept*	• "How I should be as a man" • "I wish I were a good leader" (cognitive)	*Prescriptive:* *Norms*	• "How men should be" • "Men should be caring" (cognitive) • Feeling affectionate toward caring men (affective)
	• Feeling ashamed that I am not a good leader (affective)		
	• Using drugs to soothe discomfort (behavioral)		• Keeping company with men perceived as caring (behavioral)
Proscriptive: *Ideal* *Self-Concept*	• "How I should not be as a man" • "I should not be weak" (cognitive)	*Proscriptive:* *Norms*	• "How men should not be" • "Men should not be cowards" (cognitive)
	• Depressed feelings (affective)		• Feeling disgusted with a man who won't fight to protect someone (afffective)
	• Bragging to cover up feelints (behavioral)		• Ridiculing the man (behavioral)

or throw you out of the play. If you feel strongly enough about changing the role, you might be willing to risk this outcome.

   Actors and actresses know that they have to stick to their roles to keep their jobs. Social roles are a little less defined than stage roles; nobody gives a boy an explicit script telling him how to act in masculine ways. But social roles and gender roles are every bit as

Box 2.2: *Masculine Gender Role Violation Exercises*

Choose a behavior from the list below. Evaluate your thoughts and feelings as well as the reactions of those around you as you perform the behavior.

1. Wear colored nail polish to class or some other public place.

2. Spend a half hour in a conversation with a group of people without interrupting or telling a story.

3. Tell a male friend how much you value his friendship (without being drunk).

4. If you are in a satisfying relationship with a woman, talk at length with some male friends about how much you love your girlfriend and how good she makes you feel (without talking about sex).

5. Walk to class carrying your books at your chest instead of at your side.

6. Share an umbrella with another man.

7. Make a comment about the physical attractiveness of some man.

How did it feel for you to perform these behaviors? How did others react to you? Was there a difference in the reactions of men and women? Of older and younger adults? Of people who know you well and people who do not? What does your experience of gender role violation tell you about masculinity, yourself, and the culture?

---

powerful. One may incur severe punishment for stepping outside of one's prescribed role and great social approval for staying within it. In the gender role arena, for instance, a boy who cries or plays with girls may be ostracized by his male peers. The power of gender roles is most evident when the prescriptions of the role are violated. Men can experience the power of male gender role violations by trying some of the behaviors that are described in Box 2.2.

Who are the "directors" of the "plays" when it comes to gender roles? They are everyone who can reward the individual for staying within gender role boundaries and everyone who can punish the person for stepping outside of those boundaries. Families, friends, employers, romantic partners, and others all have the power to enforce gender role norms. Sometimes their sanctions are subtle, such as a mildly disapproving look. At other times they are more overt, as in children's name calling.

Because men (and women) are socialized in a gender-typed society, they often internalize gender roles and become their own "directors" to some extent. A great many men incorporate masculine stereotypes and norms into their ideal self-concepts and attempt to live up to these standards. If one accepts such standards uncritically, then the content of masculine gender role norms becomes the yardstick by which the man judges his worth. Pleck (1981b) described such men as "prisoners of manliness" who compulsively conform their behavior to masculine role norms and lose sight of their individuality in the process.

FUNCTIONS OF GENDER ROLES

One might ask from the foregoing discussion, "Why do gender roles exist?" Answers to this question might involve explanations about reproductive roles (see Chapter 3), the history of work (see Chapter 10), or social conditions like the struggle for power and the competition for scarce resources (see Chapter 6).

Gender stereotyping also seems to be at least partly the result of the human tendency to simplify our complex perceptual worlds by thinking in categories. By the time a person becomes an adult, he or she has experienced a countless number of objects and events. To function effectively, a person must learn to separate the important from the unimportant. Part of this process involves thinking about events (objects, perceptions, thoughts, people) in terms of categories. This ability allows us to reduce data and thereby process a great deal of information. For instance, a child learns that shoes, shirts, and underwear all belong to the general category of clothing. This allows the child to understand and respond to new clothing without having to learn about its significance all over again because it is the functional equivalent of all of the clothing that he or she already understands. Being able to think in generalities helps us to predict the value of a new object in a category that we have encountered before, and thus respond to the world more efficiently.

In the same way, we have a propensity for categorizing people. Since biological sex is one of the most basic, (usually) visible, and obvious divisions among human beings, it is easy to think about people in these dualistic terms. This categorizing may guide what we notice and remember about a person, how we interpret his or her behavior, and what information we seek from this person (Stangor, & Schaller, 1996). If you meet a man for the first time, you might notice the size of his biceps but not his hips, remember how loud he laughed rather than how interested he seemed to be in you, and ask about his job rather than about his children.

We also tend to pay attention to and remember information that fits our stereotypes and ignore or discard information that does not (Judd, Park, Ryan, Brauer, & Kraus, 1995). A man who seeks sex indiscriminately may confirm a stereotype. On the other hand, people may pay little or no attention to a man who is monogamous and loving, or they may see him as an exception. Thus, stereotypes have a self-perpetuating nature (Lips, 2005).

Negative stereotypes about a group are tempered when one has frequent and meaningful contact with group members who do not confirm one's expectations. The more information we have about an individual, the more likely we are to respond to the person and not the stereotype (Swim, Borgida, Maruyama, & Myers, 1989). For example, when a heterosexual person has a close relationship with a gay, lesbian, or bisexual person who "comes out" (reveals his or her sexual orientation), the heterosexual is likely to become less homophobic (Bridgewater, 1997).

Because we tend to be sensitive to other people's expectations, there is a tendency to behave as we think the other person wants us to behave. This is especially true when we are motivated to have a person like us or approve of us (Burn, 1996). Consider the following scenario: two men are becoming friends on the basis of a shared interest and frequent social contact. After a while, each man may have the desire to expand and deepen the friendship. Doing so would involve communicating information that is more personal. Of course, neither one knows that the other has this desire, and both may believe that men should not talk about their families, feelings, or fears. Therefore, each man continues to play a stereotypical masculine role by talking about sports or work and maintaining emotional distance whenever he sees the other man. A rigid behavioral pattern is established, and the stereotypical view that men are only interested in sports and work becomes a self-fulfilling reality for these men and for people who observe them. Each man has behaved in a way that confirms the other's expectations. This example illustrates that there is a significant component of *social performance* in gender; outward behavior does not necessarily correspond with inner reality.

Stereotyping involves constructing beliefs about a person's characteristics based on presumed knowledge about a group to which that person belongs (Baron, Byrne, & Branscome, 2006). In the above example, we see the power of stereotyping in masculine gender arrangements. Both men behave on the basis of gender-stereotypical beliefs about males, despite the fact that each belongs to the group he is stereotyping, and each does not fit the stereotype. Perhaps these men view themselves as exceptions to the way that most men are and therefore continue to hold the stereotype in the face of disconfirming evidence (their own desires). It is also likely that their reluctance to act in cross-gendered ways is unconscious and rooted in the fear of a negative social reaction from the other man. Men take social risks when they act in ways that are culturally defined as unmasculine.

We tend to create cognitive structures that represent the essences of masculinity and femininity to predict events. However, in our effort to simplify, we sometimes *over*simplify by exaggerating similarities of things *within* a group, and by exaggerating differences *between* these things and those from other groups (Baron, Byrne, & Branscome, 2006). The result is an overestimation of the similarities within each sex and an underestimation of the similarities between men and women. Together with the bias toward thinking of the sexes as opposite, these over- and under-generalizations are at the root of gender role stereotyping.

One way to observe your tendency to categorize and stereotype is to use imagery. Picture in your mind the following people: a basketball player, a housekeeper, a corporation executive, and a nurse. All of these people could be male or female, but you probably pictured the basketball player and executive as males, and the housekeeper and the nurse as females. If you continue to think about these people, some other characteristics will emerge. You may find yourself thinking of the basketball player as tall, the nurse as kind, and so on.

It is important to notice that these categorizations may be somewhat useful, as there are fewer male than female nurses, more tall than short basketball players, and so on. However, problems arise when one over-attends to a category and under-attends to an individual (or to the self). Within the realm of gender, people who do not fit stereotypes often have to battle against others' tendencies to attribute gender characteristics to them and respond to them on the basis of these attributions.

Box 2.3: Alternatives to Gender Schematic Information Processing

Following are some examples that stand in contrast to gender schemata. The first three are Bem's suggestions.

1. Individual differences schema: people vary widely in their habits, attitudes, and temperament. A person may act aggressively, not because he is a man, but because he has an aggressive personality and/or finds himself in a situation in which aggression is adaptive.

2. Cultural relativism schema: "different people believe different things" (p. 271). Roman Catholics do not allow women to be priests, but some Episcopalians do.

3. Sexism schema: although beliefs differ, some beliefs about gender are wrong. Women should be allowed to be priests in Roman Catholicism.

4. Situational pressure schema: people tend to behave in certain ways when situations exert different pressures. A man may keep his feelings to himself while with his male friends, not because men are unemotional, but because other men might not give him a compassionate response. He may be very emotionally expressive as a client in psychotherapy or when he is in the company of female friends.

5. External variability schema: people do not always behave in concert with how they feel; two people can vary to a great extent in their external reactions to exactly the same internal thoughts and feelings. Two men may hold equally sexist attitudes, but one decides not to display them because he wants the approval of women.

6. Internal variability schema: two people can act the same way even though their feelings and thoughts are very different. One man may laugh at a sexist joke because it reflects how he feels about women, but another may laugh, despite the fact that he finds the joke unfunny and distasteful, in order to avoid being ostracized by the group.

There are differences among people in the degree to which they rely on stereotypes of masculinity and femininity in processing information. People who are highly attuned to these concepts in their everyday thinking are *gender schematic* (Bem, 1993). They tend to see the world in terms of gender, and, compared with *gender aschematic* people, they are more motivated to comply with gender stereotypes (Fiske & Taylor, 1991). Not surprisingly, gender schematic parents often pass this perceptual tendency along to their children (Tennenbaum & Leaper, 2002).

Although we may sometimes need to categorize people to make sense of the world, there are a variety of *schemata* (the plural of schema) other than sex that we can use. Because so many people do not fit gender stereotypes, the use of alternative and multiple schemata helps to avoid the unfortunate tendency to deny a person's individuality. Bem (1998) suggests several alternative schemata. These and others are noted in Box 2.3.

SEXISM

Sexism is differential attitudes and behaviors directed toward people based on their biological status as male or female. For example, one might comfort a female friend when she exhibits vulnerability, but avoid a male friend who exhibits the same behavior. Or the assertive behavior of a man might be described as "forceful" whereas the identical behavior, performed by a woman, might be labeled "bitchy." Sexism is an outgrowth of stereotyping, the cognitive tendency to overgeneralize about people, prejudice, the emotional responses to a group (which can be either positive or negative), and discrimination, the behavioral manifestation of these processes.

Because gender roles are sometimes subtle, because we have a natural propensity toward categorizing and stereotyping, because there are emotional and unconscious aspects to gender roles, and because we have all been socialized in a gender schematic and sexist society, we are probably all sexist in some measure.

Although it may be difficult to change sexist *behaviors*, it is often even more difficult to change sexist *reactions* that may be emotional and unconscious. Prejudiced and nonprejudiced people do not differ in *stereotype activation* (Fazio & Olson, 2003). However, the nonprejudiced person has made a commitment to be aware of and resistant to the tendency to stereotype. Over time, the stereotype activation itself decreases (Kawakami, Dovidio, Moll, Hermsen, & Russin, 2000). To reduce sexism, a person must expend efforts to understand socialization and gender role attitudes, recognize when he or she is engaging in stereotypical thinking, and resist inclinations to behave in sexist ways. Over time, this "self-training" should lead to nonsexist responses that are somewhat automatic.

Since we live in a patriarchal society in which males wield the vast majority of institutional power, the most serious forms of sexism involve the disrespect of women. A woman who makes less money than a man in the same job is a victim of *institutional sexism*. An adult woman who is called a "girl" or addressed as "honey" (two disempowering terms in most social contexts) is a victim of *interpersonal sexism*. And a woman who limits her own potential because she has received repeated messages that she is incompetent (and she incorporates these messages into her sense of self) is a victim of *internalized sexism*. Although these forms of sexism are presented here as distinct categories, they are interrelated. Sexist culture perpetuates all forms of sexism.

Some people complain that sexism also occurs in relation to males. Following are several examples:

Institutional   1. Drafting only men for military duty and combat assignments.

2. Awarding child custody to the mother when the father is equally or better suited as a parent.

3. "Bachelor Auctions" (see Box 2.5)

4. Higher car insurance rates for males.

Interpersonal	1.	Media display of negative stereotypes of men.
	2.	"Man Bashing" (see Box 2.4)
Internalized	1.	Feelings of incompetence in social relationship
	2.	Guilt around emotional vulnerability
	3.	Refusal to give in to a desire to engage in "feminine" activities

Two Forms of Sexism

In an impressive program of research undertaken with more than 15,000 people in 19 countries, Peter Glick and Susan Fiske (2001) demonstrated that sexism takes two different but related forms. *Hostile Sexism*, the hatred of women, is the kind of sexism that springs to mind when one thinks of prejudicial attitudes toward women. However, overall attitudes toward women within a population are usually quite positive. Women are believed to be nice, caring, and nurturing (Glick, 2005). At the same time these qualities are ascribed, women are also perceived as being incompetent and thus in need of men's protection, help, and financial support. *Benevolent Sexism*, which Glick and Fiske (2001) dubbed the "women are wonderful effect," serves to reward women for cooperating in a system that denies them significant resources and reduce their resistance to this inequality. It allows men to "maintain a positive self-image as protectors and providers who are willing to sacrifice their own needs to care for the women in their lives... [and] promises that men's power will be used to women's advantage, if only they can secure a high-status male protector." (p. 111). Hostile sexism can be reserved for women who challenge the status quo: powerful women, lesbians, and outspoken feminists. To illustrate: contrast the cultural attitudes between Hillary Clinton, a lawyer, powerful woman, and later a U.S. Senator, with those toward "First Lady" (a title that some find offensive) Laura Bush, a former school teacher and librarian. A great deal of vitriol has been directed toward Clinton, who defies cultural stereotypes of women, but little toward Bush, who is more stereotypical.

Glick and Fiske (2001) found remarkably high correlations between hostile and benevolent sexism within all of the cultures they studied. In countries where there was strong endorsement of hostile sexism, people also showed a strong tendency to endorse benevolent sexism. In the opinion of these researchers, these two forms of sexism act in complementary fashion as justifications of gender inequality.

Chivalry

Chivalry is a term derived from the French *Chevalier,* a heavily armed horseman in the French military (Keen, 1984). It is a set of attitudes and behaviors directed toward women by men of privilege (In medieval times, horsemen were knights and/or nobles; most common men could not afford horses). Chivalry is a form of benevolent sexism that manifests itself in a set of "gentlemanly" helpful behaviors such as holding a door open for a

---

Box 2.4: "Male Bashing"

Following are examples of the sexism directed toward men:

1. Sign in an office: "Of course God created man before woman. You always do a rough draft before the final masterpiece."

2. Lapel button: "Men are living proof that women can take a joke."

3. Book: *Men: An Owner's Manual. A Comprehensive Guide to Having a Man Underfoot.* (Brush, 1984).

4. Greeting card: Front: "Men are scum." Inside: "Excuse me. For a second there, I was feeling generous."

5. Popular tee shirt: "Boys are stupid. Throw rocks at them."

Many other examples can be found in Farrell (1986). "Male bashing" has become socially acceptable and even fashionable in some segments of society, perhaps as a result of at least two social forces: legitimate anger in women generated by the increasing awareness of men's historically exploitive domination, and the tendency to see women and men as opposites who are engaged in "the battle of the sexes."

You might ask yourself: Do I notice male bashing? Do I understand it? Do I take part in it? How does it affect the ways in which I think, feel, and act? Is equal gender disrespect really a kind of equality?

Tavris (1992) sees less concern for male bashing than for woman hating as understandable and defensible (although she does not endorse male bashing as a positive thing to do). The difference lies in the distinction between *equality* and *sameness*. Equal treatment refers to the elimination of the *consequences* of the negative action. For most women, the consequences of woman hating are in gender-based violence, lower pay than men get, and not having their voices heard, among other things. For men, who have disproportionate power and privilege as a group, male bashing is often mere inconvenience or annoyance. *Sameness* assumes gender-neutrality—the equality of opportunity and consequence, which do not exist currently between men-as-a-group and women-as-a-group.

---

woman, helping her get seated at a dining table, standing when she enters or leaves a room, and filling her wine glass at social occasions. Glick (2005) points out that these are "trivial niceties" that send the message that women are special, but that they are also incompetent, for example that they cannot open doors for themselves or fill their own wine glasses. The function of such customs is to reinforce male dominance and undermine women's resistance to it. Chivalric men believe that they are being helpful to women, but most do not help with things that really matter such as gendered pay inequity, child care, or men's violence against women.

Box 2.5: The Bachelor Auction

Bachelor auctions are events in which men offer expensive dates to the highest bidders, with the proceeds going to charity. The bachelor auction represents sexism in addition to many of the destructive aspects of masculinity:

1 The man is for sale. If women were in a similar situation, many would be rightfully outraged. Auctioning a human being also has racist undertones, as it is historically how African slaves were sold.

2 The "most eligible" bachelors are those who make the most money and have the most prestigious jobs. Not only are they "good catches" as defined socially, but they are able to offer the most expensive dates to auction. This arrangement reinforces the social norm that a man's worth as a person is determined by his income and occupational status.

3. Some women who bid on dates with these men expect the bachelor to have sex with them. This reinforces the stereotype that men are always willing to engage in sexual behavior with any willing female.

4. Men are not allowed to bid on the bachelors. Thus, the event is heterosexist.

When asked to justify such events, two rationales are usually given: (1) it's for a good cause, and (2) the bachelors do not mind; in fact, they enjoy it. Are these rationales good enough justification?

Chivalry is believed to communicate respect for women, but true respect involves listening to the other person's desires and negotiating relationship behaviors. In contrast to true respect, chivalry is a rigid set of rules based on the faulty assumption that all women are alike. Many of the men whom my students have interviewed express disappointment and anger that many women seem not to appreciate their chivalric behavior—an indication that these gestures are undertaken not for the woman's sake, but for the man's.

SEX COMPARISON

A commonly held social belief is that men and women are very different in many ways. The areas of difference most often cited include: aggressiveness, nurturance, mathematical ability, verbal ability, visual-spatial ability, achievement motivation, competitiveness, dominance, morality, conformity, and communication styles. Many television programs and popular books have capitalized on people's tendency to think in gender dualisms by displaying "experts" who make sweeping generalizations about purported sex differences.

Are males and females really different? More accurately, we might ask: *How* different are males and females? or, *How* similar are the sexes? These questions are empirical ones—we can not know the answers without careful scientific investigations.

Researchers have made comparisons between males and females on a variety of dimensions. Historically, this area of research has been referred to as the study of "sex differences" rather than "sex similarities" or "sex comparisons." The use of this term indicates that many researchers believed that important sex differences exist (Deaux, 1985), and that the scientific task is to discover and describe these differences.

The Measurement of Characteristics

If one measures enough people in a population on any dimension and then graphs the results, the picture that emerges nearly always approximates a normal curve (Figure 2.1). Most people's scores on the dimension of study cluster around the middle (average) of the distribution, and relatively few people's scores are found at the extremes. For example, if we were to give an intelligence test to 10,000 people, most would score around the average, a few people (the intellectually gifted) would have very high scores, and a few people (the developmentally delayed) would have very low scores. The majority of people would score somewhere between these two extremes.

Sex comparison research tends to treat males and females as two different populations and describe average differences between the population of females and that of males with reference to the characteristic of interest. Within each group, the distribution of scores usually approximates a normal curve. The sex comparison question is, "to what extent do the curves diverge and overlap?" A large sex difference would look like Figure 2.2. A small difference would look like Figure 2.3.

Differences are almost always a matter of *degree* because there are so few behaviors that are seen exclusively in one sex and not the other. Men may be more aggressive, but

Figure 2.1   The Normal Curve

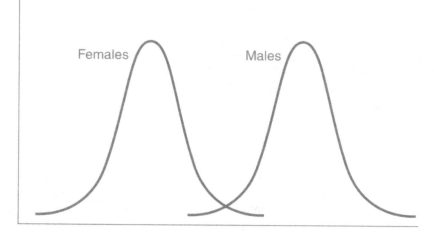

Figure 2.2   A Large Sex Difference

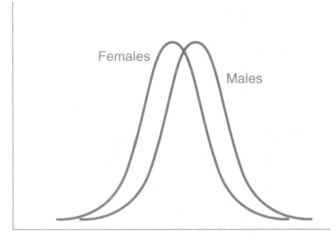

Figure 2.3   A Small Sex Difference

obviously women also display aggressive behaviors. Women may be nurturing more often, but men can also nurture. In fact, the only behaviors which are seen exclusively in one sex or the other are those associated with reproductive roles: women can menstruate, give birth, and lactate; men can impregnate (Money, 1987).

Research in Sex Comparison

An in-depth review of the voluminous sex comparison literature is well beyond the scope of this book. What follows is the barest summary of some studies that have organized large amounts of research.

Box 2.6: Sex Comparisons in Performance

In 1964, the world record for the women's marathon (a 26.2-mile footrace) was around 3 hours and 30 minutes. The men's record at that time was around 2 hours and 10 minutes. Most people at the time probably believed that this rather large difference was due to biological differences between the sexes, but if we fast forward to 2005, the women's record had improved by 1 hour and 15 minutes (2:15:25) and the men's record, less than 5 minutes (2:05:38). What appeared in 1964 to be a robust sex difference turns out to be rather miniscule by comparison, and who is to say that some talented woman might not someday eclipse the men's record?

In 2005, Harvard University President Lawrence Summers caused an uproar by suggesting that the lack of women in the sciences at Harvard might be due to biologically based differences in intellectual abilities between the sexes. His assumptions appeared to be that the world is a fair place with equal opportunities for all and that Harvard has no sex bias in hiring. Apparently he was not aware of 35 years of research comparing the sexes on a wide variety of dimensions, including a mathematics performance discrepancy that has shrunk in similar proportions to the marathon record.

Importantly, small sex differences do not tell us anything about individual men and women. Paula Radcliffe, the women's world record holder as of 2005, can outperform 99% of male marathoners. As the only female playing in a 2005 Professional Golf Association (PGA) tournament, a very young Michelle Wie barely missed the cut (qualification for the final two rounds of the tournament, based on performance in the first two rounds). Fifteen years of age at the time, Wie was undoubtedly better than 99% of male golfers and probably better than 100% of 15-year-old male golfers. In fact, she posted a better score than 48 male professional golfers in that tournament. In response, one sportswriter opined that "gender is becoming irrelevant to golf" (Jenkins, 2005, p. E7).

Ninety-eight-pound Sonya Thomas has won many competitive eating contests, beating some very large men. She has eaten seven 12-ounce hamburgers in 10 minutes, 43 tacos in 11 minutes, 23 barbecue sandwiches in 12 minutes, nearly 5 pounds of fruitcake in 10 minutes, and, in the buffalo chicken wing eating contest, she beat a 415-pound man by eating 167 wings (Carlson, 2004). In 2005, she won bratwurst and grilled cheese sandwich eating contests in addition to downing 44 lobsters in 12 minutes, easily outdistancing her competition ("Eating Champ Downs 44 Lobsters in Win," 2005).

These performances tell us that it is possible for the sex of the participant to become a secondary or even irrelevant consideration compared with other dimensions. Slowly, gender is becoming less and less of an organizing principle in society.

In 1974, Eleanor Maccoby and Carol Jacklin published the first extensive review of child sex comparison literature. They concluded that, despite the efforts of researchers to find sex differences in a wide variety of areas, very few true differences were convincingly demonstrated. Maccoby and Jacklin concluded that sex differences were found in four areas: girls had greater verbal ability, boys had greater mathematical and visual-spatial ability, and boys were more aggressive. Note that the existence of a difference does not tell us anything about *why* that difference exists. Do not fall into the trap of thinking that a male-female difference is necessarily due to biological factors.

Although the sex differences found by Maccoby and Jacklin were statistically significant, in every case the amount of difference *between* the sexes was much smaller than the variability *within* the population of males or the population of females. Graphic displays of differences resembled Figure 2.3, not Figure 2.2. This means that, for instance, although boys as a group outperformed girls as a group in mathematics, girls who did very well still outperformed the vast majority of boys; boys who did very poorly were still outperformed by the vast majority of girls. And, as evidence that even these average differences are not biologically based, recent studies of mathematics performance indicate that girls virtually caught up with boys in the 20 years following Maccoby and Jacklin's 1974 work (Vobejda & Perlstein, 1998; Murray, 1995). See Box 2.6 for a discussion of sex comparison in various performances.

Other researchers who have used meta-analysis (statistical techniques that combine data from many different studies) have reported similar results (Hyde & Plant, 1995; Cohn, 1991; Roberts, 1991; and others). Deaux (1985) noted that reported sex differences, if found at all, accounted for very small amounts of total variance, usually less than 5%. Hyde and Plant (1995) found that 25% of psychological gender differences fall into the "close to zero" range, as compared with 6% of other psychological effects. Thus, when gender differences are reported, they are four times more likely than other differences to be minimal.

What are the meanings of these similarities and differences? On the one hand, it is clear that predicting an individual's behavior based on his or her biological sex is not a very fruitful enterprise, and that people should only make generalizations about the sexes with extreme caution, if at all. On the other hand, as Deaux (1985) points out, a small difference at the *midpoint* of a distribution is accompanied by a relatively large difference at the *extremes* of the distribution. For example, although there is a very small difference between normal (average) men and women on physical aggression, there are many more highly aggressive men than there are highly aggressive women. In fact, men commit nearly nine times more violent crimes than women (U.S. Department of Justice, 2003). Thus, small sex differences have important implications when extremes of the behavior have major consequences (as is the case with violent behaviors). Clearly, however, saying that *all* men are aggressive, uncaring, disrespectful, and so on is a gross inaccuracy.

When differences exist, even when they are small, they give us clues to the strengths and weaknesses of each gender role and the characteristic struggles of men and women. These clues contribute to the awareness of the psychological importance of gender.

MODELS OF MASCULINITY AND FEMININITY

As knowledge about gender roles has increased and as sex comparison research has proceeded, theorists have created and revised theoretical frameworks for understanding the psychological implications of gender roles.

The Gender Identity Model

The earliest models of gender roles assumed that it was important for a person to display "appropriately masculine" (for males) or "feminine" (for females) behaviors. From this perspective, sex differences are understood to be based in biology and/or some sort of "natural order." The position here is that men are (and should be) different from women because of differences between the sexes in natural social roles. These differences were assumed to be so profound that they pervaded virtually every aspect of human experience. The theoretical position of this system is that the most healthy and productive men are those who are the most masculine, and that masculinity is roughly defined as the masculine stereotype (aggressive, unemotional, task oriented, etc.). These traits were thought to be opposite from "feminine" traits (nurturing, loyal, dependent, etc.).

The gender identity model carries with it a variety of assumptions about the importance of masculinity to the healthy development and general functioning of the man. First and foremost is the assumption that a fundamental developmental task for every boy is to establish an appropriate *gender role identity*, or a solid and appropriate sense of himself as masculine. Ideally, this identity is built through the boy's relationship with his father or some other appropriate male role model (see Pleck, 1981a). The most positive personality development is seen as one in which a boy spends a good deal of time with his father or "father figure," who shows the boy how to "be a man."

The gender identity model also carries the assumption that "being like a woman" (because it is defined as being unlike a man) is a negative outcome in personality development. The cause of this outcome was often believed to be an absent, distant, or passive father. A domineering or overpowering mother was also thought to thwart masculine identity, as was the "feminizing" influence of the early school years, when most teachers are women. These kinds of mother-blaming explanations were quite popular with early psychoanalytic theorists. In the last few decades, as gender roles have become more flexible, those who subscribe to the gender identity model propose that this role confusion has led to a "masculine insecurity" in young men (Lederer & Botwin, 1982).

Feminine activity is socially regarded as a threat to masculine identification. There are many parents (especially fathers) who feel that it is extremely unhealthy for their boys to play with dolls, express emotions, do domestic chores such as washing dishes, or spend a lot of time with female playmates or with women. Likewise, the failure to engage in activities defined as appropriately masculine is also seen as unhealthy. Parents and other adults may worry about a boy who shows little interest in sports or mechanical things (Antill, 1987).

What are the outcomes if appropriate male gender identity development is not achieved? Freud (1910/1989) believed that homosexuality was one possible result, and it would not be difficult to find people who agree. The logic may proceed like this: if a boy does too many feminine things, he might end up identifying with women. He would then end up being like a woman in every way, including a sexuality that is oriented toward men (and adherents to this position usually see homosexuality as a decidedly negative developmental outcome, although Freud did not). However, Kurdek (1987) reported that gay men and lesbians are more likely to exhibit a mixture of masculine and feminine characteristics as opposed to a set of characteristics usually seen in the other sex. In other words, they tend to be broader in their gender expression than heterosexuals, not *inverted*, as Freud thought. It is also worth noting that there is a great deal of variation in gender role behavior within the populations of gays and lesbians, just as there is in the population of heterosexuals.

Historically, some theorists (Toby, 1966; Adorno, Frenkel-Brunswick, Levinson, & Sanford, 1950) have proposed that insecure male gender identity leads men into exaggerated masculine behaviors that are attempts to prove their masculinity to others as well as to the self. These behaviors have been labeled *hypermasculine* and include violence, physical risk taking, and hostility directed toward women and gays. The picture that emerges is of a man who is not really masculine, but is more of a caricature of masculinity—the man who puffs out his chest, spits on the ground, beats up gays, and hates women. These activities are ways of covering up the part of the man that is a frightened, insecure little boy, because he has never come to a sense of secure masculinity. This man is like the stereotypical schoolyard bully who attacks other children because of his own poor self-esteem.

The Androgyny Model

In the 1970s, gender theorists and researchers began to question the assumptions of a gender identity model that viewed masculinity and femininity as opposites. Figure 2.4 depicts the traditional view of gender roles as a single, bipolar dimension. From this (gender identity) perspective, becoming more feminine would mean that a person was less masculine, and vice versa.

As we have seen, however, the sexes are not really opposite. Sandra Bem (1974) and many of her contemporaries believed that it was possible (and desirable) for people to have *both* masculine and feminine traits. Thus, a person could be strong *and* gentle, task oriented *and* emotionally expressive, interpersonally connected *and* independent.

Masculinity   Femininity

$\longleftarrow\!\!\!\!-\!\!\!\!-\!\!\!\!-\!\!\!\!-\!\!\!\!-\!\!\!\!-\!\!\!\!-\!\!\!\!-\!\!\!\!-\!\!\!\!-\!\!\!\!\longrightarrow$

Figure 2.4   A Bipolar View of Gender Role Identity

The person who possesses this variety of masculine and feminine attributes is defined as *androgynous*. The concept of androgyny is derived from a view of masculinity and femininity as independent dimensions (Figure 2.5). A person can be traditionally masculine—high in masculinity and low in femininity. The gender identity model would define this as the ideal for a male. The person who is high in femininity and low in masculinity is described as traditionally feminine (the gender identity ideal for a female).

The person who possesses high levels of both sets of attributes is androgynous (the ideal from the perspective of this model). It is also possible for one to be *undifferentiated*—having low levels of both masculinity and femininity. All of these categorizations are independent of the person's biological sex. Although most traditionally masculine people are men, some women also fit this description.

Androgyny theorists think of traditional femininity and masculinity as strategies for adaptation. Sometimes it is adaptive to express one's feelings (feminine); sometimes it is better to shut down one's emotions and get the job done (masculine). In stereotypical personality development, each sex acquires about half of the attitudes, skills, and behaviors necessary for coping in the world. Theoretically, the person who can incorporate both masculine and feminine characteristics into the personality will have a wide repertoire of coping strategies at his or her disposal, and this gender flexibility renders the person more

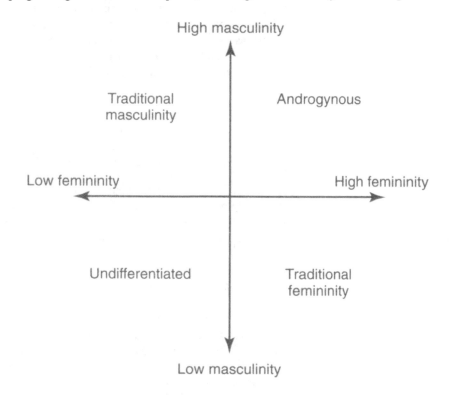

Figure 2.5   Masculinity and Femininity as Independent Dimensions

adaptive than a traditionally gender-typed person. Thus, for some theorists, androgyny is seen as a mental health ideal.

Whether or not androgyny is associated with better mental health is an empirical question, and there was a good deal of research addressing this question during the 1970s and 1980s (Cook, 1985). This research is summarized in Chapter 14.

Pleck (1981a) described the importance of the shift from gender identity models to androgyny models. In the former, traditional gender roles were seen as ideal, while in the latter, they were viewed as limiting and constricting a person's functioning. The demand to be masculine or feminine limits one's behavioral flexibility and shuts the person off from half of the potentially fulfilling experiences of the human race. The gender identity model views gender roles as emerging from within the individual, whereas the androgyny model sees gender role prescriptions as imposed through socialization.

This shift in thinking can have important effects on parenting practices. The gender identity model regards the parent's role as allowing the natural process of gender-typing to occur by exposing the child to the same sex parent, rewarding traditional behaviors, and punishing out-role behaviors. The androgyny model regards the parent's role as socializing the child to both masculine and feminine behaviors. Whereas the gender identity model sees it to be dangerous to let a boy play with dolls, the androgyny model views this activity as important for the boy in developing nurturing (feminine) characteristics.

If we look closely at this model, is it possible to take the position that androgyny is no less of a demand on the individual than masculinity or femininity? Is it possible that there is more to personality than socialization? Joseph Pleck (1981a) in his landmark book *The Myth of Masculinity*, addressed these questions in light of the available androgyny research, and proposed a new model.

The Gender Role Strain Model

While the Androgyny model emphasizes the limited adaptive quality of traditionally gender-typed behavior, the Gender Role Strain Model emphasizes that some gendered behavior, such as compulsive dominance, passivity, or emotional constriction, is downright maladaptive. In addition, some theorists (O'Neil, 1982; Pleck, 1981a, 1981b) argue that trying to become androgynous entails an attempt to live up to a set of rather stringent demands, and that perhaps these demands are even greater than the expectation to live up to traditional gender roles. For men, traditional gender roles included demands for competitiveness, aggression, and task orientation. Androgyny demands emotional expression, relationship orientation, and gentleness in *addition* to the role requirements of traditional masculinity.

Gender Role Strain is a psychological situation in which gender role demands have negative consequences for the individual or others (O'Neil, 1981a). The negative effects of masculine gender role strain can be described in terms of stress, conflict, health, and mental health problems for the individual. Violence and poor relationships are potential negative consequences for others who come into contact with the individual.

A person experiences this strain when gender role demands conflict with his or her *naturally occurring tendencies*. For example, males in most Western cultures are socialized to be unemotional. For a naturally emotional man, the demand created by this socialization may cause him to feel a good deal of pressure to conform his behavior to the cultural norm. As a result, he may experience negative consequences, such as depression or high blood pressure. The net effect of gender role strain is the restriction of the person's ability to reach his or her full human potential (O'Neil, 1981a). In the above example, the man's depression or high blood pressure may restrict his potential by lowering his functioning in his work, affecting his relationship with his partner, or even shortening his life.

Pleck (1981a) outlined a set of ten propositions defining the Gender Role Strain model. At the time, Pleck used the term *Sex Role Strain Paradigm*. Later, he revised his title to *Gender Role Strain Paradigm* based on Unger's (1979) distinction between sex and gender (Pleck, 1995). Words in italics are Pleck's propositions, directly quoted, with the term gender substituted for the term sex to be consistent with the distinction:

1. *Gender roles are operationally defined by gender role stereotypes.* As discussed earlier in this chapter and in Chapter 1, people tend to hold beliefs about how men and women are and how they should be.

2. *Gender roles are contradictory and inconsistent.* It is impossible for anyone to fulfill all of the demands of the masculine or feminine gender role. For instance, men are socialized to avoid everything feminine, but are expected to marry and be intimate with women (Jourard, 1971).

3. *The proportion of individuals who violate gender roles is high.* For men, this is true because masculine gender role demands are contradictory, but also because some demands border on the impossible and because the inner psychological needs of the person can outweigh social (gender role) demands.

   To illustrate, one gender role demand is for men to make a great deal of money. Socioeconomic conditions make it impossible for many men to do so. Men of color have to overcome societal and institutional racism in order to achieve financial success. Another masculine gender role dictate is for men to be strong and athletic, but the native endowment (natural physique, cardiovascular capacity, eye-hand coordination, etc.) of some men renders the realization of athletic success highly unlikely. Men are sometimes expected to take physical risks to defend their "honor" (or someone else's). However, safety is a basic human need, and it may often win out over the gender role (social) demand. Pleck proposes that even the most traditionally masculine, successful, physically imposing men may feel that they fail to live up to masculine gender role norms.

4. *Violating gender roles leads to social condemnation.* Men who exhibit out-role behavior may be socially ostracized or experience other punishment. For instance, a junior high school boy who plays the flute may be teased and shunned because he plays an instrument that many children may associate with femininity.

5. *Violating gender roles leads to negative psychological consequences.* A man who accepts masculine gender role norms and fails to fulfill them (which, as noted above,

is virtually inevitable) will experience negative emotional consequences such as anxiety or depression. Such men are victims of internalized sexism. For example, a man who believes that masculinity is based on having sex with many women, but who is unattractive and socially inept, and therefore unsuccessful in getting women to have sex with him, may suffer from low self-esteem based on his perceived short-comings. He might not experience this symptom if he did not embrace the traditional masculine ideological value of sexual promiscuity.

6. *Actual or imagined violation of gender roles leads individuals to overconform to them.* Masculine Gender Role Strain theorists offer this proposition as a possible cause for hypermasculinity. Pleck's proposition is that failure in gender role leads the man to compensate for negative emotions by exaggerating the masculine role behaviors that are the most obvious. He might do so by being aggressive, making negative statements about women and gays, and/or exaggerating his independ-ence. For example, sexual feelings toward other men are clearly not tolerated within dominant masculinity. Men who experience homosexual feelings may compensate for the anxiety that accompanies these feelings by attacking gay men verbally or even physically. Some empirical data in support of this hypothe-sis have been provided by Adams, Wright, and Lohr (1996), who reported that men with negative attitudes toward homosexuality tended to show some physio-logical signs of sexual arousal while watching films that depicted gay men in sexual situations.

It is important to draw a distinction between this theory of hypermasculinity and the theory proposed by the Gender Identity model. In the latter, hypermasculine behavior is thought to be the result of blocking natural (masculine) personality de-velopment. In contrast, the Gender Role Strain model is a view that hypermasculinity is a result of the conflict between individual tendencies and so-cial expectations. In the last example, the Gender Role Strain theorist proposes that, if society were to define homosexual feelings as acceptable, the man would feel less anxious about his sexuality and thus have less of a need to compensate for these feelings. If it were culturally acceptable for men to act in stereotypically un-masculine ways, there would be no need to exaggerate one's masculinity.

7. *Violating gender roles has more severe consequences for males than females.* Pleck cites a number of studies that demonstrate greater negative social sanction for male out-role behavior. For instance, "tomboys" are subject to less social disapproval than "sissies." It should be noted, however, that males can conform to gender role demands and maintain a good deal of social power, whereas females conforming to their gender role demands tend to accrue much less power.

8. *Certain characteristics prescribed by gender roles are psychologically dysfunc-tional.* For instance, aggressive behavior may lead to relationship, work, and/or le-gal problems.

9. *Each sex experiences gender role strain in its work and family roles.* The pressure to be a good provider, husband, and father sometimes conflict with one another. There

is always the demand to work harder, make more money, spend more time with one's children, and relate to one's partner better. It is quite difficult to continually do all of these things at the same time.

10. *Historical change causes gender role strain.* For example, the traditional gender role demand that men dominate women has become more stressful as women increasingly claim more of their fair share of institutional and economic power. Although changing traditional masculinity is an important thing to do, it creates anxiety for many men, who feel that they are losing the basic emotional anchor of manliness. Men in modern times find themselves increasingly encountering women in the workplace, sometimes in positions of power. As the social connections between gender and power continue to change, so will the ideologies that accompany these connections.

A Comparison and Contrast

The Gender Role Strain model has features in common with both the Gender Role Identity and Androgyny models. Both the Gender Role Identity and Gender Role Strain models stress the importance of *naturally occurring tendencies* within the individual. Gender Role Identity theorists consider these to be traditionally gender-typed, whereas Gender Role Strain theorists consider them to be more specific to the individual. In contrast, the Androgyny model de-emphasizes the importance of the naturally occurring parts of personality. Instead, the emphasis here is on the learned aspects of behavior and personality.

Androgyny and Gender Role Strain theorists both consider traditional gender roles to be archaic vestiges of history, and both consider changes in gender roles to be a positive development. Whereas Androgyny theorists stress the importance of learning all adaptive behaviors regardless of gender role definition, Gender Role Strain theorists seem to emphasize being true to one's "inner nature." From the perspective of the Gender Role Strain model, it would seem to be acceptable for a man to not be nurturing if he is not naturally so, whereas the Androgyny model seems to suggest that innate differences in such characteristics are either nonexistent or unimportant. In contrast, proponents of the Gender Identity model see advantage in the maintaining of some aspects of gender roles, although there are probably very few who would argue that current social structures are ideal. All of these models reflect ideas about human nature and behavior that theorists have wrestled with for years. We will examine these ideas further in Part II of this book.

MEASURING GENDER ROLES

The accurate measurement of gender roles and characteristics is critically important to gender research. As gender has become an object of increasing inquiry, researchers have attempted to construct such measures. As we shall see, the way that they have gone about doing so has depended on the differential endorsement of the gender role models described above.

Gender Role Identity Measures

The earliest psychological measures of masculinity and femininity were based on a bipolar, unidimensional model of gender (see Figure 2.4). Masculinity was assumed to be the opposite of femininity. It was also assumed that femininity in males or masculinity in females was an undesirable state of affairs that reflected psychological problems in the person (Derlega, Winstead, & Jones, 1991).

Terman and Miles (1936) published a scale that reflected these biases, the "M-F" scale, which was also called the Attitude Interest Analysis Test (AIST) to disguise its purpose to test takers. Morawski (1985) described the characteristics of this scale:

> Masculinity scores are gained by replying that you dislike foreigners, religious men, women cleverer than you are, dancing, guessing games, being alone, and thin women. Femininity points are accrued by indicating dislike for sideshow freaks, bashful men, riding bicycles, giving advice, bald-headed men, and very cautious people. (p. 206)

This scale became a prototype for other early attempts at gender measurement. The original Minnesota Multiphasic Personality Inventory (MMPI) (Hathaway & McKinley, 1951) was a questionnaire containing 557 statements to which the person answers "true" or "false" in relation to the self. The MMPI yields scores on various scales that were designed to measure depression, odd or unusual thought processes, antisocial tendencies, some aspects of anxiety, and other attributes, including gender characteristics.

The MMPI yields a score on a scale labeled "Mf". This scale was originally designed to differentiate male heterosexuals from homosexuals (Groth-Marnat, 2003). Questionnaire items from this scale were based on gender-typed patterns of occupational preference, preferred activities, and emotional responses. A "feminine" man would report not liking mechanics magazines or adventure stories, and liking to cook or sew.

A few other scales based on a similar conception of gender roles followed. Among these were the California Psychological Inventory (CPI) "Fe" scale (Gough, 1957), and the Feminine Gender Identity Scale (Freund, Nagler, Langevin, Zajac, & Steiner, 1974). Following is an examination of the assumptions behind such measurement techniques:

> *Assumption 1.   Masculinity-femininity is a bipolar, unidimensional construct.* A large number of researchers have demonstrated that these constructs are complex and multidimensional (Cook, 1985; Thompson & Pleck, 1995).

> *Assumption 2.   Failure to accept the "masculine role" is a sign of psychopathology.* As we have already seen, this is a false claim. Many authors (O'Neil, 1981b; 1982; Brannon, 1985; Friend, 1991; Sharpe & Heppner, 1991; and many others) have noted that the refusal to accept some aspects of traditional masculinity may be a sign of vigorous health.

Assumption 3.   The personality components of femininity and homosexuality are the same. This assumption would seem to be based on stereotypes of gay men. There have been no successful attempts to differentiate gays from heterosexuals on the basis of personality, probably because the personalities of gay people are as diverse as those of heterosexuals (Paul, Weinrich, Gonsiorek, & Hotvedt, 1982).

One of the major criticisms of the MMPI and the CPI was that they used relatively insignificant aspects of the personality (e.g., liking mechanics magazines) to make inferences about characteristics of central importance like erotic orientation, level of aggressiveness, and gender identity (Pleck, 1975), thus confusing gender with sex and sexual orientation. Reporting traditionally feminine interests such as cooking resulted in interpretations of poor adjustment and lack of masculinity.

For its original purpose, the MMPI "Mf" scale was a total failure, probably because of the flaws in theory described above. Currently, this scale is considered to be a measure of breadth and stereotypy of interest. College-educated men tend to score more "feminine" on this scale compared with the general population of men (Groth-Marnat, 2003). Under the original intent of the scale, this finding would mean that college men tend to be disturbed with gender identity problems. The reality is that these men tend to be broader and less stereotypic than the general population of men in their preferences for activities, perhaps as the consequences of higher than average intelligence and socioeconomic level, and more experiences of being exposed to a rich variety of ideas. However, some MMPI interpretations continue to make claims based on the original intent of the scale (see Box 2.7).

Box 2.7: The MMPI "Mf" Scale

Although the MMPI "Mf" scale has never been useful for describing any kind of gender-related problems, interpretation of scores to this effect persist.

Following is an excerpt from a computer service (The Minnesota Report: Butcher, 1987) that scores and provides interpretations for MMPI questionnaires. Presumably, these interpretations are written by an expert. The testing subject is a 33 year old, heterosexual, psychologically healthy man, whose "Mf" score was about average for a male college student but higher than the average male in the general population.

"He is rather insecure in the masculine role. Effeminate in both manner and dress and quite passive, he tends to be dependent on others. He may display a feminine identification pattern."

It is interesting to note that a test interpreter could make statements about a person's dress and mannerisms without having ever met or observed the person.

Androgyny Measures

In the 1970s, the conception of masculinity and femininity as independent dimensions (see Figure 2.5) created a need for new measures. By far the most popular of these measures is the Bem Sex Role Inventory (BSRI) (Bem, 1974). The BSRI is a list of 60 adjectives. Twenty of these are descriptive of traditional masculinity (e.g., "self-reliant," "analytical"), 20 are descriptive of traditional femininity (e.g., "warm," "gentle"), and 20 others are gender neutral (e.g., "conscientious," "likable"). All adjectives reflect the socially desirable aspects of each gender role due to the theory that the combination of positive traits of both roles is the ideal. The person rates himself or herself on each adjective using a seven point scale ranging from "never or almost never true" to "always or almost always true."

The BSRI yields two scores: one for Masculinity and one for Femininity. People who score high on one scale and low on the other are classified according to gender type. Thus, someone who scores high in Masculinity and low in Femininity is labeled "masculine." Although most people with this kind of pattern would be biological males, this is not always the case. Gender role orientation can be separate from biological sex, as is the case with a feminine man or a masculine woman.

Persons who score high on Femininity and high on Masculinity are labeled "androgynous." Those who score low on both scales are labeled "undifferentiated." In theory, androgynous people should be the most psychologically healthy of the four types because they have a wider repertoire of adaptive behaviors. Undifferentiated people are thought to be the least adaptable due to the relative absence of the positive characteristics associated with either sex.

A number of other androgyny measures followed the BSRI, including the Personal Attributes Questionnaire (PAQ) (Spence, Helmreich, & Stapp, 1974), the ANDRO scale (Berzins, Welling, & Wetter, 1978), and the Sex Role Behavior Scale (SRBS) (Orlofsky, Ramsden, & Cohen, 1982). There are, of course some differences among the BSRI and these other measures. However, Cook (1985), in an extensive review of methods of androgyny measurement, concluded that these differences are relatively minor, indicating that highly related aspects of gender roles are being described by all of these measures. Correlations between these measures and measures like the MMPI "Mf" scale are low, indicating that androgyny measures are tapping some construct that is relatively independent of what older gender identity scales were assessing. In addition, Masculinity and Femininity dimensions on androgyny measures are statistically independent from each other (Marsh, Antill, & Cunningham, 1989), providing some support for Bem's (1974) conception of masculinity and femininity as independent dimensions.

The 1970s and 1980s witnessed an explosion of research on androgyny. Beere's (1990) literature search produced over 900 references to studies in which researchers utilized the BSRI. An excellent description and commentary of much of this literature is provided by Cook (1985). She reviewed research on the correspondence of gender role to behavioral flexibility, adjustment, emotional stability, assertiveness, achievement motivation, and psychological health, among other dimensions. Some of this research is reviewed in Chapter 14.

Gender Role Strain and Stress Measures

James O'Neil and his colleagues have developed two versions of the Gender-Role Conflict Scale (GRCS) (O'Neil, Helms, Gable, David, & Wrightsman, 1986). These measures were developed for use with only male subjects and are designed to assess the degree to which a man endorses attitudes, behaviors, and values that have been associated with negative psychological effects. O'Neil proposes four categories of conflict (derived from factor analyses of the GRCS):

1. *Success, Power, and Competition*: the pressure to gain wealth, obtain authority, and be a winner.

2. *Restrictive Emotionality*: difficulty in expressing one's feelings or allowing others to do so.

3. *Restrictive Affectionate Behavior between Men*: limiting the expression of warm feelings for other men.

4. *Conflict between Work and Family Relations*: difficulty balancing these sometimes conflicting demands.

The GRCS-I is a set of 37 statements to which the person responds on a six-point scale ranging from "strongly agree" to "strongly disagree." Some examples of items from each area include:

"I worry about failing and how it affects my doing well as a man." (Success, Power, and Competition)

"Strong emotions are difficult for me to understand." (Restrictive Emotionality)

"Men who touch other men make me uncomfortable." (Restrictive Affectionate Behavior between Men)

"My career, job, or school affects the quality of my leisure or family life." (Conflicts between Work and Family Relations)

The GRCS-II is a series of 16 brief stories that describe situations in which conflict might be experienced. Respondents report the degree to which they would feel discomfort or conflict in such situations ranging from "very much conflict—very uncomfortable" to "no conflict—very comfortable." Following are two examples:

1. "Your best friend has just lost his job at the factory where you work. He is obviously upset, afraid, and angry but he has these emotions hidden. How comfortable/uncomfortable are you to responding to your friend's intense emotions and fear about unemployment?"

2. "There's a guy you've idolized since grade school. He's three years older than you are. In high school he was the star quarterback, valedictorian, and very active in the

Young Methodist Fellowship. Last year he graduated from college. You have just learned he is a homosexual. How much conflict do you feel between your admiration for this person and the fact that he is a homosexual?"

Stillson, O'Neil, and Owen (1991) reported that men with physical problems experienced high gender role conflict. Perhaps the demands for physical risk taking and low emotionality had adverse effects on their health (see Chapters 8 and 9). They also reported that men from varying socioeconomic strata and ethnic backgrounds are similar in patterns of gender role strain. The Fox Tribe of Iowa refers to masculinity as "The Big Impossible" (Gilmore, 1990). It seems that the masculine demands to always be "number one," sure of oneself, in control of every situation, and to never get tired are so impossible that virtually no man, regardless of his ethnicity or social status, can accept these masculine ideologies and feel that he is successful in living up to them.

Richard Eisler (1995) and his colleagues (Eisler, Skidmore, & Ward, 1988; Lash, Eisler, & Southard, 1995; Saurer & Eisler, 1990) have undertaken extensive research using a related measure, the Masculine Gender Roles Stress Scale (MGRSS), which assesses the man's "appraisal of specific cognitions, behaviors, or situations as stressful and undesirable" (Eisler et al., 1988, p. 135). For instance, men who view asking for help as feminine and weak will experience more stress than other men in situations that require this behavior. In many of these studies, researchers have demonstrated that men with high MGRS scores show high physiological arousal (e.g., elevated heart rate and blood pressure) to gender-relevant conditions such as when they are asked to endure pain and told that it is masculine to do so. This arousal pattern, combined with these men's hypermasculine unwillingness to take care of their bodies, has negative effects on men's health (Eisler, 1995). I discuss the impact of these behaviors on men's health in Chapter 9.

Newer Measures

Thompson and Pleck (1995) have thoroughly reviewed all of the measures that I have described, as well as many others. They found eleven different measures of gender-related constructs such as masculine sexism, attitudes toward masculine gender roles, masculine role norms and stereotypes, and hypermasculinity. Thompson and Pleck conclude that those scales that assess masculine *traits* (personality characteristics like gender orientation and androgyny) are conceptually distinct from those that measure masculine *ideology* (prescriptive and proscriptive beliefs). Thus, people's conceptions about how men and women should be appear to be quite distinct from the way individuals describe themselves, lending support to Pleck's (1981a) proposition that the proportion of individuals violating gender roles is high. They recommend that researchers pay close attention to the distinction between personal characteristics and social ideologies, and that they develop new strategies that go beyond paper-and-pencil measures into physiological and behavioral assessment. They also recommend that researchers pay increasing attention to *masculinities*, the variations among men with regard to race, class, sexual orientation, and other salient aspects of male subpopulations.

Andrew Smiler (2004) traced the development of measures of masculinity as they relate to the development of scholars' conceptions of gender. One important measure that was developed in the time since Thompson and Pleck's review is the Conformity to Masculine Norms Index (CMNI; Mahalik, Locke, Ludlow, Diemer, Scott, Gottfried, & Freitas, 2003), a measure of the degree to which the person's behavior and ideologies fit with stereotypical masculinity. Smiler echoes Thompson's and Pleck's suggestion for more research into multiple masculinities, noting that this work has not come very far, and also calls for researchers to move beyond personality-type measures and pay more attention to the social contexts in which behavior occurs.

The development of the ability to accurately measure the various aspects of gender is an ongoing process. As Smiler (2004) points out, these scales represent the operational definition of masculinity as it is used in research endeavors. The value of these measures will become apparent to you as you read Part III of this book, which contains descriptions of many research findings in the areas of men's violence, sexuality, mental and physical health, and interpersonal relationships.

SUMMARY

1. Gender roles contain powerful expectations for behavior that are based on a person's biological sex. They include norms and stereotypes, which have emotional, cognitive, behavioral, and unconscious components. Violating gender roles often leads to some sort of negative social sanction.

2. Gender roles are at least partly the result of people's tendencies to categorize objects and events. Roles affect what one notices and remembers about a person, how one person interprets another's behavior, and what one expects of one's own and others' behavior.

3. People tend to overestimate differences and underestimate similarities between men and women. Researchers have demonstrated very few reliable sex differences.

4. Sexism is the differential treatment of people based on biological sex. It involves disrespect of individuals. Contrary to popular belief, men are sometimes victims of sexism, although sexism against women is much more pervasive and has greater negative implications for women's quality of life.

5. Theorists have constructed new models for understanding masculinity and femininity within the last 30 years. Chief among these are the Androgyny and Gender Role Strain models, both of which view traditional sex typing as limiting and perhaps damaging to people. These models have influenced the psychological measurement of gender and the course of gender research.

3

Biologically Based Theoretical Perspectives on Males and Gender

One logical place to begin a study of male behavior and experience is within the biological paradigm. In this chapter, we explore two theoretical approaches that take biology as the starting point for explanations of gender. Sociobiology attempts to apply the theory of evolution to social behaviors, and psychoanalysis is a narrative of how basic biological survival mechanisms interact with human relationships to form the personality, part of which is gendered.

EVOLUTION AND SOCIOBIOLOGY: SEX ON THE BRAIN

Parents of large families often say that their children have differing personalities, and that these differences were evident even in the first few days after they were born. Such differences could be due to misperception or memory distortion on the part of the parents, or from prenatal events such as difficult pregnancies. But it is also possible that what these parents perceive are some real differences that are based in biology.

Developmental psychologists have long known that infants differ in *psychological temperament*. Some babies are relatively quiet and content. Others have higher activity levels or are more disposed toward crankiness. Temperamental differences are thought to be determined largely by infants' genes, hormones, and other biological forces, which continue to affect their behavior throughout their lives (Vasta, Haith, & Miller, 1992).

It is clear that males and females have differing biologies in some ways, although we should keep in mind that in *most* ways, they do not. There are differences in genetic and hormonal composition that lead to average male/female differences in height, weight, muscularity, genitalia, and secondary sex characteristics such as breasts and facial hair. There is little dispute that biological sex differences produce these usual physical differences (most of which which are *average* differences—we all know women who are taller than many men or men whose hips are bigger than many women). But, to what extent do they produce *behavioral* sex differences as well? The central question concerns to what extent "boys will be boys" because of their biological compositions, and to what extent "boys will be boys" because we socialize them to act in certain ways. Some theorists believe that biological nature is mainly responsible for gendered behavior.

A rather complex sequence of biological events is necessary to ensure that most healthy men and women will have the physiological wherewithal to reproduce. Of course, the development of these basic structures is not enough to ensure the survival of the species. Sexual behaviors are also necessary. There is little doubt that hormonal events affect brain structures and pathways, which then have strong influences over these behaviors. But what is the difference in the biological basis of *sexual* behaviors (those necessary for reproduction) on the one hand, and *gender role* behaviors (social behaviors attributed strongly to either males or females) on the other?

"Not much" would be the answer of those who support the theory of *sociobiology*, the highly controversial belief that both reproductive and social behaviors are powerfully influenced by biological forces. Barash and Lipton (1997) summarize the sociobiological viewpoint when they say, "In a genuine sense we are all animals, genetically connected to one another through an ancient lineage... that extends back to the primordial ooze..." (p. 4). They quote Delbert Thiessen, who said that, "We do not walk through nature; nature walks through us." (p. 4).

Sociobiologists argue that biological forces, which have been put into place through millions of years of human evolution, have powerful influences on social behaviors such as courtship, aggression, and parenting style. The theoretical position is that if a behavior assists in the survival of an organism or species, then the gene or gene complex associated with that behavior will be bred into the species through disproportionate representation in subsequent gene pools (Wilson, 1975).

With regard to gender role behaviors, sociobiologists propose that there are certain sex-linked social behaviors (like male dominance) which have survival value for the person, his or her stake in the gene pool, and ultimately the survival of the species (Barash & Lipton, 1997). Critics of this position maintain that it is an ideology disguised as science, and that this ideology is used to validate male power and privilege by normalizing destructive and irresponsible male behaviors (Fausto-Sterling, 1992). Box 3.1 invites you to take a critical look at sociobiological proposals.

The sociobiological position is that sex differences in behavior are the result of differences in males' and females' *reproductive investments*, which in turn affect the *reproductive strategies* of each sex. Reproductive investment refers to the amount of time and resources that are expended in producing offspring. Reproductive strategy is the behavioral pattern employed to ensure that one's genes will be passed on to the succeeding generation (Daly & Wilson, 1983).

Box 3.1: *Sociobiological Proposals*

Highly controversial biologically based explanations have been offered to account for a wide variety of purported sex-linked phenomena, including:

1. Male aggression (Kenrick, 1987): Sociobiologists see men as aggressive in the service of increased breeding opportunities.

2. All male groups and "male bonding" (Tiger, 1969): Because of their aggression, men form groups to protect themselves from harm by other men.

3. The sexual double standard and male promiscuity (Daly & Wilson, 1983): Sociobiologists see men as motivated to propagate their genes maximally.

4. Rape (Thornhill & Palmer, 2000): Sociobiologists see this socially aberrant behavior as an extreme strategy for reproduction.

5. Female nurturing (Beach, 1987): Women must protect and feed their young in the service of survival. Men are seen as being more motivated to produce large numbers of offspring than they are to protect the young.

6. Adult males' preference for younger wives (Buss, 1994): Males prefer younger women because they have more time than women to reproduce.

7. Males refusing to ask for directions when they are lost (cf. Francis, 2004): because of the evolutionary past of man-the-hunter, asking for directions indicates a lack of reproductive fitness.

What are some alternative (nonsociobiological) explanations of these phenomena? How plausible are these alternative explanations? What kinds of common behaviors have you observed that seem to run counter to sociobiological theory?

According to sociobiologists, males and females differ markedly in reproductive investment. Physiologically, males need only a few seconds to make their genetic contribution to the reproductive process. Millions of sperm can be deposited in this period of time, and a healthy young male can ejaculate several times a day. Males are capable of impregnating females for almost all of their adult lives, and sperm are an abundant resource.

In contrast, females usually only produce one ovum per month and they have a more limited number of reproductive years. Therefore, females have a greater investment in the reproductive process than males. In humans, females carry and nourish the fetus for nine months, during which time they cannot begin another pregnancy. Following birth, they must feed and protect children during the period of helpless infancy if the young are to survive. Whereas sperm are abundant resources, eggs are relatively scarce ones.

Sociobiologists claim that, because of these differences in reproductive investment, sex-differentiated reproductive strategies have evolved. To propagate his genes as much as possible, the male's strategy is to impregnate as many females as possible and prevent other males from occupying potential partners (often using aggression and other forms of dominance). On the other hand, the female must be selective in her choice of sexual partners. She chooses only the "best" genes for the fertilization of her precious eggs (Daly & Wilson, 1983). If she can also persuade an evolutionarily fit male to stick around, she can ensure a steady supply of Grade A genetic material, and even get some help with the care and protection of her offspring.

The consideration of this purported difference in reproductive strategies led sociobiologists to propose a great number of "natural" (biologically based) sex differences. As evidence for the veracity of their claims, they mainly use observations of animal behavior and experiments with animal subjects.

For example, sociobiologists have proposed that men are predisposed to seek more sexual partners, engage in sex more casually, and be more easily aroused by visual stimuli, than females (Symons, 1987). These tendencies are all the result of evolutionary forces which allow men to be less discriminating than women in their choice of sexual partners. Charles Darwin (1871) described evolution as "survival of the fittest." "Fitness" in this sense, is the male's ability to engage in intercourse with as many partners as possible. Thus, the sociobiological ideal is the promiscuous playboy, or, as Joseph Pleck (1994) mockingly referred to him, the "roving inseminator."

Note how conveniently this ideal *normalizes* the sexual double standard, male sexual irresponsibility, violence, noninvolvement with children, and a lack of a human connection with women. If we see these attributes as biologically ordained, then there is little hope in changing the standard of male dominance. Several authors (Tavris, 1992; Kimmel & Mosmiller, 1992; Fausto-Sterling, 1992; and others) have described the historic use of scientific arguments to justify the exclusion of women from public status equal to that of men, and to defend the status quo as the natural and unchangeable order of things. Gould (1981) noted that the same kind of process has been used to exclude people of color from equal participation in the public sphere.

As evidence in support of their claim, sociobiologists offer the fact that many more societies allow polygyny (men having more than one wife or partner) than allow polyandry (women having multiple partners) (Daly & Wilson, 1983). Sociobiologists downplay the effects of social forces, specifically a historical imbalance of power between the sexes, that provide plausible alternative explanations of this phenomenon.

Sociobiologists have also offered explanations for male aggressiveness, competition, risk taking, and dominance (Barash & Lipton, 1997). Just as rams butt horns to win the right to reproduce with ewes, so do men fight with one another in the competition to inseminate women. According to these theories, a male has to take a chance on being hurt or killed in competition to pass on his genes. Daly and Wilson (1983) describe the process using an animal example:

> Imagine a bull elephant seal that has no stomach for the dominance battles of the breeding beach. Very well. He can opt out: remain at sea, never endure the debilitating months of fast and battle, outlive his brothers. But mere survival is no criterion of success. Even-

tually he will die, and his genes will die with him. The bull seals of the future will be the sons of males that found the ordeal of the beach to be worth the price. (p. 92)

Sociobiologists have even offered explanations for male dominance of women. Because men can never be sure that they are, in fact, the father of the offspring (hence the phrase, "momma's baby, daddy's maybe"), they tend to be possessive, controlling, and distrustful of females. Daly, Wilson, and Weghorst (1982) note that male wife murderers and batterers cite sexual jealousy as a major rationale for their violent behavior. It is difficult to see, however, what evolutionary purpose is served by killing or beating a partner whose attentions have gone astray. Here we see purported biological explanations for men's disrespect of women (in this case, to the point of violence, even murder) when other, socially based explanations are available.

Behavioral Thresholds

I have presented sociobiology here as if social-environmental events were of little or no consequence in the formation of personality and gender role behavior. Even the staunchest of sociobiologists would not make such a claim. Sociobiology does not assume the lack of influence of cultural forces on behavior. Rather, the theory is that biology puts into motion a set of behavioral predispositions or thresholds. In other words, we are born with tendencies toward certain behaviors, and the environment can act on any tendency by encouraging it, inhibiting it, or leaving it unchanged (Kay & Meikle, 1984). Sociobiologists emphasize the power of proposed biological forces as the default options of behavior.

If sociobiological assumptions are correct with regard to the realm of gender roles, then the male is born with behavioral predispositions toward sexual promiscuity, violence, and misogyny (the hatred of women). If he is born into a culture that considers this behavior normal and desirable (such as mainstream U.S. culture, some would argue), then it will be relatively easy for this biologically set threshold to be crossed. Thus, we could expect many males in the culture to exhibit behaviors in these realms, because biological tendencies and social cultural influences work together to produce these behaviors.

On the other hand, the boy could be born into a culture that punishes these behaviors. For example, many cultures discourage promiscuity. In this case, the cultural influence would work against the biological tendency, and we would see less of the behavior. It is also possible for the cultural influence to have a relatively minor effect on the behavior, in which case the frequency of promiscuity would be somewhere between the two extremes.

It is important to note, however, that sociobiologists would predict that, in a culture that encouraged promiscuity for both sexes equally, we would see more of the behavior in men. The same would be true for a culture that inhibits the same behavior equally for both sexes. The "bottom line" of sociobiology is that there are some behaviors (like dominance or aggression) that are easier to produce in males, and some (like nurturing) that are easier to produce in females. The differences are proposed to be the result of the person needing more or less of a cultural "push" to cross the biologically determined threshold.

Sociobiology and Masculinity

Sociobiologists temper their claims with the warnings that cultural influences are also important, that no predictions for individuals are possible, and that describing biological influences is different from prescribing how people *should* act (Barash & Lipton, 1997). Nevertheless, a proposed description of a gender-typed "human nature" emerges, and the picture of "male nature" (as well as men's treatment of women) is not a pretty one. Although sociobiologists often propose that learning about sex differences in behavior will allow us to design social interventions that will result in a more gender-egalitarian and less violent world (Thornhill & Palmer, 2000), they rarely say specifically what these interventions should be, and their seeming lack of interest in modifying these destructive behaviors that they see as natural makes their motives suspect in the eyes of many of their critics.

Sociobiology characterizes the man as an aggressive, driven, immoral, impulsive, uncaring, unfaithful, distrustful, jealous, promiscuous, and cruel animal whose core motivation is to fight off other men and impregnate as many women as possible, at almost any cost, even risking his life in the pursuit of his evolutionary goals. This view serves to normalize and excuse many of the most destructive aspects of the masculine gender role: over-competitiveness, attention to task and not relationship, the unimportance of emotions other than sexual and aggressive feelings, and the risking of the body in the compulsive attempt to prove one's masculinity. However, a man can never do so, as there are always more men to fight off and more women to impregnate. He can never be sure of his own paternity, so he must be on guard against other men at all times. Eventually he will grow old and be supplanted by younger and stronger men. The picture that emerges is one of a roaming, violent, restless creature who can never be satisfied.

From the sociobiological point of view, the only hope for a civilized society is to tame the barbaric nature of masculinity. Sociobiologists see male nature as antisocial and valueless, and female nature more civilized, positive, and morally superior. They view the two sexes as inherently competitive with each other (Clatterbaugh, 1997). Gilder (1986) argues that a socialized order can only be maintained if male sexual impulses and antisocial tendencies are subordinated to female nature. He assigns the task of civilizing the world to women, who must use their erotic power to keep men in line by demanding monogamy and commitment from them in exchange for sexual access. The idea is that men have no control and that it is women's job to control them (as if women did not have enough to do!). This view would seem disrespectful toward men and downright frightening for women.

Gilder's ideal society seems to be one with traditional morals, where women refuse to have sex before marriage, and where monogamy is strictly enforced. Many sociobiologists do not believe that this arrangement will work because of the primacy of biological forces over social ones (Barash, 1982). For these theorists, "boys will be boys" forever, and therefore war, rape, and the adversarial "battle of the sexes" is unavoidable.

Critique of Sociobiology

Many people may find sociobiological theory compelling because it allows them to maintain the sexual status quo. This theory may be especially appealing for traditional men who may be motivated to dominate, disrespect, and overpower women, and to engage in competitions for dominance with other men. In bookstores, one usually finds sociobiological works in the biology section rather than the social science section despite the fact that these books are almost wholly focused on explaining social behavioral phenomena. It seems that many people view biology as "real" science and view the social sciences with a good deal more skepticism. The relative statuses of the sciences can be used by oppressors to validate the unequal social statuses of men and women. Although sociobiological propositions based on the theory of evolution are subject to serious criticism, the theory of evolution itself is well accepted, and it may be difficult for an uncritical observer to separate the two. Sociobiologists look for biological correlates of behavior in a quest to prove that sex differences are of "real" nature, not "trivial" nurture (Money, 1987a).

The major bases of critiques of sociobiology are:

1. Sociobiological methods are simplistic.

2. Sociobiological logic is circular and/or faulty.

3. The inclusion of supporting data is selective.

4. There is a consistent failure to consider alternative explanations for sex- differentiated behavior.

5. Sociobiological arguments are used to justify the maltreatment of women.

6. Genetic explanations fail to account for genes passed on from females to males (See Box 3.2).

With regard to the first objection, Goldfoot and Neff (1987) are critical of the usual methods that are used to test hormonal and other physiological mechanisms in animal studies. The typical approach is to hold constant, or to eliminate, social variables that are known to affect the behavior being studied. For example, researchers might study sexual behavior in primates by raising a male and a female primate in a cage together and observing some behavior of interest. Such research ignores the effects of known social influences such as dominance hierarchies and coalition formation within the primate troop.

With regard to the second objection, there is often an assumption in biopsychological research that animals (humans included) behave from the "inside out." If there is hormonal variation and change in behavior at the same time, the bias is to see the hormonal change as the cause of the behavioral change. There is evidence to suggest that a hormonal change may sometimes be an effect, rather than a cause, of behavioral change. For instance, although testosterone may be a partial cause of aggression, the attainment of dominance (sometimes through aggressive behavior) results in testosterone surges, both

Box 3.2: "Intergender Hitchhiking:" What's Good for the Goose Must be Bad for the Gander

Richard Francis (2004) points out an important aspect of gender genetics: both parents pass on their genetic material to their daughters as well as their sons. Therefore, the selection of a trait in one sex will be passed on to the offspring of both sexes in a process that Francis calls "intergender hitchhiking."

Theoretically, the only force that can override this natural tendency affects the animal when an advantage for one sex is accompanied by a disadvantage in the other. For instance, bright coloration in male birds results in an evolutionary benefit: they are more attractive to female birds, thus more likely to mate and pass on their genes to the next generation. However, bright coloration also makes birds more conspicuous to potential predators, an evolutionary disadvantage. Because female birds would accrue the disadvantage but not the advantage, there is a sex-specific selection for that trait, with most female bird species less brightly colored than their male counterparts.

Francis illustrates a contrast in antlers and horns, which can be advantages in mating and self-protection. He points out that antlers are physiologically costly; they are rich in blood vessels and must be re-grown every year, which requires the expenditure of a lot of nutrients. On the other hand, horns are permanent and do not require such a caloric investment. Therefore, "fe-

males with antlers are the exception, whereas females with horns are the rule." (p. 142). To parallel with humans, male nipples have no biological purpose but are homologous to female nipples. Males have nipples because they pose no evolutionary disadvantage.

Francis notes that the claim that males have greater spatial skills and memory (often attributed to men's experience as hunters over millions of years) cannot be sustained because this ability has "no obvious behavioral downside. It does not make an animal more vulnerable to predators; nor is there a behavioral energy cost." (p. 142). Brain ecologists who make sex-dimorphic arguments cannot appeal solely to the adaptive nature of traits. They must also appeal to the disadvantages for the other sex as a factor that works against intergender hitchhiking.

Ehrenberg (2005) calls into question the assumption that men have hunted throughout prehistory. She asserts that, during the Paleolithic period, any meat that was consumed was likely scavenged rather than hunted, and primate species show no sex differences in food collection behaviors. Therefore, even if hunting results in brain changes in spatial abilities, it may be too recent to have affected evolution, which is a very slow process.

for humans (male *and* female) and animals, and therefore testosterone can also be seen as an effect of aggression (Sapolsky, 1997).

Most people can find a good demonstration of the influence of an environmental event on physiology in their experience. Consider the following scenario: you are very attracted to someone. You begin dating this person and become even more attracted to him or her. At some point, you kiss this person for the first time. You can feel some strong emotional changes (excitement, sexual arousal, happiness), and we could measure concomitant physiological changes in heart rate, respiration, sexual response, and brain waves. Although hormonal and neural fluctuations "caused" your emotional experience, is it not also true that the kiss "caused" the hormonal and neural changes?

Fausto-Sterling (1992) points out that a behavior's frequent occurrence does not necessarily mean that it is genetically based. She cites an example of a primate troop that learned a behavior and passed it down to its next generation. Someone who observed the behavior (which had become universal in the troop) in the second generation, might wrongly assume that this learned behavior was instinctual and genetically based. In the laboratory, Frans de Waal (2005) has demonstrated several instances of cultural behavior transmission among primates. Fausto-Sterling's criticism is that sociobiologists assume that universal behaviors must be genetic and that genetic behaviors must be universal, a circular logic.

The largest body of critical attacks on sociobiology comes from counterexamples of human and animal behavior that do not support the theory of differential reproductive strategies. (I address the testosterone/aggression hypothesis in Chapter 13).

Several of these counterexamples cause one to question the hypothesis that it is natural for males to lack parental involvement. In some bird species, such as penguins, the male takes the major responsibility for incubating the eggs, and many birds mate for life. Male primates will protect or adopt orphaned infants, and in the pair-bonding marmoset, the father carries the young more often than the mother after the first few weeks of life (Rosenblum, 1987). Frans de Waal (1997) describes the behavior of the bonobo, a primate that is a close genetic relative of humans. Female bonobos occupy prominent positions in the primate society, which is cooperative and rarely aggressive. de Waal (2005) also notes that, contrary to the stereotype that they are aggressive bullies, most primate "alpha males" (those at the top of the troops' dominance hierarchies) are more accurately described as peacemakers or "populists."

In humans, the greater involvement of females in the care of children can be accounted for largely by cultural factors. In most cultures, girls are encouraged to partake in nurturing behavior from an early age (Whiting & Edwards, 1988). In cultures that encourage boys to take part in caring for children, no sex differences are found in adult parental involvement (Basow, 1992).

One could also construct a list of behaviors that are difficult to explain from a sociobiological perspective. Homosexuality and sexual behaviors other than genital intercourse are good examples. So are the large numbers of men who are faithful husbands and good fathers, and men who have never had a physical fight in their lives. Bleier (1984) lists a number of theoretically sound sociobiological hypotheses that are not supported by available data.

Natalie Angier (1999), challenges one of the basic tenets of sociobiology, differential reproductive investment, arguing that male promiscuity is not a sound evolutionary strategy:

> Just how good a reproductive strategy is this chronic, random shooting of the gun? A woman is fertile only two or three days a month. Her ovulation is concealed. The man doesn't know when she's fertile. She might be in the early stages of pregnancy when he gets to her; she might still be lactating and thus not ovulating. Moreover, even if our hypothetical Don Juan hits a day on which a woman is ovulating, his sperm only has a 20 percent chance of fertilizing her egg; human reproduction is complicated, and most eggs and sperm are not up to the demands of proper fusion. Even if conception occurs, the resulting embryo has a 25 to 30 percent chance of miscarrying at some point in gestation. In sum, each episode of fleeting sex has a remarkably small probability of yielding a baby... the probability is less than one percent. And because the man is beating and running, he isn't able to prevent any of his one-night stands from turning around and mating with other men... [If he were] to spend a bit more time with one woman... the odds of his getting the woman during her fertile time would increase and he'd be monopolizing her energy and keeping her from the advances of other sperm-bearers. It takes the average couple four months, or 120 days, of regular sexual intercourse to become pregnant. That number of days is approximately equal to the number of partners our hypothetical libertine needs to sleep with to have one of them result in a "fertility unit," that is, a baby. (pp. 336–337)

The major criticism of this theoretical viewpoint is that sociobiologists ignore or explain away behaviors that do not fit their model. In the search for the universality of sex-dimorphic behavior across different animal species, one may find that animal behavior is much more diverse than it appears to be at first glance. Human behavior is even more diverse, as almost any social scientist will attest. As Funder (1997) summarizes it, "a general lesson of psychology is that humans are extraordinary flexible creatures with a minimum of instinctive behavior patterns, compared with other species." (p. 193).

Hubbard (1998) notes that some nineteenth-century physicians warned girls that developing their brains through education would sap energy from their reproductive organs and render them unable to bear children. Kimmel and Mosmiller (1992) note how purported biological explanations of women's "fragile" nature were used to argue against allowing women to vote or go to college in the United States. I have earlier described a number of other destructive masculine behaviors such as rape, violence, and indifference to children that sociobiologists, whether intentionally or unintentionally, justify under the mantle of science.

The sociobiological assumption is that any behavior that exists in relatively high frequency within a population must be rooted in biology. Hubbard (1998) makes an eloquent counterargument:

> If a society puts half its children into short skirts and warns them not to move in ways that reveal their panties, while putting the other half into jeans and overalls, and encouraging them to climb trees, play ball, and participate in other vigorous outdoor games; if later, during adolescence, the children who have been wearing trousers are urged to "eat like

growing boys," while the children in skirts are warned to watch their weight and not get fat; if the half in jeans runs around in sneakers or boots, while the half in skirts totters about on spike heels, then these two groups of people will be biologically as well as socially different. (p. 150)

Despite many serious criticisms of this theory we should be careful not to "throw the baby out with the bath water." Many researchers who are not identified with sociobiology (e.g., Money, 1987a; Maccoby, 1987) agree that biology probably produces different sensitivities to behavioral influences in males and females. Social influence can exaggerate or modify these sensitivities, and possibly not in a simple, straightforward way. As Goldfoot and Neff (1987) put it, "...most, if not all, behavioral sex differences reflect complicated interactions of endocrine, physical, and social variables." (p. 191).

The quest to discover the relative strengths of biological versus social influences and the nature of the interactions between them is ongoing. It seems certain, however, that biology does not constitute a "whole program" (Money, 1987a, p. 15) for behavior. A man is not "destined" to become violent or promiscuous any more than a tall person is "destined" to become a basketball player.

THE CHILD INSIDE THE MAN: PSYCHOANALYTIC PERSPECTIVES

It is fitting that a discussion of psychoanalysis follows one on biology; the two are somewhat related. Psychoanalysis is based on the interaction of childhood psychological history with purported biological and psychological instincts. Whereas the biological perspective is that prenatal events set up propensities for behavior, the analytic perspective attempts to specify the interplay of these propensities and the important events of early childhood.

Psychoanalysis is a psychology of *meaning*. In the area of gender, it addresses questions about the deep, underlying sense of the masculine self in the adult man's life, as understood in the context of the impact of childhood psychological dramas. Many analytic writers view masculine gender behaviors as the result of the typical early experience of being a boy, one that differs markedly from that of being a girl.

There are several different versions of psychoanalytic theories, and so a good starting point is to address the question, "What makes a theory psychoanalytic?" May (1986) suggests that there are four broad commonalities among these theories. First, analytic theories emphasize the importance of *unconscious processes*. These are the areas of an individual's mind which are outside of his or her awareness, but that nevertheless have effects on the person's behavior and identity. Analytic theorists believe that these deeper regions of the psyche are more important in understanding behavior than the conscious sense of self or the person's thought processes. Psychoanalytic theory is often referred to as an "iceberg theory." Just as most of an iceberg lies beneath the surface of the water, most psychological functioning lies beneath the surface of consciousness. From this perspective, masculinity is a deep process that goes to the core of a man's being and affects a great deal of his behavior, often without his awareness.

Second, analytic theories emphasize a *developmental and historical approach* to understanding behavior. They consider the relevance of early childhood experience to be profound, and they view the adult's behavior as reflecting and reworking childhood psychological issues. The psychoanalytic view of behavior in the gender role arena is that it is mostly a result of the boy's early relationship with his parents.

Third, analytic theories emphasize the importance of *biology and body*. When we combine this emphasis with the relevance of early childhood, we see the importance of the child's awareness of self as separate from mother, the awareness of physical sex differences, and the emergence of sexual feelings in the construction of masculinity.

Finally, analytic theories emphasize the inescapability of *internal conflict*. The person is seen as inevitably caught in the middle of at least two great and irresolvable forces. A man finds himself struggling with the demands of instinct versus social demands, desire for women versus fear of women, dependency needs versus desire for independence, feminine versus masculine feelings, and the desire for something that he cannot possess. These conflicts are seen as having a never-ending quality; nobody can ever resolve them completely. The best the person can hope for is to develop a workable compromise, such as finding a comfortable way to deal with the need to be connected and the need to be on one's own at the same time.

The Freudian Legacy

Few thinkers have had as much impact on the world as Sigmund Freud (1856–1939). His prolific works, along with those of analytic theorists who followed him, provide interesting and controversial frameworks for the understanding of men and masculinity. Freud's perspective on gender can best be understood in the context of his personality theory. Therefore, I now provide a thumbnail sketch of the parts of this theory that are relevant to men's issues.

A major tenet of Freud's biological orientation is the importance of instinct in shaping personality. Instincts are innate bodily conditions which give direction to psychological processes (Hall, Lindzey, & Campbell, 1998). They include hunger, thirst, need for oxygen, body temperature regulation, aggression, and the reproductive instinct. Freud believed that, in contrast to more basic instincts like hunger and thirst, the complex sexual and aggressive instincts (broadly, love and hate) can be expressed through a wide variety of behaviors, attitudes, and emotions. For instance, one can love a person, or love learning, conversation, money, or creative pursuits. Likewise, one can express animosity toward a person, or an idea, or the self. For Freud, the personality is largely a result of the person's pattern of expressing the sexual and aggressive instincts. And, as I mentioned before, most of this psychic functioning takes place in the unconscious.

If instinctual gratification were the only problem we ever faced, life might not be easy, but it would be rather uncomplicated. However, since we live with other people, instinctual needs inevitably come into conflict with the social world. One cannot merely act out an aggressive instinct because he or she might hurt someone else and get punished for it. The person must learn how to gratify needs in a socially acceptable way. The process of maturing is one in which primitive, impulse-driven people get transformed into civilized people who are able to delay gratification until the appropriate time and place. A good deal of what we teach children in kindergarten and elementary school is in the service of learning impulse control and social rules: wait your turn, share, consider other people's feelings, and so on.

From the Freudian perspective, newborns are nothing more than instinctually driven bundles of biology with storehouses of psychic energy. Infants are helpless, and parents or caretakers work hard at fulfilling children's instincts. They feed babies, keep them warm enough, and remove irritants from their bodies when they change their diapers. Babies are incapable of doing these things for themselves; they need help to manage their instincts. The part of the personality that is primitive, instinctual, and present at birth is called the *id*. It is a collection of biological needs and undirected psychic energy.

Slowly, children begin to develop another part of personality. They become less and less helpless as they grow. Early in life, people have to feed them, but after a while they begin to grab the food themselves and put it into their mouths. This is the beginning of the formation of a new part of personality, the *ego*. The ego is more organized than the id and can deal with the real world. In the healthy person, the ego gains more and more strength as the person matures. The ego can plan, and it can hold off the id until a suitable object can be found. It becomes the center of the personality, the person's identity. (Note that the Freudian term ego is different from the common social use of the term, which implies self-absorption).

Eventually, parents begin to make social demands on children, and because children are attached to the parents, they begin to internalize these demands. In other words, we all carry our parents around with us, for better or worse. The first important imposition of social demand is toilet training, when, for the first time, the child is required to exert physical control over an instinctual process (Hall, Lindzey, & Campbell, 1998).

Robert Bly (1988) is fond of saying, "You came into this world with all kinds of energy, but your parents wanted a 'nice boy' [or a 'nice girl']." In some ways, parents care less about instinctual gratification than they care about your being socialized. They want you to be able to handle your instincts and live in the social world. Freud called the internalized parent the *superego*, and there are two parts to it. One part, the *ego ideal*, contains our parents' aspirations for us. It is this part of the superego that makes us feel good when we do something our parents value, like doing well in school. The other part, the *conscience*, causes us to feel guilty or ashamed when we go against parental wishes.

After the formation of the superego, the ego finds itself in a clash between id, which is always pulling for pleasure, and superego, which is always pushing for perfection. The healthy person has *ego strength*, which allows him or her to balance these two conflicting demands. If the id dominates the personality, the person will be impulsive and antisocial. If the superego dominates, he or she will be tense and uncomfortable due to the unrelieved tension of the instincts (Hall, Lindzey, & Campbell, 1998).

What do id, ego, and superego have to do with masculinity? We can make a number of important connections of both the positive and the negative aspects of masculine gender roles.

The analytic ideal is a paragon of positive masculinity: the person who can love and work. Such a man can achieve a satisfactory balance between his biological and his social sides. He is able to be responsible both in his work and his dedication to his partner and family. Note here that the analytic ideal is quite the social conformist, but note also that there are many men who fit this description: dedicated, principled, hard working, caring individuals who enjoy life and contribute to the greater good.

In psychoanalytic terms, the man described above has high ego strength, which was built by his having learned to deal with problems and assert his will. He is also a person with a strong ego ideal and a reasonable conscience. He can be goal directed and achieving. Socially, society encourages the development of these structures in men.

Some men are not so fortunate, however. Destructive masculinity can be conceptualized as being the result of poor superego development, rigid, harsh, or destructive content of the superego, or poor ego strength.

Theoretically, the id is constant. It is biological and innate, so it exerts about the same amount of influence on everybody. Differences among people reflect differences in the way the id is handled and directed. In the case of poor ego and superego development, the id is the most powerful part of the personality, and so it is allowed to run amok. The result is a person who is antisocial and destructive, giving vent to sexual and aggressive impulses without restraint. Sometimes, parents and the society at large teach girls to worry about everyone else except themselves and boys to only worry about themselves. Both of these lessons are problematic because they both lead to a poor balance of id and superego.

We can conceptualize violent criminals as people with poor ego and superego development. Most of these people are men. In fact, males commit nearly 90% of violent crimes in the United States (United States Department of Justice, 2004). The major inhibitor of destructive id impulses is the superego, which makes the boy feel guilty when he is destructive and good when he is prosocial. According to Freud, male superego development depends critically on a boy's identification with his father or "father figure." If the father is absent, emotionally distant, or overly punitive, the identification is weakened. Unfortunately, a lot of fathers fit this description. According to psychoanalytic theory, a lack of ego ideal in the boy leaves him aimless and unable to reward or restrain himself appropriately.

It is also possible for id and superego to be strong but the ego to be weak. In this case, the result is a pattern of behavior in which the person does things which are harmful to someone else, feels guilty about it and expresses regret, but then repeats the same bad behavior later. Baseball great Babe Ruth fit this pattern. He was well known for his public misbehavior. Occasionally, he felt guilty about his negative effects on people, especially on children who looked up to him as a hero and role model, and he would make heartfelt public apologies for his misdeeds. Nevertheless, he would continue to engage in embarrassing incidents, not because he was insincere in his apologies, but because, if one applies Freudian theory, he lacked the ego strength to restrain the id in a society that fails to hold elite athletes accountable for their behavior.

In other cases, the content of the superego may be especially harsh, rigid, and/or destructive. This may happen if the parents' demands on the child are extreme. If the parent inculcates the demands of destructive masculinity into the boy, he will have a punitive superego that can make him feel chronically unworthy and unmasculine. This is the case for many men, for whom the superego demands that he be competitive, wealthy, in control at all times, and dominant over women.

The Oedipus Conflict

We can see another important perspective on masculinity in Freud's model of psychosexual development. Freud believed that instinctual energy (called *libido*) courses through stages of psychosexual development that are defined in relation to certain parts of the body (called *erogenous zones*). Each stage entails a crisis which the child must resolve in order to achieve healthy psychosexual development.

Following the oral and anal stages, in which boys and girls go through similar developmental challenges, children enter the phallic stage, and Freud proposed that sex differences emerge at that time. The phallic period (roughly, between age three and six) is the first primitive manifestation of what will later become adult sexuality. Children at this age become very aware of and concerned about sex differences. Masturbatory activity and some forms of sexual play among children at this age are not unusual.

Freud believed that, for both boys and girls, sexual interest at this stage centers around the penis (hence the term phallic, which refers to the penis, rather than a term that refers to the genitalia of either sex). He also believed that, during this time, the child begins to experience unconscious sexual feelings toward the other-sex parent. It is not unusual for the girl to say she is going to marry her father or a boy, his mother. As a result of the desire for the other-sex parent, the child unconsciously perceives the same-sex parent as a rival for the affection of the other parent. This is a psychologically dangerous and uncomfortable love triangle, and the child must resolve this difficulty. Freud called this crisis the *Oedipus conflict*, after the king of Thebes in Greek mythology who kills his father and marries his mother.

A boy feels desire for his mother, who is affectionate and caring. Strong sexual feelings are centered in his genitals, and he betrays this fact by touching his penis often. Parents often punish this masturbatory activity, and the boy gets the message that he might get punished by having his penis removed. This *castration anxiety* is also fueled by the rivalry with his big, powerful father, who might punish him for having these feelings toward his mother. When the boy first sees female genitalia, he perceives the female as a castrated male and unconsciously perceives that this could happen to him (Freud, 1924/1989).

At the height of the Oedipal conflict, the boy senses that gratifying his desire for his mother would mean losing his penis, and it's just not worth it. In the normal resolution of

---

Box 3.3: *Freud's Antifeminist Legacy*

Freud's theoretical construction of the Oedipus conflict was partly based on the famous case of "Dora" (Freud, 1905/1963), an 18-year-old patient whom Freud saw for 11 weeks of psychoanalysis in 1900 in order to treat a number of psychological and psychophysiological symptoms (e.g., migraine headaches and depression) (Gay, 1989). Dora reported to Freud that, when she was 14 years old, Herr K., a close friend of her father, had embraced and kissed her against her will. Dora was quite disgusted and unnerved by Herr K.'s behavior. She told her parents about it and requested that they break off their friendship with Herr K. and his wife. Dora's father confronted Herr K., who emphatically denied that he had made sexual advances toward Dora, and Dora's father believed his friend rather than his daughter.

Eventually, Freud came to believe that Dora was really in love with Herr K., and he insisted that Dora's disgust was a disguise for her real feelings of sexual arousal. In historical perspective, we now know that it is not unusual for adult men to make such advances upon young girls nor for girls to respond as Dora did. Hare-Mustin and Maracek (1990) point to the importance of Freud's reframing of Dora's experience in the patriarchal context of privileging men's perspectives over women's. In effect, Freud blamed the victim for her emotional reaction and relegated her perspective to a secondary position to his own, implying that he (and men) knew Dora (and women) better than she knew herself. As psychoanalysis became scientific orthodoxy, its antifeminine character further justified the marginalization of women.

---

this psychic conflict, he gives up these sexual feelings for his mother and displaces them on to a more appropriate object, such as the girl next door. Part of this solution involves the boy's development of a psychological identification with his father. Identification allows the son to feel less threatened by his father and also to experience romantic feelings with the mother vicariously through the father. This is an important step in superego development, as the boy begins to internalize the father's values and characteristics. The sexual love for the mother is converted into feelings of tender affection.

Freud thought that girls experience themselves as castrated males, and that therefore when they desire their fathers and see their mothers as rivals, their love is mixed with bitter feelings because they want a protruding sex organ like their father's. Thus, according to Freud, girls suffer from *penis envy*. The resolution to girls' conflict is similar: She gives up her desire for her father and displaces it. Freud thought that penis envy was converted into the desire to bear a child. He also thought that, because girls do not experience the powerful motivator of castration threat, they do not give up their father desire as easily and they do not identify with their mothers as fully. As a result, they have less developed superegos. Freud once stated that women are morally inferior to men for this reason (Freud, 1915/1989).

Many theorists have roundly criticized Freud for this view of women (for a feminist historical perspective, see Box 3.3). The great feminist analyst Karen Horney (1932) countered that women envy men's privileged social positions, not their penises. In support of this hypothesis, Nathan (1981) demonstrated through cross-cultural research that penis envy dreams among women are more common in cultures where women have low social status. Horney's view is that a girl's psychosexual development centers around her own genitalia, and not the male's. Hare-Mustin and Maracek (1990) noted Freud's sexism in his characterization of "women's bodies as *not having* a penis rather than as *having* the female external genitalia." (p. 32, emphasis original). Freud himself felt unsatisfied with this part of his theory, as he knew many women whose moral development equaled or surpassed that of men. At one point, Freud stated that it was the task of women analysts to describe the female psyche (Freud, 1915/1989).

Oedipus and Masculinity

Theoretically, the childhood Oedipal crisis colors the adult man's approach to relationships with women (originally represented by mother) and authority figures (originally represented by father). Fine's (1987) view of the Oedipal situation is that confusion results when parents or other adults punish the boy's sexual expression. He loves his mother, but he can not approach her sexually, and an early split between sex and affection can result. These are the roots of the so called "Madonna/Whore complex" (the religious Madonna, not the singer). The man feels that virtuous women, those whom he respects, are not sexual (the Madonna was conceived without original sin—absolutely pure), and that sexual women ("whores") are not worthy of respect. Thus, he has a tendency to degrade a woman if she is sexual with him. This sexuality/love contradiction causes extreme problems in the man's relationships with women and perhaps in his sexual functioning. The boy who successfully resolves the Oedipal conflict becomes a man who can love and be sexual with the same woman. The boy who does not may grow up to be misogynist, promiscuous, or sexually dysfunctional as he plays out the unresolved Oedipal drama again and again. As Freud (1924/1989) said, "the finding of an object [Freud's term for the thing or person that fulfills the instinct] is in fact a refinding of it." (p. 288).

Fathering may have an important effect in the Oedipal situation. If the father is caring and attentive to the boy, he will facilitate his son's positive identification with him and mitigate the son's castration anxiety. If, however, the father is harsh, punitive, and demanding with his son, the identification process will cause the boy to become intropunitive, and castration anxiety may be exaggerated. The boy grows up fearful and without a strong sense of himself as masculine. He may act "macho" to cover up his insecurity. He may be aggressive to defend against the unconscious threat of castration (Tyson, 1986), or he may derogate women in order to feel better about his masculinity. Lisak (1991) noted that sexual assault perpetrators have feelings of bitterness toward their fathers, who caused them feel inadequate and unmasculine.

Critique of Freud

Many criticisms of Freud are leveled at his assumption that sexual instinct is the primary determinant of personality. Even some of his closest followers abandoned the sexual theory, although most maintained their belief in the importance of the unconscious and early childhood events. If we look at the parent-child attachment as one that is not primarily sexual, very different conclusions about male functioning become possible. And, even if one accepts the premise that sexuality is the basis of human personality, some of Freud's conclusions are open to debate. The description of castration anxiety as being fairly resolvable is one of the most questionable.

Freud's position is that the Oedipal crisis in the boy is touched off by his realization that he could lose something valuable. In the girl, it is stimulated by her imagining that she has already lost it. If you have lost something valuable, it is greatly disappointing at first. After a while, you usually accept that it is gone and move on. If, however, you have a deep-seated fear of losing something, you are obligated to anxiously protect it all of your life. The penis is also in somewhat of a vulnerable place, being outside of the body. It seems that castration anxiety would follow many more men into adulthood than penis envy (if it exists at all) would follow women.

In 1932, Karen Horney published a classic essay on male psychology entitled, *The Dread of Women* in which she argues that the process of psychosexual development produces in the boy a profound yet unconscious fear of the feminine, and that much typical male behavior in adulthood is a reflection of this dread. Horney argued that the vagina, with its ability to engulf, is a psychic threat to the male. The threat of castration by the father does not approach the threat of engulfment from the mother. Horney illustrated this in metaphor: "Sampson, whom no man could conquer, is robbed of his strength by Delilah." (Horney, 1932, p. 84).

If, as Freud believed, the other-sex parent is the love object in this stage, then the size difference between parent and child leads to a difference in how boys and girls experience themselves. Girls, Horney believed, begin to have unconscious desires to take in the penis. If the father is the love object, then her vagina is too small for him, and so she fears that he could hurt her. The boy, with his mother as love object, senses that his penis is much too small for her, and reacts with feelings of inadequacy. He anticipates that his mother (and later other love objects) will ridicule and deride him.

The implications of Horney's theory for masculine psychology are far reaching. Horney proposed that every man has a deep sense of apprehension that a woman can destroy his self-respect, and that his penis (and thus his manhood) is not large enough nor good enough. Masculinity, then, is never on very solid ground. Rather it is fraught with dread, and the man must make extreme efforts to manage his anxiety around his masculine adequacy. He has basically two options: he can withdraw from women or compensate for these uncomfortable feelings.

Withdrawal solutions include staying away from women either physically or emotionally. Compensation solutions involve going to extremes to prove one's manhood over and over again. Part of this strategy may involve debasing and controlling women. By doing so, the man can deny the power of the woman to hurt him. At the extreme of masculine inade-quacy, we see desperate behaviors like rape and domestic violence, which can be seen as aggressive reactions to the extreme dread of the feminine. Horney goes so far as to suggest that patriarchy, men's institutional oppression of women, is a reaction to this inadequacy in the collective male psyche. Horney's theory also provides a possible explanation of the core attitude of antifemininity that characterizes traditional masculinity.

IDENTIFYING WITH MOM: EGO PSYCHOLOGY AND MASCULINITY

Many of the theorists who followed Freud disagreed with him on one major point. They believed that some aspects of ego functioning were independent of the id. For these theo-rists, the ego is not something that merely serves to direct and control the instincts, it also drives the person to deal with basic psychological tasks like developing a sense of self, re-lating to others, learning to work, and developing values. Many of these "neo-analytic" theories center around the person's motivation to develop a sense of identity.

People's behavior varies across different situations and roles, but identity is the part of the person that ties all of this varying behavior together. The formation of this sense of self begins in infancy with the child's realization that he or she is separate from the mother. As the individual progresses through adolescence and adulthood, the expression of identity can be seen through a variety of decisions around relationships, work, sexuality, values, and preferences.

Gender identity is the part of overall identity that defines for the person what it means to be male or female. After children learn that they are not a part of their mothers, boys learn that they are similar to their fathers and different from their mothers in a basic way, and girls learn the converse. Children as young as two to four years of age become very upset if someone says to them "What a nice girl (or boy) you are," using the incorrect sex label. This is evidence that gender identity is learned very early and that it has a strong emotional component (Lewis, 1987). The strength of the emotion associated with gender identity attests to its central place in overall identity, although the origin of that centrality (biological, social, and/or cultural) is open to question.

Because of sex-differentiated child rearing, the formation of gender identity is thought to proceed very differently for males and females, with important implications for the personalities of adult men and women. Gender identity is formed mainly through the child's interactions with his or her parents, and women are the primary care-takers of infants in most cultures. The amount of time a typical mother spends with the infant far outweighs the typical father's time (Cohen, 1998). Thus, the most striking sex difference in early parent-child interactions is that girls are usually raised by the same-sex parent, boys by the other-sex parent.

Ruth Hartley (1959) first proposed that the impact of this sex difference in early expe-rience is considerable. In the formation of gender identity, girls learn "I am what mom is." They experience themselves as continuous with their mothers and define themselves through the process of attachment. Boys, on the other hand, do not learn "I am what dad is" so much as they learn "I am what mom is not." The boy experiences himself as different from the mother and defines himself through the process of separation. "I am what mom is not" defines the content of gender identity in a negative way. Rather that starting out with some sense of masculinity, the boy starts out with a sense of antifemininity.

Before they perceive sex differences in early childhood, children of both sexes feel continuous with their mothers, and the identification process has already begun. For girls, it is a process that continues in the same direction throughout childhood, because their mothers are the same sex as them. For boys, however, gender identity development critically depends on switching tracks. From this view, boys must put rigid boundaries between themselves and their mothers to define themselves as masculine. If we believe that some identification with the mother has already taken place, then the separation process entails a repression of the mother identification.

These dramas get played out again and again, according to analytic theory. The result of this separation process is that the boy's gender identity rests on his putting psychological barriers not just between himself and mother, but between himself and anything feminine. Included are "feminine activities" and, of course, girls and women themselves. Having already identified with the mother, the boy must also repress the feminine parts of himself, usually represented by his emotional experiences and feelings of relatedness to others. Girls are under no such pressure. They do not have to deny the masculine in order to define themselves as feminine (Chodorow, 1978). This is one possible explanation for the tolerance of "tomboys" but not "sissies." Martin (1995) reported that stereotypes of tomboys resembled stereotypes of traditional boys. However, the stereotype of the sissy did not resemble that of a traditional girl. Instead, it was defined narrowly and related to many negative characteristics.

The mother-identified parts of the boy are relegated to the unconscious because they pose a threat to the ego. When "feminine" experiences like sentimental feelings or a desire for attachment surface from the unconscious, they are associated with anxiety, which the boy must then defend against. In a typical scenario, a man may go to a sentimental movie, begin to identify with a character and feel some strong and vulnerable emotions. He may sense that this experience is a threat to his masculinity and detach himself from vulnerable emotion by putting his mind on something else. Eventually, he may begin to avoid these types of movies. Culturally, traditionally masculine men in the United States often avoid movies that have feminine themes, calling them "chick flicks" that hold no interest for them.

The early childhood gender-typed mix of separation and attachment is considered by some to result in an enduring approach to the world. Nancy Chodorow (1978) described women as "selves in communion," meaning that they tend to experience themselves in the context of relationships, and men as "selves in separation," oriented toward independence and task completion.

From this standpoint, a straightforward solution to male antifeminine anxiety is an increase in fathers' involvement in child care. Coltrane (1998) provides some anthropological evidence in support of the hypothesis that antifemininity results from boys' lack of meaningful contact with their fathers. He notes that cultures in which men participate in child rearing (and in which women have the power to control property), there are "significantly fewer displays of manliness, less wifely deference, less husband dominance, and less ideological female inferiority. . ." (p. 81). One psychoanalytic interpretation is that, because fathers are more psychologically available to sons, there is less need for compulsive separation from the mother, thus less fear of women and femininity, and thus less of a need to compensate for this fear through hypermasculine posturing and mistreatment of women.

SUMMARY

1. There is little doubt among developmental psychologists that biology affects personality and behavior, although there is little consensus about the extent of these effects. Because there are differences in male and female biology, there is a good deal of speculation and research about the behavioral implications of these differences.

2. The controversial theory of sociobiology is the position that biology profoundly affects behavior by establishing predispositions toward certain activities. These predispositions have survival value for the organism and its genes, and thus they were established through the process of evolution.

3. From the sociobiological viewpoint, major behavioral sex differences are thought to reflect different male and female reproductive strategies. Males who impregnate a large number of females are "successful" from an evolutionary standpoint because they insure maximum and varied reproduction of their genes. In contrast to females, males can participate in the reproductive process with a minimum investment of time and resources. Differences in reproductive strategies are thought to underlie important differences in male and female "nature."

4. Social scientists have leveled a number of theoretical and methodological criticisms against sociobiology. Many critics charge that sociobiologists selectively include data that supports their theories while ignoring other data. Few, if any, theorists consider biology to forge an immutable sexual destiny, but there are major disagreements about the relative strengths of nature and nurture. Critics charge that sociobiology is a patriarchal ideology disguised as science.

5. Psychoanalytic approaches to the understanding of masculinity emphasize biological, unconscious, and early childhood determinants of behavior.

6. Freud emphasized the role of sexual instinct and its conflict with social forces. If the young boy does not develop a strong social structure (superego), he will become impulsive, destructive, self-absorbed, and antisocial.

7. According to Freudian theory, the most important period for the development of masculine gender identity is the phallic stage, in which the boy experiences strong sexual feelings for his mother and views his father as a rival. He fears that he will be castrated for these desires, and so he transfers his sexual feelings onto a more appro-

priate object. If the Oedipal crisis is resolved poorly, the boy may later have sexual problems and/or problems relating to women.

8. Karen Horney viewed the Oedipal period as a time when males developed deep-seated feelings of insecurity associated with the feminine. She thought that misogyny and even violence toward women are desperate attempts to compensate for masculine inadequacy.

9. Ego psychology theories emphasize the processes of attachment and separation in early childhood. Because boys are usually raised mainly by their mothers, they must put rigid boundaries between themselves and the feminine in order to attain a strong sense of masculinity. Males tend to avoid "feminine" behaviors because they are accompanied by anxiety, causing difficulty when situations call for such behavior.

4

Socially Based Theoretical Perspectives on Males and Gender

"IT'S THE WAY I WAS RAISED": SOCIAL LEARNING PERSPECTIVES ON MASCULINITY

Why do relatively few men know how to sew and relatively few women know how to repair cars? The simple answer is, of course, that a lot of women and men learned these behaviors as they grew up. But what influenced their learning? For many, it was parents, older siblings, or family friends. Common stories involve young boys watching their fathers work on cars or young girls watching their mothers sew. Gradually, the child takes an interest and begins to learn skills with the guidance and encouragement of the parent. This process takes place within a culture and a family environment that defines certain tasks, activities, and self-concepts as gender-specific.

What happens if a boy takes an interest in his mother's sewing? The same kind of process might occur, but other scenarios are also very possible. His mother and/or father might say, "You don't want to learn that; sewing is for girls." The boy's playmates might ridicule him if they find out that he likes to do such a "sissy" thing. His mother might not be as encouraging to a son as to a daughter, making it more likely that the son would gradually lose interest. The most common scenario is that the boy would not pursue his interest in the first place, because he perceives sewing as something that only females do.

At a deeper level of analysis, the answer to our original question is that, although the social environment encourages gender-typed activities, it does not encourage (and often discourages) cross-gender activities, especially for males. If the boy has a strong interest in sewing, he may pursue it in spite of the social forces that work against it, but the pursuit of more traditionally masculine activities surely offers less resistance. One of my female students reported that a male friend of hers asked her to teach him how to crochet but not to tell his friends, an illustration of both the awareness of negative sanctions for cross-gender behavior and how a strong enough interest can cause one to resist gendered social pressure.

The basic assumption of social learning theory is that the most important influence on behavior is learning. The example above illustrates many learning processes: reward, punishment, observation, imitation, and gender-schematic thinking. From this position, gendered behavior is produced by *differential treatment*, the systematic, although sometimes unintentional, provision of sex-specific environmental influences. Social learning theory provides a picture of how people are socialized by families, peer groups, schools, and cultures.

Reward and Punishment

Many behavioral patterns are built through the experience of reward and punishment. Thorndike (1898) stated the simple *Law of Effect:* behaviors that are followed by pleasant states of affairs tend to increase in frequency (because they have been rewarded, or reinforced), while those followed by unpleasant consequences tend to decrease (because they have been punished). We are motivated to recognize situations in which rewards or punishments are available and act accordingly.

We also tend to make generalizations based on similarities among situations, and discriminations based on differences among situations (Skinner, 1974). For instance, you might receive social approval (a reward) for telling a joke to one group of friends, and so you tell it to another group of friends. In this case, your behavior has generalized because the situations are similar. On the other hand, if you were to refrain from telling the joke in class, you would have discriminated and displayed a change in behavior based on differences between situations.

We find ourselves in a variety of situations during our lives. Some are quite similar to one another; others are more unique. We acquire behavioral habits by operating in varied environments. Over time, these habits become part of us—so ingrained that they are difficult to change, or even to notice, without considerable effort.

Many researchers have focused on the sex-specific application of reward and punishment by various socializing agents: parents, schools, and peer groups. Certain behaviors are typically rewarded or punished in males, and this gender-typed socialization process creates dispositions toward masculine behaviors and away from feminine ones.

Childhood Environments

Together with co-author John Lynch (Lynch & Kilmartin, 1999), I proposed the following:

Imagine that you are visiting the house of some friends who are the parents of an eight-year-old boy. Shortly after you arrive, the boy tells you that he wants to show you his room, so you walk upstairs with him as he proudly opens the bedroom door.

What do you expect to see? Certainly not dolls, ruffles, pastel colors, or floral decorations. Boys' rooms contain far more sports equipment, animal furnishings, and transportation toys than girls' rooms. If you play with the boy, are you more likely to "horse around" or to have a make-believe tea party? If you talk to him about growing up, are you more likely to ask him about his future career or about his plans to become a parent? When he is old enough to take on some household chores, will he be cutting the grass or babysitting? When he goes out to play in his single-sex peer group, will the interactions he has with his male friends have a different character than that of his sister's peer group? What gender typed images is he likely to see on television?

We could go on and on with these questions, and the answers to all of them are obvious. In many important ways, boys and girls grow up in distinctly different worlds. Socializing agents make male-female distinctions in the kind of decor one is supposed to enjoy, the kinds of work one is supposed to do, the kinds of colors one is supposed to like, the kinds of hobbies one is supposed to have, and a wide variety of other experiences and behaviors. (p. 55)

The experience of the rewarding or punishing aspects of environments depends on being exposed to those environments, and there is good evidence that boys sometimes find themselves in markedly different settings than girls. If you were to look at most middle class children's bedrooms, you would probably have little difficulty guessing the sex of the child. Girls' bedrooms often contain dolls (Snow, Jacklin, & Maccoby, 1981) and are often decorated with flowers, lace, or other stereotypically feminine design. Boys' bedrooms often contain sports equipment and transportation toys (Pomerleau, Bolduc, Malcuit, & Cossette, 1990).

Parents tend to communicate gender stereotypes in children's play and household chores (Lytton & Romney, 1991). Parents in Western cultures (especially fathers) play with boys more roughly, perhaps as a result of the perception that boys are stronger and tougher (Culp, Cook, & Housley, 1983), but this pattern is not universal (Hewlett, 2005). Children who choose gender-typed toys tend to get more positive responses from their parents than those who do not (Caldera, Huston, & O'Brien, 1989).

Developmental psychologists often view play and family activity as a rehearsal for later social roles. For instance, putting puzzles together is rehearsal for task completion and problem solving. "Playing house" is a rehearsal for relationships and domestic work. Here again, parents tend to be gender-typed in their treatment of children. Boys are taught to develop structures, to experiment with new approaches to solving problems, to attend to task and performance, and to master the situation. Girls are encouraged to be cooperative and compliant (Block, 1984). In household chores, parents often assign boys activities that take them away from the residence, such as yard work, animal care, or taking out the garbage, whereas girls are assigned more domestic chores such as baby sitting, cooking, or doing dishes (Lytton & Romney, 1991). The net result of children's play and household chore activity, according to Block (1984) is that we give boys "wings" and give girls "roots."

Gendered Behavioral Patterns

Another consistent research finding is that boys get punished for cross-gender behavior earlier in life and more harshly than girls (Martin, 1990). A girl can associate with a male group without fearing a loss of status. Boys who play with girls, however, are often ridiculed by and ostracized from male social groups (Maccoby, 1998). Parents do not worry about "tomboys" until they reach puberty, but parents show grave concern about "sissies" before kindergarten age (Nelson, 1985). Because of punishment for "feminine" behaviors, boys may begin to view femininity and females with contempt. The mainstream cultural definition of masculinity as antifemininity has its developmental origins in this devaluing of activities, self-concepts, and behaviors that are thought to be reserved for females.

Comparisons of fathers' and mothers' gender typing of children reveal that fathers tend to be more stereotypic in their definitions of gender appropriate activities, especially with their sons (Lytton & Romney, 1991). Perhaps as a consequence of their less frequent contact with children, they embellish a lack of information by the use of stereotypes (Basow, 1992). Not surprisingly, the level of the son's gender stereotyping is strongly related to the father's level (Tennenbaum & Leaper, 2002).

Many cultural forces, including the typical family, encourage boys to control their feelings and conform their behavior to external standards like performance in sports. In sharp contrast, these same forces often encourage girls to "look inside" and think about their feelings (Block, 1984). Adams, Kuebli, Boyle, and Fivush (1995) found that parents refer to most emotions much more frequently when talking with daughters than they do with sons. At 40 months of age, these researchers found no sex differences in children's use of words that describe emotions. However, by age 70 months, girls' language contained more emotional terms than boys'. Thus, parents tend to teach girls about the salience of feelings in the early stages of language acquisition, and they teach boys to attend to other aspects of experience. In adulthood, this lack of emotional socialization may contribute to social definitions of masculinity that emphasize the external: job status, money, material possessions, athletic performance, power over others, and even the attractiveness of one's partner. It is important to note that this style is not only a remnant of childhood rewards from evaluating externally; the encouragement is ongoing. Many social and other rewards come to men whose behavior conforms to masculine cultural images.

Although the encouragement to look outside of the self may cause problems such as an impoverished emotional life and lack of meaningful relationships, it is also responsible for some of the most positive aspects of traditional masculinity. Boys are rewarded from an early age for going out into the world, solving problems, achieving, and competing. Although competition and ambition can get out of hand, this orientation to the world is associated with good occupational functioning and enhanced self-esteem, especially when it is balanced with socioemotional orientations.

Boys are generally rewarded for controlling their emotions (with the curious exceptions of anger and sexual feelings), but they are sometimes discouraged from controlling their behavior (See Chapter 8 for a discussion of gender and emotion, Chapter 12 for an analysis of masculinity and aggression.). Girls are taught to stay close to adults both at home and at school, whereas boys are rewarded for independence and being active (Serbin, Zelkowitz, Doyle, Gold, & Wheaton, 1990). This differential socialization can cause problems for boys in elementary school settings that emphasize behaviors like co-operating, sitting still, and listening, which are contradictory to these gendered expecta-tions (Richardson, 1981). In an early article, Kagan (1964) described school as a "girl's world" that rewards behavior control and conformity, which are taught to girls at an early age. These contradictory demands for boys may contribute to their higher incidences of behavior and academic problems (Richardson, 1981). Many more males than females ap-pear to be choosing not to attend college (especially in minority racial populations and lower and middle socioeconomic classes), and some speculate that this is because college seems to be unmasculine (Lewin, 1998). At the same time, we should be careful not to think of schools as favoring girls. There is ample evidence that there is an interaction be-tween sex and race, with teachers tending to give White boys the strong message that they are more important than girls. However, Black males receive less support in the academic environment than any other group (Basow, 1992).

Gender typing of children is greatly accelerated by typical early educational experi-ences, which Luria and Herzog (cited in Maccoby, 1987) refer to as "gender school." The gender role of boys is largely shaped by two forces: male peer culture and the differential treatment of boys and girls by teachers.

Children often segregate themselves into same-sex play groups. They will mix when adults reward them for doing so or punish them for not doing so, but frequently re-segregate when adult sanctions are removed (Maccoby, 1998). Social scientists have observed sex segregation in many different cultures (Whiting & Edwards, 1988). In boys' play groups, we see a great deal of reward for aggression, beginning at an early age (Fagot & Hagan, 1985). Boys groups tend to demand rigid conformity to masculine behavior by punishing cross-gender behavior very harshly (Maccoby, 1998). Thus, the peer culture strongly reinforces what a boy has often learned at home and in the culture at large.

Despite teachers' efforts to treat boys and girls the same, there is ample evidence that they often do not do so. Boys receive more positive and more negative attention in the classroom than girls (Sadker & Sadker, 1985). Boys' behavior is more likely to be taken seriously than that of girls, and boys learn that what they do has tangible consequences. Parents tend to give boys both more praise and more punishment than girls (Lytton & Romney, 1991). One of the reasons for greater frequencies of punishment is that boys get into more mischief than girls, perhaps as a result of a relatively higher average activity level (Maccoby, 1998).

The punishment of boys is relevant to the study of men and masculinity for several rea-sons. First, various cultural forces like the family and peer group often employ this pun-ishment to enforce masculine gender role behaviors, some of which are associated with a number of personal and social problems (See Part III of this book for an analysis of these issues.). Second, boys are more likely to be punished physically, while girls are more likely to be punished with social disapproval (Lytton & Romney, 1991). Physical punishment has the effect of actually *increasing* aggression in children over the long run (Patterson, Reid, & Dishion, 1992). There may be somewhat of a vicious cycle for the acting-out boy. He is active and undercontrolled as a result of temperament and socialization. He is physically punished for his behaviors, and these punishments are likely to result in further aggression.

Third, fathers tend to do more punishing than mothers (Block, 1984). The boy's experience of physical pain in the presence of the father may inhibit positive feelings and identification, especially if the father is not around much and/or there is a dearth of positive father-son interactions (Lynch & Kilmartin, 1999). In the worst-case scenario, the mother spends much more time with the son, but the punishment duties are relegated to the father. The son who is told, "Wait until your father gets home." does not learn that he gets punished when he does something inappropriate. Rather, he learns that he gets punished when his father gets home, and he may well develop feelings of fear, anger, and resentment toward his father.

Observation, Imitation, and Cognition

A person does not need to actually perform a behavior and be reinforced or punished for learning to take place. A good deal of behavior is learned through observing and imitating others. Moreover, a person is not merely a passive recipient of behavioral consequences. He or she makes judgments about situations, categories, and values. What a person thinks about a situation may be as important in determining behavior as the actual reward or punishment contingencies present in the situation (Rotter, 1954).

It is not unusual to see people behaving like their parents without even being aware of it. Parents often reward children for imitative behavior. For example, a father who proudly says, "That's my boy!", after his son emulates something the father has done, has provided a social reward. Although the provision of such a reward serves to strengthen the behavior, the child may spontaneously imitate the parent or other model without being rewarded (Bandura & Walters, 1963). The acquisition of language in a child is a parallel process. Children are pattern-seeking organisms who appear to have an innate predisposition to learn language (Chomsky, 1957). Although rewarding a child for using new words will likely accelerate language acquisition, this reward is not necessary, as children learn most language through the process of mere imitation.

In their classic research, Bandura, Ross, and Ross (1961) described several factors that influence whether or not a person will imitate the behavior of another person (the *model*). First is the amount of exposure to the model: The more time a person spends with the model, the more likely he or she is to imitate this person's behavior. As we shall see, this is an important factor in male development because of the historically small amounts of time that boys usually spend with their fathers. Movies and television can also provide models, and frequent exposure to characters in these media can have an important effect on behavior. In fact, children who spend large amounts of time watching television tend to be more gender-typed than other children (Signorielli & Lears, 1992).

Second, imitation is increased when the person perceives himself or herself as sharing salient characteristics with the model. In other words, you are more likely to imitate someone if you see yourself as being similar to that person in important ways. As sex is a basic division among human beings and is often highlighted as important by cultural forces, it is not surprising to find that children imitate same sex models more readily than models of the other sex, and this process begins to occur as early as three years of age. Boys imitate females less often than girls imitate males (Bussey & Bandura, 1992). This difference may be due to a number of factors, including differential punishment for cross-gender behavior, the antifemininity bias in masculine gender roles, and the higher social status of males in most cultures, which empowers females who act in masculine ways but disempowers males who act in feminine ways.

Third, observing whether a model is reinforced for a behavior affects whether or not a person will imitate the behavior. For example, if you were to see someone put money into a vending machine and not receive any goods, you would be less likely to put your money into the machine. Boys who observe men being rewarded for gender-typed behavior are more likely to imitate the behavior through the process of *vicarious reinforcement*. In television and movies, male characters are often rewarded for using violence to solve problems, and the viewing of this "justified" violence may be even more damaging than viewing villainous violence, as boys learn that physical aggression is a part of being one of the "good guys." (See Chapter 12.)

Finally, because people are sophisticated pattern-seeking organisms, cognitive processes affect the performance of behaviors. As people grow, they become increasingly adept at seeing similarities and differences among models and among situations. They learn how to put behaviors into categories and to apply these categories to new situations. Children may notice that males perform certain behaviors more often than females in similar settings. The child may then abstract an unarticulated concept of masculine behavior (Perry & Bussey, 1979) and pattern his behavior on this concept. If the child is male, he is then more likely to imitate these behaviors. Because of this abstraction, however, he is less likely to imitate a male whom he perceives as behaving in a feminine way (Eisenstock, 1984).

From a social learning perspective, "gender identity" is formed through the abstraction of masculine and feminine categories of behavior together with the understanding of physical sex differences and the imitation of same-sex models. As the boy increasingly behaves like his father and other males, his identification as masculine becomes more and more stable (Lips, 2005). This view contrasts with psychoanalytic theory, which views gender-typed behavior as following, rather than preceding, gender identification.

David Lynn (1959; 1966; 1969) was one of the first modern writers to theorize about the implications of the historical inaccessibility of fathers as role models. When they are young, children tend to spend much more time with mothers than with fathers. When they enter school, the most salient adult models are teachers, most of whom are also female. Therefore, girls get a good deal of exposure to same-sex models. In constructing ideas about femininity, they have a lot of information on which to base their imitation.

In sharp contrast, boys do not get nearly as much of an opportunity to observe their fathers and other adult males. Therefore, they must extrapolate a good deal in constructing a sense of what masculinity is. Boys must fill in large gaps of information, and they tend to do so by using other, more available male models such as peers, older boys, and males in the media. These are sometimes not good sources of realistic, secure, positively defined masculinity. Goldberg's (1977) description of gender identity development is that girls identify with a real person, whereas boys identify largely with a fantasy. This fantasy may be heavily laden with unrealistic, hypertrophied aspects of stereotypical masculine gender roles. For example, two-thirds of African-American boys aged 13–18 believe that it is realistic for them to become professional athletes, an impossibility for more than 99% (Simons, 1997).

Hartley (1959) first noted that this lack of male models together with harsh, early demands to "be a man" creates a volatile combination of social forces for the boy. He learns that behaving in a masculine ways is important, because masculine gender role demands are sometimes backed up with threats of punishment. At the same time, he does not have much information about how to do so. Thus, he experiences a good deal of anxiety and inadequacy about his masculinity. To make matters worse, he is supposed to be certain of what to do. Asking for help or even expressing feelings of doubt is considered feminine.

Lynn (1969) theorized that the boy's typical reaction to this anxiety is to adhere to stereotypical masculine gender roles in a very rigid way. For many males, the combination of antifemininity, masculine anxiety, and punishment for cross-gender behavior leads to a compulsive conformity to cultural definitions of masculinity, such as the stereotypical masculine behavior of refusing to ask for directions when lost.

Since boys often identify with a hypermasculine fantasy, they often feel compelled to become that fantasy. Boys tend to role-play occupations that are highly unlikely for them (Greif, 1976; Simons, 1997), such as astronaut or professional athlete, whereas girls' play is usually around more realistic and universal roles such as mother or caretaker. As a result, the transition from boyhood to adult roles may be somewhat discontinuous for many males (Archer, 1984). Perhaps this is one reason why many adult men place such importance on professional sports or "macho" media figures who provide an avenue for vicarious fulfillment of hypermasculine fantasy.

A sense of invulnerability is an important aspect of many of these unrealistic masculine fantasies. If the boy identifies with a fantasy of his father (as many sons do), and if his father is inexpressive of vulnerable feelings such as fear (as many fathers are), then it is easy for the boy to have an image of his father (and, by extension, of any man) as someone who never gets hurt in any way. Of course, a father experiences fear like any other human being, but he may hide his reactions. The son is likely to figure that fearful feelings do not exist in "real men." Inevitably, the boy experiences fear, as everyone does from time to time, and he may feel unmasculine and inadequate at these times because he compares his inner experience with his father's appearance (Lynch & Kilmartin, 1999).

Gender Schema Theory

Sandra Bem (1981b; 1985; 1987; 1993) constructed a theory of gender-dependent information processing with an important emphasis on cultural factors. Bem believes that cognitive development and gender role development are parallel in some regards. She also argues that gender-typed information processing is taught to children by a culture that emphasizes sex differences for virtually every domain of behavior. If our culture were not so gender-typed, children would learn to use other categories to organize their experiences.

Because we deal with so much information, we must categorize and organize it in order to avoid a sensory overload. To do this, we develop *schemata* (the plural of *schema*), which are cognitive structures that allow us to anticipate and understand events. As a child observes males and females in a gender-typed environment, he or she gathers information about gender. The child makes associations among different aspects of masculinity and femininity and uses these resulting associations to organize new information. The structure and meaning of events are stored in gender schematic terms. In addition, the person applies the gender schema to the self and behaves in gendered ways.

According to Bem, children categorize events according to gender only because we live in a culture that communicates to people that sex is important in occupation, clothing, hobbies, children's toys, and other areas where it need not be viewed as important. For instance, at a recent high school graduation ceremony, a female graduate was not allowed to participate because she ordered blue graduation robes in defiance of the school tradition in which females wear white robes and males blue robes. The excluded graduate stated that a senior class sponsor told her that the school makes this distinction because "white represents purity, while darker colors signify strength." (Krishnamurthy, 1998, p. C1). Bem would say that drawing a distinction between the sexes in such a non-sex–dependent activity as an educational ceremony encourages children to use sex as a cognitive guide for understanding the world. It is not unlike having African Americans wear black robes and Caucasians white ones. Few people would consider it appropriate to call attention to racial differences when the accomplishments of all are identical, and it would seem equally inappropriate to do so with sex differences.

The lesson of language acquisition may provide some clues to the often rigid conceptions of gender in children. Children's understanding of the deep structure of language is more sophisticated than we might think (Chomsky, 1957), and their mistakes tell us so (Pinker, 1994). For instance, instead of saying "I went to the store" or "My candy tastes better than yours", a child might say "I *goed* to the store" or "My candy tastes *gooder* than yours." (A child would never say "went the to I store." Their errors are not random.) These predictable mistakes are called overregularizations—they are evidence that the child has learned the rules of, in these instances, past tense and comparative adverbs, but they have applied them incorrectly by overgeneralizing them to situations in which they do not apply.

Because we live in a gender schematic society, people observe patterns of conduct and tend to abstract categories of behavior within the conceptions of male and female. And, just like language acquisition, the early stages of this process are largely nonconscious—if you asked a very young child about the rule for past tense, he or she would probably not be able to tell it to you (even if you went to great lengths to explain the question in the child's language). However, you would hear many examples in the child's

Box 4.1: Sexist Language, Non-Sexist Language, and "Political Correctness"

Consider the many sex-specific terms contained in the English language. To cite only a very few: mailman, meter maid, chairman, hat check girl, mankind, newspaper boy, fireman, hostess, freshman, coed. English also has a tradition of using the generic masculine. When writing or talking about people in general, people often use masculine pronouns. Thus, the sentence "Every person needs to plan for his retirement." may be intended to refer to both men and women.

Many proponents of gender egalitarianism have leveled strong criticisms against the uses of sexist role terms and the generic masculine. They suggest gender neutral terms like: police officer, humankind, fire fighter, and waitperson and a change in the linguistic convention of the generic "he" to constructions such as she/he or s/he. Some have even suggested the adoption of a new set of pronouns that are gender neutral such as "hir" or "tir." Social conservatives have often been critical of these proposed changes, citing the following arguments:

1. Everybody is used to the old way of doing things and knows what the communicator is referring to. Therefore, there is no reason to change. To change a pronoun is to change standard English, which nobody should do.

2. Using terms like "he or she" rather than "he" is bulky and interrupts the flow of writing and speaking.

3. The movement toward nonsexist language is just another example of political correctness (P.C.), a movement designed to make people feel guilty for not being a member of an oppressed minority group.

Are these arguments compelling enough to justify maintaining the status quo? Proponents of nonsexist language offer the following:

1. Language is not a static entity. It changes in response to the needs of the culture. If I were to tell you a story, you would naturally envision the events in your mind's eye. There is evidence that, when readers or listeners apprehend the generic masculine, they imagine males (Lips, 2005). Most children are not aware that masculine pronouns can potentially refer to females (Hyde, 1984). Therefore, the use of this construction constitutes poor communication when one is trying to refer to people of either sex.

2. It is true that these terms are sometimes bulky and awkward, but people should be willing to tolerate this mild discomfort rather than passively communicating that males' experience constitutes a standard and females' experience a variation. As Basow (1992) stated, "use of the generic he is not just an arbitrary custom, but a continuing statement about the social roles of

men and women." (p. 142, emphasis original).

3. "Political correctness" is a pejorative term used by people who are in power and seek to maintain it. Calling someone P.C. is an attempt to shame them for their sensitivity and respectfulness. It is parallel to the vilification of the terms "feminist," which social conservatives have characterized as man-hating, bitter women. Yet the Merriam-Webster Dictionary (2005) defines feminism as, "the theory of the political, economic, and social equality of the sexes." The demonization of the term is a political strategy to influence people to refuse adoption of the principle to maintain the status quo of male dominance.

everyday language, proof that he or she has learned the rule nonconsciously. A rigid gender schema would seem to represent the same kind of overregularization. In the case of the language error, adults are likely to correct the child, who would then eventually learn that there are exceptions to the rule. But adults may be less likely to correct children's gender "mistakes," especially if they are gender schematic themselves.

Thorne (1995) described several elementary school situations in which teachers and other adults needlessly called attention to students' sexes. These included statements like "the girls are ready and the boys aren't" (p. 110), or classroom contests in which a team of all boys competes against a team of all girls. In these situations, adults model the use of gender schemata and make it more likely that children will also acquire them. Thorne (1993, 1995) also described various aspects of children's play that maintain gender boundaries, including teasing for playing with other sex children, "cooties," and "invasion" of same sex play groups by other sex children.

We see many examples of gender schemata in the English language. For instance, there are work titles that differ depending on the sex of the person who occupies the role. The linguistic distinctions between waiters and waitresses, policewomen and policemen, actors and actresses, and comedians and comediennes may lead people to believe that the sex of the role occupant is an important distinction for human beings at work. The increased use of nonsexist terms such as firefighter, chairperson, and mail carrier should encourage people to use different, nongendered ways to categorize. Box 5.1 further explores the issue of sexism in language.

Bem describes gender schema as a "nonconscious ideology" (1987) and a set of "default options" (1993) for behavior. Most people are not aware that they organize their perceptions on the basis of gender, nor are they aware that alternative conceptualizations are possible. As she eloquently stated, "Look through the lens of gender and you perceive the world as falling into the masculine and feminine categories. Put on a different pair of lenses, however, and you perceive the world as falling into different categories." (Bem, 1987, p. 309).

From this view, the only time when it makes sense to be gender schematic is in the realm of biology, and yet gender schema is extrapolated into many other domains. Bem (1985) tells an amusing story of her four-year-old son wearing a barrette to nursery school. A schoolmate told him that he must be a girl because he was wearing a barrette.

Four-year-old Jeremy informed his classmate that being male only means "having a penis and testicles," and he "finally pulled down his pants as a way of making his point more convincingly." (p. 216).

Bem (1993) suggests that some of the destructive aspects of gender stereotyping could be alleviated by providing people with alternative ways of thinking about the world and the self. She suggests an "individual difference" schema (that people within any group vary widely), and a "cultural relativism" schema (that different people believe different things). In this way, sex can be understood as a biological category that is not important in every setting. Bem clearly emphasizes the role of education in social change, and her theory can be applied to the social change agenda of men's studies.

It is often said the "the fish is unaware of the water" because it has never experienced anything else. Because many aspects of culture have long considered masculinity as a normative referent for experience, many men have not been very aware of the gender-schematic nature of their approach to the world. Men have remained unaware of the culture of patriarchy because it benefits them, just as fish benefit from water. Women and other marginalized groups of people are usually more aware of sexism, racism, classism, and other forms of unequal resource allocation because they usually suffer the adverse effects of these arrangements, and often on a daily basis. A fish has the luxury to remain unaware of the water. A drowning mammal does not.

To become conscious of one's ideologies would seem to require psychological- mindedness, nondefensiveness, introspection, and a willingness to listen to others' points of view. Males have been socialized away from every one of these activities. As femininity has long been associated with loss of power and status for men, there has been a good deal of reward for men's attending to the world in gender schematic fashion. Men who begin to break out of this stereotyped information processing are finding that they can evaluate themselves with standards that are less punitive and more reasonable. If Bem is correct that gender schematic processing is destructive and unessential to human development, then we ought to support countervailing educational and therapeutic activities such as consciousness raising, gender awareness curricula, women's studies, and men's studies.

Situational Influence

The social learning approaches that I have described emphasize the role of external social forces that shape the individual's behavior. The person internalizes gendered tendencies toward feeling, thinking, and behaving by generalizing from these social experiences. From these perspectives, gendered behavior is a product of the history of social influences in interaction with the individual's patterning of behavior and his or her conceptual world.

The situational influence perspective also emphasizes the role of external forces in shaping behavior, but in contrast to social learning perspectives that focus on historical influence, this perspective stresses the power of the *immediate situation* in shaping behavior.

A person often finds himself or herself in the company of others, and there is powerful pressure to behave in certain ways in these situations. For example, when you go to a restaurant, you are highly likely to wait to be seated, be polite, ask for the food that you want, and pay the bill when you are finished. You are highly unlikely to push people aside because they are sitting where you want to sit, get your own food from the kitchen, put it on the floor and stir it up with your feet, and leave without paying for your meal. Except for very unusual people, restaurant behavior falls within a rather narrow and predictable range. Under most circumstances, most people act in ways that situations dictate.

The characteristics of situations have strong influences on all behavior, including gendered behavior. Note that this perspective is not incompatible with the other social learning perspectives that I presented earlier. Your behavior in the restaurant is also a product of your *perception of the situation*, which has been strongly influenced by social learning. Children in restaurants often behave in ways that are considered inappropriate for adults, partly because they have not learned the normative adult perception of the situation.

Men (and women) often experience pressure to behave in ways that they perceive as appropriate to the social setting. For example, in many men's social groups, it is not unusual for men to describe women in denigrating terms. There is tremendous pressure in these situations for individual men to laugh, or at least remain silent in reaction to these comments. In a survey of college males, Berkowitz (1997) discovered that 75% reported feeling uncomfortable with these kinds of comments, yet only a very small minority of men express their discomfort or confront the man who makes the offensive comment. Doing so would require a man to resist the group pressure to go along with the attitude being expressed, and this study attests to the considerable power of this group pressure. In the typical male peer group situation where a misogynist (anti-woman) attitude is displayed, it is not necessarily the attitudes of individual men that allow this behavior to go unchallenged, it is the influence of a social context that carries its own momentum.

Of course, groups are made up of individuals who can affect the social atmosphere and its influences. In the above example, it is quite possible for an individual man to recognize his discomfort and confront the man who made the misogynist comment. In doing so, he might be successful in changing the social pressure of the group in the direction of disapproval of these kinds of comments. As we shall see, it is likely that he will find support for his view from others in the group who hold attitudes that are similar to his. Education and training to help college men break out of the passive bystander role in these kinds of situations are a promising development in efforts to decrease violence against women. (See Chapter 12.)

Beginning in the 1960s, social psychologists began to describe and measure the considerable influence of interpersonal situations. Three landmark studies, two of them involving the willingness to engage in violence, demonstrated the power of social contexts. The first was Stanley Milgram's (1963) series of laboratory experiments, in which research participants were led to believe (erroneously) that they were inflicting dangerous electric shocks on other research participants. In the situation in which the "victim" was in another room (although his protests could be heard by the "attacker"), more than 50% of research volunteers were willing to inflict 450-volt shocks to the victim in response to strong pressure from an authority figure in a white lab coat. Milgram's experiments demonstrated the power of *compliance*—change in behavior as the result of direct and explicit social pressure.

In the early 1970s, Phillip Zimbardo and his colleagues (Haney, Banks, & Zimbardo, 1973) set up a mock prison in the basement of the Stanford University psychology building. Male students volunteered to be randomly assigned to the roles of prisoners and guards. The prisoners were "arrested," given numbers, dressed in prison garb, and put behind bars. Within a short time, a significant number of guards became abusive toward the prisoners, who responded with a variety of symptoms: panic, physical illness, depression, and apathy. The experiment was terminated earlier than originally scheduled because of the danger to prisoners. Zimbardo's experiment demonstrated the power of social roles—people assigned to social statuses are motivated to act in accordance with these statuses.

(I should note here that, in the opinion of many people, both of these experiments were unethical, as researchers placed volunteers in dangerous psychological and physical situations. Modern safeguards have since been enacted to prevent experiments like these from taking place today).

Solomon Asch (1965) demonstrated that group pressure can cause a person to report incorrect perceptual judgments. Experimenters presented a series of three lines and asked research participants in groups of eight to say which of the lines was closest to the length of a standard line. The people in the group consistently gave answers that were obviously wrong, because they were actually accomplices of the experimenter who were hired to pose as volunteers. The study was designed to investigate the frequency with which the actual research participant will go along with the group. Only 20% remained independent of the group opinion on every trial, even though one line was unquestionably more similar to the standard than the others. (When people were asked to make the same judgment without influence from others, they gave the correct answer nearly every time.) Asch's experiments demonstrated the power of *conformity*—change in behavior in response to implicit and unspoken social pressure (in contrast to the explicit, direct pressure in Milgram's experiments).

These studies, as well as many others, tell us that people do not always behave from the "inside out." It would be foolish to characterize Milgram's "attackers" or Zimbardo's "guards" as cruel, or to characterize Asch's judges as stupid or blind. All of these people responded to the direct or indirect social pressure of the moment.

Because gender is a central organizing principle in many cultures, social situations often carry different expectations for males' and females' behavior. Social psychological concepts and research can help us to understand the considerable influences of the immediate situation and the potential for changing these influences.

Social *norms* are implicit or explicit social rules that specify appropriate behavior in social settings. For the most part, mainstream U.S. culture includes the social norms of being on time, being polite, responding when asked a question, and stopping a car when the traffic light is red. These standards for behavior are subject to change in response to specific situational influences. For instance, you might not respond to a question from a stranger in a crowded city or stop at a red light during a medical emergency.

The personality approach sees gender as a collection of ingrained attributes. Yet, as Pleck (1995) theorized, and much research has demonstrated, most people's personalities who do not match traditional gender role definitions. Eagly (1987) proposed that, rather than being descriptions of typical males and females, gender stereotypes are really descriptions of social norms—widely accepted beliefs about the gender appropriateness of behaviors.

People are motivated to conform to social norms in order to avoid disapproval and rejection from the social group. Burn (1996) refers to the motivation for avoiding social disapproval as *normative pressure*. Several studies have demonstrated that cross-gender behavior is associated with a loss of popularity, particularly for boys (Martin, 1990; Archer, 1984). Because social norms for males' behavior are defined as the avoidance of femininity, there is an unspoken pressure in many mixed-sex and male-only social groups for men to restrict their display of vulnerable emotions, caring for others, and affectionate behavior toward other males.

Observers of these groups are at risk for committing the *fundamental attribution error* by assigning the causes of such behaviors (or nonbehaviors) to men's personalities rather than to the situation at hand. People who come from an individualistic culture like that of the mainstream United States tend to understand others' behavior largely as a result of the individual's personality. Thus, you would be tempted to say that men do not behave in feminine ways because they are not vulnerable, affectionate, or caring. In reality, an individual man may be all of these things, but he is proscribed from displaying these characteristics by his understanding of social norms for men. Imagine a man in a typical social group saying any of the following:

"Bill, I *love* your outfit."

"Don, it's been so long since I've seen you; I've missed you so much."

"I've been so unhappy lately; I think it has to do with my relationship with my girlfriend."

In most social groups, men who were to say things like this would be unlikely to elicit a positive response from others, whereas gender norms allow women to say all of these things. The man may love Bill's outfit, miss Don a great deal, and be very distraught and depressed about his relationship with his girlfriend, but social display rules make it difficult for him to say so.

People depend heavily on information from others in constructing their attitudes regarding social issues. We often behave like others not only to avoid social disapproval, but because we do not know how to think, feel, or act in a given situation. We tend to follow others' leads and make assumptions about what is correct from watching others behave. The desire to be right adds *informational pressure* to normative pressure. Together, these two forces constitute powerful motivations to conform to social gender expectations. For most people, this conformity is unconscious and automatic. Unless an individual is strongly aware of social pressure and gender roles, he or she is likely to follow along with the social program (Burn, 1996).

There is considerable evidence that gendered behavior contains a strong component of conformity, compliance, and/or role performance. The endorsement of traditional masculine values and attitudes is surprisingly weak (Thompson & Pleck, 1995) and, for both men and women, public behavior is much more likely to be gender stereotypical than private behavior (Burn, 1996). You may see a man behaving in stereotypical "macho" fashion when having a drink with his buddies, but that does not mean that his internal sense of self matches his behavior or even that he privately endorses the very attitudes that he is displaying.

It is not uncommon for men to behave in ways that are usually considered unmasculine when the situation permits it or calls for it. For example, male athletes often hug and even pat one another on the rear end. Men cry publicly at funerals and when they retire. They express vulnerability and dependence privately with their intimate partners. They talk about their feelings with female friends. From the situational perspective, we could expand a great deal of social behavior beyond traditional gender boundaries simply by giving people permission to think, feel, act, and experience themselves in nontraditional ways.

One very important component of social situations is the different levels of power within the group of participants. Communication models of gender tend to emphasize that women's language is more affiliative and tentative than men's and that men's is more direct and authoritative than women's (Tannen, 1990). However, Tavris (1992) points out that power differences can account for these effects without appeal to gender. People in power do not have to worry about offending their subordinates, and so they can communicate in very straightforward and direct ways. On the other hand, subordinates need to be concerned a great deal about how their superiors will receive their communications, and so they find it necessary to be more tentative and periodically ask for superiors' opinions to gauge the response that they are getting from more powerful others. This self-protective tendency can be interpreted as affiliative, as it pays attention to relationships. Listen closely to the differences in how bosses speak to their employees and how employees communicate to their bosses, and you will easily see this effect. A power analysis casts gender differences in communication as the result of generalized power differentials between the sexes in a male-dominated society. Returning to Bem's (1993) analysis, gender-schematic information processing obscures the fact that other aspects of human experience are in operation.

In contrast to the essentialist perspective of sociobiological approaches, and, to a lesser extent, psychoanalytic approaches, social learning approaches emphasize the social constructionist view that gender roles are the products of environmental influences that are wholly subject to change. Essentialists tend to see gender as "the way it is"—an immutable fact of life and nature. Social constructionists counter that essentialists only believe that gender is "the way it is" because people, not nature, made it that way, and that there is ample evidence that gender roles can and do change.

SUMMARY

1. The basic assumption of social learning theory is that the major influences on behavior are learning processes such as reward, punishment, imitation, and information processing. From this perspective, gender typing is produced through the differential treatment of males and females by various socializing agents.

2. There is evidence of differential gender treatment of children in bedroom decor, toys, assignment of household chores, encouragement of gender-typed behaviors, discouragement of cross-gender activities, and levels of praise, punishment, and attention.

3. Historically, many males have suffered from a lack of exposure to positive masculine models. Some theorists believe that boys identify largely with hypermasculine fantasies rather than with real persons. As a result, they often strive to reach unrealistic standards of manliness.

4. Bem argues that gender typing is a result of an overuse of sex categorization in the culture. The habitual use of gender schema encourages people to see the world in masculine and feminine terms. The uses of other schemata draw attention away from sex categorization in settings where sex distinctions are relatively unimportant.

5. The situational influence perspective stresses the power of the immediate social setting in shaping behavior. People are motivated to conform and comply with actual or perceived gender demands in order to avoid social disapproval. Social pressure to act in concert with socially defined gender roles is often greater for males than for females.

5

Masculinities I: Ethnic Identities and Men's Ways of Being

Consider the following:

- Unlike peoples in most parts of the world, Tahitian (south Pacific) and Semai (central Malaysian) people have very little differentiation of social roles based on sex (Gilmore, 1990).

- In much of the Middle East and South America, men express their emotions as freely as women. There is a great deal of cultural variation in the gendered expression of emotion, with some cultures considering women to be the "emotional sex," some allowing wide latitude for expression in both sexes, and some expecting both men and women to control their emotions (Tavris & Wade, 2001).

- As societies become more industrialized and urban, gender arrangements tend to become less traditional (Best & Williams, 1993).

- During World War II, U.S. women took over most traditionally masculine factory work. After the war, they were encouraged to quit their jobs to make room for returning male soldiers in need of work (French & Poska, 2006).

- Gender arrangements tend to be more egalitarian at higher levels of education and social class (see Adler, 1993).

- A man with long hair or an earring would have been socially condemned in the United States in the 1950s.

- In combat situations, an estimated 85% of soldiers have tried not to kill, instead firing their weapons into the air or running away (Grossman, 1995).

- The kinds of employment that are considered "women's work" and "men's work" vary to a significant degree from culture to culture (Tavris & Wade, 2001).

As we can see from these examples, gender roles vary according to social settings; they are not transhistorical, cross-cultural, or cross-situational. Social conceptions of gender are influenced by a variety of factors, including ethnic patterns, economic conditions, religion, language, family socialization, cultural expectations, and the spirit of the times.

In this chapter and the next, I describe the features of masculinities within specific sub-groups as a product of critical factors that affect men's ways of being: culture, race, age, ethnicity, sexuality, socioeconomic class, and historical era. My purpose is not to provide an exhaustive review of all of the ways in which masculinity is defined across time and place—to do so would require several volumes. My goal is to give you a sampling of the variations in masculinities and a sense of theorists' speculations about the sources of these variations. Keep in mind that these cultural forces exert pressure on men to behave and experience themselves in certain ways, but that the reactions of individual men to this pressure are widely variable. For example, mainstream U.S. masculinity exerts pressure on men to deny emotional vulnerability, value athletics, and strive for economic success, but there are certainly men who are emotionally expressive, do not like sports, and/or are not oriented toward making a lot of money.

CULTURE AND MASCULINITY

Questions of cultural variations in gender and their development are not particularly new ones. More than a half century ago, anthropologist Margaret Mead (1949) wrote:

> How are men and women to think about their maleness and their femaleness in this twentieth century, in which so many of our old ideas must be made new? Have we over-domesticated men, denied their natural adventurousness, tied them down to machines that are after all only glorified spindles and looms, mortars and pestles and digging sticks, all of which were once women's work? Have we cut women off from their natural closeness to their children, taught them to look for a job instead of the touch of a child's hand, for status in a competitive world rather than a unique place by a glowing hearth? In educating women like men, have we done something disastrous to both men and women alike, or have we only taken one further step in the recurrent task of building more and better on our original human nature? . . . These are questions which are being asked in a hundred different ways in contemporary America. (p. 13)

Mead's words could easily have been written today. As we have already seen, people continue to debate these same questions in the twenty-first Century. We may never an-

Anthropologists like the one above strive to understand the effects of cultural influences, including gender ideologies, on behavior and identities.

Photo by Dr. Bruce Knauft, Department of Anthropology, Emory University.

swer them completely and for all time, but social scientists have begun to provide clues to their answers through careful research.

There is no question that cultures vary greatly in the ways that they exert pressure on people to think, feel, and act in certain ways. For instance, in mainstream U.S. culture, it is common for people to make eye contact during conversations, but in many Asian and Native American cultures, eye contact is a sign of aggression and disrespect. The standard vacation for a U.S. worker is two weeks per year, but many western Europeans take three times that amount or more. Industrialized societies tend to be strictly organized around time; being more than a few minutes late is a violation of standards of acceptable conduct. But in polychronic cultures (most rural, agriculturally based economies), being a day or even a week "late" is quite acceptable (Tavris & Wade, 2001).

Cultural rules regarding sex, gender, and sexuality are no exception to the phenomenon of cultural variation. Sandra Bem (1993) noted, "The analysis of how conventionally gendered women and men are made is…a special case of how cultural natives are made…. Preprogramming an individual's daily experience into the default options of a particular culture is apparent in the most superficial analysis of how children have been made into unmistakably different kinds of social beings in different cultures and different historical epochs." (p. 139).

Cultural gender arrangements constitute a set of the "default options" to which Bem refers. Through its customs, language, and power interrelationships, cultures transmit expectations about how men and women should process their experiences, think of themselves, and behave. Becoming a gender non-conformist requires a person to resist a considerable amount of cultural momentum. Bem points out that doing so is made more difficult by the fact that the process of enculturation tends to transfer values, beliefs and attitudes to its natives in nonconscious ways as a *subliminal pedagogy*—a set of meanings that are so embedded in social practices that they are virtually invisible to most people. She states that children learn about "their culture's way of construing reality without yet being aware that other construals are possible" (p. 140) through this process of cultural transfer, which "is initiated every time the active, pattern-seeking child is exposed to a culturally significant social practice." (p. 141). It is quite difficult to resist a cultural pressure that you cannot even name—to answer a question when you cannot even articulate the question. One of the goals of gender studies is to articulate the context of gendered default options so that people can more freely choose between these options and alternatives, including those that they otherwise would not have known were available to them.

Cultural Variation in Gender Roles

Anthropologist Margaret Mead (1935, 1949) is generally credited with popularizing the interest in cross-cultural gender variations. In *Sex and Temperament in Three Primitive Societies* (1935), she described widely variant cultural ideals among different tribes in New Guinea for the often gender-typed behavior of aggression. According to Mead, the Mundugumor tribe is characterized by aggressive behavior in both men and women. The Arapesh tribe values non-aggression for both sexes. The Tchambuli expect females to be aggressive and males to be passive, the complete opposite of most Western cultures.

Pleck (1987) emphasizes that Mead did not intend to describe *actual* sex differences within each culture, even though many writers have interpreted her work in this way. Instead, she sought to describe cultural differences in gender *ideologies*, or *ideal types* from the perspective of each dominant cultural climate. In fact, she included chapters describing the ways that each culture deals with people who deviate from the ideal. Do not be misled into thinking that *all* Arapesh men or *all* Mundugumor women behave in the same ways. As Pleck points out, "Mead's real point was that a man or woman perfectly adapted to the [gender]-role norms of one culture could be a misfit (a term Mead used repeatedly) in another." (p. 27).

One commonality across cultures is that misfits tend not to be treated very well by the rest of the society (If you want to experience the social disapproval that befalls a gender misfit, try some of the gender role violations that I suggested in Chapter 1). Mead's great contribution was to challenge the essentialist notions of male and female by proposing that the *content* of the gender ideal and, by extension, the content of the gender role violator's or misfit's behavior and sense of self, vary among different cultures. Thus, she sparked a new awareness of cultural relativism in gender.

In the time since Mead's work, anthropologists, cross-cultural psychologists, sociologists, and other social scientists have sought to specify the content of gender ideologies among various groups, and to describe similarities and differences in the ways in which cultures address the distinction (or lack of it) between male and female. Again, keep in mind as you read each description that researchers are describing cultural gender ideologies, and that individuals within every culture vary in their actual behavior.

Many people assume that there are only two sexes (male and female), two gender roles (masculine and feminine), and two sexual orientations (homosexual and heterosexual). However, researchers have pointed out that there are more than two sexes (Fausto-Sterling, 1996, 2000; Lorber, 1994). In addition to unambiguous males and unambiguous females, there are hermaphrodites, male pseudohermaphrodites ("merms"), female pseudohermaphrodites ("ferms"), male-to-female transsexuals, and female-to-male transsexuals. Although much of Western culture has virtually ignored intersexed individuals, some cultures have extensive regulations for dealing with them. Fausto-Sterling (1996) suggests that, if cultures were to acknowledge intersexuality, then the apparent male-female dichotomy, from which gender and sexual orientation arrangements proceed, would have to fall away and be replaced by other ways of categorizing people.

If the biological category of sex is not as unambiguous as is generally believed, then the psychological and behavioral categories of sexual orientation and gender are even more murky. There are wide variations in preferred sexual behaviors, attractions, relationships, and fantasies. The categories of homosexual, bisexual, and heterosexual do not capture the richness and intricacy of sexual orientation.

There are also several cultural exceptions to the two-gender standard. One frequently cited example is the North American Indian *berdache*, an anatomically normal male who behaves much like the females of the tribe. These people are not considered to be deviant males; they are not scorned or shamed for their behaviors. Thus, we cannot consider them gender misfits. Instead, berdache is a third gender within the tribe (Williams, 1996). Several other cultures also have third genders, such as the *nadle, alyha*, and *hwame* of the Mohave Indians, the *hijiras* of northern India, and the *xaniths* of Oman, all of whom fulfill culturally approved social and sexual roles apart from the usual masculine and feminine genders (Doyle & Paludi, 1998). Cultures with more than two genders are more the exception than the rule, but they provide an expanded view of the possibilities.

Within two-gender cultures, there are many commonalities among conceptions of male and female. In most cases, men are more aggressive than women, handle the large-game hunting, and avoid activities considered to be feminine (Gilmore, 1990; Adler, 1993; Tavris & Wade, 2001). Women tend to do a majority of household work and child care, are considered to be more emotional, and have lower social statuses than men, although their status is not uniformly low across classes or cultures (di Leonardo, 1991).

Perhaps the most important and ambitious anthropological work on men and gender in recent times is David Gilmore's (1990) *Manhood in the Making*. Gilmore studied many

---

Box 5.1: *Traditionality and Nontraditionality of Cultural Conceptions of Gender*

Modern (egalitarian)
   Netherlands
   Germany
   Finland
   England
   Italy
   Venezuela
   United States
   Canada
   Singapore
   Malaysia
   Japan
   India
   Pakistan
   Nigeria
Traditional (male dominated)

Williams and Best (1990) rank order of gender roles in 14 countries. Note that differences between ranks may be statistically nonsignificant.

---

cultures around the world and described important commonalities and differences in social conceptions of masculinity. He found a "family resemblance" in masculinities for most (but not all) of the world. In the majority of the cultures Gilmore studied, masculinity was characterized by strength, risk taking, avoidance of femininity, aggression, and sexual initiative. These findings echo those of Williams' and Best's (1990) study of 14 countries and Adler's (1993) collection of gender descriptions in 31 countries. Gilmore also noted that, in most of the world, masculinity is regarded as an achievement—something that the culture must build into males through various socialization processes (hence the title of the book). The dominant conception is that men do not become masculine simply by growing into adulthood. Instead, they must endure some sort of ordeal, often involving considerable physical pain (see Box 5.1). The ubiquity of these rites of passage into manhood may tell us that many cultures have evolved social processes that dissuade men from their natural inclinations to avoid pain and express their feelings. The existence of these processes is evidence that men fulfill specific functions within social groups and that emotional or physical vulnerability are often viewed as being incompatible with these functions.

There are many variations within the basic masculine themes that Gilmore described. For instance, there seems to be more of an emphasis in fathering children as an expression of masculinity in Circum-Mediterranean cultures than in most others. The culture of Truk Island (in the south Pacific) is marked by heavy drinking and brawling among men. The Trukese consider fighting to be sexy. The Samburu (East Africa) stress the element of generosity in masculinity. Several cultures, such as the Mehinaku of Brazil and the Sambians of Papua New Guinea, view the willingness to engage in dangerous hunting or fishing as a sign of manliness.

One of the most striking aspects of Gilmore's work is his description of two cultures, Tahiti (in Polynesia) and Semai (in central Malaysia) in which gender ideologies are very different from most of the world. He describes Semai as a gentle, noncompetitive culture with little or no sexual jealousy or overt aggression. According to Gilmore, visitors to Tahiti are often struck by the

> bizarre [by Western standards] lack of sexual differentiation on the island.... Tahitian women had a remarkably high status and were permitted to do almost everything that the men did.... Men are no more aggressive than women; women do not seem 'softer' or 'more maternal' than the men... there is no stress on proving manhood, no pressure on men to appear in any significant way different from women or children. Men have no fear of acting in ways Westerners would consider effeminate. During dances, for instance, adult men will dance together in close bodily contact, rubbing against each other without any anxiety..." (p. 202–203).

Williams and Best (1990) note a degree of difference in gender ideologies on a continuum ranging from traditional (male-dominated) to modern (egalitarian) (see Box 5.2). Together with Gilmore's descriptions, we can conclude that, although most of the world holds similar cultural views of the roles of men and women, there are variations in the degree to which particular cultures subscribe to traditional ideologies, and in some cases, there are radical departures from what is commonly expected of men and women in most societies.

EXPLANATIONS OF CULTURAL SIMILARITIES AND DIFFERENCES IN GENDER IDEOLOGIES

The finding that gender ideologies often bear some resemblance to one another tempts us to embrace essentialist notions of gender. Many theorists (e.g. Buss, 1989; Barash & Lipton, 1997) use the finding of cross-cultural similarity as an argument for the pre-eminence of biological bases of gendered behavior. We are inclined to say that, if people are so similar on gender dimensions world wide, then there must be something in genes, hormones, brain structure and function, and/or some other biological essence that make them so. On the other hand, the findings of cross-cultural differences, especially the striking exceptions of Tahiti and Semai, and the various "third genders," tempts us to embrace social constructionism, as we are inclined to say that, if some places are so different, then gender must be very malleable (not only at the individual level, where it undoubtedly is, but also at the cultural level). An essentialist argument must include an explanation of differences; a social constructionist argument must include an explanation of similarities.

Box 3.2: Male Initiation Rituals

Gilbert Herdt (1982) states that "Femininity unfolds naturally, whereas masculinity must be achieved, and here is where the male ritual cult steps in" (p. 55). Many cultural rites of passage for males involve undergoing painful and frightening experiences in the service of making them into warriors who will face danger without vulnerable emotion. Following are some rites of passage described by Gilmore (1990):

Samburu (East Africa): Adolescent boys are subjected to "bloody circumcision rites" to which they "must submit without so much as flinching under the agony of the knife. If a boy cries out while his flesh is being cut, if he so much as blinks an eye or turns his head, he is shamed for life as unworthy of manhood, and his entire lineage is shamed as a nursery of weaklings." (p. 13). The cutting may last four minutes or more.

The New Guinea highlands: Boys must endure "whipping, flailing, beating, and other forms of terrorization by older men." (p. 14).

Tewa (native American peoples of New Mexico): Boys are taken away from their homes, undergo ritual purification, and are beaten by Kachina spirits (their fathers in disguise). The stiff yucca whip causes bleeding and leaves permanent scars.

Sambia (New Guinea): In addition to physical beating, boys undergo a bloodletting ritual in which "stiff, sharp grasses are thrust up the nostrils until the blood flows copiously." (p. 156).

There are also some nonviolent rites of passage, like the Jewish bar mitzvah, which is centered around ordeals of learning and reciting tenets of faith. There are also rites that involve physical discomfort but not violence, such as the African Ju/'hoansi, where young men go into the bush and experience extremes of hunger, thirst, cold, and extreme fatigue. Raphael (1988) provides another description:

Thonga (South Africa): "...youths are continually beaten during their three-month initiation ritual. They are also denied water and forced to eat unsavory foods, such as the half-digested grass found in the bowels of an antelope. They are made to lie naked on the cold winter nights, sleeping only on their backs while being bitten incessantly by bugs in the ground." (p. 5).

Many cultures have less formal rites of passage, such as challenges around enduring humiliation and taking risks in all-male groups. Some fraternity, lodge, military, and street gang initiations are a few examples. Rites of passage may be important indicators of cultures' masculine ideologies. Whether they are violent or not, most involve separation from the mother and other women of the group, a strong message that masculinity is formed in the context of homosocial experiences and relationships. There is also a pervasive sense that childhood is left behind. In fact, many rituals involve the symbolic death of the boy as a part of the birth of the man (Gilmore, 1990; Raphael, 1988). In part, this "death" may involve the turning away from feeling, experience, and connection toward the world of independence and task-orientation. Some authors (e.g., Horne, Jolliff, & Roth, 1996; Bly, 1990; Raphael, 1988) have mainly positive views of male initiation rites, seeing them as necessary, and, in some cases, biologically based. There is a sense of boys coming to power as they are accepted into the world of men. But would males need to have this separating experience of power if females were just as powerful as males?

Social psychologists often view initiation rites in the context of cognitive dissonance, the tendency to have one's behavior match one's values and attitudes (Aronson, 2004). When a person conforms his or her behavior to extreme demands, he or she is then motivated to endorse the values and attitudes that are connected with these demands. In other words, if I endure a hardship, it is vital to my sense of self to believe that the outcome was worth the pain, otherwise I am a fool. Cognitive dissonance explains the intense loyalty to a group that many people exhibit when they have gone to great lengths to become a part of that group.

Very few essentialists would deny that culture has a powerful effect on human behavior, and so their explanations of difference are constructed around a culture's ability to dissuade its natives from whatever the theorist considers to be human nature. On my view, most essentialists spend very little time dealing with exceptions to their predictions, preferring to chalk up these differences as a reflection of expected variation in behavior and unspecified sociocultural forces.

Social constructionists seem to fare much better in explaining the similarities in gender ideologies across cultures. The basic argument is this: cultural similarity is no guarantee of a hard-wired biological basis for behavior. Instead, these similarities may well reflect *cultural redundancies*, sociocultural forces that have affected many cultures in similar ways. Various theorists have proposed specific kinds of these forces, mainly historical and economic ones. Theoretically, exceptional cases such as Tahiti and Semai are marked by either the absence of the usual cultural forces or the presence of unusual ones.

As I mentioned in Chapter 1, an important historical view of gender considers the centrality of patriarchy, a 5,000-year-old system by which men have dominated women in public and private life. Many historians and anthropologists believe that this system evolved in reaction to societies' economic needs. As Bonvillain (2001) proposes, "Gender is a basic criterion for the assignment of economic work in most cultures and is therefore deeply entwined in a society's mode of production." (p. 1)

In her landmark book, *The Creation of Patriarchy*, Gerda Lerner (1986) argues that male domination of women is largely embedded in the development of agriculture. Prior to the Neolithic period, humans lived in hunter/gatherer societies that were largely nomadic. In these foraging societies, children were not the economic resource that they later became. Their existence meant that there were more mouths to feed on a daily basis, and children only became valuable if they could develop to a point where they could produce more food than they consumed. Because it was difficult for people in these societies to accumulate surpluses of food or to stay in one place, children stretched resources and inhibited mobility.

U.S. President George W. Bush walks hand in hand through the flower garden at his ranch in Crawford, Texas with Crown Price Abdullah of Saudi Arabia. Although Bush is conventionally gendered and handholding between men is proscribed in mainstream U.S. culture, the same behavior is a commonplace gesture of friendship in Saudi Arabia.

Photo © AP Images.

The character of work and survival changed radically with the development of the ability to cultivate crops and maintain food surpluses. At that point, children became a labor resource, and having lots of them meant that a family or social group could till more land and thus have a much better chance of accumulating wealth. The relative burden of moving the children to more plentiful sources of food fell away, as groups could stay in the same places for generations. Land also became a valuable resource to be defended.

According to Lerner, hunter/gatherer societies were relatively gender-egalitarian, as women, who often did more gathering than men, produced more than their share of the wealth (food). With the advent of agriculture, however, women became most valuable for producing children, and similarly to land, they became a resource to acquire. The society then had an interest in controlling women's reproductive capacities, and, by extension, their sexuality. The means of *production* for women became the means of *reproduction*. Lerner describes the process by which women

> were exchanged or bought in marriages for the benefit of their families; later, they were conquered or bought in slavery, where their sexual services were part of their labor and where their children were the property of their masters. In every known society it was women of conquered tribes who were first enslaved, whereas men were killed. It was only after men had learned how to enslave the women of groups who could be defined as

strangers, that they learned how to enslave men of these groups and, later, subordinates from within their own societies. (pp. 212–213)

Gender ideologies, including laws, customs, and religions based on the "counterfactual metaphor of male procreativity" (p. 220) flowed from these fundamental changes in the character of work. Over the course of 2,500 years, cultures established systems by which the male came to be valued over the female in virtually every sphere of public and private life. Lerner makes it clear that the oppression of patriarchy for women and the privilege for men have never applied equally to all people, but rather that it interacts with social class to have profound effects on people's lives and resulted in women-as-a-group living in a "relatively greater state of un-freedom than men" (p. 214) from that point to the present day.

Nancy Bonvillain (1998) provides some anthropological evidence in support of Lerner's theory. Bonvillain describes two cultures in which social gender arrangements changed in concert with economic developments. The Ju/'hoansi (ju-TWAN-si, also known as the !Kung in anthropological literature) of the Kalahari Desert in Africa were mainly a foraging people with egalitarian gender roles, an arrangement that Bonvillain ties to men's and women's relatively equal contribution to the band's subsistence. (Actually, women provided more of the total caloric intake for the group than men.) One marker of this gender equality is the lack of a sexual double standard—females are as free to express their sexuality as males. (Recall Lerner's contention that the double standard is an expression of the patriarchal control of women's lives.) For the Ju/'hoansi, the social and interpersonal costs of having extramarital affairs are equal for men and women. Two other important features of this culture reflect the absence of patriarchal arrangements; wife-beating and rape were very rare—perhaps non-existent—and fathers' participation in child care was considerable. Coltrane (1998) notes that the level of fathers' child care involvement is inversely related to the level of masculine aggressiveness in the culture. One could argue that this connection is both cause and effect of gender equality.

In the early twentieth century, Ju/'Hoansi economic arrangements began to change as European Boers came to the area, appropriated land, established agriculture, and hired natives as farm laborers. At the same time, the British established schools and various missionaries came to the area. Both wielded considerable influence over the ideologies of the natives. By the 1960s, most Ju/'Hoansi were involved in farming and herding, which are mostly carried out by men. A division of labor developed, with women relegated mainly to domestic chores. Men became the owners of the herds and fields, and women's work became regarded as subsidiary. The sexes experienced a greater degree of separation than ever before, with men became more mobile and women more home bound. As a result, work roles came to be defined more rigidly along gender lines, men came to higher status as a group compared with women, and gender arrangements moved toward models found in much of the world. The antifeminine ethic evolved, with men increasingly refusing to do "women's work."

The Arctic Inuit provide another example of change from what was an unusual cultural gender arrangement. Inuit society was marked by a limited male dominance, that is, there were some features of patriarchal tradition (e.g., violence against women, physical and social segregation of the sexes) and some indicators of women's power in the culture (i.e., no sexual double standard, considerable child care participation by fathers, low division of labor, and *uxorilocal* residence—a couple initially lived near the wife's family following marriage). Bonvillain ties the male dominance aspect to men's provision of most meat and fish and the egalitarian aspects to the considerable contribution of women's labor to the group's subsistence in the harsh environment of the Arctic—women do some hunting and fishing, and they do the majority of sewing, a critical survival function because clothing that protects people from the elements must be expertly made and replaced often.

Inuit economies underwent a transformation in the early twentieth century, when trapping animals for fur replaced whaling as the main source of income. As the Inuit moved from a subsistence hunting society to one in which wealth could be accumulated, men spent increasing amounts of time away from home, checking traps and trading furs for food and other commodities. Male dominance increased and gender roles moved toward the arrangements I have described as "traditional" throughout this book, although they are anything but traditional for the Inuit.

Bonvillain tracks concomitant economic and gender changes in several other societies, such as the plains Native North Americans, the Igbo of Nigeria, and the Jivaro of Peru. She concludes that gender equality depends on women and men having control over the acquisition and use of resources and postmarital residence rules favoring women. These conditions have been relatively absent in most of the world for centuries.

The history of masculinity is also a history of warfare and other danger. When the survival of the society depends on dangerous hunting, intertribal competition for food, or fighting off intruders, those tasks fall to men for three major reasons. First, men have relatively greater upper-body strength than women and are thus better suited to many aspects of these tasks, especially prior to the development of modern weapons and labor saving devices. Second, men's physical role in the reproductive process is minimal. They do not become pregnant or nurse children, and so their time can be invested in other tasks. Third, men are, in a sense, expendable. The survival of a society, in terms of producing children, requires many fewer men than women.

But facing danger is not natural. The self-preservation instinct provides a strong motivation to run away from it. Therefore, a society has to offer men great incentives for risking death, and the rewards for men who survive generally take the forms of power, status, and sexual access. Women must cooperate by being subservient for this arrangement to function. Men must be stripped of their vulnerable emotions in order to perform this work, which involves going against their natural inclinations. Thus, they have to be "made" into masculine men by some "unnatural" process. Herdt (1982) believes that harsh male initiation rites serve this purpose of making men into machines. The rewards for succeeding as a man are great; so are the costs of failing.

Therefore, a social constructionist explanation of cross-cultural similarities in masculinity is that many cultures have found it necessary to defend land and compete for scarce resources to survive, and that the gender ideology of men as risk taking, aggressive, powerful, and dominant provided a cultural context for men as hunters and warriors. Gilmore (1990) explains it thus: "Manhood is the social barrier that societies must erect against entropy, human enemies, the forces of nature, time, and all the human weaknesses that endanger group life." (p. 226)

We return to the exceptional cultures of Tahiti and Semai as evidence in support of this argument. Although most cultures have historically been served by male dominance and aggression, these two cultures have not. Gilmore (1990) notes that the economic and social conditions that have existed in most of the world were never present in these cultures. Tahiti is an island paradise where there is no dangerous or strenuous work. The food sources are fish and agriculture. Unlike the situation for the Mehinaku of Brazil, fishing in Tahiti is not dangerous, nor is hunting. There is always a plentiful supply of food. There is no shortage of arable land or domesticated animals. As Tahiti is an island remote from the rest of the world, there has been no need to defend its borders and therefore no culture of warriors. Thus, the economic forces that promote competition and aggression are noticeably absent.

The Semai have plentiful land and no private ownership. Although only men hunt, this activity is not dangerous or strenuous—small wild pigs are the largest game pursued. Trapping and fishing provide a much larger amount of the food supply, and, again, the fishing is not difficult or dangerous—children often fish by hand. There has been no warfare. Gilmore summarizes the striking differences between most of the world and these two cultures, describing Tahiti and Semai as places where:

> There is no want of natural resources and thus no economic incentive to strive or to compete, no agonistic ethos, no open market for skills. Because the economy is cooperative, ambition is devalued. There are no serious hazards in the external world that the men are expected to defend against.... Neither society feels threatened by invaders; neither engages in warfare. There is little pressure for worldly success. There is no concept of a secluded private sphere of women and children that men must protect. Men have no interest in defining themselves as different from or superior to women, or as their defenders. In short, there is little basis for an ideology of manhood that motivates men to perform under pressure or to defend boundaries. (pp. 217–218)

From this perspective, it seems that the "default options" of traditional gender that Bem describes are constructed from social, historical and economic conditions, that traditional masculinity is constructed as a psychological and social response to perceived and/or actual threat, and that the natural human default options are cooperation and gender egalitarianism.

If social and economic conditions are responsible for producing traditional gender roles and ideologies, will these arrangements change if and when the conditions that produced them change? There is evidence that this is indeed the case. Best and Williams (1993) study of 14 countries demonstrated that gender ideologies are strongly related to the social and economic development of the culture. The modern conditions of urbanization and industrialization are accompanied by more modern gender arrangements. Many of the authors in Adler's (1993) edited volume, *The International Handbook of Gender*

Roles, noted that this phenomenon seemed to hold within a culture—that urban people and people with non-traditional occupations tended to be more gender-egalitarian than their rural and traditional counterparts within the same countries.

The finding that two things go together (modern work roles and modern gender roles) does not necessarily mean that one causes the other, but we can make a strong argument for this relationship as a causal one with the use of a functional analysis. Industrialization greatly diminishes the need for a sexual division of labor. The skills required by most modern work do not require physical strength or risk taking. We have also seen profound changes in reproduction. Reliable contraception is increasingly allowing people to control when and if they will have children (Tavris & Wade, 2001), who are not the economic resource they were in agricultural societies. Thus, it is possible for people to have children for reasons other than economic ones, and people tend to have many fewer children as a result. Women or men are capable of performing all child care duties, as demonstrated by a small but growing number of stay-at-home fathers in the United States. Overall, modern societies can offer many more options in the world of work than traditional societies could, and change in gender ideologies occur as a result. Social constructionists view traditional gender arrangements in the modern world as historical artifacts that will continue to evolve into modern arrangements over time, just as patriarchy began to evolve in response to social and economic changes some 5,000 years ago. The recent interest in studying gender is but one indication that social changes are taking place. We may be coming full circle, as the economic bases of urbanization and industrialization recapitulate the resource control that women had in foraging societies.

DIVERSITY AMONG AMERICAN MEN: THE IMPACT OF ETHNICITY AND SOCIAL CLASS

We have seen the impact of various cultural forces on the social construction of masculinity, and I have noted both continuity and discontinuity in gender ideologies across cultures. I now turn to a more detailed description of some of these social factors within various groups in the United States.

Historical Considerations

The content of masculine gender ideology in mainstream U.S. culture is not a static entity. It has evolved in response to changes in the spirits of the times across history. Two comprehensive descriptions of historical changes in masculinity as culturally construed in the United States are Anthony Rotundo's (1993) *American Manhood: Transformations in Masculinity from the Revolution to the Modern Era* and Michael Kimmel's (1996) *Manhood in America: A Cultural History*.

Rotundo conceptualizes changes in social conceptions of masculinity in three phases. The first, *communal masculinity*, characterized colonial times. It emphasized a man's usefulness to the community more than his economic success. The major expression of masculinity was in meeting the needs and expectations of one's family and neighbors. There was a fundamental value of male superiority that was based in the belief of men's supposedly greater ability to reason and control emotions. These beliefs were the bases of laws and other social arrangements that gave men and women unequal status. For example, women were not allowed to vote in the United States until well into the twentieth century.

In the late eighteenth century, the service orientation of communal masculinity gave way to the economic orientation of *self-made manhood,* with its emphasis on business and professional success and the accumulation of wealth. Rotundo believes that this change came about as an effect of an increased political and economic climate that emphasized individuality over the collective. People believed that unfettered competition would reward the most deserving men. The ethic of controlling one's passions gave way to an emphasis on channeling them into expressions of dominance and independence. Although men were seen as the more virtuous of the sexes under communal masculinity, they came to be seen as selfish and aggressive under self-made manhood, and people came to regard women as virtuous people whose social role was to civilize and control the animal passions of men.

During this period, there was an increasing emphasis on what both Rotundo and Kimmel refer to as the *doctrine of separate spheres*. This cultural assumption that men and women are fundamentally different led to the belief that the sexes function best in settings (spheres) that conform to their supposedly natural proclivities. Women's domain was defined as the home; men's as the world-at-large. People considered the world to be an evil and dangerous place from which "fragile" women must be protected. A man came home from work to renew himself for the next day's battle. As Rotundo so eloquently puts it:

> the social fabric was torn every day in the world and mended every night at home. Men's sphere depleted virtue, women's sphere renewed it. . . While men of the colonial era had struggled to reconcile ideals of public virtue and personal interest, those ideals realigned themselves along a male-female axis in the nineteenth century. (pp. 23–24)

Kimmel (1996) describes the self-made man as a restless person who had to prove himself every day, but who could never demonstrate his worth once and for all. Therefore, he had to compete with other men both at work and in the other "homosocial preserves" (all-male environments) such as men's clubs and sporting events. No matter how much he did or how successful he was, it was never enough. As an astute foreign observer of U.S. culture in the nineteenth century, Alexis de Toqueville described the restlessness of the American man:

> An American will build a house in which to pass his old age and sell it before the roof is on; he will plant a garden and rent it just as the trees are coming into bearing; he will clear a field and leave others to reap the harvest; he will take up a profession and leave it, settle in one place and soon go off elsewhere with his changing desires. (quoted in Kimmel, 1996, p. 25)

The homosociality of which Kimmel speaks became a very important proving ground for masculinity in the nineteenth century, and it continues to hold this function in the present day. Because the doctrine of separate spheres sharply distinguished the domains of men and women, too much influence from women's sphere, the home, was believed to feminize, and thus emasculate men. They experienced an increasing need to prove themselves to other men in places away from the home—in sports, at clubs, and, for children, in an aggressive "boy culture" (Rotundo, 1993). The colonial emphasis on connection to home evolved into an ethic of somewhat of a disconnection, increasingly emphasizing the social definition of masculinity as antifemininity.

The nineteenth century also saw the rise of homophobia as a consequence of the rise of masculine competition and antifemininity. Kimmel writes that, "Homophobia is more than an irrational fear of homosexuals... . Homophobia is the fear of other men—that other men will unmask us, emasculate us, reveal to us and the world that we do not measure up...." (p. 8). Homosocial preserves were at once de-pressurizing and re-pressurizing; they were an escape from the pressures of the working world and women's sphere, the home, but they were also an immersion in highly competitive, rough, and aggressive all-male environments. A boy wants to go off with his male friends in order to escape from the feminizing influence of his mother, but there he must conform his behavior to masculine standards or risk being ostracized as a "sissy."

The late nineteenth and early twentieth centuries saw the rise of *passionate manhood*, which Rotundo describes as, "...in some respects an elaboration of self-made manhood, but it stretched those beliefs in directions that would have shocked the old individualists of the early 1800s" (p. 5). The major change was the view that being competitive and aggressive moved beyond the world of work to become regarded as ends in themselves. Rotundo describes this social change:

> Where nineteenth-century views had regarded the self and its passions suspiciously as objects of manipulation (self-control, self-denial), twentieth-century opinion exalted them as a source of identity and personal worth (self-expression, self-enjoyment). Play and leisured entertainment—once considered marks of effeminacy—became approved activities for men as the nineteenth century ended.... A man defined his identity not just in the workplace but through modes of enjoyment and self-fulfillment outside of it. In a world where the passions formed a vital part of the self, older forms of virtue—self-restraint, self-denial, became suspect. (p. 6)

We see common threads of more modern conceptions of masculinity in all of these historical phases: independence, antifemininity, toughness, competition, homophobia, and aggression. Yet the relative emphases of these masculine ethics changed from era to era. In the final chapter of this book, you will read about the present-day evolutions in masculine ideologies. Social constructionists view all of these changes as reflections of the economic and social needs of a society, a connection we will explore further in the descriptions of masculinity and work.

There are important interactions between the social demands that come with gendered status and those that come with memberships in other socially defined groups. Following are brief descriptions of masculinities in the contexts of several ways in which society perceives people as different in important ways. In this chapter I explore the connections between masculinity and ethnicity, in the next chapter, three other forms of identity: sexual orientation, socioeconomic class, and age.

Ethnicities and Masculinity

Ethnic identity is a strong identification with one's cultural group. The United States is a collection of many ethnic peoples, and each group has cultural modes of language, customs, food, religion, and dress that make it distinctive. Ethnic identities also include psychological characteristics like world view, moral values, and rules about appropriate behavior. These cultural characteristics are passed from one generation to the next within family systems, and there is evidence of the effects of ethnicities even many generations after immigration (Greeley, 1981). *Acculturation* is an identification with the dominant culture, which in the United States could be described as white, heterosexual, middle-class, Christian, and western European in origin.

The ways of being of ethnic and acculturated values sometimes come into conflict, but researchers have demonstrated that ethnic identity and acculturation are not opposite ends of a single continuum. In other words, an individual does not necessarily become less ethnically identified as he or she becomes more acculturated. Rather, these two processes are relatively independent. A person with a strong ethnic identity and weak acculturation is termed *ethnic separatist*. A person with a strong ethnic identity and strong acculturation is termed *bicultural*. An immigrant who conforms to the "melting pot" ethic, the value on rapid acculturation and abandonment of ethnic identity, is termed *assimilated*. And, some *marginal* people have weak identification with both the dominant group and their culture of origin. Individuals vary with regard to degree of ethnic identity and acculturation (Tavris & Wade, 2001).

Gender roles are obviously important components of ethnicities. As we have already seen, societies have many different ways of handling perceived divisions of labor, sexuality, and personality characteristics between the sexes. For example, German-American fathers are known for their interpersonal distance, low emotionality, and strong discipline, often including the use of physical punishment. The traditional German man was the unquestioned head of the family, and his main role was that of economic provider. Wives were expected to do domestic chores and maintain order within the home. They are considered to be more emotionally available to children than their husbands (Winawer & Wetzel, 1996). Many German-American families continue to follow this model of male dominance, even though the German culture from which they descended has evolved into one of the more gender-egalitarian cultures in the modern world (Williams & Best, 1990).

Italian-American men resemble German-American men in most respects, but the cultural standards for emotional expression are a distinct exception. Italian Americans tend to have close-knit nuclear and extended family ties, and families are viewed as a source of help for problems and central to an individual's decision making. Going outside of the family for help with personal difficulties is strongly discouraged (Giordano & McGoldrick, 1996). Thus, we see significant variations, even within two well-established European-American cultures, but there is also a high degree of similarity between these two groups in cultural concepts of masculinity.

Similar gender issues may find different modes of expression across different ethnic groups (Rybarczyk, 1994). For example, British men often express homophobia by avoiding physical contact with other men. On the other hand, Portuguese-American men usually feel quite comfortable embracing each other, although they express homophobia by bragging to one another about sexual exploits with women (Moitoza, 1982).

One way to observe cultural differences in the conceptions of "men's work" and "women's work" is to visit traditional ethnic restaurants. In Greek or Indian restaurants, seating customers and waiting on tables are considered men's work. In Polish and Ethiopian eateries, women perform these functions (Rybarczyk, 1994). And these arrangements change over time. The first time I visited Spain in the early 1990s, waiters were nearly exclusively males. On my most recent trip there in 2005, women were as visible as men in these jobs.

In order to illustrate the effects of ethnicity on masculinity, I will briefly describe some of the research on the three largest groups of ethnic men in the United States, Latino, African-American, and Asian men, all of whom have prominent ethnic identities.

Latino Men

The term *Hispanic* is used by the U.S. government to refer to all Spanish-speaking ethnic groups. This term can refer to people of any race from as many as 20 distinct ethnic groups, including Cubans, Puerto Ricans, Spaniards, Dominicanos, and Mexicans (Valdés, Baron, & Ponce, 1987). The histories and ethnic identities of these groups are often very different from one another. For example, many Salvadorans and Nicaraguans emigrated to the United States during civil wars in their home countries. Compared with some other Latinos, they were more likely to come from low socioeconomic backgrounds and had relatively little preparation for moving to the United States. In contrast, many Chilean and Cuban immigrants have more educational advantage higher socioeconomic status, and many had made arrangements and established local support before emigrating. Central Americans are much more likely than most other groups to have experienced war and to have been forcibly displaced from their homes (Comas-Díaz, 1993).

By far, the largest group of Hispanic peoples in the United States are Latinos/Latinas, people whose ethnic backgrounds are in the Spanish-speaking countries of the Americas. Compared with the dominant Anglo culture, which tends to be centered in the nuclear family, Latino culture places more emphasis on extended families. The value of *familismo* (familism) emphasizes these kinship relationships in the context of values like interdependence, cooperation, and affiliation (Falicov, 1996).

Latino cultures largely endorse hierarchical family arrangements whereby fathers are expected to be authoritarian and mothers submissive. There are strong traditions of gender-differentiated ideologies, with men thought to be strong, brave, independent, and rational. Women are thought to be intuitive, gentle, submissive, and dependent (Comas-Díaz, 1993). However, there is considerable variation among individual families. Many are egalitarian, and women dominate in others (Falicov, 1996). Comas-Díaz

(1993) also notes that traditional gender roles among Latino/Latina immigrants are undergoing change in reaction to exposure to mainstream U.S. culture, and also because wives tend to have an easier time finding employment than their husbands. Again, we see the influence of economic power on gender relations.

Considerations of race are usually intertwined with socioeconomic class issues. Hispanics' average income is little more than half that of Whites in the United States (Suro, 1998). Most Latinos immigrated to gain employment, and many did so without going through standard immigration channels. These "illegals" are often forced to accept "off the books" jobs with poor working conditions in which they do not have access to standard labor protections such as worker's compensation. Partly as a result of their fear of being detected and perhaps deported, "illegals" often strive to call as little attention to themselves as possible. At the same time, some aspects of Latino culture emphasize behaviors that co-exist easily with this low-key style. Most notable among these is the traditional value of *respeto* (respect) that stresses deference and submission to authority (Comas-Díaz, 1993), and the practice of dissimulation (hiding one's true feelings and motives in social situations). Some theorists believe that these qualities reflect an "oppressed servant" mentality that developed from centuries of foreign domination in much of Latin America (Rybarczyk, 1994).

The stereotype of the Latino male centers on *machismo*, the display of strong and aggressive masculinity. In mainstream U.S. society, this term is usually used to describe the negative qualities of physical aggression, sexual promiscuity, dominance of women, and excessive use of alcohol (Gutierrez, 1990). Some authors have argued that machismo is little more than a negative stereotype of Latinos that the mainstream culture uses to rationalize prejudice and discrimination (Lips, 2005), and that the cultural definition of machismo more accurately describes the positive qualities of courage, generosity, dignity, respect for others, and love for family (Valdés, Baron, & Ponce, 1987). At the same time, there is little doubt that the ethic of male dominance exerts considerable influence over gender relations in Latino/Latina culture (Garcia, 1991). Maxine Baca Zinn (1980) theorizes that machismo is a compensation for Latino immigrants' feelings of economic and political powerlessness within a mainstream culture that discriminates against them. This analysis mirrors the assertions of many theorists (e.g., Kimmel,1995; Gilmore, 1990; Pleck, 1981a) that hypermasculine behavior is generally performed in the service of defending against feelings of powerlessness, rather than in gaining power for some specific purpose. In other words, these behaviors appear assertive and goal oriented, while in reality they are more defensive and emotion focused.

Machismo may be more of a public display rather than a common personality trait. Baca Zinn (1995) has noted that a number of nontraditional gender traits are quite common in Mexican-American men, such as shared decision-making, nurturing fatherhood, and participation in family-oriented social and recreational activities. At the same time, patriarchal ideologies remain fairly strong in Latino culture, reflected largely in the continued tradition of father as undisputed head of the household. Latino masculinity is an illustration of many common themes of continuity and change, cultural diversity within a group often perceived as unitary, individual behavior within the context of group ideology, and the interactions among race, class, and gender.

African-American Men

Because racial characteristics such as skin color are visible, race often plays a prominent role in social relations. In contrast, ethnicity is usually more fluid, sometimes changing in response to acculturation, selectively expressed (e.g., at family functions and religious ceremonies, but perhaps not at work), or concealed (e.g., by changing one's surname) (Rybarczyk, 1994).

In many cases dominant cultures consider people of minority races to be different from others in important ways. *Racism* is a set of behaviors, values, and attitudes that reflect a belief in the innate superiority of one race over another. This belief need not be conscious in order to have profound effects. Institutional racism in the United States has resulted in segregation, discrimination, stigmatization, and alienation for minority peoples. All of these maltreatments have profound influences on people's behavior and senses of self.

Any description of African-American men must be imbedded in the contexts of slavery as well as racism, which is both historical and ongoing, both personal and institutional. African-American men's gender identities and their expressions of masculinities have been shaped in response to racism and its social consequences such as isolation from mainstream culture, underemployment, poverty, and unequal treatment in legal systems. Racism often results in predictable psychological responses such as low self-esteem, suspiciousness of people from the dominant culture, and anger (Aronson, 2004).

African-American men have struggled for many generations in response to a mainstream culture that has denied them personhood and dignity. Prior to the late 1960s, adult African-American men were often referred to as boys, a label that denies their status as adults (Franklin, 1984). (Note here that many people persist in referring to adult women as *girls*, a sexist parallel to this racist practice). Many people have described the situation of African-American men as a national crisis, as this population is beset by high rates of unemployment, drug and alcohol abuse, premature death by violence and preventable diseases, crime victimization, and incarceration (Gibbs, 1992). Nearly one out of every three (29%) African-American males is incarcerated in state or federal prison at some time during his life, compared with about one in six Hispanic males and one in 25 White males (The Sentencing Project, 2004). African-American men are eight times more likely to be incarcerated than African-American women, about the same sex ratio as is found in the general population (Jacobs, Siegel, & Quiram, 1997).

Lemann (1991) proposes that the lack of employment opportunity has created a cycle of poverty and powerlessness for African Americans. Although they achieved emancipation from slavery in the nineteenth century, economic opportunities have been slow to arrive. In the late 1800s, many people found subsistence living in the exploitive system of share cropping. Even these jobs became untenable following the dramatic improvement of farm technology in the 1940s. As a result, many African Americans migrated from the rural South to northern cities to seek work in industry. This was the largest migration in U.S. history, and 81% of African Americans continue to live in large urban areas (Hines & Boyd-Franklin, 1996). The availability of industrial work has decreased in recent years, creating high unemployment and underemployment among African Americans within a context of race-driven discrimination in education, housing and employment (Wilson, 1987). Individualistic explanations of problems in these communities (i.e., that African Americans are not as bright, hard working, or ambitious as everyone else) are victim-blaming rationalizations that ignore the 400-year history of racism in the United States.

Eliot Liebow's (1967) classic sociological work, *Talley's Corner*, described the social atmosphere of street corner life for African-American men of the lower socioeconomic class. These men desperately wanted to succeed economically and socially, and their definitions of masculinity were similar to those of mainstream culture—protector, provider, dignified man. At the same time, lack of real opportunity, together with the daily humiliations suffered at the hands of Whites, resulted in expressions of frustration, anger, and despair. According to Gibbs (1994), the colorful idiomatic Black language of "talkin' and testifyin'" developed as a way of voicing resentment about unfair social conditions.

According to Franklin (1984), many African-American men have attempted to maintain a sense of gender identity in this context by emphasizing the masculine characteristics that do not depend on economic success (toughness, risk-taking, athleticism, violence, and exploitation of women). The effect of this standard of masculinity can be seen in high rates of incarceration and violent deaths among young African-American males (aged 15 to 24), who are more likely to be murdered than to die from any other single cause. The murder rate for this group more than doubled between the 1960s and the 1990s (Gibbs, 1994).

The development of a masculine gender identity among African-American males tends to take a different path from that of their Euro-American counterparts, who often grow up with the social message that "power and control are their birthright" (Lee, 1990, p. 126). Lacking much of an opportunity to achieve socially defined masculinity, but with this goal nonetheless important, African-American men have often constructed alternative masculinities.

Majors and Billson (1992) describe a frequent approach, the cultural signature of *cool pose*, a social style that many African-American males adopt in order to survive psychologically. Cool pose involves a set of ritualized behaviors that involve toughness, detachment, control, and a stylish, sometimes flamboyant presentation. Majors and Billson describe it thus:

> The purpose of posing and posturing—being cool—is to enhance social competence, pride, dignity, self-esteem, and respect. Cool enhances masculinity. Being cool also expresses bitterness, anger, and distrust toward the dominant society for many years of hostile mistreatment and discrimination. Cool pose helps keep the dominant society off balance and puzzled and accentuates the expressive self. (p. 105)

This kind of psychological response is a show of pride and strength and a refusal to display vulnerability. However, it may come at some cost to close relationships, which require attachment and emotional expression. Cool pose is also used to teach men to restrain their anger, since expressing it directly to someone more powerful can lead to negative consequences. Social training for doing so takes the form of "playing the doz-ens"—a ritualized game of insulting one another. An older African-American man traces the survival value of being able to do so back to the days of slavery:

> It was a game slaves used to play, only they wasn't just playing for fun. They was playing to teach themselves and their sons how to stay alive. The whole idea was to learn to take whatever the master said to you without answering back or hitting him 'cause that was the way a slave had to be, so's he could go on living. (Guffy, 1971, in Majors and Billson, 1992, p. 101)

The social stress on African-American men is also reflected in the high rates of physi-cal ailments such as hypertension, heart disease, stroke, and cirrhosis of the liver, all of which have psychosocial and behavioral components. (See Chapter 9.) The suicide rate for young African-American males has tripled in the last 30 years (although it remains considerably lower than that of White males), and deaths from high-risk behaviors like smoking, drug abuse, and reckless driving affect this population disproportionately (Gibbs, 1994). Williams, Baufort, and Shekelle (1985) suggest that tobacco use and street drug abuse are common ways of dealing with the stress of a harsh environment and the ac-companying feelings of hopelessness.

It is important to note that most African-American men survive quite well in a society that seeks to marginalize them, and that some thrive. Duneier (1992) points out that this silent majority of men hold down jobs, enjoy meaningful friendships and primary rela-tionships, and lead responsible and satisfying lives.

Many social conservatives would have us believe that racism is a thing of the past. However, evidence clearly indicates that African Americans continue to struggle in a dominant culture that marginalizes them, and that the cumulative effects of segregation, economic inequality, and the reality of centuries of slavery has been to maintain a hostile and unpredictable environment for African-American males. An understanding of con-temporary social constructions of African-American masculinity is achieved largely through an analysis of a systematic inequality that pervades the educational, economic, criminal justice, health care, and virtually every other institution of mainstream U.S. so-ciety (Gibbs, 1994).

Asian-American Men

In the same way that the categories of Hispanic and Latino encompass a wide variety of cultures, Asian men are a diverse group of people. Despite mainstream Americans' seem-ing view of Asians as indistinguishable from one another (Chan, 2004), Asian-Ameri-cans' origins are in a wide variety of places such as China, Japan, Korea, Vietnam, Laos, Malaysia, and India, to name a few, each culture with its unique history and gendered tra-ditions (Liu, 2002).

As with all ethnicities, the conditions of immigration strongly shape the conscious-ness of the culture. For example, in the late nineteenth and early twentieth century, the U.S. immigration policy allowed for an influx of Chinese men but very few Chinese women (Many of these men were married and left their wives behind of necessity.). As a result, the sex ratio in this ethnic group in 1890 was an astounding 27 males for every woman, and there were similar, although not as pronounced, patterns for Japanese, Korean, and Filipino people. Because Asians were not permitted to date or marry outside of their race, heterosexual Asian men were effectively desexualized and "bachelor societies" developed in a redefinition of the family. Immigration policies were not made gender egalitarian until years later, and many Asian wives and (then adult) children emigrated to join their husbands and fathers after decades apart. During World War II, the U.S. government incarcerated ("interned") more than 100,000 Japanese and Japanese Americans, undermining their dignity and effectively erasing the economic gains of a generation and creating a pervasive sense of hopelessness. Later, many Asian men served in the war and helped to reduce prejudice against Asian peoples (Espiritu, 1997).

Much of the literature on Asian American masculinities focuses on the negative media images of Asian men, who are often portrayed as asexual at the same time as Asian women are portrayed as hypersexual and exotic. Elaine Kim (1990) asserts that both of these stereotypes "exist to define the White man's virility... and superiority" (p. 70), Asian women as the sexual possessions of White men and Asian men as subservient. Fong-Torres (1992) suggests that the combination of racism and sexism contributes to the relative absence of Asian men on television news programs while Asian women are quite visible. Asian men are also portrayed as evil (the "sinister oriental") and/or violent (e.g., the martial arts expert).

Yen Le Espirtu (2001) notes that there are now two "distinct chains of emigration from Asia: one comprising the relatives of working-class Asians...the other of highly trained immigrants. In other words, today's Asian American men both join Whites in the well-paid, educated white collar sector of the workforce and join Latino immigrants in lower-paying secondary sector jobs" (p. 37). Whites' inability to distinguish Asian peoples may lead to a perception of Asians as relatively privileged. This may be true for many Chinese and Japanese whose well-educated grandparents and great grandparents immigrated into the country, but it is not true for the vast majority of, for instance, first-generation Hmong, many of whom struggle merely to survive.

In summary, we see some of the same issues in Asian-American men as in other ethnicities: diversity within a group considered by the mainstream to be homogenous, a tension between ethnically defined masculinity and that of the dominant culture, and the intersection of racism and prejudice with gendered strivings.

SUMMARY

1. Social conceptions of gender are influenced by a variety of factors, including ethnic patterns, economic conditions, religion, language, family socialization, cultural expectations, and the spirit of the times. Mainstream gender roles constitute the "default options" of a culture. Becoming a gender nonconformist requires a person to resist a considerable amount of cultural momentum, a task made more difficult by the nonconscious quality of gender ideology. Gender roles contain a set of meanings that are so embedded in social practices that they are virtually invisible to many.

2. There is a "family resemblance" in masculinities for most (but not all) of the world, often characterized by strength, risk taking, avoidance of femininity, aggression, and sexual initiative. In most of the world, masculinity is regarded as an essence that males achieve, not merely grow into.

3. In a minority of cultures, gender ideologies are strikingly different from most of the world. These cultures are marked by unusual social, historic, and economic situations.

4. Patriarchy, the male domination of women, largely originated in the development of agriculture. Changes in economic conditions have fostered changes in gender ideology, with more modern societies exhibiting correspondingly modern (egalitarian) gender arrangements.

5. The dominant ideology of masculinity in the United States has undergone significant changes during the past two centuries, from an emphasis on service to one on individualism to an emphasis on competition for its own sake. The colonial emphasis on connection to home evolved into an ethic of somewhat of a disconnection, increasingly emphasizing the social definition of masculinity as antifemininity.

6. The United States is a collection of many groups of ethnic peoples, and each group has cultural modes of being that are passed from one generation to the next within family systems, and that have effects on behavior for many generations after immigration. Gender roles are important components of ethnicities.

7. Latino/Latina cultures place a strong emphasis on extended families and largely endorse hirarchical family arrangements and gender-differentiated ideologies. Machismo, the display of strong and aggressive masculinity, carries both negative and positive connotations. Machismo may be more of a public display rather than a common personality trait. A number of nontraditional gender traits are quite common in Latinos.

8. Race also has an important impact on the expression of masculinity. African-American men, who are subject to widespread and longstanding racial oppression, experience a variety of unique problems, including high rates of unemployment, premature death, and incarceration. "Cool pose" is one reaction to being denied masculine power and privilege. The majority of working class African-American men, who are well adjusted in spite of social circumstances, have been ignored by social scientists and the media.

9. As a group, Asian-American men struggle with some of the same issues as other minorities: a mainstream view of a diverse group as homogenous, some disconnection between definitions of masculinity in the dominant culture and the ethnic culture, and a need to negotiate the boundaries of gender and identity within a context of racial and ethnic prejudice.

6

Masculinities II: Intersections of Masculinity with Other Forms of Identities

Masculinities become more complicated and interesting when they combine with other forms of identity such as socioeconomic status, age, physical ability, and sexualities. In this chapter, we explore some of these intersections. As with Chapter 5, my aim is to give a sense of the effects of cultural masculinity as it relates to the most common social statuses, not to undertake an exhaustive review.

Social Class

Gender stereotypes are somewhat variant at different levels of education, occupation, and income. For instance, Ehrenreich (1983) has noted that working-class masculinity in mainstream U.S. culture is more overtly aggressive and angry than professional-class masculinity. Power is central to social definitions of masculinity, and many see economic power as the best kind to have. Lacking this essence, low-income men may turn to other sources of power: the physically and the interpersonally dominant. Connell (1995a) describes the difficulty in achieving standard masculine "success":

> in the marginal class situation, where the claim to power that is central to hegemonic [dominant] masculinity is constantly negated by economic and cultural weakness. . . these men have lost most of the patriarchal dividend. . . One way to resolve this contradiction is a spectacular display, embracing the marginality and stigma and turning them to account. At the personal level, this translates as a constant concern with front or credibility. (p. 116)

Therefore, masculine posturing, misogyny, and violence are ways of counterbalancing a deep-seated, perhaps nonconscious sense of weakness. Connell once again echoes the theme of negative masculinity as a defense against powerlessness and the need for marginalized men to construct alternative models to a masculinity that includes the high social status that comes with wealth. Many of the authors in editor Lenore Adler's (1993) collection of international gender role descriptions noted that men and women tended to have more egalitarian statuses in the more educated and higher socioeconomic classes.

However, we should not paint too rosy a picture of economically successful men. Because masculinity is defined as being "number one," many of these men may view their levels of success as not good enough. As a result, they may see themselves as deprived, as their relative privilege is often invisible to them. One marker of masculine insecurity is family violence. A common view is that child abusers and wife batterers commit violent acts in order to defend against chronic low self-esteem by dominating less powerful others. Gelles (1997) notes that there is a connection between low socioeconomic class and family violence. Unemployed and underemployed men beat their wives at double the rate of fully employed men, a testament to the centrality of earning to the masculine self-concept. However, the fact that poorer men are more likely to be violent should not obscure the fact that family violence is present in all social strata nor the fact that most poor men are not violent. Economic conditions interact with individual psychology and other social forces to encourage or inhibit family violence and other toxic masculine behavior.

Because of centuries of institutionalized inequality, socioeconomic class is often intertwined with race and sex. United States median income levels show sharp disparities by race. In 2003, among people who worked full-time year-round, Hispanics' median income ($25,403) was less than two-thirds of Whites' average income ($37,580). The economic situation of the average African American ($30,554) was not much better. Asians median income ($40,443) was slightly higher than that of Whites. Women earn an average of 76% of what men earn (median for males: $41,503; for females: $31,653) (United States Bureau of the Census, 2003). Negative stereotypes of women and people of color are both cause and effect of these imbalances, as people other than White men are often disadvantaged in hiring and promotion practices. Their lack of visibility in high-status occupations then fuels negative gender and race ideologies.

Sexual Orientation

The dominant definition of U.S. masculinity includes heterosexuality as one of its central characteristics. Therefore, gay, bisexual, transgendered, and transsexual men, like men of color and economically disadvantaged men, tend to construct their identities in ways that are different from mainstream masculine ideologies. These orientations entail much more than just the sexual behavior of the person. They also involve considerations of personal identity, culture, and lifestyle, hence their inclusion in this chapter.

Cultures vary widely in their attitudes toward non-heterosexual behavior, from severe negative sanction to tolerance to encouragement. For example, ritual homosexuality between older men and younger boys is obligatory in Sambia (Herdt, 1982; Gilmore, 1990) and other societies in eastern Melanesia. However, most Western cultures have long traditions of repressing and discouraging sexual behavior between same-sex persons. In many cases, these attitudes were codified into laws prohibiting such contact. In the United States, four states prohibited most common same-sex sexual behaviors, even though it was legal for heterosexual couples to engage in these same behaviors. Sodomy laws were ruled unconstitutional by the U.S. Supreme Court in the landmark Lawrence versus Texas case in 2003 (sodomylaws.org, 2005).

The right to same-sex marriage is another recent legal controversy in the United States. A variety of rights and privileges available to married heterosexual people are not available to couples of the same sex, such as spousal health insurance, social security benefits, family and medical leave, and emergency health care decisions. The U. S. General Accounting Office (2004) has identified more than 1,000 federal protections and rights in which marital status in part determines eligibility. In 2003, Massachusetts became the first state to allow same-sex marriage, and legal battles for the right to marry are ongoing in many jurisdictions. (See Chapter 15.)

The label *homosexual*, as a description of a person (not merely a behavior) emerged in the U.S. in the 1880s (Rotundo, 1993). Barbara Sherman Heyl (1996) describes the effect of this new term:

> Until that time the moral and legal debates on homosexual behavior centered on just that—behavior. The shift in focus defined homosexuality as a 'state of being' that could exist prior to and without any overt homosexual act and, from somewhere inside the person, compelled a lifelong habitual preference for same-sex partners. Homosexuals became a highly stigmatized category of persons. (p. 121)

Anthony Rotundo (1993) traces the late eighteenth-century shift from a linguistic tendency of describing the behavior (e.g., "sodomy," "unnatural acts") to the use of a variety of new and pejorative words that label the person—"degenerate," "pervert," "fairy." As a result of the social polarization of homosexuals and heterosexuals, people whose sexual desires were oriented toward their same sex began to think of themselves as distinct social groups. They formed communities in large cities in order to find support in a mainstream environment that persecuted them, and to develop relationships with people who would nurture their social and sexual identities.

Anti-gay sentiments are centered in antifeminine ones. Masculinity is socially defined as antifemininity—what could be more socially feminine than loving a man? Rotundo puts the emergent notion of homosexual identity into the context of masculine ideology:

> The image of the male homosexual played an especially important role in the redefinition of middle-class manhood that was taking place at the turn of the [twentieth] century. The effeminate homosexual provided a negative referent for the new masculinity, with its heavy emphasis on the physical marks of manliness. The emergent homosexual image soon acquired an awesome power to stigmatize. By the turn of the century, men were using the same terms of scorn for homosexual males that they used for artistic, tender-minded, or reformist men. (p. 278)

Thus, "homosexual" and "feminine" became parallel and negative concepts in reference to masculine character. Prior to that time, males engaged in romantic nonsexual friendships with one another, writing passionate letters and often sleeping in the same bed. But romantic friendships disappeared with the new homophobia of the late nineteenth century, as it dramatically increased men's motivation to distinguish themselves from the feminine. Close male-male friendships developed into "buddyships" in which men bonded around sports, work, and antifemininity rather than sharing their emotional lives. Thus, homophobia had, and continues to have, negative effects on both gay and heterosexual men.

Nonheterosexual men are not immune to the social pressures of masculinity, and they must find solutions to the contradictions of these pressures and their sexualities. The strategies they use in dealing with these two considerable forces are many and varied. John Loughery (1998) points out that, contrary to stereotype, there has never been any set of personality and lifestyle attributes that we could describe as characteristic of *the* gay man.

Although some nonheterosexual men have traditionally masculine characteristics, they are more likely than heterosexual men to consider and adopt a broader range of gendered behavior (Heyl, 1996). It is possible that an awareness of being different frees an individual to consider more than the usual options, and/to develop a sense of identity by clarifying and affirming what he is not, that is, a masculine man as defined by the society (Herek, 1985). As heterosexual men may affirm their in-group identities by contrasting themselves with the out-group of men of other sexualities, a parallel process may take place with regard to the gendered behaviors of members of the out-group. In other words, the statement of what one *is* often begins with a statement of what one *is not*.

Within gay communities, *gay identity* is not an exclusively sexual one. It also includes emotional, lifestyle, and political aspects of living (Levine & Evans, 1996). These lifestyles range from the stereotypical "camp" and "drag" (flamboyantly feminine performances) to the embracing of traditional masculine features (save heterosexuality) that Martin Levine (1998) referred to as *gay macho*.

Ruth Fassinger (1998) proposed a stage model of lesbian/gay identity development which describes typical paths of individual and group identity changes that many gays and lesbians experience as they learn more about themselves and deal with both the mainstream and gay cultures. In the first stage, the individual becomes aware that he or she feels different sexual feelings than most others seem to feel. Around the same time, he or she also comes to a heightened awareness of the existence of a variety in sexual orientations in others. In the second stage, the person explores erotic desires for same-sex others and the possibilities for being a part of an identified group of gay or lesbian people. This stage involves self-acknowledgment of these desires and may or may not include actual sexual behavior. At the group level, the person thinks about fitting in to a social group of like-minded others.

The third stage involves deepening commitment to one's sexual orientation and the choices that grow out of it. At the group level, the person becomes more personally involved with the social reference group and often painfully aware of the societal oppression of nonheterosexuals. He or she begins to understand both the positive and negative consequences of embracing a lifestyle that is condemned by many.

Fassinger labels the fourth stage Internalization/Synthesis. In this final stage, the person is able to integrate his or her sexual attraction and attachment to same-sex people into the overall identity as an individual and as a member of a social group. Fassinger believes that the individual and group aspects of identity are "mutually catalytic," meaning that consideration of one's personal identity tends to highlight group issues, and vice versa.

Coming out is an important event in the psychological and social life of gay men. It refers to the process of revealing one's sexual orientation to others. The opposite of being out is being closeted (keeping one's sexual orientation secret). The pervasive mainstream cultural assumption of heterosexuality makes being closeted the default option, and it also means that coming out is not an event that takes place one day and leaves the person "out" once an for all. There are many decisions about whom to come out to, how, and when, and there are different degrees of being out. Some people are out to virtually everyone they know. Others may be out to nearly everyone except their families of origin, to one parent but not the other, in a community but not at work, and all the endless variations in between.

The Stonewall Riot is the community parallel to the individual's coming out. The Stonewall was a popular gay bar in the Greenwich Village area of New York City. On June 28, 1969, police cleared the bar of patrons and shut it down for suspected liquor law violations. As the police emerged from the bar, a crowd of angry gay men threw objects at them and a riot ensued. Herdt and Boxer (1991) describe Stonewall as a watershed historical event in gay political activism, one that crystallized a gay liberation movement that had begun quietly in the 1950s. In other words, it was the gay community's coming out, and it moved the focus of the gay world "from the secretive bar to the far more elaborate gay and lesbian communities of major cities around the world." (p.1). Herdt and Boxer describe individual coming out and community pride as emblematic of the transition from *homosexual* (secret) to *gay* (public and affirmative).

The last 35 years have seen a new level of cultural identity for gay, lesbian, and bisexual people. Gay cultures have become more elaborated and, in some cases, more accepted. The American Psychiatric Association removed homosexuality from its official list of mental disorders in 1973 (The World Health Organization followed suit, but not until 1993) (van Hertum, 1992), and the American Psychological Association (APA) has taken many gay-affirmative public positions in the last 30 years, for instance an affirmation of full legal rights for gay and lesbian people (American Psychological Association, 2005). Some municipalities have passed ordinances prohibiting housing and employment discrimination on the basis of sexual orientation, and by the end of 2004, 216 of Fortune 500 corporations had extended spousal benefits to include same-sex partners, a tenfold increase since 1995. 410 of these corporations included sexual orientation in their non-discrimination policies (Joyce, 2005).

At the same time, there is a visible social conservative backlash against gay rights. To cite only a few of the many examples, in 1993, the state of Colorado passed a law (later ruled unconstitutional) prohibiting municipalities from passing gay rights ordinances

(Moses-Zirkes, 1993). In 1998, the city of Orlando, Florida and Disney World sponsored "Gay Days," a gay-affirmative festival. In response, fundamentalist Christian televangelist Pat Robertson warned that the city should beware of hurricanes, tornadoes, and meteor strikes as divine retribution for supporting homosexuals ("In light of Gay Days festival, Robertson warns of storms," 1998). In a recent survey by the Chronicle of Higher Education, 38% of male and 23% of female first-year college students agreed that, "It is important to have laws prohibiting homosexual relationships." ("Freshman Profile," 2005). Gay, lesbian, bisexual, and transgendered people's struggle for recognition and equality is ongoing.

Herdt (1991) describes the differing experiences of four age cohorts of gay men in the United States. The first extends from 1900 to 1940. These were men who nearly all grew into adulthood without ever coming out. Now in their sixties and beyond, many of those who survive remain closeted.

The second cohort spanned the time period from World War II to the 1969 Stonewall riot. According to Herdt, many of these men came to awareness and fulfillment of their same-sex erotic desires for the first time while serving in the armed forces. The Mattachine Society (an underground network of gays) was founded in the 1950s and provided a new level of community, as did the emergence of gay bars in the 1960s. Still, gay communities largely remained secretive, and partly as a result, many men experienced their sexualities in negative terms (Levine, 1991). The hiding of such an important part of the self is often associated with feelings of shame.

Gay Pride Day marks the June anniversary of the Stonewall riot, which ushered in a new age of coming out and political activism. Men in the third, post-Stonewall cohort felt more free to express themselves in gay-affirmative ways, and gay neighborhoods like Greenwich Village in New York and Castro in San Francisco grew in size and visibility. There was mass coming out and an ethic of "free love" and recreational sex.

The AIDS epidemic ushered in the most recent cohort in the early 1980s, bringing radical changes in sexual behaviors and lifestyles. Martin Levine (1991) describes the new sexual ethic of the gay community: "Most men now perceive coupling, monogamy, and celibacy as healthy and socially acceptable." At the same time, gay communities began to make concerted efforts to support young gay men in the process of coming out. The sieges of AIDS and homophobic backlash appear to have brought the gay community together, and gay life is increasingly marked by a service orientation to the rest of the community and a renewed political activism (Pharr, 1997a).

Laud Humphreys describes the products of gay community transformation:

> The dozen largest urban areas of North America now have readily identifiable gay neighborhoods with heavy populations of same-sex couples. Each of these districts features not only openly gay bars and restaurants, but clothiers, bookstores, laundromats, a variety of shops, doctors, lawyers, dentists, and realtors that cater to a gay clientele. (quoted in Levine, 1991, p. 74)

Martin Levine (1991) contends that gay lifestyles are largely shaped by the culture and social structures that surround it. The relative social and geographical separation of many gay communities from mainstream cultures is a response to the heterosexual assumptive world of the mainstream culture and the stigma that it continues to attach to gay roles and behavior.

Attitudes toward Homosexuality

The social acceptance or nonacceptance of homosexuality varies from culture to culture and from one historical era to another (Gregersen, 1982). The beliefs that gays are mentally ill, immoral, vulgar, or dangerous are probably connected to the strong conservative Christian roots of mainstream U.S. culture. Early Catholic theologians, most notably Augustine, pronounced that sexual activity had procreation, not pleasure or self expression, as its purpose (Nelson, 1988). Since homosexual behavior could not possibly produce offspring, it was seen as immoral. The Victorian ethic of repressed sexuality led one to ask, "Why would a person have sex if he or she did not 'have to'?" There is no good answer, from the perspectives of these values, except to vilify the homosexual. Social conservatives such as the Religious Right have characterized homosexuality as immoral and a sin against God (Rosin, 1998; Rosin & Edsall, 1998). The Boy Scouts do not allow openly gay members (Thompson, 1998), and some psychologists have developed a therapy designed to convert gays to heterosexuality (Edwards, 1996) (See Chapter 11.).

There have been some fluctuations in attitudes toward gays in mainstream U.S. culture. In the 1970s, support for gay legal rights increased, perhaps as a function of more generally liberal political and sexual attitudes. The 1980s witnessed a resurgence of negative attitudes toward gays. AIDS struck the gay male community first, and there was a tendency among some people to believe that this horrible disease was a result of gays' lack of morality. Some prominent fundamentalist Christian leaders publicly stated that AIDS was a punishment from God for homosexuals' sins. People tend to believe in a "just world"—that bad things happen to bad people (Aronson, 2004), and gays became a convenient scapegoat for this deadly disease.

In the United States, gays have long been victims of various forms of oppression, such as violence, interpersonal insult, the outlawing of homosexual behavior, and discrimination in housing, insurance, and employment (Blumenfeld, 1992). The U.S. military discharged a number of gay soldiers after they returned from the Persian Gulf War in 1991 (Lambert & Simon, 1991) (see Box 6.1). In 1992, the State of Colorado passed a law preventing its municipalities from passing antidiscrimination laws that protect gays and lesbians. The Roman Catholic Church reaffirmed its stance that homosexuality is a mental illness, and supported discrimination against gay people in the 1990s (Stepp, 1992). More recently, the Vatican announced a ban on priests with "deep-seated homosexual tendencies" or those who are involved in "gay culture" (USA Today, 2005). In the early 1990s. the city charter of Springfield, Oregon not only allowed, but actually *required* discrimination on the basis of sexual orientation (NGLTF, 1993). Gays who openly display affection for their partners risk being assaulted.

Some people seem to believe that same-sex erotic orientation is a "choice." In light of the kinds of phenomena described above, who would choose a life in which one encoun-

---

Box 6.1: *Gay Soldiers*

When Bill Clinton was elected president of the United States in 1992, he spoke in favor of allowing gay and lesbian people to serve in the military. Although they have always been in the service, they have had to hide their sexual orientations or risk being discharged. The current "don't ask; don't tell" policy requires gays and lesbians in the military to remain closeted. Various arguments for and against having gays in the military have been proposed. A few of these are listed below for thought and discussion. Which ones are convincing to you? What assumptions underlie each argument? What is your position?

Arguments for Allowing Gays in the Military

1. The military is a workplace. A worker should be judged by job performance. Sexual orientation has nothing to do with being a good sol-

dier, as evidenced by the thousands of gay men and women who have served well in the military.

2. Many other countries allow self-acknowledged gay men and lesbian women to serve in the armed services. This has not seemed to have an adverse effect on the functioning of the military.

Arguments against Allowing Gays in the Military

1. Gays in the military make heterosexual soldiers uncomfortable, and this affects their job performance.

2. Being a good soldier in life-and-death situations involves "bonding" with fellow soldiers. People with different sexual preferences can not "bond" effectively with one another. This puts many military personnel, and in fact, the entire nation, in danger.

---

ters threats of physical, psychological, and institutional violence on a daily basis? In my view, it is remarkably insensitive to believe that gay people can and should change their sexual orientations. If you asked the typical heterosexual man, he would probably say that he believes strongly that his sexuality is determined by his biology in a powerful way. There is no reason to believe that a gay man's sexuality originates from a different source.

Homophobia and Masculinity

Homophobia is the irrational fear and intolerance of homosexuality and homosexual persons (Smith, 1971). It is a widespread phenomenon that manifests itself in a variety of ways, including the avoidance of nonsexual intimate behaviors between men, derogatory terms for and jokes about gays, societal bigotry against homosexuals, and even unprovoked violence against persons perceived as gay.

Sexual attraction between people of the same sex carries a powerful taboo in most Western societies, especially if the two people involved are male. Empirical evidence clearly points to the conclusions that men tend to be more homophobic than women, and that gay male behavior meets with even more disapproval than lesbian behavior (Whitely & Kite, 1995). Moreover, homophobia seems clearly related to the acceptance of stereotypical gender roles. Heterosexual men and women who hold positive attitudes toward egalitarian gender roles tend to be more accepting of homosexuals (Kurdek, 1988). People who hold more traditional attitudes often feel threatened by gender role deviance, and they tend to view an alternative sexual lifestyle as one of the most extreme forms of this deviance (Kerns & Fine, 1994). Research has documented clear relationships between homophobia and both the endorsement of the double standard of sexual behavior and discomfort with changing gender roles (Lehne, 1998). Thus, homophobic sentiments are strongly intertwined with traditional gender ideologies.

Box 6.2 illustrates a few extreme reactions to homophobic feelings. These descriptions attest to the deep levels of anxiety that tend to arise when men consider the possibility of same-sex erotic feelings. One method of dealing with this anxiety is to defend against it by placing very rigid boundaries between the self and other men. The man who claims to have absolutely no clue about male attractiveness or who becomes violent when dealing with gay men wants it to be absolutely clear to everyone (including himself) that he does not have an ounce of homosexuality in his body.

Why would men go to such great lengths to deny even the slightest possibility of homosexual feeling and thought? After all, it's not like we have been given a huge sexual

---

Box 6.2: Homophobic Behavior

The depth of homophobia reaches almost incredible proportions in many men. Consider the following true stories:

1. A teenage boy received disapproval from the male peer group because he revealed that he had kissed his girlfriend after she had performed oral sex on him. The message was that you do not want any connection between your mouth and a penis, even if the contact is indirect, and even if the penis is your own!

2. A businesswoman having lunch with a colleague (in his thirties) pointed out a man in the restaurant and commented that he was attractive. Her male colleague replied, "I wouldn't know."

3. Many men, especially young men, have been heard to comment that they would become violent if approached by a gay man.

4. During the 1992 controversy around allowing gays and lesbians into the military, a military man wrote a letter to the editor of a small town newspaper. He spoke against integrating the military with persons of alternate sexual orientations, saying, "Military personnel have the right to live in a nonthreatening environment." He seems to have forgotten that a large part of the military mission is to face threat. Perhaps being on a battlefield is experienced as less threatening than being in the same room with a gay man.

partner "menu" in this life. You can love men, women, or both. It would make sense that the possibility has at least crossed the minds of even the most heterosexual of men. Yet these experiences are so disturbing to many men that they feel compelled to use somewhat desperate measures to protect the self from the perceived threat of homosexuality.

Homophobia is both the *substance* and the *enforcer* of culturally dominant forms of masculinity (Lehne, 1998), patriarchy, and sexism (Pharr, 1997b). You might recall from Chapter 2 that one of the central messages of masculine socialization is "don't be like a girl." A male proves his masculinity by behaving in opposite ways from females. Any "feminine" behavior casts doubts on one's masculinity, and what could be more feminine (in a heterosexist culture) than loving a man? Moreover, only about 30% of people in the United States say that they know an openly gay person, and so it would seem that homophobia is less likely to stem from actual experiences with gay people and more likely to be based on stereotypes (Herek, 1998).

The childhood male peer group uses homophobia to enforce gender conformity (Plummer, 2001). The male who behaves in stereotypically unmasculine ways is often labeled a "queer," "fag," or "pansy," and ostracized from the social group. He may be given these pejorative homosexual labels for sexual behavior such as getting an erection in the boys' locker room, but more commonly he is labeled for failing to live up to masculine role norms. Regardless of the boy's sexual orientation, his heterosexuality may be called into question if he refuses to be violent, express a love of sports, or participate in the derogation of females. Males who want to maintain the approval of other males often find it necessary to display rigid, defensive attitudes toward homosexuality and homosexuals.

On a personal level, homophobia functions to trap men into rigid gender roles and limit their friendships with other men. Gay men are not immune to homophobia, and the anxiety created by these feelings sometimes compounds an already difficult process of understanding the sexual self in the context of a heterosexist culture. The gay man who has learned to hate homosexuality in his childhood may find himself dealing with feelings of self-hatred in adulthood (Strong & DeVault, 1997). On one level, he knows that these feelings are irrational. On another, they seem quite real and difficult to ignore.

The intolerance of homosexuality is thought by many to be a way of projecting unacceptable feelings about the self onto others. Vague feelings of same-sex attraction threaten the sense of masculinity, and ultimately self esteem. If the person can psychologically place these unacceptable feelings outside of the self, then he can hate the feelings without hating himself. Herek (1986) reported that people who hold defensive attitudes toward gays also showed a generalized tendency toward this externalizing defensive style. It is not surprising that we see this style often in males, who are usually socialized to deal with conflicts externally rather than to "look inside" and think about how they feel (Lynch & Kilmartin, 1999).

The hypothesis that homophobia is a defense against homoerotic feelings received some support in an important study by Adams, Wright, and Lohr (1996), who measured physiological responses to erotic stimuli. These researchers used the results from a homophobia questionnaire to divide self-reported heterosexual men into two groups: men with high levels of homophobia and men with low levels. Then, they showed these men videotapes of heterosexual, lesbian, and male homosexual sex. Using a device known as a *penile plethysmograph*, which records changes in the circumference of the penis, they measured research participants' physiological arousal in response to the videotapes. Although both groups of men showed signs of sexual arousal while viewing the heterosexual and lesbian tapes, only the high homophobia group showed arousal in response to the male homosexual tapes. The researchers surmised that homophobic men deny or are unaware of their own homoerotic arousal.

The external defensive style prevents a man from learning anything about himself and encourages him to react to the pressure of masculine insecurity by overconforming to the masculine gender role (Pleck, 1981a). This hyperconformity is dehumanizing and has serious negative implications for physical health, psychological health, and relationships with other people. When men lower their defenses against homophobia, they often find that homosexuality is not the huge threat that they perceived, and they feel somewhat freed from the pressure of constantly proving to themselves and others that they are masculine (heterosexual) men. Homophobia is highly emotional and deeply rooted (see Box 6.3). Some suggestions for dealing with homophobic feelings are presented in Box 6.4.

Box 6.3: Are You Homophobic?

Like any form of prejudice, homophobia has cognitive, emotional, and behavioral components. These sometimes conflict with one another. For example, you might believe that gay people should not be treated any differently from others, but at the same time, you might feel uncomfortable around openly gay people and avoid them. A parallel in racial prejudice would be a white person's discomfort around people of color. Although one may be very egalitarian in one's ideology, racism, sexism, and heterosexism often operate at emotional and/or unconscious levels.

Most, if not all, of us were raised in a heterosexist, homophobic environment. Therefore, one should not be ashamed for having emotional reactions to gay people. On the contrary, the openness to these reactions reveals a willingness to be honest with the self, to learn something about the self and about others who are perceived as different, and to work toward dealing with homophobic anxiety.

My most memorable personal experience with homophobia occurred a few years ago after I had given a lecture on men's issues. During a subsequent question and answer period, one of the students said, "You have said that men who step outside of the traditional masculine role are often perceived as homosexual. You also said that talking about male emotion and experience is outside of the role. Since you do just that in your lectures, do your audiences tend to think you're gay?" She stopped just short of simply asking, "Are you gay?" While I thought that I understood and had dealt with my homophobia, the suggestion that I might be gay produced a strong wave of anxiety coming from the deepest part of my gut. This feeling alerted me that I had more personal emotional work to do on this problem.

In assessing your own feelings and attitudes toward sexual orientation, think about the following:

1. How and when did you first learn about homosexuality? What attitudes toward gays were conveyed by your family and your peer group? What nicknames for gays did you learn when you were growing up? What connotations for these names did you perceive? How did you feel about homosexuality when you were a child?

2. Imagine that you are having a conversation with several friends and someone tells a disrespectful joke about gays. How do you react, emotionally and behaviorally? Do you feel pressured to join in, to confront the person, to withdraw?

3. Imagine that a family member or close friend has just revealed to you that he or she is gay. How do you react? Will your relationship change, and if so, in what ways? Does your reaction differ depending on whether you imagine a male or a female?

4. If you are heterosexual, role play or imagine that you are gay or bisexual and "coming out" (revealing your sexual orientation) to a close friend. How do you go about the task? What feelings are present? If you are gay, lesbian, or bisexual, you may have had this experience or at least thought about it. What feelings come up? How would (or did) you deal with the emotions and with the task?

Aging Men

What is the pattern of continuity and change in the gendered behavior of men as they age? If you think about the older men that you know, you may be acquainted with some who have seemed to change and some who have not. Actor Jack Palance, in his seventies, demonstrated his physical fitness by doing one-armed pushups on stage after receiving an Academy Award, a "macho" display that one does not expect to see from an old man. On the other hand, there are many older men who seemed to have shifted from this kind of behavior as they have aged into styles that we might describe as androgynous. And, of course, as I have stated many times, there are many who never really fit the mainstream masculine image in the first place.

There is some evidence of adult developmental changes in gendered behavior that appear to be driven by significant changes in family status, physical changes, social position, career, or health. Middle-aged and elderly men are likely to encounter several psychological events such as parents' deaths, retirement, changes in parental status, and adjustments in relationships. These gradual and abrupt life changes have the potential to affect their gender ideologies and behaviors.

A common misunderstanding about adult developmental change is the belief that men encounter a predictable "midlife crisis," and that they then make profound changes in the ways that they approach their work, relationships, and leisure pursuits as a result of the psychological pressure produced by this emotional upheaval. Two very popular books in

Box 6.4: Dealing with Homophobic Feelings

What can an individual do to work against homophobia at a personal level and against heterosexism (the cultural-institutional manifestation of homophobia)? Below are several suggestions:

1. If you are heterosexual, do not avoid contact with gay people. Like everybody else, they gays and lesbians are also students, sons and daughters, athletes, coworkers, friends, and so on. You may find that you have something in common with a gay person. Direct interpersonal contact with feared people tends to reduce that fear (Aronson, 2004). Don't wait for your homophobia to go away before having contact with a gay person. Do it *despite* these uncomfortable feelings.

2. Work toward understanding that occasional same-sex erotic feelings are probably more a rule than an exception, and that homophobic feelings are a consequence of growing up in a heterosexist culture.

3. Support gay rights.

4. Refuse to participate in interpersonal or institutional gay-bashing.

5. Learn about the gay rights movement and gay and lesbian people's struggles.

6. Participate in an antiheterosexism workshop (See Blumenfeld, 1992.).

7. Work to understand the freeing effects of breaking out of homophobia and rigid gender roles.

Sears and Williams (1997) and Pharr (1997b) provide a number of useful interpersonal, educational, and institutional strategies for overcoming homophobia.

---

the 1970s (D. J. Levinson, Darrow, Klein, M. H. Levinson, & McKee, 1978; Sheehy, 1976) proposed and popularized the idea that this "crisis" is universal and based on chronological age. In other words, one could expect that, around age 40, a man is very likely to do things like change jobs, get divorced, buy a sports car, and find a young woman to date. Subsequent research demonstrated that the so-called male midlife crisis is non-normative. Although some men's behavior at midlife might be characterized in this way, no such crisis occurs among most men (Kilmartin, 2004a). When there is a crisis during this time of life, the chances are that it is brought on by changes in the man's job situation or relationships, not merely by the fact that he is aging. Even crisis-level changes in important areas such as these are no guarantee that a full-blown life crisis will ensue. Most psychologically healthy people manage to handle a crisis in one area of their life without causing crises in others.

Psychoanalyst Carl Jung believed that people's gendered sense of self tends to expand during the second half of life (Hall, Lindzey, & Campbell, 1998). Jung's belief came largely from essentialist notions about personality development, but it is also quite possible to assess gender shift (or lack of it) as a result of social environmental forces. For instance, most men encounter several life changes in their forties or fifties that may affect their gender ideologies and behavior. Physical declines are inevitable and may include minor hearing loss, graying hair, decreased muscularity, weight gain, and more frequent aches and pains. Men who are athletes see their abilities diminish and/or have to "retire" from some sports. There may be changes in workplace status, such as big promotions or declines in duties. Men whose work involves physical labor may find themselves having more difficulty keeping up with younger men or avoiding injury on the job. Children grow up and move out of the house. There may be a realization that some of the things they dreamed about as younger men are not going to take place. Rybarczyk (1994) summarizes the impact of these events: "The consequences of these changes can be positive (e.g., new roles, new goals) and negative (e.g., feelings of disappointment). For men whose self-concepts rely heavily on youth-oriented masculine traits, these changes undoubtedly force a redefinition of their gender identities." (p. 114).

We have to be cautious with generalizations about older men from research, because of the inevitable confounding of generation (also known as cohort) and age. Comparisons of the current generation of older adults and the current generation of younger adults cannot demonstrate age differences, only age and cohort differences as they occur together. The level to which each factor contributes is a matter of speculation. For example, we could assume that older men are less likely to exercise than younger men because this is currently the case. However, it is quite possible that this generation of younger men might exercise at the same level when they become older. Separating cohort and age effects is difficult, if not impossible (Rybarczyk, 1994).

There is also a lack of research on all but White, middle-class U.S. men. Minority men may experience aging in very different ways. There is very little examination of the interactions between these statuses and adult psychological development. For example, many working class retirees may not fit the stereotype of the person who spends a lot of time traveling, playing golf, and enjoying other leisure activities, as they may not have the money to do so.

Gutmann (1987) proposed that gender role differentiation becomes minimal in later life and that this gender shift is a universal, not a culture-specific phenomenon. Based on anthropological studies of several different cultures, he concludes that women tend to become more powerful and assertive as they age and men tend to become more passive and more involved in domestic matters. Like sociobiologists, Gutmann (1977) believed that these changes are a result of evolutionary adaptation, however he never considered the possibility that cultural redundancy could produce this universal phenomenon, if in fact it is universal.

A number of researchers disagree with Gutmann's proposed universal midlife gender transformation. Peskin (1992) followed a small sample of college graduates for more than 25 years and found little evidence of such a shift. Huyck (1992) found that these gender changes tended to be confined to relationships between spouses, with men and women becoming more similar in their behaviors as time went on. Feldman, Biringen, and Nash (1981) demonstrated that gender changes were more related to parenting status than to a person's chronological age.

These contradictory findings have led some theorists to conclude that age-related shifts in gendered behavior result largely from the expansion of social role opportunities for older men. For example, most men can spend more time at home after they retire, and thus they are freer to pursue more activities associated with traditional femininity, like cooking and gardening. Social forces that encourage men to be traditionally masculine may not apply as much to older men, and, even if they do, older men may become less invested in maintaining a masculine image (O'Rand, 1987).

Aging men face special challenges in dealing with the influence of masculine social demands. Even those who were once "successful" in traditional masculine realms often find it difficult to live up to dominant gender standards. Traditional masculinity is defined as very physical, work oriented, and independent, yet older men experience physical decline, retirement, and the increasing need to depend on others and ask for help. It seems that very few older men can hold on to the macho ethic and survive, either physically or psychologically.

Considerable evidence points to the negative effects of certain aspects of traditional masculinity on the lives of older men. They are less likely than women to see a physician or psychotherapist (Addis & Mahalik, 2003), more likely to downplay their symptoms even if they do seek help (Komiya, Good, & Sherrod, 2000), and overwhelmingly more likely to commit suicide (Arias, 2004). Men who attempt to deal with old age using the psychological approach of traditional masculinity often find themselves lonely, ill, and depressed. I often refer to "macho old men" as *developmentally unsuccessful*, as they have not learned the behaviors they need to negotiate this stage of adult development.

But the picture of elderly men is not usually so bleak, as most adjust well to changes in gender identity. They take on new social roles and often come to appreciate aspects of their lives that were previously "off-limits" because they were defined as feminine (Gutmann, 1987). As a result, they report a wider range of self-expression and less worry about whether they are being masculine enough to suit others' wishes.

Masculinity becomes more complicated when it intersects with other identities. I have described a number of social, economic, cultural, and historical factors that affect social conceptions of masculinity, and yet have barely scratched the surface of the richness of these topics, which are being explored at the cutting edges of social science. The writers of these many disciplines are convincing in their argument that gendered behaviors, self-concepts, and social institutions are not formed by a unitary path from singular cause to singular effect, and that a full understanding of our gendered world can only be gained through a full understanding of the effects of cultural forces.

SUMMARY

1. Gender stereotypes are somewhat variant at different levels of education, occupation, and income. Lacking the central masculine characteristic of economic power, low-income men may turn to other sources of power and dominance. Socioeconomic class is often intertwined with race and sex, as average incomes are widely discrepant among groups.

2. The dominant definition of U.S. masculinity includes heterosexuality as one of its central characteristics. Therefore, men of other sexual orientations tend to construct their identities in ways that are different than mainstream masculine ideologies. Besides the sexual behavior of the person, minority sexualities also involve considerations of personal identity and lifestyle. Gay, bisexual, and transgendered men are more likely than heterosexual men to consider and adopt a broader range of gendered behavior.

3. Individual and group identity goes through a series of transformations for gay men as they learn more about themselves and deal with both mainstream and gay cultures. Coming out is an important process for gay men. Historical events such as the Stonewall riot and the AIDS epidemic have had powerful effects on individual and community gay identities. Large urban areas contain gay neighborhoods that provide support and community.

4. Because men sometimes confuse sexual and intimate feelings, they may feel very anxious when natural feelings of closeness to other men arise. Homophobia, the irrational fear of homosexuality and homosexuals, results in a number of negative personal and social consequences, including gay bashing, institutional bigotry toward gays, and the limiting of male-male friendships. The threat of being labeled homosexual enforces conformity to traditional masculine gender role prescriptions under the threat of ostracization from the male peer group. Because we live in a heterosexist culture, most people experience some degree of homophobia.

5. Aging may be connected to changes in gendered ideologies and behavior. These may be driven by significant changes in family status, physical changes, social position, career, or health. Age-related shifts in gendered behavior may also result from the expansion of older men's social role opportunities. The so-called "male midlife crisis" is not a normative event.

7

The Inner Reality: Phenomenological Perspectives on Male Development

Every man lives in two worlds. One is the physical, external world with which he interacts. The other is a unique, private, inner world where he feels, thinks, perceives, and interprets, and where he ascribes meaning to his life. It is here that he experiences himself as nobody else can, and it is here that he constructs his own reality. His self-awareness and private world are unique; he is a phenomenon.

Phenomenological psychologists emphasize the importance of the person's subjective psychological environment. At any given moment, an individual may experience perceptions, sensations, interpretations, and feelings about the self, others, objects, or ideas. For the phenomenologist, the subject of study is the totality of the subjective, immediate experience of the individual, termed the *phenomenal field*, and its effect on behavior. For men, the application of phenomenological theory provides a rich avenue for the enhancement of gender awareness and self-understanding.

Phenomenological theories stress the ability of the person to create and fulfill the self by following inner nature and making choices that affect his or her life in a positive way. In this chapter, I apply two phenomenological theories to the understanding of men: the humanistic approach of Carl Rogers, and the existential theories of Rollo May and others.

HUMANISTIC THEORY

As we have seen, biological and psychoanalytic theories emphasize the primitive, survival aspects of the person. These theories often characterize human nature as animalistic and selfish. Social learning theories emphasize the aspects of the person that are shaped by the environment. These theories tend to describe human nature as essentially neutral.

In contrast, humanistic theory emphasizes the person's ability to create and express the self. Humanists are unabashedly optimistic about human nature. They believe that the most powerful force in a person's life is *self-actualization*, the fulfillment of an individual's positive, unique, human potential. In other words, the core motivation of the human being is to become whatever his or her nature is to become.

Carl Rogers (1961) believed that all living things, if given the right environmental conditions, would grow and thrive. He termed this drive toward fulfillment the *actualizing tendency* and theorized that it is biologically based. There is a genetic blueprint not only to survive and reproduce (as analytic and biological theories stress), but also to grow and develop.

Self-actualization is the psychological outgrowth of the actualizing tendency (Rogers, 1959). Just as a healthy plant grows larger and extends itself, a healthy person progressively and vigorously expresses a unique self. Just as a plant will grow on its own in a favorable environment, so will a human being. You do not have to seize control of a plant or a person in order for growth to occur. It is enough to merely provide the right conditions.

All organisms need physical nutrients in order to display the actualizing tendency, and people need a "psychological nutrient" in order to become self- actualized. The approval of important people early in the person's life allows him or her to develop approval of the self, or *self-esteem*. The person who has a solid, positive sense of self is able to be aware of and fulfill his or her potential.

When children first come into the world, they get a lot of approval. Parents and others hold them, attend to their needs, smile at them, and communicate joy about their existence. Rogers called this basic approval *positive regard*. It is roughly equivalent to a non-possessive love. The child who experiences positive regard feels valued by others. Later in life, he or she internalizes these attitudes and comes to value the self. In other words, the person develops *positive self-regard*.

As a child grows, he or she acquires a larger behavioral repertoire as a result of the actualizing tendency that causes the body and the brain to develop. Behaviors are a way of expressing the self, but some of these expressions may not be particularly pleasing to others. For instance, a two-year-old boy who expresses his curiosity about some expensive object may grab and inadvertently break it. If parents or caretakers respond by communicating disapproval of the child (not merely the child's behavior, but his value as a person), they have, in effect, withdrawn their love from the child because of his behavior. They can do this by striking the child, by saying "bad boy" (which says "you are a bad person"), or by saying something like, "Daddy doesn't like you when you do that." These expressions of disapproval can also be indirect or nonverbal, as when the parent gives the child a "dirty look" or becomes emotionally cold.

Rogers called this kind of parental behavior *conditional positive regard*, or placing *conditions of worth* on the child. It is a communication to the child that he or she is only worthwhile under certain conditions. As a result, the child begins to construct the self in terms of actions, thoughts, and feelings which have been approved. If events like the one described above were to happen repeatedly, the boy would come to deny the parts of himself that are associated with curiosity.

A healthier environment is one in which the child experiences *unconditional positive regard*, which is a warmth, respect, and acceptance that does not depend on the behavior of the child. It is possible to communicate disapproval of a behavior while communicating approval of the person. In effect, the parent is saying, "You are valuable no matter what you do" (without conditions). The child is worthwhile for the mere reason that he or she has shown up on the planet. You should not confuse this position with *laissez-faire* parenting, where the parent provides no guidance to the child. Rogers' position is that parents can make a clear distinction between disapproving of a behavior and disapproving of the personhood of one who enacts the behavior.

There are several negative consequences for the person who experiences conditions of worth in large doses. First, feelings of inadequacy result in anxiety and defensiveness as the person denies and rejects the disapproved parts of the self. Second, self-actualization is blocked because the self-concept is narrowed. Rogers believed that the full experience of the self provided the vital information needed to strive toward human potential. It is difficult to fully express the self when one has lost touch with significant parts of it. Third, defensiveness against and rejection of these aspects of the self render the individual less able to appreciate others, and misunderstandings in relationships often ensue.

The net result of conditional regard is that the self-actualizing tendency becomes misguided and full functioning is inhibited. The following example will serve to illustrate Rogers' theory: A child who grows up with an overprotective parent receives disapproval for any minor risk taking, such as going outside if it is a little cold or trying something for the first time. This child denies the parts of the self that are associated with exploring new environments and with healthy assertion of the self. When this person becomes an adult, he or she does not develop a satisfying career or relationships outside the family (despite having the resources to do so), because he or she has internalized the parent who disapproved of the independent parts of the self. The person feels an undue amount of anxiety around what most people find to be reasonable risks, and thus he or she fails to activate a good deal of his or her potential.

Humanistic Theory and Masculinity

The application of Rogers' theory to male development provides an excellent framework for understanding the negative aspects of masculine gender roles. Often, boys are socialized in a way that is fraught with conditional positive regard. As a result, a great many men have hidden away large parts of themselves, sometimes with dire consequences.

The Gender Role Strain Model (Pleck, 1975; O'Neil, 1982) presented in Chapter 2 is based on humanistic theory. Gender role strain occurs when cultural gender demands conflict with naturally occurring tendencies in the person. This conflict creates a discrepancy between the "real self" and the "ideal self-concept" (Garnets & Pleck, 1979). In other words, gender role strain occurs when "who I am" is not consistent with "who I should be."

In Rogerian terms, gender role demands are enforced by conditional positive regard. In the typical scenario of male socialization, a boy's "masculine" behavior meets with approval and other behavior results in the withdrawal of approval. The boy learns that he is valued when he acts masculine, and that he loses some of his worth when he does not. He may cry when he is sad and be told, "Don't be a sissy; big boys don't cry." He then withdraws value from this emotion.

As a result of consistent disapproval of certain aspects of his experience and behavior, the boy begins to deny the part of the real self that is considered unmasculine by important people in his life. He attempts to match his behavior to the gender demands that allow him to gain the positive regard of these significant others in his life, and later, himself. The price that he pays is in self-alienation. As the full experience of the true self is necessary for self-actualization, the attempt to live up to gender demands that are not a part of the self limits the potential for full functioning (Leafgren, 1990). The gender role strain position is that, for the most part, a man often cannot be himself and "be a man" (as traditionally defined) at the same time. The more a man comes to value traditional masculinity, the more he will lose his individuality and his path to fulfillment. Loss of significant parts of the self results in behavior that is destructive to the self and/or others (O'Neil, 1990).

Because every man is unique, and because some men are raised with harsher gender demands than others, the degree to which an individual man experiences gender role strain will vary. For example, there is generally an expectation for boys to participate in athletics. For a boy who is naturally athletic and drawn to sports, this demand would not create much strain. However, a boy who is not athletic or interested in sports would experience a high degree of strain, which would be accompanied by feelings of low self-esteem and misgivings about his masculinity. If his parents and other important people in his life are especially harsh in pressuring the boy to be athletic, he experiences even more strain. The level of gender role strain is a function of the level of gender role demand in interaction with the degree of conflict between naturally occurring tendencies and gender role.

We can see an extreme example of the conflict between the real self and gender role demands in some transvestites. Many male cross-dressers report that they experience traditionally feminine aspects of themselves such as gentleness, passivity, and emotional sensitivity, when they wear women's clothing. They feel compelled to express these parts of personality, but feel that they can only do so when dressed as women (Renaissance Education Association, 1987). These are people who feel a good deal of gender role strain due to lack of congruence between gender role and naturally occurring tendencies. Note that this conflict would not be present if social disapproval for males' being feminine and/or for wearing clothing designed for women did not exist. (I should note here that motives for cross-dressing vary from person to person, and the expression of the feminine is not the primary goal for all transvestites.)

Gay and bisexual men also find themselves in the position of having to deal with considerable gender role strain. They are sexually oriented toward men, but society defines masculinity as antifemininity and same-sex attraction as feminine. Therefore, they face social disapproval for expressing themselves in a homophobic society and/or the self-alienation of denying a sexuality that is central to their identities.

Pleck (1981b) advanced the theory that gender role strain can lead a male to exaggerate his masculinity. Unable to gain approval because he does not naturally fit the cultural ideal, he tries to overcompensate by forcing himself into the gender role. This high level of gender role strain and the hypermasculine reaction to it result in an extreme degree of self-alienation. There would seem to be a great many men who compulsively conform to masculine standards of behavior because they do not want to risk the social disapproval (and the internalized self-disapproval) for behaving in unmasculine ways. Paradoxically, they receive approval for behaving in ways that fulfill the masculine values of independence and courage, yet they find it extremely difficult to be truly independent or emotionally courageous by defying a gender demand when they feel that it is important for them to do so.

Even though the level of gender role strain varies from person to person, certain gender role demands would seem to conflict with naturally occurring tendencies in every man. It is impossible for a real self to be congruent with the literally inhuman aspects of traditional masculinity. There are also certain gender role demands that conflict with naturally occurring tendencies in many, though perhaps not all, men.

Emotion is universal across the human race. Various structures in the brain have the function of processing emotional experiences. In Rogerian terms, feelings are a part of the "true self" for everyone. It is as natural to express them as it is to express every part of the self. Strong emotion is accompanied by strong physical sensations. One can feel emotions virtually demanding expression from the most primal part of one's organism. For many young boys, however, the expression of emotion (except for anger, and, later, sexual feelings) is met with disapproval, and the boy denies the parts of the self connected with most vulnerable emotions. As he incorporates gender role demands into his ideal self-concept, the experience of emotion becomes associated with lowered self-esteem, and he is motivated to move away from his feelings.

As a result of this undervaluing of the emotional self, many men report difficulties in expressing their feelings (Moore, 1990). The extent of this difficulty is described by Joyce Johnson (quoted in Naifeh & Smith, 1984): "I'd learned myself by the age of 16 that just as girls guarded their virginity, boys guarded something less tangible which they called Themselves. They seemed to believe they had a mission in life, from which they could easily be deflected by being exposed to too much emotion." (p. 1).

Emotion is a huge part of human experience. Denying this primal aspect of the self requires a great deal of psychological effort, and the amount of strain and self-alienation that results can be considerable (O'Neil, 1990). In fact, the problems associated with restricted emotionality require an entire chapter (Chapter 8) to detail. For now, it will suffice to say that this issue pervades virtually every aspect of many men's lives. As O'Neil (1982) put it, "the capacity for accurate recognition and communication of feelings is a prerequisite for coping with life's problems" (p. 24). Yet many men have been stripped of this basic capacity by social forces that seek to make them into machines.

Safety is another universal human need. Part of the actualizing tendency is to protect the self from physical harm. Many males, however, are taught to deny this basic human need in the service of striving to meet standards of masculinity (Jourard, 1971). The conflict here is between the self-protective aspects of the real self and the masculine demand to "take it like a man." This eschewal of safety needs is related to the earlier issue of emotion. Fear is an information sense. It is the emotional experience that tells us that we are in a situation where our safety is threatened. If the male's self-worth is undermined when he feels fearful, then he is motivated to deny or suppress that fear. For example, if a large man is running at you at full speed, your basic self-protective instinct makes you fearful and tells you to get out of the way. However, if you are a middle linebacker and the man coming at you is carrying a football, then you are motivated to do the very opposite.

The denial of safety needs affects men's physical health (see Chapter 9). The fact that a man can be reluctant to acknowledge a symptom, even a life threatening one (Courtenay, 1998a), attests to the depth to which masculine conditional positive regard has moved him away from his real (self- protecting) self. He would rather die than be considered unmanly. It is quite common for men to ignore other physiological needs in the areas of sleep, diet, exercise, and alcohol intake (Courtenay, 1998a).

Many a man has risked physical harm in order to preserve his sense of masculinity. You can see gender role strain in a typical school or neighborhood situation where a bigger, stronger, boy challenges a smaller, weaker one to a fight. The human part of the smaller boy tells him to run away, but the masculine part tells him to stay and defend his "honor," even though he is sure to get hurt.

Contact sports and war are two arenas where men have traditionally tested their masculinity. Football is dangerous, and it hurts. Playing this game requires that one suppress the self-protective and pain-avoiding parts of the self. Even as young boys, athletes are encouraged to play in spite of pain and to risk their bodies in order to win games. Winners receive a great deal of approval, whereas losers are often shamed or ignored.

War, of course, is the ultimate in the suppression of the self-preservation instinct. Although there may be more reasons to fight in a war than just to prove one's masculinity, men who have refused to do so have historically been branded as cowards and shamed as unmanly (Levy, 1992). Young men in war find themselves living with abject fear in virtually every moment. It is probably not a coincidence that modern men's movements began near the end of the Vietnam War, when thousands of men experienced the ultimate in gender role strain.

Many theorists argue that a degree of dependence on others is also a universal human need (Jourard, 1971). Here again there is a conflict between the human and the masculine, and again we find a connection to emotionality. A man can never be completely independent and thus he will sometimes feel helpless and alone. Gender role strain results from these feelings, which the man must deny if he accepts traditional standards of masculinity.

Many men find it nearly impossible to ask for help when they need it, even when it is readily available. People often laugh at some men's reluctance to ask for directions when they are lost. It seems like an obvious problem-solving strategy and a simple thing to do, yet the power of early prohibitions against dependence prevents it. Being lost on a trip is somewhat trivial, but refusing to ask for help in some other areas may have important implications for the man's functioning. These areas include the masculine reluctance to seek information about sexuality (Rappaport, 1981), mental health (Addis & Mahalik, 2003), and relationships (Gordon & Allen, 1990).

There are several other areas where gender role strain is evident for many men:

1. *Power, control, and competition*: The socialized tendency for men is to dominate others. Doing so requires a man to bury the parts of the self that are associated with empathy, mutuality, and cooperation. Many theorists believe that this orientation leads to damaged interpersonal relationships (Messner, 1992), role strain (O'Neil, 1990), and sexual conflicts (Gross, 1992).

2. *Homophobia.* The role demand for men to restrict interpersonal closeness to males due to the risk of being labeled homosexual requires one to deny naturally affectionate feelings toward other men (May, 1988). Many theorists believe that homophobia has the effect of severely limiting the intimacy of male-male relationships (see Chapter 6).

3. *Achievement, success, and money.* Many people associate men's personal value with their accomplishments and social standing. At the extreme, this involves a denial of the parts of self associated with pleasure, relaxation, and family life (Skovholt, 1990). Validation of masculinity from this source is dependent on economic conditions, social position, and talent, as well as education and access to resources (Pleck, 1981a). Many socially marginalized men experience the demand for economic success but have few avenues for achieving it.

4. *"Femiphobia"*. Men are encouraged to avoid any behavior that might be considered feminine. This requires them to suppress any parts of their personalities that are culturally associated with women's characteristics. O'Neil (1990) believes that fear of femininity is at the root of all other role strain. (The term *femiphobia* was coined by O'Donovan, 1988.).

5. *Athletic prowess.* Boys are often shamed and ridiculed if they do not play sports or do not play them well. Athletic participation is the most important factor in boys' high school social status (a form of positive regard), and nonathletic boys are more likely than athletic ones to doubt their masculinity (Richardson, 1981).

6. *Sexual initiative and performance.* Men are expected to seek sex actively, and to be insatiable, promiscuous, and sexually goal oriented. This masculine sexual orientation involves denial of the parts of self that make affectional ties to others (Nelson, 1985) and the more sensual aspects of the man. Engaging in unwanted sexual activity is normative for men. Most college men report that they have had sex when they did not want to because of male peer pressure or the desire to be popular (Berkowitz, 1997). Sexually aggressive men, who are considered to be under a great deal of role strain (Pleck, 1981a) tend to set nearly impossible sexual expectations for themselves and may feel chronically unsatisfied with their amount of sexual experience.

The bottom line of gender role strain is that conditional positive regard leaves the male out of touch with his "inner world" and overconcerned with the external world (Leafgren,

1990). His socialization has impaired his ability to deal with psychological conflicts, except by denying that they exist.

The self-actualizing tendency, however, is a potent human force. Going back to the comparison between humans and plants, Rogers (1980) says:

> I remember that in my boyhood the bin in which we stored our winter's supply of potatoes was in the basement, several feet below a small window. The conditions were unfavorable, but the potatoes would begin to sprout—pale white sprouts, so unlike the healthy green shoots they sent up when planted in the soil in the spring. But these sad, spindly sprouts would grow two or three feet in length as they reached toward the distant light of the window. The sprouts were, in their bizarre, futile growth, a sort of desperate expression of the directional tendency I have been describing in... dealing with clients.... I often think of these potato sprouts.... The clue to understanding their behavior is that they are striving, in the only ways that they perceive as available to them, to move toward growth, toward becoming...they are life's desperate attempt to become itself...his potent constructive tendency.... (p. 118–119)

Despite unfavorable conditions, most men strive, in the only ways that they perceive as available to them, to achieve some degree of emotional expression, intimacy, self care, and sexual satisfaction. Most men put their power, status, and competitive needs into some kind of perspective with the rest of their identities. In other words, most men cling to their humanness in spite of the forces that seek to wrest it away and turn them into machines. Rogers would say that this tenacity is the manifestation of the self-actualizing tendency.

Rogers would also be optimistic with regard to the ability of men to deal with the effects of their harsh childhood socialization and adult environments. Because he believes that the self-actualizing tendency exists in every man, Rogers also believes that it will emerge under the right conditions, just as the potato shoots he described would turn healthy if deposited in rich soil. Given an environment in which men can discover and express their true selves, they can drop their masculine facades and make the transition from "seeming" to "being."

At least two factors that work against this potential change. First, the emotional "scar tissue" from childhood and adolescence is considerable for many men, making it difficult for them to feel safe in dealing with this inner world that has become so alien. Second, we live in a sexist culture which continues to base approval on traditional masculine characteristics and behavior. Nevertheless, the primacy of this psychological work has encouraged many men to deal with these obstacles.

EXISTENTIAL THEORY

Existential theory of personality is based on the writings of existentialist philosophers such as Sartre, Kierkegaard, Heidegger, and Nietzsche. It bears a strong resemblance to humanistic theory in many regards, but it departs in others. The existential view of the person provides an interesting perspective on men, particularly with regard to the positive attributes of traditional masculinity.

The major similarities between humanistic and existential theories are the emphases on self-awareness and self-determination. Like humanistic theorists, existentialists believe in the importance of being in touch with the inner life and using it as a guide for action. The major difference in these two theories is in the area of conflict within the person. For the humanist, the self-actualizing tendency is only stifled by conditional positive regard, a force that originates from outside of the person. If the environment supports the real self, then the person can move unencumbered toward fulfillment. Growth only entails risk if positive regard is conditional. In contrast, existential theorists see conflict within the person as an inevitable feature of the human condition. For them, growth always entails risk.

Existentialists like Rollo May (1958) believe that moving toward fulfillment is not just a matter of a person following his or her actualizing tendency. It requires more effort than that. Because the person has many different possibilities and potentials for growth, he or she must decide which ones to pursue and which ones to leave by the wayside. It is in these decisions that conflict emerges. At every moment, the person is forced to make choices that involve giving something up. If you decide to go to class, you can not stay in bed. If you decide to stay in bed, you can not go to class. If you decide to spend an afternoon with other people, you can not spend it by yourself.

Although these are relatively trivial choices, other decisions are more profound in their effect on our lives. If you decide to marry, you can not stay single, and vice versa. Maybe you can experience the other alternative later, but maybe there will not be a "later." Since we have a limited amount of time to spend in this world, our choices are finite and vitally important. For the existentialist, it is the pattern of choice that determines the personality, and the person is wholly responsible for his or her choices. This means that you are what you do, and that you create who you are. By making choices, a person ascribes purpose and meaning to his or her life. It is an intensely personal meaning, not some meaning that is bestowed by outside forces such as biology or other people. The decisions that one makes define one's values and individuality.

Life is a frightening thing, because we must continually make choices without having all the necessary information on which to base these decisions (May, 1958). When you chose a college to attend, you probably gathered information about aspects of several schools, but you could not know everything about every school and be able to perfectly predict the outcome of attending one or the other. You made your best guess and you lived with it. For the existentialist, life is a series of such guesses; hopefully they are educated ones. These choices are made every day and at every moment. Not only did you choose to attend a college, you choose to be in school every day that you stay. If you choose to marry, you will also opt to stay with your partner (or not) every day.

Decisions are satisfying when we make good ones, although we can never know whether or not we have made the best one. We would need to see into the future in order to do so. Even when you make a choice that turns out well, you may be left with a lingering feeling that perhaps another alternative might have been better. When you make a poor decision, you are left with the negative feeling that you had a chance but did not take advantage of it.

Every choice involves two basic alternatives: you could choose to face the unknown future, or you can stick with the routine, predictable past. For example, you can face the problems of going out on your own and defining your world (future), or you can define your world simply by what your parents or other people tell you is important (past).

Choosing the future is a frightening thing because it always involves risk. You might make a decision that does not turn out right, and this could result in your losing something valuable. If you left home to go to college, you probably felt pretty apprehensive when you first arrived there. After all, you might not like it, you might not do well, and you might lose touch with your friends at home. You had to risk the loss of peace of mind, self-esteem, and the companionship of people whom you value. Existential psychologists call this feeling of apprehension *ontological anxiety*, or fear of the unknown (Maddi, 1996).

Choosing the routine, predictable past is not frightening, but it is boring. When you merely stick with what you know, you get the feeling that you are missing out on something, and that the routine does not seem to have any meaning in life. For instance, you could choose to work for the rest of your life at a job that is unfulfilling and unchallenging. If you did, you might find that your life had become unsatisfying and meaningless. Existentialists call this feeling of boredom and regret *ontological guilt*. It is the stifling sense of missed opportunity.

Ontological anxiety and ontological guilt are the painful and inescapable realities of the human condition (May, 1958). Ontological anxiety will always be with us because we are faced with the necessity of making new choices every moment, and our prediction of the outcomes of our decisions is always imperfect. Ontological guilt is inescapable because we have too many potentials to be fulfilled in one lifetime. Choosing one thing always involves giving up another, and we are always left with the sense that we might have missed something important.

Although it never goes away completely, we can minimize ontological guilt by making wise choices and vigorously participating in our lives (Tillich, 1952). If you are pursuing a rewarding and interesting career, you do not feel so badly about the other things you could have done. If you are courageous enough to assert your being in the face of ontological anxiety, then ontological guilt will not rear its ugly head very often.

Courage is the hallmark of psychological health for the existentialist (Frankl, 1960). Choosing to grow despite the uncertainty of one's decisions is what allows a person to be most fully human and fulfilled. It is "daring to be great." Courage should not be confused with bravado. Courage involves taking a risk in order to attain something valuable. Bravado is pretended courage; it is often seen in "macho" behavior, where a man is facing risk solely to avoid being considered unmasculine.

Existential values should not be misconstrued as a prescription for recklessness. Existential psychology places value on the willingness to make your best guess and go with it, not the willingness to make a random guess, or to fail to consider the consequences of your actions. Spontaneity is not the same as impulsivity, and making an educated guess is much more than merely "rolling the dice."

But from where does the "educated" in "educated guess" come? If one's being is so unique and individual, what information can a person use to guide decision making? The answer to these questions comes back to the humanistic theory discussed earlier. If the person's being is unique and individual, then he or she must use it as a guide for decision making. The full experiencing of the self involves a vigorous sense of body, emotions, thoughts, sensations, an appreciation of the physical world, and an ability to examine the self in a nondefensive way. The person who has a full experience of self is said to be living an "authentic" life.

Authenticity helps point the way to existential choice. Intentionality and courage actualizes the choice. For instance, occasionally people leave high paying jobs, even if they are good at what they do. When asked why they left, they often say, "That job just wasn't me." Their self-awareness told them that their job no longer had a place in their lives, and they were courageous enough to search for something more important.

Existentialism and Masculinity

From the existential perspective, traditional masculinity has a number of marked advantages and disadvantages (as does traditional femininity). Men are socialized in some ways that help them assert their existential selves. Other influences get in the way of this process. Because responsibility for the self is inescapable, each man is charged with the struggle for overcoming these negative influences and living an authentic life.

We can conceptualize these negative influences in much the same way as in the application of humanistic theory. If the vigorous experience of the self provides the data on which to base existential decision, then many men are basing their decisions on limited information. The socialization of boys to avoid emotion leaves a large gap in the experience of the self. This lack of awareness allows men to see emotional situations only in intellectual terms and may often force them to wallow in emotional problems.

Masculine gender roles contain a wide variety of prescriptions for behaviors that emphasize the outward appearance of the man: stoicism, job status, wealth, material possessions, control, dominance, achievement, and independence. Traditional masculinity is defined by how the man looks, not by his inner experience.

Many men who chase the masculine dream find it to be disillusioning and self-alienating. This is especially true for men who have reached middle adulthood. Some have exerted considerable effort in attempting to live up to the masculine mystique, and they may have done fairly well at it. Others have given up on trying to meet the harsh standards of masculinity.

In middle adulthood, the body begins to decline and the man must acknowledge his mortality and vulnerability. At the same time, he may have become tired of holding up the heavy burden of the masculine facade in his work and social life. These changes may prompt him to re-examine traditional masculine values. One of Vaillant's (1977) middle-aged interviewees described his crisis: "One part of me wants power, prestige, recognition, success; the other part feels all of this is nonsense and chasing the wind" (p. 228).

Many men choose to emphasize family and leisure roles at midlife (R. J. May, 1988) or to otherwise reevaluate their lives (Levinson, Darrow, Klein, Levinson, & Mckee, 1978). In existential terms, their self-experience tells them that they need to make adjustments in their choices in order for their lives to remain meaningful. Choosing to define himself by gender role standards may prevent a man from pursuing options in many areas such as work, leisure, relationships, and sexuality. Some men gather the courage to break out of the narrow definition of self and exercise options that they previously avoided.

There are a number of positive aspects to traditional masculinity from the existential perspective. Courage is surely one of them. Throughout history, men have been willing to face challenges and overcome obstacles. Again, however, we need to make a clear distinction between real courage and engaging in a dangerous behavior as an end it itself (such as participating in the running of the bulls in Pamplona, Spain). Men have poured themselves into physically and psychologically dangerous ventures, and pushed the limits of their capabilities, because they believed that what they were doing was worthwhile. To do so is to risk failure in order to attain fulfillment.

Men have also been raised to believe in the necessity of decision making and action, which are also existential ideals. Sometimes the most courageous thing a person can do is to get to work and do what must be done. Farrell (1990) goes so far as to define problem solving and the offering of solutions as "male nurturance."

Many of men's accomplishments have required them to tolerate a good deal of discomfort, which the existential person must do in order to carry out difficult decisions. Millions of working men have suffered horrible physical conditions in order to support their families. From an existential standpoint, these men made the choice to stay in these circumstances moment after moment and day after day, because they defined their purpose as the role of provider and breadwinner.

The healthy existential person is someone with vision who can imagine possibilities and future. In boys' play, problem solving, and other aspects of their socialization, the culture often encourages this kind of imagination (Block, 1984). The fact that males are encouraged to go out into the world independently and deal with it helps them to see and choose from a wide variety of options.

An existential men's studies perspective would argue for an expansion rather than an eradication of traditional masculinity. The existential man who wants to move beyond the constraints of traditional gender roles can do so by expanding masculine ideals into psychosocial realms. To be truly independent means that he sometimes goes against what others define as appropriately masculine. Risk-taking does not only include things like running into burning buildings, we can expand it to include emotional risk-taking, like telling someone that you are afraid and need their support. The value of providing for a family can expand beyond material providing into including emotional nurturing and the kinds of daily caretaking activities that have traditionally been relegated solely to mothers. From a base of independence, courage, and risk taking, men can expand to becoming independent from unreasonable gender role demands, having the courage to enter the traditional realm of the feminine, and taking emotional risks.

We return to the discussion of gender as a set of "default options" from Chapter 1. In moving from "going along with the program" to making informed choices about one's behavior and life, it is very helpful to have an awareness of what the program is. If gender is a cultural pressure that it sometimes makes sense to oppose, it is very difficult to resist a pressure that one cannot name. Gender awareness gives men a language for symbolizing their experience, and this language is a helpful guide to existential choice.

SUMMARY

1. Phenomenological psychology emphasizes the importance of the individual's sense of self and the ability of the human being to attain personal fulfillment. Carl Rogers believed that all living things have an actualizing tendency which propels the organism toward growth. Self-actualization is the psychological outgrowth of the actualizing tendency in human beings. Under the right environmental conditions, self actualization allows a person to fulfill his or her unique potential.

2. The healthiest psychological environment is one in which important others communicate loving and valuing to the person in all circumstances (unconditional positive regard). When a person gets messages that the self is not of value when certain types of behavior are evident, they experience conditional positive regard.

3. Because feedback from others is critical in shaping the personality, the person who receives a great deal of unconditional positive regard will internalize this attitude and come to value the self. Large doses of conditional regard cause the person to deny the parts of the self associated with disapproval. Because vigorous experiencing of all parts of the self is necessary for self-actualization, conditional regard inhibits the fulfillment of human potential.

4. The application of Rogers' theory to masculine socialization reveals that many males grow up with a good deal of conditional regard. "Masculine" behaviors often meet with approval and "feminine" behaviors with disapproval. Boys begin to value the masculine parts and deny the feminine parts of the self. This denial leads to self-alienation.

5. The Gender Role Strain model is based in humanistic theory. Boys whose naturally occurring personalities contradict social standards of masculinity tend to experience many negative consequences. They may become hypermasculine to force themselves to strive for the cultural ideal.

6. The denial of emotion is central to many masculine gender roles and creates a good deal of strain for many men. Other areas of strain include safety needs, the avoidance of physical pain, dependence, power needs, homophobia, femiphobia, achievement, athletics, and sexuality. Despite this strain, most men are able to assert their unique human selves. Rogers would be optimistic about men's healing.

7. Existential theory resembles humanistic theory in its emphases on self awareness and self determination, but it departs in its emphases on personal responsibility, conflict, and risk. From the existential perspective, self-definition is a matter of individual choice, which always involves the possibility of losing something valuable. The human condition is one of ontological anxiety, or fear of the unknown, and ontologi-

cal guilt, the sense of missed opportunity. Although both are unavoidable, one can minimize the latter by choosing to push forward despite the experience of fear and uncertainty. The authentic person is one who is attuned to the self and courageous enough to make difficult choices.

8. From the existential viewpoint, traditional masculinity contains positive and negative influences. The negative influences are the encouragement to deny the emotional self and the emphasis on the outward appearance of the man. The positive aspects include the masculine willingness to face challenges, overcome obstacles, take action, make decisions, take risks, endure discomfort, and push the limits of one's potential.

8

It Never Lies, and It
Never Lies Still:
Emotion and Masculinity

Few human experiences are as basic and ubiquitous as emotion. A person responds to almost any internal or environmental event with some degree of feeling, and the experience of positive emotions is probably one of the most important motivators in life. People seek money, love, knowledge, physical pleasure, relationships, or human service because they believe that these things will provide some degree of emotional fulfillment. The U.S. Constitution holds the "pursuit of happiness," an emotion, as an inalienable human right. Just as the brain structures associated with emotion are at the center of the brain, emotion is at the center of human experience.

As an old psychoanalytic saying goes, "Emotion never lies, and it never lies still." Directly or indirectly, feelings tend to find some sort of manifestation. Strong emotions seem to have a life of their own. You can feel them physically; they seem to cry for expression. If you accept the premise that emotional *experience* strongly encourages emotional *expression*, then it must take even stronger forces to suppress the outward display of emotion. These powerful influences can be found in masculine gender socialization, masculine ideologies, and situational expectations for men to avoid the expression of vulnerable feelings.

Even the casual observer will notice that many men have difficulty understanding, dealing with, and expressing emotions. Restrictive emotionality is one of the most frequently discussed issues in men's studies, and it is thought to underlie a number of other problems for men, including relationship difficulties (Lynch & Kilmartin, 1999), physical illness (Pennebaker, 1995), mental health problems (Hendryx, Haviland, & Shaw,

1991), and violence (Pollack, 1998). Masculine gender roles often encourage men to resist the awareness of affect, avoid emotional vulnerability, and disguise their feelings, especially when those feelings involve hurt, fear, sadness, or any experience that signals weakness or lack of control. Some men believe that tear ducts on men are like nipples—we only have them through a biological accident.

In this chapter, we explore the origins, consequences, and remedies of restrictive emotionality by addressing the following important questions:

- Are there demonstrable sex and gender differences in emotional experience, expression, and self-disclosure?

- What typical masculine socialization experiences and social situations lead to restrictive emotionality?

- What have researchers learned about the effects of emotional constriction on the person?

- What are the possibilities for helping men to improve the quality of their emotional lives?

SEX AND GENDER DIFFERENCES IN EMOTIONAL EXPRESSION

We must keep in mind that, although every culture exerts pressure on its members to handle emotion in prescribed ways, these "rules" vary widely from culture to culture. For instance, many Asian cultures expect both men and women to control their emotions. Many Middle Eastern and South American cultures expect both men and women to express their emotions. Some cultures expect women, but not men, to express emotions. And in some cultures, men are considered more expressive of certain emotions than women (Tavris & Wade, 2001).

It is also worthwhile to repeat an important consideration from earlier chapters. Although a culture exerts pressure on people to feel, think, and act in certain ways, individual responses to cultural influences are widely variable. Even in cultures that expect women to be highly emotional and men to be stoic, there are very expressive men and very inexpressive women.

Leslie Brody and Judith Hall (2000) delineate several important conceptual categories in the study of gender and emotion. First, many researchers have studied gender *stereotypes* of emotionality. These studies describe people's *beliefs* about men's and women's emotional lives. There is also a body of research on *self-descriptions* of emotionality—people's reports about their experiences. And there is an important distinction between the *experience* and the *expression* of emotion. A person might feel quite strongly but try not to communicate that feeling for any number of reasons.

It is no surprise that, in studies of gender stereotypes, most people believe that women are more emotional than men. Fischer and Manstead (2000) noted that this stereotype exists in 30 of the 33 cultures that they observed. In fact, this difference in emotionality is one of the central defining features of the masculinity-femininity dimension (O'Neil,

1981a; Bem, 1981). These findings are especially robust for judgments of emotional *expression*. Although people tend to also believe that women *experience* stronger emotions than men, they do not see the gulf between the sexes as being as large as that of expression (Brody & Hall, 2000). Therefore, the prevalent beliefs are that women feel a little bit more than men, but that they display their emotions a great deal more than men.

Self-descriptive studies may be strongly biased by gender stereotypes. Psychologists have known for a long time that *social desirability* affects self-report, even in basically honest people (Kenrick, Neuberg, & Cialdini, 2005). People are motivated to present themselves in a positive light. As gender stereotypes carry with them strong values, males and females are more likely to portray themselves as masculine and feminine, respectively.

With these limitations in mind, we find a number of researchers who have demonstrated that women report greater experiences of positive emotions (happiness, well-being, joy) than men. At the same time, females also report higher levels of many negative feelings, especially those that are *intropunitive* (self-punishing), such as shame, guilt, sadness, anxiety, and fear (Brody & Hall, 2000). Although males reported feeling contempt more often, there was no difference between men and women in the intensity of contempt (Brody, 1993). Studies on sex differences in the experience of anger show mixed results, with some finding no differences and others finding differences depending on the target of the anger (Brody & Hall, 2000).

An important finding is that there is a high positive correlation between the reported experience of positive feelings and the reported experience of negative feelings (Diener, Larsen, Levine, & Emmons, 1985). According to self-descriptions, it is apparent that high emotionality is a mixed blessing, allowing one to fully experience joy and contentment, but also leaving the person vulnerable to intense negative feelings. The same is true for low emotionality—it allows a person to escape from intense feelings of fear and anxiety, but apparently at the cost of sacrificing positive emotional experiences. Positive and negative emotions are therefore a kind of "package deal."

Within the domain of emotional expression, there is little doubt that males tend to display most feelings less frequently and less intensely than females. Interesting data have emerged from developmental studies in this area. Infant boys appear to actually be more expressive than infant girls (Brody & Hall, 1993). Preschool children show no sex differences in expression, but consistent differences begin to emerge by age six (Adams, Kuebli, Boyle, & Fivush, 1995), and these differences become well established by middle adolescence (Balswick, 1982). Stapely & Haviland (1989) found that adolescent boys were much more likely than girls to deny that they *ever* had emotional experiences. Other studies have demonstrated sex differences in expression of feelings for college students (Snell, Jr. 1989), and other adults (Saurer & Eisler, 1990).

Although females tend to display generally higher levels of emotions than males, the expression of anger, pride, and loneliness are more frequent in males (Brody & Hall, 2000). Balswick (1982) reported that the available research evidence indicates a strong trend for men and women to behave in accordance with gender stereotypes. However, psychological gender is more predictive of level of emotional expression than biologi-

cal sex. In other words, knowing a person's level of stereotypical masculinity and femininity allows for a better understanding of his or her emotional expressiveness than
simply knowing whether the person is male or female (Brody, Hay, & Vandewater,
1990). People who believe in the stereotype that men are "naturally" unemotional are
more likely to report stereotypical emotionality for themselves (Deaux, 2000). Likewise, men's high levels of adherence to masculine ideology, which includes the belief
that men *should be* unemotional, are associated with low expressiveness (Bruch, Berko, & Haase, 1998).

There are also average sex differences in the manner of emotional expression. Females
are more likely to communicate their feelings through facial and other nonverbal expressions, and by talking. Males are more likely to act out their feelings (Brody & Hall, 2000;
Lynch & Kilmartin, 1999). Females also tend to be better than males at identifying others'
feelings from facial, body, and voice cues (Manstead, 1992). These findings indicate that
women, on the average, are more sensitive than men to people's feelings, even when
those feelings are expressed indirectly.

We should also keep in mind that context is a critical factor in the display of emotion
(Shields, 2000). Masculine men may embrace one another when they are teammates and
win the game, cry with one another at funerals or war veterans' reunions, and may otherwise show feelings usually defined as unmasculine by the culture when the immediate social setting allows for such display. Social forces exert influence on people both in
immediate context and the "big picture" of the larger culture (Deaux, 2000).

The Special Case of Anger

Although masculine stereotypes and ideologies contain the expectation for men to be in
control of their emotions, the expression of anger is a notable exception. Curiously,
men's anger is often seen as being completely out of control. Moreover, an angry man is
expected to express his anger through acting out, sometimes in violent ways. Because
anger is socially acceptable for men, traditionally gender-typed men tend to convert
most other emotions into anger, often resulting in destructive behavior and a lack of
awareness of the original emotion (e.g., jealousy, sadness, disappointment) that was
converted into anger (Lynch & Kilmartin, 1999). Don Long (1987) referred to anger as
the "male emotional funnel system." Parents have a tendency to highlight the experiences of anger and the related emotions of contempt and disgust with their sons much
more often than with their daughters (Brody & Hall, 1993), and psychological masculinity is associated with aggressive, unacknowledged, and uncontrolled anger (Kopper
& Epperson, 1996).

Although emotional expression can have positive health and mental health consequences, the expression of anger is quite risky from a health perspective. Carol Tavris
(1989) noted that the expression of anger is sometimes dangerous and self-destructive.
Many people believe that, when a person is angry, he or she needs to "blow off
steam"—to act out the anger in some way. But a conventional belief can be wrong. In
many circumstances, the unrestrained expression of anger tends to make a person angrier,

and also tends to damage relationships. In extreme situations, the expression of anger can get a person killed, as in the increasing incidence of "road rage," in which more than 95% of the participants are boys and men (Joint, 1995).

Researchers have identified chronic anger as an important contributor to a number of physical health problems: hypertension, heart attack, and recently, stroke (Williams et al., 2002) (see Chapter 9). The research on anger expression tells us that "counting to ten" is often a much better strategy than "blowing off steam," in both the long and the short term (Lynch & Kilmartin, 1999).

Self-disclosure

Self-disclosure is the verbal communication of personal information from one person to another (Cozby, 1973). It includes an important emotional component. There is ample evidence that self-disclosure is basic to mental health (Pennebaker, 1995). The person who is able to reveal his or her thoughts and feelings to others has the opportunities to express the self, receive social support, gain insight into the self, understand his or her emotional nuances, and form close relationships. In order to do so, however, the person must tolerate some degree of vulnerability. In other words, the revelation of the self to important others involves some interpersonal risk, but it also helps the person to be understood, connected, and in touch with the self. Moreover, being in touch with the self helps one to better understand others (Jourard, 1971).

Across a wide variety of cultures, women disclose to more people than men, using emotionally descriptive language more often when they converse and write (Brody & Hall, 2000). Men show a tendency to only disclose to their intimate partners (Rime, Mesquita, Philippot, & Boca, 1991). Men who display this pattern may put themselves at risk for losing their sole source of social support should the relationship end or come into serious conflict. As is the case with emotional expression, gender may be a better predictor of self-disclosure than sex. Androgynous individuals of both sexes exhibited equally intimate levels of disclosure (Balswick, 1988).

There also appears to be differences in topics that males and females disclose about as well as the sex of the person who more often receives the disclosure. Stapley and Haviland (1989) reported that adolescent boys disclosed more about their activities and achievements than girls, and that they found these areas (where performance is assessed) to be more emotionally charged than other areas. Girls reported relationships to be more emotionally charged, and they disclosed more in this area. In general, girls tend to reveal personal information and boys tend to reveal what they are doing or thinking (Polce-Lynch, Myers, Kilmartin, & Forssmann-Falk, 1998).

The "target" of a self-disclosure refers to the person to whom the disclosure is directed. Here the data are unambiguous. People of both sexes disclose more often to females than to males (Timmers, Fischer, & Manstead, 1998). We could view this as a sex similarity (higher disclosure to females) or a sex difference (same-sex vs. other-sex target). Gender-typed males tend to reveal very little personal information to other males, although they disclose about the same to females as androgynous men do (Winstead,

Derlega, & Wong, 1984). Males overwhelmingly express more affection toward women than toward men (Brody, 1993).

In summary, there are fairly robust findings to indicate that males, especially gender-typed ones, are less expressive and disclosing than females for emotions other than anger, that they tend to reveal thoughts more than feelings, and that these self- revelations are not often made to other males. Theorists have proposed a variety of explanations for the roots of these differences.

ORIGINS OF RESTRICTIVE EMOTIONALITY

Emotional constriction is one of the hallmarks of traditional masculinity. Males are usually socialized to deny and suppress feelings from an early age. The masculine values of toughness, self reliance, task orientation, logic, fearlessness, and confidence are usually perceived to be antithetical to the expression of emotions, especially those associated with vulnerability. Anger would seem to be a potentially empowering emotion, and therefore it is socially allowable for men (Shields, 2000).

There are a number of cultural and social forces that encourage men to restrict their emotionality. O'Neil (1981a) believes that the antifemininity norm is at the heart of men's fears of emotional expression. He describes the following four commonly held masculine beliefs:

1. Emotions, feelings, and vulnerabilities are signs of femininity and therefore to be avoided;

2. Men seeking help through emotional expressiveness are immature, weak, dependent, and therefore feminine;

3. Interpersonal communication emphasizing emotions, feelings, and intuitions are considered feminine and to be avoided;

4. Emotional expression may expose inner fears and conflicts that could portray the man as unstable, immature, and unmanly." (p. 206)

Some psychoanalytic interpretations of masculine inexpression appeal to the early childhood denial of psychological identification with the mother. Because boys are often raised by their other-sex parent, they must put rigid boundaries between themselves and their mothers in order to define themselves as masculine. If the boy's mother is emotionally expressive and his father is not (a fairly common case), then emotions are experienced as "feminine" and they threaten masculine identification. When the boy feels something, he becomes anxious about his masculinity and learns to deny and devalue these emotions. Theoretically, girls' gender identity is based on attachment to the mother, whereas that of boys is based on separation from her (Chodorow, 1978). As a result, girls tend to become more relationship oriented and boys more task oriented.

Relationships do not really have outcomes, per se. They are experiences, just as emotions are, and the maintenance of attached, intimate relationships requires emotional self-disclosure (Jourard, 1971). Tasks, on the other hand, are often defined by outcome.

They tend to be more cognitive in nature, and the important thing is not to experience the task, but rather to get it done. A task-oriented approach to the world may often involve the view that emotions are a nuisance to be disposed of as soon as possible. The engineering honor society at the General Motors Institute proudly claims the name, "The Robots" (Penwell, 1992), reflecting the value on eschewing emotion. During a nationally televised post-game interview, a basketball coach cried as he described how moved he was by his team's courage. A sportscaster then commented, "He needs to get control of those allergies [emotions] (Lynch & Kilmartin, 1999).

If the boy's father is emotionally inexpressive, then this style may become a part of the boy's identification with the father. Sons whose fathers are highly involved parents are more emotionally expressive than other boys (Brody, 1997) and boys who have emotionally expressive fathers display their feelings at similar levels to girls (Balswick, 1988). In families where both parents are expressive, boys will not tend to view emotional expression as an exclusively female trait, and therefore the natural inclination to display feelings will emerge, since it is not associated with threats to masculinity.

We could also easily view the finding that expressive fathers tend to have expressive sons as merely a product of imitation. Fathers tend to use more demanding language than mothers and, especially with sons, use more pejorative language ("you knucklehead") (Brody & Hall, 1993), hardly a style conducive to the display of vulnerable feeling. If we look at the availability of male role models in mainstream U.S. culture, it is easy to see how inexpressiveness perpetuates itself generation after generation. Fathers' inexpressiveness is imitated, and male heroes in popular culture are often paragons of traditional masculinity. Movies and television often contain male characters who are task oriented, tough, inexpressive, and violent.

An interesting research finding is that parents display a wider range of their own emotions to their daughters than to their sons (Brody & Hall, 1993). Therefore, girls usually have more opportunities than boys to observe and imitate expressive models. In one longitudinal study (one in which a group of children is followed over a number of years), Adams, Kuebli, Boyle, and Fivush (1995) demonstrated that parents' more frequent use of emotional language with girls appeared to create a sex difference in children's use of similar language. The researchers found no sex differences at 40 months of age, but clear differences emerged by 70 months. These 30 months are a time of highly accelerated language acquisition, and parents' reluctance to speak to boys about their emotions may communicate the belief that feelings are not important.

There is also considerable evidence that interpersonal and behavioral influences within the family lead boys away from the world of emotion. Parents talk about emotion more to daughters than to sons, except for anger and disgust. When children feel badly, mothers are more likely to talk directly about the feeling with daughters and to talk about the causes and consequences of the feeling with sons. The former encourages expression; the latter, control (Brody & Hall, 1993). In these interactions that highlight certain aspects of experience, pattern-seeking children learn which of these aspects deserve their attention. For girls, it is often the emotional world. For boys, it is likely to be the world of task, control, and detached analysis.

Rewards and punishments for self-disclosure may also affect the frequency of this behavior. It is clear that "unmasculine" behaviors such as crying often meet with disapproval from parents and peers (Brody, 2000). Most men have a storehouse of memories of times when their emotional expression was punished. The crying little boy whose father says to him threateningly, "*I'll* give you something to cry about" can quickly extinguish that behavior. There is solid research evidence that the extensive socialization to control emotional expression leads to an *overlearning* of this tendency (Barr & Kleck, 1995). In other words, emotional inhibition becomes a habit that is applied automatically across a variety of situations.

The male peer group can be especially brutal in its enforcement of the restrictive emotionality norm (Lynch & Kilmartin, 1999). In extreme groups, such as street gangs, this norm is rigidly enforced with threats of violence. Besides punishing expressiveness, male groups may also reward emotional inexpressiveness. For instance, in some fraternity initiation rites, a group symbol is burned into the arm of the initiate, and he is applauded for remaining stoic and unresponsive. Many male initiation rites around the world encourage emotional suppression, an important skill for warriors (Herdt, 1982).

We can see from the above research findings and examples that restrictive emotionality is not only the product of a *history* of these sanctions. Gendered reward and punishment contingencies exist in many settings in which adult men find themselves. Not only did men get punished for emoting when they were children, they often get punished for displaying their feelings as adults. From blue collar to corporate workplaces, for example, emotions other than anger are not often tolerated in men.

Women in the corporate world sometimes find that expression of weakness is disadvantageous to their careers. A female banking executive relates that, among her female colleagues, the rule is, "you die before you cry." I suspect that, for males in these and other work settings, this rule goes without saying. My experience of the corporate culture is that, for many women executives, emotional restriction is situation specific. They tend to confine inexpressiveness to the workplace because it is defined as appropriate there, but they continue to view expressiveness as useful elsewhere. For many men however, emotional constriction may be more cross-situational. There are precious few settings when they feel safe enough to disclose. For women, "die before you cry" is a hyperbole that stresses the career importance of avoiding the display of weakness in a male dominated setting. For men, dying may be literally what they are doing (see Chapter 9).

Role Theory

As I have noted several times, social roles are powerful determinants of behavior. It is in this theoretical area that we find one of the most convincing explanations of male inexpressiveness. People tend to assume roles in organizing their behavior, and they tend to avoid out-role behavior (Turner, 1970). As we have seen, masculine and feminine roles are generalized social roles that function to influence a wide variety of social behaviors. This may be especially true for gender-schematic people, who tend to rigidly organize their worlds into male and female categories (Bem, 1993).

Box 8.1: Culture and Nature

I made a recent trip to Long Beach, California, and on my way from the airport, the cab driver pointed out an island that was the site of a large power plant. He commented, "That island wasn't there ten years ago. They built that island." In an area where land is scarce and people want to build a large power plant, one solution is to create more land, certainly a feat of problem-solving and engineering. The Hong Kong airport, conceived largely by Western construction and engineering firms, was built in the South China Sea.

These solutions to the problems of scarce land reflect the view of nature as an entity that humans should *control*, if at all possible. In mainstream U.S. culture, emotions (like all of nature) are no exception to the control-over-nature approach. The common masculine view is that, to think clearly and reason soundly, you have to set your emotions aside and solve problems using only your cognitive faculties.

There is little doubt that too much emotion can lead to actions that have the potential for harm to self or others. But is *no* emotion the path to "rationality"? Is it desirable, or even possible? Antonio Damasio (1994) thinks not. He reviews a good deal of research on emotion and cognition and concludes that, "Reduction in emotion may constitute an equally important source of irrational behavior." (p. 53). Rather than being separate from reasoning, emotion is an integral part of reasoning.

Masculine roles involve a set of expectations for task-oriented behaviors that emphasize logic and rationality, and de-emphasize emotional experience (although the rational and the emotional may well constitute a false dichotomy—see Box 8.1). From early childhood, social forces encourage boys to value masculine traits and behaviors and devalue feminine ones. The ideal of masculinity is physical courage, toughness, risk taking, competitiveness, and aggression, traits seen as incompatible with emotional expression (Balswick, 1988). For example, men are socialized to view all other men as competitors. One does not exhibit vulnerability to a competitor (Skovholt & Hansen, 1980). Since self-disclosure often involves vulnerability, males tend to avoid it, especially in the company of other males.

Besides being incompatible with masculine expectations, emotional expression is defined as feminine. Men are less likely to disclose their feelings to others because out-role behavior may meet with social disapproval and/or self-disapproval. In addition, masculine gender demands are applied earlier in life and more intensely for boys than feminine ones are for girls (Basow, 1992). Thus, behavioral role sanctions are stronger for men than for women. Consider what your reaction might be if you overheard the following conversation (Brannon, 1985, p. 307):

"Mike, I've been so upset since we had that argument, I could hardly sleep last night. Are you sure you're really not mad at me?"

"Heck, Jim, I'm so relieved... I was just afraid that you'd be mad at me!"

For many, this example is comical—so out of the ordinary that it seems absurd. But it is important to note that, even if this conversation does not take place, these two men may well *experience* this kind of upset even if they do not *display* it. Because of the social dominance of men, out-role behavior is viewed as a loss of masculine power and privilege, and not to be tolerated. Hence, pejorative terms like "sissy" or "wimp" are applied to men who exhibit emotionality, submissiveness, or dependence. Masculine privilege not only devalues and restricts women, it devalues and restricts the feminine-defined parts of men.

We can also understand emotional expression within the context of relationships. One broad social expectation is for *reciprocity*, the tendency to respond to other people as they behave toward us (Baron, Byrne, & Branscome, 2006). For example, when someone expresses anger toward you, you tend to respond with anger. When haggling over the price of something, a salesperson who reduces an asking price influences a buyer to increase his or her offer.

With regard to self-disclosure, the reciprocity norm influences people to disclose at a level similar to that which they receive (Cohn & Strassberg, 1983). Since males are less often the targets of disclosure than females, then it is not surprising that they tend to themselves disclose less. Males exhibit higher levels of emotional disclosure to females than to other males, perhaps reflecting the influence of the reciprocity norm.

The other side of the coin from reciprocity is *complementarity*, the tendency to balance the expression of the other person. For instance, dominant behavior on the part of one person in the relationship influences the other person to be submissive (Strong, 1986). L'Abate (1980) argued that male inexpressiveness is a complementary reaction to female "overexpressiveness." Although there is evidence that complementarity may operate in certain circumstances, it is influenced by complicated interactions among many setting and relationship variables (Kilmartin, 1988).

Sattel's (1976; 1998) explanation of male inexpressiveness is very different than those presented thus far. He argues that men are inexpressive simply because they want to maintain power. By being emotionally withholding, men force women to "draw them out" and do the emotional work in the relationship. As evidence, Sattel (1976) offers that men are often expressive early in relationships with women as a way of seducing them. Later, they become inexpressive as a way of asserting control, since masculinity and male privilege demand dominance. Sattel goes so far as to suggest that inexpressiveness is directly related to the power of a person's role. Husbands are more likely than wives to respond to marital conflict by "stonewalling"—minimizing their facial expressions, eye contact, and listening (Levenson, Carstensen, & Gottman, 1994). Lakoff (1990) contends that men's and women's typical communication patterns are better understood in terms of superior and subordinate, noting that similar patterns develop between supervisors and workers, Whites and people of color, prisoners, and guards. Both women and men in positions of authority use power-assertive language, reveal their feelings less often (except for anger), and display similar nonverbal behaviors (Tavris, 1992). Social status and power are extremely important variables in the study of emotional expression (Deaux, 2000), with gender often operating as a generalized power variable.

In summary, it seems that there are a variety of social, cultural, and interpersonal forces that influence men to be inexpressive. The available evidence is that these forces do a pretty good job of inhibiting what seems to be a natural, often healthy inclination to disclose and express feelings. Since emotion is pervasive, the results of compulsively restricting it may also be pervasive.

CONSEQUENCES OF RESTRICTIVE EMOTIONALITY

It is said that "emotion never lies, and emotion never lies still." Affective experience is central to human experience, regardless of whether or not one attempts to deny its existence. Feelings that are not expressed directly often find indirect forms of expression. Many men deal with emotions by placing feelings outside of themselves, through externalizing defenses, by "acting out" emotional conflicts, and/or through physical symptoms.

We have seen that, from early childhood, girls are encouraged to look inside of themselves and think about how they feel, and boys are encouraged to look outside of themselves and think about what to do (Brody & Hall, 1993). Strong "feminine" emotions are experienced as threats to masculinity, and these threats are sometimes difficult to ignore. The traditional male deals with these feelings with strategies that allow him to perceive them as nonexistent. In this way, he preserves his masculinity by defending against feminine experience and behavior.

Families' acceptance of emotion in children is associated with higher levels of social and psychological adjustment (Bronstein, Briones, Brooks, & Cowan, 1996). It appears to be critical to children's mental health for their families to allow them to experience and express their feelings. Although some families squelch emotions in both children of both sexes, they are much more likely to do so with sons than with daughters.

Mahalik, Cournoyer, DeFranc, Cherry, and Napolitano (1998) found that men with rigid masculine expectations used more immature and neurotic ego defenses than more gender-flexible men. Some psychologists see the main function of masculinity itself as a generic defense against vulnerable feelings (Lynch, 1998). An example will help to clarify these styles. If you are rejected by a romantic partner, that event can precipitate painful feelings of sadness due to the loss of the valued person, as well as anxiety due to doubts about your adequacy. There are several ways to deal with these feelings. You could talk about them with a close friend and gain support, express the sadness through "having a good cry," convert these feelings into anger and engage in some aggressive behavior, or deal with the feelings as though they were an intellectual problem. The latter two strategies are preferred by masculine men. The former two are feminine styles which, despite their effectiveness, can not be accessed by these men, since doing so would constitute a threat to masculinity.

Because of the overwhelming quality of these emotions, the traditionally gender typed man might punch a wall, drink heavily, or compulsively and desperately seek a new partner. In all of these strategies, solutions come from outside of the self. The man can take out his frustrations on an object or find something (alcohol or another person) that will hopefully soothe him, as he is not good at soothing himself.

There are several negative consequences to this external style. First, if the soothing person or object is not available, the man finds it difficult, perhaps impossible, to deal with his loss. Second, little new learning can take place. He does not have the skills to introspect and think about himself, and thus he has difficulty in learning what caused the troubling situation and how he might behave differently. If he always deals with emotions externally, he can learn little about what is inside. Third, these kinds of behavior may have a tendency to alienate other people.

A relationship breakup involves a powerful experience of emotional loss, and one must assimilate that loss into one's sense of self in order to recover healthy functioning. This course of recovery from loss is known as *grieving*. It is a process by which a one expresses, works through, eventually accepts the feelings that have accompanied the loss, and comes to a point of resolution that allows one to move on with one's life. John Lynch and I (1999) describe the problem that traditional masculinity creates for the grieving process:

> Grieving has a life of its own. It is quite natural to feel and behave in certain ways—such as crying, reminiscing, and expressing a wish that one had treated the person better—in response to loss. Every culture has funeral rituals that help people to initiate the grief process following the ultimate loss, death. The grieving process takes time; one cannot spend an hour grieving and be done with it once and for all. Depending on the loss, it can take months or even years. The man who has lost his partner is aware that something is wrong, but many men avoid grieving because it involves the expression of vulnerable feelings, and also involves acknowledging that he feels connected to her. These two behaviors are culturally defined as unmasculine, and so he tends to make efforts to distract himself so that he does not have to deal with his pain. He pays a price for doing so, as he is likely to develop symptoms, which are his body's and his mind's way of telling him that something is wrong. If he does not heed these signals, he will continue to have these symptoms. When there comes a time for him to again become involved in a relationship, he will be predisposed to acting out the psychological issues that arise from an incomplete grieving process. (p. 176)

Alexithymia

Inexpressiveness begins as part of a social role, but continuous participation in a role over time can have an enduring effect on the person. Actors who play the same stage role for long periods of time report that they incorporate some aspects of the role into their personalities (Brannon, 1985). The man who continually acts like he has no feelings over many years may virtually lose his ability to experience emotion.

Sifneos (1972) coined the term *alexithymia* to describe the style of habitual inexpressiveness. It comes from the Greek (*a*=lack, *lexis*=words, as in lexicon, and *thymos*=emotions). Literally, the word alexithymia means "no words for feelings." Alexithymic persons have such an impoverished emotional life that they can not even identify feelings, much less express them. Nemiah, Fryberger, and Sifneos (1976) described alexithymia as having four features: " a) difficulty identifying and describing feelings; b) difficulty distinguishing feelings from bodily sensations; c) reduction or absence of symbolic thinking (lack of imaginative ability); d) an external, operative cognitive style" (p. 227–228.).

The alexithymic dimensions of poor identification and expression of feelings have been shown to be strongly related to symptoms of anxiety and depression in medical students (Hendryx, Haviland, & Shaw, 1991) and college students (Bagby, Taylor, & Ryan, 1986). Haviland, Shaw, Cummings, and MacMurray (1988) found a depression-alexithymia relationship in a group of newly abstinent alcoholics. A number of researchers have also discovered that alexithymia is related to a variety of physical problems (Cooper & Holmstrom, 1984; Taylor, 1984; and many others), as well as to narcotic abuse (Solomon, 1982).

This large body of research provides strong support for the hypothesis that emotion never lies still. People who do not deal with feelings directly do not make them go away. The alexithymic style often becomes destructive to the person either physically, psychologically, or both. Although only a small percentage of men are truly alexithymic, and some women also suffer from this problem, the connections between alexithymia and masculinity can hardly be denied. Ronald Levant (1998) describes a "normative male alexithymia"—a sub-clinical level of emotional inexpression found in many men. Although the origins of alexithymia are complex (Taylor, 1984), harsh masculine gender socialization can only encourage its development. In a large, four-city, multicultural sample, Levant and colleagues (2003) found a strong relationship between alexithymia and masculinity ideology.

Other Consequences

The hypothesis that "emotion never lies; emotion never lies still" is supported by a number of studies indicating that men are more likely than women to express negative emotions through physiological processes such as heart rate reactivity and elevated blood pressure. When this style of reaction becomes ingrained and habitual, it can have a negative effect on men's physical health (Jansz, 2000) (see Chapter 9).

Theorists and researchers have also proposed a variety of other consequences for restrictive emotionality. Many of these are in the realm of interpersonal relationships, where self-disclosure is a crucial factor in building trust and connectedness. Not surprisingly, much of the available data come from studies of heterosexual married couples.

In his classic work, *The Transparent Self*, Sidney Jourard (1971) contended that disclosing the private self is one of the primary functions in marriage. There are several studies (Campbell & Snow, 1992; Schumm, Barnes, Bollman, Jurich, & Bregnighis, 1986; Hansen & Schuldt, 1984; and others) that have demonstrated a link between positive self-disclosure and partners' reported marital satisfaction.

Husbands tend to disclose less than their wives (Notarius & Johnson, 1982), and inequality of disclosure is related to lowered levels of marital satisfaction (Balswick, 1988; Davidson, Balswick, & Halverson, 1983). It appears, then, that two of the factors in having a good marriage are that partners disclose a good deal and that they disclose about the same amount. It is quite common for a wife to complain that her husband won't "let her in," and that this is a source of frustration for her.

Emotional restrictedness may also affect sexual enjoyment and/or functioning (O'Neil, 1981a). Since emotions and physical sensations are associated with each other, the man who suppresses emotion also loses touch with his sensuality. It is difficult for traditional men to see sex as something to be experienced, rather than as a task with a goal (orgasm). At its best, sex is an expression of positive emotion, and therefore an inexpressive style limits the enjoyment of the man and his partner.

Fathering is another area affected by male inexpressiveness. In order to be a good father, a man must sometimes go against gender demands that require him to be unemotional, unconnected, and task oriented. He finds himself in situations that call for expressiveness in the form of nurturing, play, giving comfort, and being affectionate (Lynch & Kilmartin, 1999). The inexpressive man may feel inadequate in doing these things for which he has had very little practice.

Male inexpressiveness has been hypothesized to be a major contributing factor to the reluctance of men in seeking medical or psychological help (Addis & Mahalik, 2003). Restrictive emotionality also has relationship and societal consequences. *Empathy* is the emotional awareness of another person's distress and thus an inhibitor of violence. In other words, if you can put yourself in the victim's place in an emotional way, you will be less likely to hurt him or her intentionally. However, it is impossible to understand someone else's feelings if you do not understand your own. David Lisak (1993) coined the term *empathy for the self* in his work with male victims of childhood abuse. Lisak found that those men who were able to acknowledge the emotional and physical pain of their experience as victims showed a strong tendency to not become violent as adults. In contrast, those who denied their pain tended to later act it out in a violent way. For a survivor of childhood abuse, being able to understand his own vulnerable feelings—having empathy for the self—allowed him to have empathy for other people, and thus not harm them. In other words, it appears that a person must have an experiential referent in order to connect emotionally to others' pain.

Men who have embraced task-oriented and inexpressive gender role characteristics may find it easy to perceive people as if they were things, and subordinate human welfare to a task that they define as more important. When such men are in power, their potential for destruction is great. War, racism, sexism, violence, exploitive business practices, the pollution of the planet, and other forms of victimization are all at least partly the result of a failure of compassion and empathy. Men have not been the exclusive perpetrators of these human wrongs, but they have certainly contributed more than their share. The social encouragement to become unfeeling machines, together with the disproportionate allotment of power to males, shoulders some of the responsibility for this state of affairs.

TOWARD SOLUTIONS

We have seen that restrictive emotionality has many psychological, physical, interpersonal, and societal consequences. The good news is that we are not doomed to live with them. A number of therapeutic, educational, and social interventions have been designed to help men become more comfortable with affect. Since feelings such as satisfaction, love, and emotional connectedness are critical to quality of life, and because restrictive emotionality has negative consequences, it is not surprising that many men desire to become more aware and expressive of their emotional worlds (Dosser, 1982).

We have already seen that inexpressiveness arises, at least in part, from situations in which males are discouraged from being emotional. Therefore, one solution is to create environments that give men permission to break the social norm of non-disclosure, thus allowing the natural human propensity for expression of feeling to emerge.

One popular method for creating such settings has been through the establishment of men's consciousness raising groups. In these groups, men who want to learn expressive skills come together into an unusual all-male situation. Rather than having the common men's group norms of competition, task orientation, and macho rigidity, group members strive to create an atmosphere of cooperation, empathy, and self-disclosure. It is important that groups such as this critically examine the effects of masculine gender role demands on their lives as part of their activities (O'Neil, 1996).

Since these groups are usually formed outside of academic or therapeutic settings, not much research evidence of their effectiveness has been accumulated (Balswick, 1988). Many men, however, report that they find these experiences meaningful and helpful (Eichenfield, 1996). Considering that social roles are powerful influences on behavior, it stands to reason that establishing expressiveness as a role expectation has some real potential. Whether consciousness raising groups are able to establish this role norm, and whether behavior changes generalize to settings outside of the group remains to be seen.

Therapists and researchers have designed other interventions and accumulated some evidence of their effectiveness. Moore and Haverkamp (1989) designed a structured group approach for increasing emotional expressiveness in 30- to 50-year old men. Group activities included training in listening skills, reading assignments, and general discussion around masculine gender role issues such as competition, power, control, and relationships.

Many men exhibited strong emotional reactions within the context of the group, and participants showed significant gains in emotional expressiveness, according to several measures. Although we can not be sure how long the changes endured, or whether they generalized to other settings, the evidence is clear that men can change affectively, at least in the short term, when they are motivated to do so. Moore and Haverkamp also noted that some group members were continuing to meet together informally as of six months after the formal group ended. Many group members also reported that their new skills were helpful in their marriages, careers, families, and the management of their health concerns. These reports provide anecdotal evidence that participation in nontraditional groups has significance for motivated men.

James O'Neil (1996) has designed the Gender Role Journey Workshop, a six-day mixed-sex exploration into gender roles and their impact on participants' lives. Male participants find that the workshop experience helps them to increase their level of emotional expressiveness, an outcome they report as satisfying. In one- and two-year follow-up surveys, most participants report that the workshop continues to positively affect their lives.

Dosser (1982) also designed an intervention program for increasing male expressiveness. He suggests that, in addition to communication skills training and consciousness-raising activities, assertiveness training is also helpful. We do not usually think of traditional men as lacking assertive skills, but the expression of feeling is a type of assertion (Lange & Jackubowski, 1976) which men are often lacking. *Assertiveness* refers to the ability of the person to claim his or her rights as a human being. Men have the right, and often the desire, to say, "I love you," "I feel close to you," or "I need your help and support," but the confines of traditional masculinity make it difficult to do so. Many men also have problems with the appropriate expression of anger (Lynch, 2004).

Ronald Levant (1997a; 1998) developed a five step, skill-based model for individual treatment of men who display normative male alexithymia. He informs his client that "We're going to learn the skills that nine year old girls learn as a matter of course," (Levant, 1997a) but that the culture has conspired to prevent men from attaining. In the first phase, the therapist educates the client about the connection between masculine socialization and inexpressiveness and helps the client develop the ability to tolerate emotions. Step two is the development of an emotional vocabulary. Levant has the client list as many words for feelings that he can generate over the course of several days. The third step is practice in identifying others' emotions by learning to read their facial expressions, vocal tone, and body language. He can do this in conversations and in watching movies and television and attempting to take the perspective of the characters. In the fourth stage, the client keeps a daily log where he tracks his emotional responses, concomitant physical sensations, and the contexts in which the feelings arise. The final step involves practice to reinforce the emotional skills he has learned. Levant (1998) reports that this new emotional awareness is empowering and exciting for many men. One client remarked that "it was as though he had been living in a black-and-white television set that had suddenly gone to color." (p. 48).

Balswick (1988) adds that increases in male expressiveness can also be realized through societal changes. We are seeing some movement in this direction in the United States in recent years. As women increasingly share the involvement in economic activities, many men are increasing their family involvement, with its emphasis on expressive activities, albeit at a slower pace (Marsiglio & Pleck, 2005). Balswick suggests that, in the traditional structure of the family, women are economically dependent on men, while men are emotionally dependent on women. Just as some women are beginning to attain economic independence, some men are beginning to work toward emotional independence. This kind of self-sufficiency does not mean disconnection or stoicism, but rather the man's expressive management of his emotions in the context of relationships and self-awareness.

SUMMARY

1. Even though emotion is at the center of human experience, masculine gender roles define it as feminine and discourage it in men, with the exception of the expression of anger. However, the display "rules" for emotion vary with changing social contexts.

2. There is a great deal of evidence that men, especially gender-typed men, tend to be less expressive and self-disclosing than women. This difference is first evident in childhood. Differences in topic of disclosure also emerge at this time, with boys more focused on thinking and performance, and girls more focused on feeling and relationships. Both sexes show a greater willingness to disclose to females than to males.

3. The origins of restrictive male emotionality are in the gender role definitions of vulnerability, inner conflict, dependence, and the definition of feeling as an unmasculine experience. These norms are often enforced by family and peers, as well as by media images of masculinity. Boys with expressive fathers, however, tend to themselves be expressive. Norms for adult male inexpression are enforced in many work and interpersonal settings. Men who exhibit cross-gender behavior may suffer negative consequences in these settings.

4. The reciprocal nature of role behavior also encourages men toward low levels of self-disclosure, as they are less often the targets of disclosure than women. There have been suggestions that low male disclosure is a balancing reaction to women's overexpressiveness, and that low disclosure is a power maneuver in relationships.

5. Emotional constriction may have a number of negative consequences for men and those around them. Men who are uncomfortable with their feelings are prone to using external defenses and acting out. These methods of coping are often less effective and efficient than self-disclosing and asking for help.

6. The extreme of inexpressiveness is alexithymia, which involves a poor awareness of and ability to describe feeling states. Alexithymia has been associated with a wide variety of physical and mental health problems. The hypothesis that "emotion never lies, and emotion never lies still" is supported by the research in this area.

7. Restrictive emotionality also appears to have negative effects on relationships in general and marriages in particular. Low levels of disclosure and partner inequity in disclosure are associated with a lack of marital satisfaction. Sexual dissatisfaction and dysfunction may also be linked with restrictive emotionality. The role of father sometimes calls for expressive skills, which many men are lacking.

8. There are many men who have expressed a desire to improve their abilities to express and disclose. Interventions for this purpose include consciousness raising, structured group activities, individual psychotherapy, and assertiveness training. There is good evidence that these interventions are effective, although more research in this area is needed.

9. Male inexpressiveness should also increase as a function of more liberal gender roles. Since restrictive emotionality is strongly influenced by the expectations of social settings, the creation of nontraditional settings with alternative expectations holds a great deal of promise for improving the quality of men's emotional lives.

9

Surviving and Thriving:
Men and Physical Health

In the not-too-distant past, before it was possible to know a baby's sex before birth, it was common to ask expectant parents if they had a preference for either a boy or a girl. One of the most frequent responses to this inquiry was, "We don't care as long as 'it's' healthy." As it turns out, "it" has a greater chance to be healthy if she is a girl, as sex and gender have a significant relationship to physical well-being. As we will see, the reference to females as "the weaker sex" is misleading when it comes to serious health problems and longevity.

There are sex differences in the epidemiologies (statistical incidences within a population) of many physical problems. For example, males are more likely than females to contract early-onset heart disease, emphysema, and most forms of cancer. On the average, men die at a significantly earlier age than women. Many researchers believe that these sex differences in disease and longevity cannot be explained solely by biological differences between the sexes.

A good deal of evidence has led theorists to suggest that certain aspects of traditional masculinity are at least partially responsible for men's problems with disease and longevity. In this chapter, we describe some of these problems and review the relevant psychological literature on sex and gender as it relates to physical health.

SEX DIFFERENCES IN LONGEVITY

The most recent available United States statistics for life expectancy are for 2002. The National Center for Health Statistics reported that the average life expectancy for African American males born in the United States in 2002 was 68.8 years, compared with 75.6

162

years for African American females. For Whites, the expectancies were 75.1 years and 80.3 years for males and females, respectively (Arias, 2005). As you can see from these data, relative to their female counterparts, minority men are especially at risk for early death. They are more likely than majority men to live in hazardous, stressful, and/or impoverished environments, as well as to lack access to health care (Ro, Casares, Treadwell, & Thomas, 2004). Although life expectancies for all groups rise steadily over the years, men in the United States have died an average of five to seven years sooner than women since the decade of the 1950s (Arias, 2005).

Table 9.1 details sex ratios for U.S. deaths in 2002. As you can see, more males than females die at every stage of life until age 65 (the ratios change directions at that point because so many more women than men have survived to that age). At ages 15–24, the ratio of male to female deaths is a staggering 237:100. At best, U.S. males die "before their time" at about a 6 to 5 ratio to females. At worst, the ratio is more than 2 to 1. Contrary to the social belief that males are heartier and more resistant to disease, the evidence is indisputable that males are more vulnerable than females at every age.

At birth, there is a slight imbalance in the ratio of males to females. Conception favors males because Y-chromosome bearing sperm (androsperm) are more motile than X-chromosome bearing sperm (gynosperm), and thus they are more likely to fertilize the ovum. There are somewhere between 120 and 160 males for every 100 females at conception (Stillion, 1995). However, male fetuses are more likely to have problems *in utero*, leading to spontaneous abortion (miscarriage). By birth, the large sex imbalance that was produced at conception has shrunken considerably; there are between 104 and 106 male births for every 100 female births (Stein, 2005). Because males die at higher rates than females, parity (an equal number of males and females in the age group population) is

TABLE 9.1

Ratio of Male to Female Death and Survival Rates (2002 U.S. Data)

Age in Years	Male: Female Death Ratio	% surviving to next age	
		Male	Female
1–4	123:100	99.1	99.3
5–14	117:100	98.9	99.2
15–24	237:100	98.0	98.8
25–44	205:100	94.6	97.0
45–64	156:100	81.2	88.6
65–100	93:100	1.4	4.0
over 100	34:100		

Calculated from data from National Vital Statistics Reports, Center for Disease Control (Arias, 2005), http://www.cdc.govnchs/data/nvsr/nvsr53/nvsr53_06

reached somewhere between the ages of 25 and 34 (Basow, 1992). From this age range and up, women outnumber men. Women are much more likely than men to survive beyond age 80, and nearly three times as likely to live to be 100 (Arias, 2005). Eleven out of 12 U.S. wives outlive their husbands (Dolnick, 1991).

SEX DIFFERENCES IN DISEASE

There is some evidence to suggest that women get ill more often and report feeling sicker than men on a day-to-day basis. For instance, they are more likely than men to report being bothered by headaches, bladder infections, arthritis, corns and calluses, constipation, hemorrhoids, and varicose veins. We cannot be sure to what extent these differences are real, and to what extent they reflect the social permission for women to report illness. When it comes to serious (life-threatening) diseases, which are, of course, hard to ignore, men outnumber women in almost every category (Arias, 2005).

The two diseases that most often cause death are heart disease and cancer. About 28% of all people eventually die of heart disease. The male:female ratio for cause of death by heart disease is about 96:100 (Arias, 2005), a very small sex difference that actually favors males. When one looks at these data *by age group*, however, a very different picture emerges. Between the ages of 25 and 44, the ratio of male to female deaths from heart disease in 2002 was 239:100 (National Center for Health Statistics, 2004). Three out of four people who die from heart attacks before age 65 are males (American Heart Association, 1995). Thus, although many people die of heart disease, males tend to die much earlier than females. Males are also three times more likely than females to have a non-fatal heart attack or to be diagnosed with heart disease before age 65 (American Heart Association, 2005).

With regard to cancer, sex ratios differ depending on the location of the cancerous tumor in the body. As a cause of death, men lead women in every category except breast cancer. The greatest differences are in mouth and throat cancer (250:100), lung and respiratory cancer (263:100), and cancer of the urinary organs (201:100) (Harrison et al., 1995). Prostate cancer affects one in every six men (American Cancer Society, 2005), and it kills an average of 107 men each day (Boodman, 1998). According to the American Cancer Society (1994), male deaths from cancer increased more than 20% between the 1960s and 1990s, while the rate of female cancer deaths has remained unchanged during the same period. Men are nearly twice as likely to die from lung cancer as women (American Cancer Society, 2005). Lung cancer is one of the most deadly forms of the disease, and because it is so strongly related to smoking and environmental toxins (87% can be linked to tobacco and airborne carcinogens), lung cancer is also one of the most preventable cancers (Gordon & Cerami, 2000).

Table 9.2 details sex ratios for leading causes of "early" (before age 65) deaths. Although data from all ages tends to obscure sex ratios due to the greater number of females alive at older ages, this table provides a good picture of the causes of deaths that we might consider premature, and males lead females in every category.

TABLE 9.2

**Ratio of Male to Female Early Deaths (before age 65)
Leading Causes of Death (2002 U.S. Data)**

Cause of Death	Male/Female ratio
Heart disease	230:100
Malignant neoplasms (cancer)	110:100
Cerebrovascular disease (e.g., stroke)	117:100
Chronic lower respiratory diseases	106:100
Accidents*	185:100
Influenza and Pneumonia	138:100
Diabetes	138:100
Human immunodeficiency virus (HIV)*	239:100
Suicide[#]	407:100
Homicide[#]	341:100

*All ages
Calculated from Arias (2005). Except:
[#]calculated from Kochanek, Murphy, Anderson, & Scott (2004)

OTHER CAUSES OF DEATH

Table 9.2 also includes data from all ages for causes of death other than diseases: accidents, suicide, and homicide. You will note that the sex differences in these areas are very large. Thus, an alarming number of physically healthy men die from causes that are somewhat preventable. In fact, homicide is the leading cause of death for African American males between the ages of 15 and 34 and the second leading cause for 10–14 year olds (Anderson & Smith, 2005). Although it is a disease, most deaths from Human Immunodeficiency Virus (HIV) infections can be prevented through the avoidance of two types of behavior: unsafe sexual practices and sharing of intravenous drug syringes.

WHY DO MEN LIVE LESS LONG THAN WOMEN?

The above might strike you as an awkwardly worded title. It would be smoother to ask "Why do women live longer than men?" However, it appears that the difference in lifespan may be due more to men's lives being shortened rather than women's lives being lengthened.

Around the beginning of the twentieth century, men's lives and women's lives, on the average, were about the same length. In modern industrial nations such as the United

States, there has been a dramatic reduction in the risk of death from pregnancy and child-birth, which were relatively dangerous at the beginning of the twentieth century (Stillion, 1995). The decrease of this risk resulted in the lifespan sex differential. It could be said that both women's and men's lives were shortened 100 years ago, and that we have found ways to stop shortening women's lives. Hopefully, the same can be done for men. How-ever, it may become apparent to you that this is a complicated process.

There are two basic types of explanations for the sex difference in average lifespan. The first is a *biogenic* explanation. From this viewpoint, men die earlier because of ge-netic, hormonal, or other biological differences between the sexes. The second type of ex-planation is a *psychogenic* one, in which sex differences in lifespan are attributed to gender differences in psychological and social areas such as behaviors, socialization, and methods of problem solving.

Note that these two types of explanations do not necessarily compete with each other. It is possible for both biogenic and psychogenic factors to contribute to sex differences in lon-gevity. In fact, there is good evidence to suggest that both factors are operating in many cases. The question is one of the relative contribution of each factor. There has been a trend among researchers in recent years to speak of *biopsychosocial* models that take biology, in-dividual psychology, and the effects of other people and social systems into account in con-structing comprehensive pictures of behavioral phenomena.

It is also possible for biogenic and psychogenic factors to interact with one another. For instance, a man who is at high risk for heart disease because of his physiology (biogenic fac-tor) might be less likely than a woman to see a physician for regular checkups because he sees doing so as an admission of weakness and vulnerability, which he considers unmascu-line and therefore undesirable (psychogenic factor). The man in this example might have a shorter life than would be the case if either factor were operating in isolation.

In the above example, the biogenic factor might be the major contribution. It would also be possible for a psychogenic factor to make a major contribution while still interacting with a biogenic factor. For instance, a man might drink alcohol heavily in response to the pressure of meeting masculine gender role demands, thus damaging his body and shorten-ing his life, or he might use tobacco to enhance his masculine image, with a similar result.

BIOGENIC EXPLANATIONS

As I mentioned earlier, male fetuses are more vulnerable *in utero* than female fetuses, and the death rate for males aged 1–4 exceeds that of females. These data are ample evidence that biological factors operate in the lifespan sex differential, as it would be difficult to ar-gue that masculine socialization could have a profound effect on mortality at such an early age. Explanations of biological factors include genetic and hormonal sex differences.

Genetic Differences

The difference in males' and females' genetic makeup is that females have two X chro-mosomes and males have one X and one Y chromosome. When there are recessive disease genes on the X chromosome, having a second X chromosome turns out to be a genetic advantage. The second X chromosome often contains a dominant corresponding gene that protects the female from contracting the genetic disease. For example, if there is a gene for hemophilia on one X chromosome, the female will not contract the disease unless there is also a hemophilia gene on the other X chromosome, an extremely rare occurrence.

Because the form of the Y chromosome does not correspond exactly with that of the X chromosome, the male is not always afforded such protection. Genetic abnormalities on the X chromosome are much more likely to appear in the male because of the absence of a second (corrective) X chromosome. Some "X-linked" abnormalities like color blindness or baldness are relatively innocuous. Others are more serious. For instance, there is some speculation that dyslexia (a learning disability) and hyperactivity might be X-linked. A few genetic abnormalities, such as hemophilia, can be life threatening.

In the search for explanations of the sex differential in longevity, genetic differences make a very small contribution because of the rarity of life-threatening X-linked diseases. As Waldron (quoted in Dolnick, 1991) stated, "Most of the common X-linked diseases aren't fatal, and most of the fatal X-linked diseases aren't common" (p. 12).

Hormonal Differences

A major sex difference in hormones is in males' higher levels of testosterone and females' higher levels of estrogen. These two hormones account for physiological sex differences in average muscle size, body fat percentage, and metabolic speed. There is evidence to suggest that testosterone may render men somewhat more vulnerable to certain diseases, and that estrogen may have some protective effect.

The most demonstrable effect of these two hormones is in the area of heart disease. In recent years, the effect of cholesterol on heart disease has been the subject of much research and discussion. There are two kinds of cholesterol, high density lipoprotein (HDL), called "good cholesterol" because it protects against heart disease, and low density lipoprotein (LDL), called "bad cholesterol" because of its damaging effects.

In prepubescent males and females, HDL levels are about equal. At puberty, HDL levels drop rapidly in boys, but they hold steady in girls. This change coincides with the large surge of testosterone in boys and estrogen in girls. It is assumed that adolescent testosterone production is responsible for the reduction of HDL cholesterol, while estrogen has little or no effect on HDL levels (Dolnick, 1991).

LDL ("bad") cholesterol begins to rise in both males and females after puberty. However, males show a more rapid increase, leaving them more susceptible to heart disease. After menopause, when women's estrogen level is greatly reduced, LDL levels show this same kind of sharp increase. Therefore, researchers assume that estrogen has a protective effect against LDL cholesterol, while testosterone probably has little effect (Dolnick, 1991). These hormonal effects are important ones because heart disease is the leading cause of death. However, there is also some evidence that testosterone may shorten men's lives in other ways that are not fully understood.

Male cats who are neutered (a process that drastically lowers testosterone) live a good deal longer than those who are not (there is no corresponding effect for spayed female cats). Part of this difference is due to the fact that unneutered cats are more likely to fight, as testosterone is related to aggression in cats. Thus, these cats are more likely to die in fights. When cats that died in fights are eliminated from the data, however, a large lifespan difference between neutered and unneutered cats remains (Hamilton, Hamilton, & Mestler, 1969). Still, we can not be sure of the possible life-shortening effects of fighting, even if the cat does not actually die in a fight. Human boxers and football players do not live as long as most men, but we cannot necessarily attribute this difference solely to participation in the sport.

If we wanted to make a true experimental study of the effects of testosterone on human longevity, we could take a group of males, castrate them, and see if they live as long as their counterparts. This kind of experimentation is obviously not possible for ethical reasons. However, there have been times in history when castrations were performed on humans for various reasons, as recently as 1950! In China and the Ottoman Empire, castrated males (eunuchs) were employed as palace guards. They could guard harems of women without the possibility of sexual liaisons. In Europe, boys were castrated in order to keep their singing voices in prepubescent ranges (Daly & Wilson, 1983). In Kansas, mentally ill men and men of very low intelligence were sometimes castrated in order to reduce their aggressiveness (Hamilton & Mestler, 1969).

Historical anecdotes tell us that Chinese, Turkish, and Italian eunuchs seemed to live longer than other men, but no data on lifespan were collected. However, a research team studied 297 men who had been castrated at a Kansas institution for the mentally impaired. When compared with a matched group of inmates, the eunuchs' lives were an average of 14 years longer (Hawke, 1950).

What is the relative contribution of biogenic factors to sex differences in longevity? Estimates range from two-thirds of the approximate five and a half year difference (Dolnick, 1991) down to one-quarter (Waldron, 1976), and, because of the aforementioned interactions with psychogenic factors, apportioning ratios to either type of cause may be difficult and misleading. Almost all researchers would agree that biogenic factors are in operation. However, almost no researchers would say that these are the *only* factors that exist.

PSYCHOGENIC EXPLANATIONS

There are at least four ways in which psychological processes can contribute to illness, injury, and/or the shortening of a man's life. First, behaviors can be directly self-destructive. Suicide is obviously the best example of this type of psychogenic factor, but one might also consider the use of tobacco products or the excessive use of alcohol and other drugs in this category. These behaviors involve the person's active harm of his or her body. It is also possible for the person to passively harm his or her health by neglecting to perform behaviors that maintain health. For example, a man with high blood pressure who refuses to take the medication to control it, or someone who does not see a physician even though he has detected a symptom of cancer (when he has medical resources available to him) adversely affects his health through his behavior.

Third, some behaviors involve physical risk of illness, injury, or death. These behaviors include: sharing needles in intravenous drug use, drunk driving, and engaging in dangerous sports. Fourth, some psychological processes seem to have adverse effects on the body. For instance, the effects of stress on physical health are well documented, and there are also certain personality characteristics that are predictive of some physical conditions. I have separated these four categories of psychogenic factors for purposes of discussion.

Self-destructive Behaviors

Suicide. Suicide is, of course, the ultimate self-destructive behavior, and the overwhelmingly most common motive for it is to escape from one's pain. Although females in the United States are more likely than males to make suicidal gestures or attempts, U. S. males complete suicide attempts over four times more often than females (Arias, 2004). Adolescent girls make 90% of suicide attempts in that age group, while adolescent boys make 80% of completed suicides (Stillion & McDowell, 1996). Among 15–24 year olds, males commit suicide nearly six times more often than females (Anderson & Smith, 2005). Among older people, the ratio of male to female suicides is similar, and elderly suicide is on the rise (Colburn, 1996), with an alarming 33% increase among elderly males in the United States during the 1980s (Lester, 1997).

There is some conjecture that more women than men use suicide attempts to "cry for help" rather than as determined efforts to die, which are more common in men (Harrison, 1978). Women are also more likely to use suicide methods that have relatively low potential for death, such as overdose or wrist slashing, whereas men are more likely to use violent and highly lethal methods such as firearms or motor vehicles (Nolen-Hoeksema, 1998). Firearm suicides accounted for 60% of all male suicides (Anderson & Smith, 2005), compared to 39% of all female suicides (USBC, 1992). The lethality of method does not account for the whole difference, however. Males complete more suicides with every method (Canetto, 2000).

Traditional masculinity has several connections to suicidal behavior. Foremost among these is a gender-differentiated socialization for dealing with psychological pain. Whereas women have been taught to think about and express feelings, gain social support, and take care of themselves, men are socialized to act on problems, be hyperindependent, and disdain emotional self-care. The hypermasculine man in severe emotional distress is often alone with his pain. He cannot express it, and he cannot ask for help with it. If the pain becomes great enough, it may seem to him that suicide is his only option.

A second factor is the success, status, problem-solving orientation in gender-typed males. The masculine value of "getting the job done" may actually relate to the "job" of taking one's life. Stillion and her colleagues (1989) report anecdotal evidence from emergency room personnel that males who do not complete suicide attempts are often distressed over their "failure."

Finally, there is the masculine norm of independence. Needing and requesting help is antithetical to traditional masculinity. Teenagers who feel connected to their families are much less likely to engage in suicidal behavior (or violence and drug abuse), and the adolescent suicide sex differential may be related to families' demands for hyperindependence in boys (Pollack, 1998). Despondent men often feel alone with problems that seem unsolvable and pain that seems intractable. For these men, suicide may seem like the only alternative. It is apparent that, more often than females, males are unwilling to ask for help either before their problems escalate to the point of suicide contemplation, or by giving messages through a suicide gesture rather than a serious attempt.

It is also interesting to speculate about the two periods of development in which the suicide sex ratios are most unbalanced, adolescence and old age. Adolescence is the most gender-typed time of life, the time in which the boy begins to establish himself as a man, sometimes without healthy guides for doing so. Males who feel "unsuccessful" at meeting masculine demands may be at high risk for depression and suicide. In part because masculinity and heterosexuality are so intertwined, gay male teenagers are particularly at risk. Researchers estimated that 25–30% of gay adolescents have attempted suicide on at least one occasion (Hetrick & Martin, 1988).

In old age, the traditional hallmarks of masculinity begin to fade away. Men are culturally defined by physical abilities and the work role. The older man must face the facts that his body is declining and, after he retires, that he is no longer a valued contributor in the working world. If his sense of self is overly consumed by this narrow standard of masculinity, body and work role decline can seriously undermine his sense of self-worth. Additionally, the man may also be faced with a loss of independence at some point during his physical decline, which is also antithetical to the traditional masculine role.

The combination of pain and masculine bravado can indeed be a quite volatile one. In a strongly worded statement, Stillion and her colleagues (1989) describe this association:

> If we wanted to write a prescription for increasing suicide risk, we could not improve on the traditional male socialization pattern. Take one male child, who has higher levels of aggression and activity than his female peers. Put the child into competitive situations. Tell him he must win at all costs. Teach him that to admit fear or doubt is weakness and that weakness is not masculine. Complete the vicious circle by assuring him that his worth is dependent on winning games, then salary and promotion competitions, and you have the perfect recipe for enhanced suicide risk. (p. 243)

William Pollack (2000a) pointed out that, although more people die from suicide than from homicide in the United States, homicide prevention accounts for ten times the financial expenditure of suicide prevention.

Use of Tobacco.   Tobacco products are the only commodities legally sold in the United States that, when used as intended, will usually kill the consumer. The most common results of extended tobacco use are bronchitis, emphysema, asthma, and cancers of the respiratory system, mouth, and throat. In 1982, men outnumbered women in deaths by a three and a half to one ratio for bronchitis, emphysema, and asthma, and a two and a half to one ratio for lung, mouth, and throat cancer (Harrison et al., 1995).

In 1976, Waldron estimated that one third of the sex difference in longevity was attributable to the sex difference in smoking. Deaths from bronchitis, emphysema, and asthma are proportional to the number of cigarettes smoked (Harrison, 1978). Because the sex difference in smoking has been shrinking steadily since 1960, we might expect some of the disease proportions to also change (Harrison, et. al., 1995; Waldron, 1995). However, male smokers tend to engage in more dangerous smoking habits than women, including smoking more than 25 cigarettes a day, inhaling deeply, using products with high tar and nicotine content and/or cigarettes without filters (Courtenay, 2000a). Will Courtenay (2000b) summarizes the connections between gender and tobacco use:

> Cigarette smoking is considered the single most preventable cause of illness and death in the United States.... . Tobacco use accounts for roughly one in five deaths overall, and one in four deaths among those aged 35 to 64 years. *Twice as many male as female deaths are attributed to smoking*, and men's higher lifetime use of tobacco is considered a primary reason for their higher rates of cardiovascular disease and stroke. One quarter of all heart disease deaths are associated with smoking. The risk of heart disease and stroke among smokers is more than double the risk for nonsmokers, and the risk of sudden cardiac death is up to 4 times greater.... . Three of four men who get any kind of cancer are smokers. The lung cancer death rate for men is 2 1/2 times higher than the rate for women, and 9 of 10 male lung cancer deaths can be directly attributed to cigarette smoking. Men who smoke double their risk of prostate cancer. Regularly smoking cigars doubles a man's risk of lung cancer and increases his risk of oral cancer between 5 and 10 times. Smokeless tobacco users increase their risk of developing oral cancer by *nearly 50 times*. (pp. 8–9, emphases added)

"Smokeless" tobacco (chewing tobacco and snuff) is used by males almost exclusively. According to a Public Health Service survey, one out of six males had used these products within the past year. The average first use of smokeless tobacco is at age nine, and one quarter of users had their first taste of chewing tobacco before age five! There are 30,000 new cases of oral cancer each year in the United States, with an average of 8,000 deaths and a mortality rate of one-half of new cases within five years of diagnosis (Colburn, 1993).

Socialization of destructive masculine behaviors can certainly be implicated in tobacco use. Advertisers have long used masculine mystique approaches (e.g., the Marlboro Man) to sell their products by associating tobacco with desirable images of masculinity (self-assuredness, independence, and adventurousness). About 6 times more males than females smoke on prime time television, and *Sports Illustrated*, the number one magazine read by adolescent males, contains more tobacco advertisements than any other magazine (Courtenay, 2000a). Advertisers know that they can sell a great deal by playing on people's insecurities and then offering a product that promises to remove their misgivings about their adequacy. When one is asked to live up to vague and impossible standards of masculinity, what man would not feel insecure? This advertising is both reflective and encouraging of certain cultural values for men: Do whatever you want; don't worry about dying.

Neglectful Behaviors

Men sometimes shorten their lives or become ill because they fail to perform the behaviors necessary to maintain their health. For example, 30–50% of hypertension (high blood pressure) patients stop taking their medication, leaving them at increased risk for heart attack (Hackett, Rosenbaum, & Cassen, 1985). Men are disproportionately represented in this group.

Men can also create problems by failing to seek help or take time off from work when it is indicated, such as when they are injured, sick, emotionally distraught, or when they have not had a physical examination for a long time. Traditionally masculine men may see taking necessary medication and seeking help as admissions of weakness, vulnerability, and dependence, which go against the masculine cultural prescriptions to handle problems on one's own, focus outside of the self, be strong and invulnerable, and "take it like a man." Negative or extreme masculinity is related to poor health practices (Helgeson, 1990; Courtenay, 2000a; Eisler, 1995).

In a national survey conducted by the American Medical Association and the Gallup Poll, 40% of physicians endorsed the belief that over one-half of men aged 50 or older undermine potential lifesaving treatment for prostate or colorectal cancer (which kill an estimated 200,000 men per year in the United States), by ignoring symptoms, delaying treatment, or refusing to discuss symptoms. Embarrassment was cited as the major reason for failing to discuss medical problems (Royner, 1992). Women give more information and ask more questions during doctor visits than men. The average number of questions that a woman asks during a 15-minute visit is six; men average zero (Pleck, 1995)! Half of men do not know the symptoms of prostate and colorectal cancer, nor those of prostate enlargement, which affects 75% of men over the age of 50 (Friend, 1991).

Risk Behaviors

Men sometimes choose to engage in behaviors that involve the risk of injury, death, or legal sanction. For instance, habitual excessive drinking puts one at increased risk for liver disease and accidents. Drunk driving, drug dealing, sharing hypodermic needles, use of firearms, high-speed driving, engaging in gang violence, and working in dangerous jobs are other risky behaviors. Again, many more males than females participate in these behaviors (Patrick, Colvin, Fulop, Calfas, & Lavato, 1997). For instance, more than 90% of those arrested for alcohol and drug abuse violations are men (Kimbrell, 1991). Males die in car accidents more than twice as often as females and are nearly three times more likely to die in an accident in which they are driving while drunk. They drown nearly four times as often (National Safety Council, 1997)—more than eight times as often for males aged 14–34 (National Safety Council, 1996). Males account for 82% of spinal cord injuries (National Spinal Cord Injury Association, 2005).

Risk behaviors associated with masculinity are summarized in Box 9.3. Males are less knowledgeable than females about health in general and about symptoms of specific diseases, less responsive to health information, and less likely to utilize the health care sys-

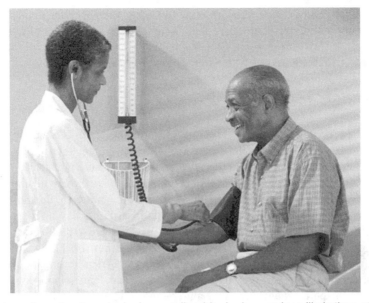

Men who adhere to stereotypical masculine ideologies are less likely than other men to do this: have regular medical checkups.

Photo courtesy of the National Institutes of Health, Washington, D.C.

TABLE 9.3

Masculine Risk Behaviors

overuse of alcohol	tobacco use
dangerous sports	criminal activity
refusing to see a physician	use of recreational drugs
refusing to wear a seat belt	engaging in physical fights
carrying weapons	consuming high amounts of fat
sleep deprivation	physical overexertion
refusing to wear sunscreen	failing to obatin health information
risky sexual practices	linoring symptoms of disease
taking risks in the workplace	lacking basic nutritional knowledge
eschewing social support	consuming high levels of dietary cholesterol
physical inactivlty	reglecting to do testicular self-examinations
dangerous driving practices	using anabolic steroids
refusing to wear a motorcycle helmet	driving drunk
working in dangerous occupations	

Sources: Courtenay (2000a, 2000b)

tem (Courtenay, 2000a). Men who subscribe to traditional masculine gender ideologies show a greater willingness than other men to engage in a wide range of risk behaviors (Courtenay, McCreary, & Merighi, 2002; Sabo, 1998). Our discussion will focus on three areas of risk: dangerous sports, war, and unsafe sexual practices.

Dangerous Sports

To say that sports and masculinity are strongly interconnected in U.S. culture seems like an understatement. The almost religious fervor with which many men approach athletics is evidence that sports have more importance to men than mere physical fitness. Ten of the 11 sports that are most dominated by male participation are those with high risks of injury (the exception is golf) (Kruckoff, 1993). For children under 14, the most dangerous four sports (football, baseball, basketball, and skateboarding), all with disproportionate numbers of male participants, are responsible for an estimated 410,000 emergency room visits in an average year (Wilson, Baker, Teret, & Garbarino, 1991).

An unfortunate minority of men and boys have suffered debilitating injuries and even death as a result of overexertion, physical contact, or accidents in sporting events. The most dangerous sports would seem to be auto racing and professional boxing. The object of the latter is to pummel one's opponent into unconsciousness. More than 50 professional boxers (such as Dipo Saloko and Robert Benson) have even died in the ring (Newfield, 2001). Others—such as former heavyweight champion Muhammad Ali, who now suffers from Parkinsonian symptoms—have suffered irreparable brain damage as the cumulative result of many years of repeated head traumas. For several years prior to his death in 1999, former heavyweight Jerry Quarry needed help putting on his shoes and cutting his food because of neurological impairment. It is estimated that 20% of professional boxers suffer some degree of permanent brain damage (Trafford, 1996), resulting in symptoms such as "memory loss, inattention, impaired hearing, paranoid ideas, and 'a decrease in general cognitive functions.'" (Newfield, 2001, p. 20).

Few men participate in auto racing and boxing relative to other violent sports such as ice hockey and football. The populations that engage in risky sports such as sky diving, hang gliding, scuba diving, mountain climbing, hunting, and contact sports is overwhelmingly male (Courtenay, 2000b). In 2004, ten football players died from injuries and overexertion (Mueller & Cantu, 2005). Heat-related illnesses killed 15 football players between 1996 and 2001 (Shapiro, 2001). There were 18 catastrophic injuries (such as permanent brain injuries or paralysis) in 2004 (Mueller & Cantu, 2005). 424,665 football players were treated in hospital emergency rooms for football injuries in 1995 (National Safety Council, 1996).

According to the ESPN documentary series (1994) *Outside the Lines*, the average number of concussions in the National Football League (NFL) is one per team per game. A concussion is a traumatic brain injury (where the brain is thrown against the inside of the skull) that temporarily disrupts the functioning of the brain. It renders the victim more susceptible to subsequent concussions, and multiple concussions can result in permanent neurological damage. Former Jets wide receiver Al Toon estimated that he suffered as many as 13 concussions during his eight-year professional career (Alloy, Jacobson, & Acocella, 1999) and reported that his head "has never been clear" since that time (ESPN, 1994). Approximately one quarter of a million high school football players suffer concussions each year (Alloy, Jacobson, & Acocella, 1999). Five percent of high school and college players who play football for three years sustain concussions (Reid, 2002). However, as many as three out of four college football players do not report their head injuries to team trainers or coaches because they do not think their symptoms are serious ("Many concussions go undetected, unreported," 2004).

Football is one of the ultimate expressions of hypermasculinity in the United States. It involves sacrifice of the body for a task and denial of basic instincts for self-preservation and safety. The average NFL player engages in 12,000 impacts per season (ESPN, 1992), the worst of which are the equivalent of a 25 mile per hour head-on automobile accident (Gugliotta, 2003), and these players die an average of 12-15 years before the average life expectancy (ESPN, 1992). In 2001, there were 290 National Football League players weighing at least 300 pounds, and it was estimated that the momentum generated by a 340-pound player running at 15 miles per hour (the equivalent of the 40 yard dash in 5.1 seconds, average for these players) is the same as a 17-pound bowling ball shot from a cannon at 300 miles per hour (Mihoces, 2002).

Television commentary of football injuries (and sports injuries in general) almost always involves reference to the task: "Will he return in the second half?"; "How will they contain the pass rush without their best blocker?"; "Will the other team exploit the substitute?" Imagine a television commentator reacting to an injury with "That must be disappointing and painful; I wonder how he feels about that?"

Contrary to popular belief, men are no more physically active than women, and the health risks from sedentary lifestyles are well documented. Among those who are physically active, males are much more likely than females to engage in "weekend warrior" kinds of exercise—infrequent but strenuous activity—that actually increases the risk of death from heart attack, perhaps as much as 100 times (Courtenay, 2000b). In response to the 1997 deaths of three wrestlers, the National Collegiate Athletic Association (NCAA) banned wrestlers from using dehydrating practices, such as wearing rubber suits and working out in high temperatures, to lose weight (Knight, 1998).

Another recent trend is the use of anabolic steroids to enhance muscle mass and athletic performance. It is estimated that 260,000 high school students and half of all NCAA Division I football players have used steroids. These substances are associated with a number of health problems, including high blood pressure, elevated cholesterol levels, liver damage, hyperthyroidism, cancers of the kidney and prostate, shrinkage of the testicles, obstructive lung disease, baldness, acne, mental health symptoms, and sterility (Sabo, 2005; Hancy, 1996; Klein, 1995).

War

Generation after generation, we have marched young men off to be killed in wars. In U.S. society, dying or being maimed in war is considered an act of heroism rather than as the victimization of a young man. Although participating in the defense of one's country might be considered to be a loving thing to do, only relatively recently have U.S. men been given a choice as to whether or not they would serve in the armed forces.

The wars of the twentieth century have been described as "holocausts of young men" in which millions of men were killed and over 100 million men were injured. The average age of World War I and II casualties was 18.5 years (Kimbrell, 1991). Thus, the victims of war tend to be the youngest men, who feel (and often are) less powerful, and who feel the strongest need to establish a sense of masculinity. Poor men and men of color, who are marginalized by mainstream U.S. culture, have also been disproportionately represented among the war dead. Many men who survived the modern, technological war in Vietnam returned with physical and emotional scars of profound proportions. It is perhaps no coincidence that the modern men's movement began at about this time, when it was becoming obvious that soldiers were finding it difficult to "take it like a man."

The recent wars in the Middle East brought up the question of whether women should be able to serve in combat. There seemed to be little awareness that perhaps *nobody* should be in combat. A letter to the advice columnist Ann Landers (Ziff, 1990) argued against women participating in combat because of its hardships. In this letter, the author states that, "combat means sleeping in a muddy foxhole, eating a can of beans for your main meal of the day, urinating and defecating wherever you happen to be, and keeping your toilet paper on your head under your helmet because it's the only dry spot on your entire body when it rains. Combat means watching your buddy step on a land mine and get blown to pieces." It is implicit in this person's letter that it is acceptable to subject men to these hardships.

Unsafe Sexual Practices

Males are nearly four times more likely than women to contract AIDS (Avert, 2005). It is only possible to get this disease through introduction of the Human Immunodeficiency Virus (HIV) into the bloodstream. This may happen by unfortunate accidents such as receiving an HIV-tainted blood transfusion, but the overwhelming majority of HIV infections occur through the sharing of hypodermic needles by intravenous drug users and through unsafe sexual practices.

It is not difficult to find connections between sexual risk behaviors and cultural prescriptions for masculinity. Foremost among these are the expectations that males will be sexually promiscuous and adventurous. Condom use reduces the risk of infection, but there is a good deal of resistance to using condoms, perhaps because their use involves an acknowledgment of one's vulnerability, as well as a caring for the self and the sexual partner. These orientations go against masculine norms. Poppen (1995) found that, among college students, males were much more willing than females to engage in risky sexual behavior, both with regard to partner choice (e.g., having more partners and partners they did not know well) and sexual risk behaviors (e.g. non-use of contraceptives and condoms). As Kimmel and Levine (1989) put it, "Abstinence, safer sex, and safer drug use compromise manhood. The behaviors required for the confirmation of masculinity and those required to reduce risk are antithetical." (p. 347). Men tend to underestimate their health risks across every domain of dangerous behavior (Courtenay, McCreary, & Merighi, 2002).

Adverse Physical Effects of Psychological Processes

Only recently has science begun to understand in some detail the connections between psychological and physiological processes. The relatively young field of behavioral medicine is focused on understanding and treating physical disorders that are thought to be strongly influenced by the person's psychological functioning (Gentry, 1984). Masculine socialization may well contribute to some physical disorders that are disproportionately experienced by men (Eisler & Blalock, 1991). Chief among these are cardiovascular disorders and peptic ulcers.

Cardiovascular Disorders

It has long been suspected that coronary artery disease and hypertension have strong relationships to stressful work settings and certain behavioral patterns of response to those environments. Hypertension is quite common among workers in highly stressful occupations (e.g., air traffic controllers, police officers). It is also common among those described as projecting an image of being easygoing but at the same time suppressing a good deal of anger (Hackett, Rosenbaum, & Cassen, 1985). It is not surprising that many African American men have problems with hypertension, given the emphasis in many African American cultures on "cool pose"—an outward appearance of calmness (Freiberg, 1991). At the same time, many of these men experience the anger that is created by membership in an oppressed group and by harsh masculine socialization. These men may experience the powerful internal conflict between these feelings and the demand to be "cool", and this conflict may be partially manifested in high blood pressure.

Several decades ago, cardiologists Meyer Friedman and Ray Rosenhan coined the term *Type A behavior* to describe a personality pattern commonly found in people who had suffered myocardial infarction (heart attack). This pattern described the classic compulsive, hostile, competitive, emotionally inexpressive "workaholic." Friedman (cited in Hackett et al., 1985) defined Type A as, "a characteristic action-emotion complex which is exhibited by those individuals who are engaged in a relatively chronic struggle to obtain an unlimited number of poorly defined things from their environments in the shortest period of time and, if possible, against the opposing efforts of other things or persons in this same environment." (p. 1154). Recent research indicates that the hostility component of Type A is more predictive of coronary heart disease than the other characteristics (Benson, 2003; Miller, Smith, Turner, Guijarro, & Hallet, 1996), and chronic anger and hostility is estimated to increase the risk of heart attack by a factor of three (Smith, 2003). Hostile personality is associated with four to five times the risk of death from all causes for the age group 25–50, thus it also carries risks beyond heart disease (Weiss, 1997), most notably, stroke (Williams et al., 2002).

Again we see vestiges of the destructive aspects of traditional masculinity in this pattern: the aggressive attempt to measure up to vague standards of achievement and competition. Type A individuals tend to be hyperindependent; they seize authority and dislike sharing responsibility. Contrary to popular belief, they tend to be less successful than those who are more relaxed and less aggressive (Hackett et al., 1985). Type A behaviors are significantly related to masculine gender typing (Grimm & Yarnold, 1985). Negative or extreme masculinity is also related to heart attack severity (Helgeson, 1990).

Helgeson (1995) proposes that certain aspects of traditional masculinity interact with biological factors to produce high levels of coronary risk. Not only is traditional masculinity associated with Type A behavior, but it is also linked with low levels of social support and poor health care practices, which are both linked with masculine hyperindependence as well as with coronary risk.

It is clear that men are biologically predisposed toward certain physical health problems. This predisposition interacts with certain aspects of masculine socialization, as well as with the negative effects of dangerous, historically male environments. Women who expose themselves to these environments and exhibit traditionally masculine behaviors increase their health risks (Rodin & Ickovics, 1990). Thus, it is hazardous to be male, and it is also hazardous to be negatively masculine. Lippa, Martin, and Friedman (2000) found that people of both sexes who score high on measures of masculinity were more likely to die at every age than those who scored low. Thus, in addition to sex, gender is a significant factor in mortality. In fact, this relationship is a strong one. As the researchers note, "The increase in mortality risk in masculine individuals...was comparable to increases in mortality risk associated with physiological factors such as elevated blood pressure." (p. 1568).

Moreover, according to Stanistreet, Bambra, and Scott-Samuel (2005), who undertook a comparative study of 51 countries, high levels of patriarchy in a society are associated with higher mortality in men. The authors opine that, "The same practices that represent men's capacity to oppress women and promote their interest in doing so are also systematically harming men." (p. 874). A specification of these factors awaits further research; we do not yet know exactly how patriarchy harms men's health.

Sidney Jourard said it best in his landmark 1971 article, "Some Lethal Aspects of the Male Role." Jourard described a set of human needs: to know and be known, to depend and be depended upon, to love and be loved, and to find some purpose and meaning in one's life. The masculine role is poorly designed to fill these human needs. It requires us to "be noncommunicative, competitive and nongiving, and to evaluate life successes in terms of external achievement rather than personal and interpersonal fulfillment" (Harrison, 1978, p. 13). Jourard's belief was that this not only limited the quality of our emotional lives, but that it also had the effect of slowly destroying us physically. Only recently have researchers and practitioners begun to address the gendered aspects of health and well-being for men. Some of these efforts are described in Chapter 15.

SUMMARY

1. There are many health problems that are more common in men than in women. Men's average lifespan is more than five years shorter than that of women as a result of a number of factors.

2. Biogenic explanations for sex differences in disease and longevity include male chromosomal vulnerability, the damaging effects of testosterone, and the protective effects of estrogen.

3. Psychogenic explanations for sex differences in disease and longevity include the masculine denial of vulnerability, self-destructive behaviors, eschewal of self-care, risky sexual behaviors, and the cultural expectation to take part in dangerous sports and in war.

4. Stressful work environments and typical masculine responses to them also take their toll on health and longevity. There is a growing awareness that living up to masculine gender demands involves the denial of some basic human needs, and that the results may be illness, injury, and\or premature death.

10

Men at Work:
Jobs, Careers, and Masculinity

If there is anything that men have been about throughout history, it is work. From the assembly line worker to the chief executive officer, most men in the Western world define themselves according to their jobs. An important part of the masculine socialization process is oriented toward preparing males for the working world. Many scholars (e.g., Lerner, 1986; Basow, 1992) have argued that gender roles are mainly a result of the historical division of labor between men and women. From this perspective, it is not surprising that the last several decades have witnessed changes in the ways that people think about gender as the working world undergoes significant evolution. Women are entering the paid work force in record numbers and rightfully demanding that they be treated as equals. Many men are having trouble adjusting to increasingly mixed-sex environments, especially those in which women are in positions of authority. More and more labor-saving devices are becoming available, and the competition-oriented, individualistic working culture is giving way to team building, quality circles, and environments where cooperation is valued. As a result, there are fewer and fewer places for the physically powerful working man or the hard-nosed manager, and more and more places for the technician and the executive with "people skills."

Although much of the mainstream masculine value system encourages being a good worker, it may do so at a considerable cost. Additionally, some aspects of masculine gender role socialization are counterproductive to functioning in many modern workplaces. And although changing gender roles create considerable stress for many, they also provide exciting opportunities for men (and women) in the working world. In this chapter, we investigate the relationships between masculinity and work. In order to provide a context, we look first at changes in the sex-based division of labor, with special attention to relatively recent economic developments in the United States.

A HISTORY OF WORK AND THE SEXES

You will often hear people speak of the "traditional" family in which the husband works outside of the home and the wife works full time on child care and other domestic duties. Stephanie Coontz (1997) points out that this conception of the family has only existed for about 150 years. Moreover, the work of a significant proportion of U.S. families has not fit this pattern, even in the decade of the 1950s, the heyday of the dichotomous breadwinner-homemaker ideology. In the 60 years prior to the turn of the twenty-first century, the percentage of U.S. working households with single-earner married couples went from 66% to 25%, and is predicted to decline further, to 17% by 2030 (Clay, 2005).

In a section of her book entitled "The Late Birth and Short Life of the Male Breadwinner Family," Coontz (1997) dispels the myth that sex-based labor division is traditional, except in a very narrow historical frame: "One of the most common misconceptions about modern marriage is the notion that coprovider families are a new invention in human history. In fact, today's dual-earner family represents a return to older norms, after a very short interlude that people mistakenly identify as 'traditional.'" (p. 54).

For the vast majority of human history, labor chiefly consisted of hunting animals and gathering edible vegetation. Societies based on other forms of labor are a relatively recent phenomenon, comprising only about two percent of the time in which people have inhabited the Earth (Collins, 1979). In these hunter-gatherer societies, which still exist in some parts of the world, women nearly always contributed equal or larger amounts of the community food supply compared to men. There is some evidence that gender roles in these societies tended to be more egalitarian and cooperative than in most modern cultures, as men and women worked together as economic partners. As Nancy Bonvillain (2001) notes, "In many foraging bands, women's and men's interdependent contributions to their households were reflected in equality of social relations and social status." (p. 17).

When people learned to plow, plant, and domesticate animals, some 6000 years ago, the character of gender arrangements changed. Plowing required one to be relatively far from home, thus it became largely the man's job. Producing offspring meant more help in the fields, and thus there was economic advantage to control women's sexuality and reproduction (Lerner, 1986).

Another important change characterized agrarian societies. There was no longer a need for people to be nomadic. In hunter-gatherer societies, survival depended on moving to where vegetation and game were available. In agrarian societies, people could stay in one place and produce food with a little cooperation from nature. There was a certain harmony with the earth, and husbandry, the cultivation and respect of nature, became a dominant value (Keen, 1991). Sons spent a good deal of time working with and learning from their fathers. Thus, there was a sense of intergenerational continuity (Stearns, 1991). Civilizations and communities took on a relatively permanent, and therefore more elaborate, character.

Land was now useful and valuable for long periods of time, generation after generation. It became something a person owned, dealt, protected, and willed to heirs. Land meant food, and food meant wealth. Institutions were created to deal with land transac-

---

Box 10.1: *The Gods Must Be Crazy*

The Gods Must Be Crazy illustrates the social changes that resulted from property ownership. This movie describes a civilization of Bush People in the Kalahari Desert of South Central Africa. In their community, there are no scarce resources to compete for, and therefore no ownership. In the movie, a scarce resource (humorously, a Coca-cola bottle discarded from a small airplane) is introduced into the culture, and results in competition and aggression. This movie provides an interesting commentary on modern societies.

---

tions. The most notable institution was *patriarchy*, the system by which males dominated public and private life. *Primogeniture* was the patriarchal arrangement by which sons inherited property from their fathers and passed it on to their sons. This system established male social and economic dominance, as well as the control of women's sexuality by men (Lerner, 1986).

Susan Basow (1992) described changes in the !Kung society of Africa, a foraging society which has moved to the agrarian way of life during the last few decades. She noted that women's mobility is more restricted and that they contribute less to the food supply than before. Children's play groups are becoming more sex segregated, and aggression has increased. Basow argues that agrarian society is historically responsible for gender inequity, and that these types of societies are the bases for every industrialized society in the world.

Property ownership and patriarchy changed masculinity in important ways. Men created institutional laws to protect their land, but physical force also came to be used, hence the transition of man the planter to man the warrior. In hunter-gatherer societies, men bonded together in order to share resources in the hunt, and the kill was shared by all the community. After property ownership, men's bonds were in the service of killing other men. Therefore, organized violence became a hallmark of masculinity. Sam Keen (1991) speculated that the masculine ethic of cooperation gave way to an ethic of conquest at this time, and that the quest for harmony became a quest for control. He also noted that men from victorious armies routinely raped the women of the conquered territories. Thus, we see in these societies the origins of negative masculinity: violence, over-competitiveness, dominance over women, and physical risk.

Patriarchy also dictated that men should control their children's (especially their male children's) lives. Fathers had to see that their sons learned to act properly, since they would someday control the family wealth. In Western cultures, this gave rise to an ethic of discipline, which was sometimes administered physically. The punitive nature of this relationship created a tension between affection and resentment for both father and son (Stearns, 1991).

The division of labor in agrarian societies was not nearly as sharp as it has been in the last one and a half centuries in the industrialized world. Typically, family members worked alongside each other in farming or small businesses. The co-provider family remained the norm, as it has been throughout most of human history (Coontz, 1997).

The turn of the nineteenth century witnessed the dawn of the Industrial Revolution. Hand tools were increasingly replaced by machines, and production became more large-scale and centralized in factories. Industrialization continues to spread throughout the world.

Since patriarchy was firmly established by this time, since the vast majority of industrial work was at a distance from the home, and since a good deal of this labor required physical strength, factory work became largely men's work. Women were expected to withdraw from the paid labor force following marriage and to work full-time at domestic duties and child care. Men began to specialize in paid employment outside of the home and abdicated their traditional child care duties to their wives. In times of male labor shortages, more women worked outside of the home, but their work was devalued, and they were pushed aside by men when jobs became scarce.

In the transition from co-provider to single-earner families, women's contributions to economic life tended to become less direct. Although most families could no longer survive by farming, crafting, and trading, they could not rely solely on ready-to-use goods that they purchased from the husband's earnings. Many families could afford fabric but not clothing, flour but not bread, seeds but not vegetables. Among many other duties, the wife's work was to turn these raw materials into useable goods with her cooking, sewing, gardening, and other skills. Thus, women's work was critical for family functioning, but men's work became increasingly associated with wage earning (Coontz, 1997).

The development of many masculine gender role norms can be laid at the doorstep of industrialization. First and foremost is the establishment of the breadwinner role, which Gould (1974) described as the beginning of "measuring masculinity by the size of a paycheck." Socially, masculine attractiveness is based largely on economic power. Many men attempt to project a masculine image through external success, not internal fulfillment. Gould noted that if a man "flashed a roll of bills, no one would see how little else there was of him." (p. 97).

A second and equally important development of industrialization was a renewal of the antifeminine element of masculinity. The increased polarization of men's and women's work led to a belief that work outside and inside the home are the natural environments for men and women, respectively, an ideology that many writers refer to as "the doctrine of separate spheres." Doing "women's work" became an increasing threat to masculinity, as did spending too much time in the home and in the company of women. Exclusively male lodges and other social and recreational organizations became popular as avenues for fulfilling a perceived need for safe haven from women's "sphere." Men became increasingly hostile to femininity, and, by extension, to women themselves. Scott Coltrane (1998) and other anthropologists have noted the connection between the level of sex segregation in a society and the frequency of men's violence against women.

The Industrial Revolution ushered in the age of specialization. In agrarian societies, a man plants, reaps, takes care of animals, and is able to see the fruits of his labor. In contrast, the industrial worker may spend the better part of a lifetime putting a single bolt on each of a million machines. Karl Marx first described the dehumanizing character of such a job. Although agrarian man could take pride in the *process* of planting, growing, and harvesting, industrial man is focused on *outcome*, the amount of money produced.

For most men, this was not a lot of money, as the few powerful men exploited the many less powerful men. Most men became (and still are) "work objects" (the term "object" in reference to a person was first coined by Marx). Objectification is the denial of the person's humanness. Just as many women have historically been treated as sex objects, men have been exploited as work objects. However, women were, and are, also work objects, as their domestic labor went largely unpaid and viewed as secondary to men's labor (Coontz, 1997).

Men have also been war objects. When the work of the wealthy and powerful involves organized violence, it often becomes the task of poor young men. Most victims of recent wars are young men, sometimes even teenaged boys, the least powerful males in the society. A disproportionate number of victims were men of color. The more privileged of men were (and are) often allowed to opt out of combat, or of military service altogether.

The stereotype of men as socially and economically powerful does not fit the experience of most men. Although men as a group retain more economic power than women, the vast majority of men have jobs, not careers. They sacrifice and labor day after day, under the pressure to be a good provider for their families. The necessity of doing so makes many men vulnerable to exploitive employers. Emotional expression is also of little value to the factory worker.

Perhaps the most profound effects of industrialization on masculinity were that it effectively banished men from their homes (Keen, 1991), and devalued domestic work. It is no surprise that many men who subscribe to the breadwinner ideology are not very relationship oriented. They spend the vast majority of their time on tasks away from their families and view any work that takes place in the home as "women's work." When the father returns home at the end of the day, he finds it difficult to flip the switch that turns on all of the emotional and relationship attitudes that he has suppressed all day at work. As Robert Bly (1990) put it, "When a father, absent during the day, returns home at six, his children receive only his temperament, and not his teaching." The result is the disconnection of father and child (Keen, 1991) and an intergenerational pattern of masculine alienation.

The ethic of paternal discipline carried over from agrarian societies, but now fathers had to assert this role after coming home from the industrial workplace. This may have involved more physical punishment both as a function of diminished contact with children (Stearns, 1991) and work strain on the father (Stearns, 1990). Many sons now had to deal with fewer positive contacts with fathers in addition to harsher discipline.

Far from being a "natural" economic arrangement, the male breadwinner role was a relatively recent development, a historical artifact of the transition from agricultural to industrial society. Although the ideal of male breadwinner-female homemaker began to take hold early in the nineteenth century, a majority of families did not have this arrangement until the 1920s, and, despite many people's nostalgia for the 1950s, only about 60% of children in the United States grew up in this kind of family even during that decade. As a result of a decrease in real wages and a sharp increase in the cost of housing, the single-income arrangement is untenable for most families. Married women who are employed full-time now contribute more than 40% to the family income. In historical context, no sooner had the male as sole breadwinner family arrived on the scene that it began to disappear (Coontz, 1997). Gender roles are (and will most likely continue to) change in conjunction with changes in the sex-based division (or, increasingly, the non-division) of labor. Contrary to popular belief, there is mounting evidence that the majority of two-earner families find considerable satisfaction in both work and domestic life (Barnett & Rivers, 1996).

Although many people throughout the world continue to be employed in industrial and preindustrial settings, large segments of the population are involved in work that is characterized as postindustrial. This recent trend is a movement away from the production of goods and toward the provision of information and services. In these settings, physical strength is not highly valued, as labor-saving devices have been developed and thus men have no biologically based advantage over women. Because a single income is no longer sufficient for most families, and because many women want to claim their right to be full economic partners in society, these settings are becoming increasingly heterogeneous.

Work outside the home is no longer the exclusive province of men, and thus social changes are taking place. We will return to a discussion of these changes later in this chapter. Before doing so, a description of men's issues around work seems appropriate.

NET WORTH EQUALS SELF-WORTH: THE SOCIALIZATION TO WORK

Masculine gender socialization is largely oriented toward preparing boys for work. Boys are often asked at a young age, "What do you want to be when you grow up?" They learn that the right answer is not "a husband, father, and friend", but rather a worker of some kind. Males tend to develop an occupational "dream" in childhood and strive to attain it in adulthood (Levinson et al., 1978). Boys are impressed very early in life with the idea that gainful employment is manly. The masculine values of competition, task completion, and independence serve to provide attitudes conducive to functioning in a wide variety of work settings.

Sports and play are a training ground for the world of work. Boys' sports usually have elaborate sets of rules, score keeping, and clear cut winners and losers (Pasick, 1990). Sports results are quantifiable in terms of wins and losses, batting averages, and other statistics that invite comparisons between players and teams. The amount of adulation a boy receives for being an athletic success is matched by the amount of adulation a man receives for being a career success. We see connections between sports and work in the language of the business world: "Who are the players?" "They have a good batting average." "Let's see if we can get them to play ball with us." An easy business deal is sometimes referred to as a "slam dunk."

The messages are clear. In the athletic world, you are a valued person if you are a winner. Later, being a winner translates into being a *bread*winner—a vocational success. In fact, many men's very definition of their masculine value depends on their occupational statuses. As Pasick (1990) pointed out, "For males in our culture, simply passing through puberty is not sufficient to enter adulthood." (p. 39). One can not "be a man" without masculine (economic) power. The important factor is the outcome, not the process. Success for men is often defined in terms of being "better" by getting promotions, having high job status, and making more money. Women tend to be more oriented toward providing a helpful service (Bridges, 1989), although there is a great deal of variability in occupational values both within the population of men and within the population of women.

The man-as-breadwinner association of masculinity with work and money can hardly be denied. Anybody that works knows that it is a two-edged sword with both advantages and disadvantages. The work tradition has gotten men where they are today, in both a positive and a negative sense.

Positive Masculinity and Work

Ruth Hartley's classic (1959) essay on masculine socialization includes the statement that, "On the positive side, men mostly do what they want and are very important." (p. 463). The social status and economic power that men-as-a-group have enjoyed from work is unmistakable. The fact that men are less often the victims of job discrimination than women has given many men opportunities for self-determination. It has even been argued that, just as many women face a "glass ceiling" (an invisible barrier to entry into high management positions), majority men have sometimes been advantaged by a "glass escalator" (Williams, 2001). As of 2002, women occupied the Chief Executive Officer (CEO) position in only six of the 500 top U.S. companies and held only 15.7% of officer-level corporate executive positions (Downey, 2002). Of course, this gendered workplace advantage is rarely in evidence for minority men, who have been occupationally marginalized throughout U.S. history.

Work can be quite satisfying. Men who are fortunate enough to have careers (reimbursable means of expressing an important part of the self) as opposed to jobs (labor done solely for economic survival) may find the challenge and satisfaction of their work to be one of the most fulfilling aspects of their lives. It also goes without saying that money goes a long way toward making life easier and more enjoyable. Traditionally, men's orientation toward task completion and self-reliance, together with work opportunity, has made economic and career success a strong possibility for many. The "winners" may get some of the best that life has to offer: status, material wealth, and the opportunity to make a difference.

Men who have not been able to enjoy satisfying work have nevertheless been able to take pride in fulfilling the breadwinner role, a traditional expression of masculine love. Historically, many men have felt a deeply emotional investment toward this role, which also has clear social value (Stearns, 1991). Mark Kiselica (2005) describes his feelings about his father's work ethic:

> My father is the most wonderful man I have ever known. He overcame a tragic childhood—including the death of his dear mother when he was only about 8 years old, a ne-

Men's physical labor has traditionally been a source of pride and an opportunity for male camaraderie.

Photo © Bettman / Corbis

glectful and exploitive alcoholic father, debilitating injuries to his leg and hip, poverty, and a lack of education—to be the most wonderful parent any child could ever wish for. My father worked two jobs—one as a maintenance mechanic in a factory, the other as a painter—always in excruciating pain, and literally had to drag himself out of bed every day in order to limp off to work so that he could earn a living to support our family, consisting of my mom and my four siblings and me. And he did all of this, never once complaining, all out of his love for his family. He is a truly heroic man, and I will always adore him.

Negative Masculinity and Work

Although vocational success carries with it great rewards, they can come at a cost to the man's relationships, leisure pursuits, and health. It is also important to note that many, perhaps most, men do not feel successful, and the association of success and masculinity for these men may lead to chronic feelings of inadequacy. Following is a list of some potentially damaging effects of the masculine gender role in the world of work:

1. *You only hurt the ones you love*: Many men work in frustrating environments, for example the assembly line worker who is bored and unable to find much job satisfaction, the mechanic who faces difficult problems and time pressure, or the middle

manager who faces pressure from both his subordinates and his superiors. Some have not learned how to deal with the emotional aspects of work frustration. They have been raised to ignore emotion, especially if it is connected to feelings of weakness or powerlessness. Some of these men deal with these feelings by projecting them outside of the self. Because spouses and other family members are most available for these projections, they may bear the brunt of these negative emotions, and this can lead to strained family relationships. A spouse interviewed for Weiss's (1990) study illustrates the effects of "bringing work home":

> He is so proud, telling people that he works things out for himself and he doesn't worry his family.... Well, that really isn't the case. Because what happens is, (if) he has a problem, whatever it is, whether it's a business slowdown or a difficult supplier or whatever, he is just a *bear*... to live with until he has worked it out.... If we say, 'What is the problem?,' he will say, 'What do you mean, what is the problem?' (p. 99)

Box 10.2 illustrates a negative interaction between a man's work and family life.

Box 10.2: Work, Family, and Masculinity

A television commercial for a bank's financial planning services shows a middle-aged man standing in a nicely appointed suburban kitchen and speaking to the camera as sentimental music plays in the background:

"For years, I worked my fingers to the bone, going to the office nights and weekends, so that Beth and the girls could have what we wanted. Then one day it hit me: I've made it! Now I want for all of us—especially the girls—to enjoy all that we have for a long time to come."

There are several interesting aspects to this 30-second commercial. First, there is the man's satisfaction of having achieved some vocational success. This is one of the most fulfilling aspects of the traditional masculine role. Second is his commitment to the provider role, which is traditionally the way that men have expressed love for their families.

A few other messages are beneath the surface. First, making money is not enough. This is an advertisement for financial management services. A "real man" must know what to do with money after he has earned it. This is another role demand that entails the acquisition of a variety of skills, and which may or may not be compatible with his job skills. Second, and most importantly, "Beth and the girls" may not know who this man is. If he has been working nights and weekends, he probably has not had much time to maintain a close relationship with his wife, and he has probably missed the chance to be closely involved with his daughters as they grow. The former opportunity may be recoverable; the latter will never be.

As an aside, the phrase, "especially the girls" is puzzling. For some reason, their welfare supersedes that of his wife in his mind.

2. *What price glory?*: The competitive, pressure-packed nature of masculine occupational striving is associated with a wide variety of physical and mental health problems such as heart disease, ulcers, back pain, alcoholism, and suicide (Harris, 1992). Men are much more likely than women to work in hazardous environments, and an overwhelming proportion of workplace injuries and deaths involve male victims.

3. *The burden of proof*: A conventionally gendered man proves his masculinity by succeeding in work and being "number one." However, a single success, no matter how significant, does not last. There is always another goal to set and accomplish. If a man is fortunate enough to become "number one" at something, he can only remain in this position by continuing to compete with and vanquish his opponents. Thus, the validation of masculinity involves attempting to prove something that is essentially unproveable. Satisfaction, for many men, becomes a dangerous feeling, since it may inhibit further competition. In the world of sports (the leading masculine metaphor for work), we hear sportscasters lauding players and coaches who can never be satisfied. We hear athletes talking about next year's season less than an hour after they have won the championship! Box 10.3 illustrates the cultural expectation that men should never be satisfied.

4. *You've got to break a few eggs to make an omelet*: A man who wishes to "work his way up" in an organization may have to subordinate his individuality to the wishes of his superiors. Of course, nearly everybody alters their behavior to adapt to social situations, so it is a matter of degree. To what extent are men willing to move against their personalities and values in order to "fit in" at work?

Many business organizations expect gender stereotypical behavior from men, and men who do not display such behavior often forfeit the opportunity for advancement. Therefore, the man who refuses to act like "one of the boys" may not succeed, regardless of his level of competence. If he plays the masculine role to gain approval, he may experience a high level of gender role strain. In corporate culture, a large part of this strain is based in the organization's encouragement for men to emphasize the work role over the family role (Bowen & Orthner, 1991).

The extent to which a man will compromise his behavior to fit the work environment involves a decision that each individual must make. Is he willing to engage in derogatory humor, wear ties and white dress shirts, lie to customers? Because men are socialized against introspective skills, they may have difficulty in accessing the information necessary to make these decisions.

Crites and Fitzgerald (1978) described the constriction of human qualities in order to meet organizational demand as a "straitjacket of success" that requires a the man to "be able to obey rules and follow orders, regardless of how silly and unnecessary they may seem... to control and hide true feelings when faced with an incompetent superior... (to be) intensely loyal to an employer, yet able to transfer that loyalty when you change jobs." These prescriptions produce men who are "expedient, shallow, conforming but competitive, and ultimately ruthless" (p. 44).

Box 10.3: *Masculinity, Work, and Satisfaction*

A television commercial for a corporation depicts a football coach berating his team at halftime for their performance. After several highly critical statements, one of the players looks up and says, "Coach, aren't we ahead by 21 points?" The coach replies, "That's what I mean... the moment you're satisfied as a football *player*, we're finished as a football *team*."

This is a commercial for a corporation, which is trying to communicate that its people are never satisfied. It is no mistake that the advertiser chose football, the most hypermasculine of pursuits, to illustrate the corporate ethic. You must never be satisfied with what you do. It will never be enough. Moreover, satisfaction is sometimes defined as *dangerous*. A satisfied person is thought to lose the competitive "edge."

According to humanistic theory, extreme conformity to outside demands leaves one feeling alienated and out of touch with the self-actualizing tendency. The man may sacrifice some of his human potential in order to strive for external success. This conflict is common among working men (Cournoyer & Mahalik, 1995; O'Neil, 1981a, 1981b).

5. *Cast your fate to the wind*: Job or career success are often dependent upon factors that are beyond the man's control, and perhaps, his understanding. The American myth that working hard enough always brings success may be a reality for the talented and privileged, but the "average Joe" depends at least partly on opportunity and the vicissitudes of the market. The combination of subscribing to the American myth and equating economic success with masculinity leaves the average man feeling emasculated.

6. *You can't win if you don't play*: Equating masculinity with vocational accomplishment has especially damaging effects on men who encounter significant barriers to meaningful employment. In many poor segments of society, few opportunities for work, education, or training are provided, yet the men in these subcultures tend to subscribe to the "money equals masculinity" value (Liebow, 1969). Is it any wonder that some of these men turn to illegal activities such as drug dealing? They may see such activities as their only opportunity to validate their masculinity through economic success. The high rates of incarceration, violence, and drug use among economically disadvantaged men of color are not the result of negative influences in ethnic subculture. Rather, they are the result of the oppressive nature of mainstream U.S. culture, which imparts its masculine values to these men while at the same time blocking most avenues for them to participate in the American Dream.

Employed men who lose their jobs through economic downturn, injury, or even retirement face a battle to retain their masculine self esteem. Kamarovsky (1940/1971) published a classic study of 59 unemployed men and their families.

Box 10.4: *Death of a Salesman*

Arthur Miller's classic (1949) play, *Death of a Salesman*, is a brilliantly insightful examination of the relationship between masculinity, work, and family. Willy Loman, the lead character, is a salesman in his sixties. His job skills are deteriorating, and thus his value to his employer is decreasing rapidly.

Because Willy is relatively poor, and because his self-esteem is almost wholly invested in his work identity, he is suffering emotionally. He is a traditional man who refuses to admit vulnerability, and so he tries to delude himself into believing that the best is yet to come. He frequently fantasizes about his brother Ben, a successful and adventurous man who reminds Willy of the differences between the brothers' wealth: "When I was seventeen I walked into the jungle, and when I was twenty-one I walked out. And by God I was rich."

Willy Loman wholly subscribes to the value that wealth equals masculinity and self-worth. Underneath, he has the painful feeling that he has not been courageous or industrious enough. He says, "The world is an oyster, but you don't crack it open on a mattress." To make matters worse, Willy's two sons, Biff and Happy, are also unsuccessful. Because Willy cannot deal directly with his feeling of failure, he deals with it indirectly through his sons, alternately berating them for their irresponsibility and pumping them up with unrealistic dreams of instant success. Biff occa-

sionally tries to fight through his father's denial, but the effect is to flood Willy with overwhelming pain.

Willy's feelings of emasculation and depression peak in intensity when he loses his job and can no longer deny that his sons are also not on the path to success. He takes the provider role so seriously that he contemplates suicidet to bequeath $20,000 (a huge sum of money in the 1940s) in insurance money to his family. In an imaginary conversation with Ben, Willy says, "A man can't go out the way he came in, Ben, a man has got to add up to something." Willy has come to feel that he has only added up to an insurance policy, and thus that he is worth more dead than alive.

Because of his sense of loss and hopelessness, his feelings of failure as a father and worker, and his ardent desire to live up to the masculine ideal of the good provider, Willy finally commits suicide by intentionally having a car wreck. Ironically, he does so in the same week that the final payment on the family house is made, a joyous occasion for most couples. In some ways, Willy was a success: he provided an acceptable standard of living for years, and purchased a house "free and clear." But traditional standards of masculine success demand much more, and Willy did not feel free or clear. *Death of a Salesman* details the tragedy of a man who would rather die than re-define his masculinity.

Many of these men were ridiculed, blamed, and rejected by their families for failing to fulfill the provider role. They also tended to blame themselves and to suffer from depressive symptoms. Unemployment remains a strong predictor of gender role strain (Stillson, O'Neil, & Owen, 1991).

Retirement presents a difficult transition for many men, as they must leave the activity through which they have defined themselves for most of their lives. Although most men report a satisfactory adjustment to retirement, as many as 15–20% of men report being unhappy (Parnes & Nestel, 1981). Box 10.4 depicts the tragic story of an unsuccessful man at retirement.

7. *What have you done for me lately?* As I pointed out in Chapter 4, early masculine socialization shapes behavior, but ongoing social contingencies maintain it. Successful men have their masculinity affirmed frequently across many social settings. Conversely, less than successful men are socially devalued. Fogel and Paludi (1984) reported that occupationally unsuccessful men are viewed less favorably than unsuccessful women.

Socially, successful men are defined as the most desirable partners for dating and marriage. It is not surprising that men learn to connect sexuality with money. It is said that "Power is an aphrodisiac." A business deal is sometimes referred to as, "getting into bed with" the partner. In a classic article on work and masculinity, Gould (1974) remarked on the association of men's money and their sexual desirability:

> Women have been taught that men who achieve success are the best 'catches' in the marriage market. Women have also been taught that the right motives for marriage are love and sexual attraction. Thus, if a woman wants to marry a man with money, she has to believe she loves him; that he is sexually appealing—even if the real appeal is his money.... Many women learn to make this emotional jump: to feel genuinely attracted to the man who makes it big, and to accept the equation of moneymaking power with sexual power. There are many phenomenally wealthy men in the public eye who are physically unattractive by traditional criteria; yet they are surrounded by beautiful women and an aura of sexiness and virility (p. 97).

8. *When enough is never enough*: Men who overemphasize the work role sometimes fall prey to what are commonly referred to as workaholism or success addiction. A *workaholic* is someone who works because it provides a feeling of self-worth that they can not find anywhere else (Wilson-Schaef & Fassel, 1988). Pasick (1990) describes two major negative outcomes for workaholics. First, their families and other relationships suffer, if only from a lack of time in interpersonal contact. Second is the constant tension and worry that workaholics tend to experience around their job performance. Box 10.5 describes the relationship of a workaholic and his family.

9. *The lonely hunter*: A singular striving for success is often incompatible with the formation of relationships. I have already pointed out the negative aspects of the suc-

Box 10.5: The Blue Collar Workaholic

A therapist related the story of a woman who "dragged" her husband into marital therapy under threat of divorce. He was an automobile mechanic who worked a 40-hour-per-week job and had a free-ance business in his home garage on evenings and weekends. His side business provided more than enough work and a good deal of money, but he rarely spent more than a few minutes with his wife or family before the phone would ring or someone would pull into the driveway in need of repairs.

When the therapist asked him why he worked such long hours, the man said, "I don't want to retire at 65 like my father; I'm going to retire at 45." It was clear that this man was chasing a quantifiable and probably mythical definition of success, to the detriment of his family. One has to question the rationality of extreme overwork towards reaching a goal of *not working*.

cess-mascuinity connection on the family. This connection also inhibits the formation of close relationships with other men.

Ochberg (1988) describes an interesting pair of role demands on a group of career men he interviewed. He investigated aspects of these men's relationships with male coworkers and concluded that men are encouraged to present the *illusion* that they are personal with one another while at the same time maintaining limits. Friendliness is expected, but men who get too close are seen as losing control of their situations. According to Ochberg, "Striking this balance between detachment and the appearance of friendliness is actually more of a strain than being either genuinely personal or genuinely indifferent." (p. 11). Although most of the men Ochberg interviewed reported a desire for personal relationships with their colleagues, they work hard to resist it because the man who is a colleague today may be a subordinate tomorrow, and they believe it to be difficult to discipline or give orders to a friend. Ochberg reports studies indicating that "Successful executives show that they have an unusual ability to cultivate friendships with those who are ahead of them on the corporate ladder, and disentangle themselves from attachments to people who once were their peers, but whom they have since left behind." (p. 11).

WORKING IN THE MODERN WORLD

The world of work in the postindustrial world has undergone many changes in recent years. There are increases in women's participation in nearly every segment of the paid labor force, and these increases are accompanied by slight decreases in men's participation. Several men's issues have arisen in response to these changes.

Probably the most important development in the work arena for men is that breadwinning and providing can no longer be considered exclusively masculine. In modern societies, most men have not gained much satisfaction from their work. They validated their masculinity through the *results* of their work: money and providing. As women continue to make gains in the amount of money they earn as a group, men who hold antifeminine ideologies will often have to find masculine validation elsewhere, although many do not know where to turn. As Bernard (1981) put it, "The good-provider role may be on its way out, but its legitimate successor has not yet appeared on the scene" (p. 12). Men who have been marginalized (e.g., men of color and older men) have experienced the greatest difficulty living up to the breadwinner role demand (Wilkie, 1991). There is a small but positive movement toward men's gender-egalitarian beliefs as a result of a decreasing emphasis on the breadwinner role (Zuo, 1997).

Male-Female Relationships in the Workplace

The dominance and antifemininity norms of traditional masculinity can cause men difficulty when their work peers, superiors, or subordinates are women. Gender-typed men tend to react to a woman in a "man's job" with some mixture of anger, fear, confusion, and anxiety (Astrachan, 1992). The traditional view of woman as underling and sex object is dysfunctional in a number of increasingly common work situations, a few of which are detailed below:

1. When a man and woman are required to work together cooperatively, unreasonable dominance by the man is damaging to employee relationships and the quality of the work.

2. When a man and a woman are competing for promotion, he may feel emasculated if she wins.

3. When hiring, promotion, and pay increase decisions discriminate against women, individuals are victimized and organizations suffer emotional distress, lowered productivity, and sometimes economic hardships brought on by litigation or job action.

4. When a man's supervisor is a woman, he may be uncooperative, anxious, resentful, or disrespectful if he persists at retaining sexist values. This can be damaging to the man's job performance and to the organization. As a group, men tend to have negative attitudes toward female managers (Schein, 2001), especially when the manager acts in a stereotypically masculine way (Rudman & Glick, 2001).

5. Sexual harassment in the workplace is pervasive (McAllister, 1996). The man who sexually objectifies women at work and acts on this attitude is engaging in an illegal act, harming other human beings, and sometimes damaging his own potential for vocational success.

SEXUAL HARASSMENT

In October of 1991, a U.S. Senate committee held hearings on the confirmation of Judge Clarence Thomas to the Supreme Court. Anita Hill, a University of Oklahoma law professor, testified that Thomas had pressured her for dates and made frequent lewd comments in the workplace while he was her supervisor in the early 1980s. Hill's accusations and the reactions to them by the all-male Senate Judiciary Committee elevated public awareness of sexual harassment (Jaschik-Herman & Fisk, 1995). In 1992, several women reported similar behaviors by Oregon Senator Bob Packwood (who resigned because of the scandal) (Taylor, 1995), and the allegations of sexual harassment by Paula Jones against President Bill Clinton (along with his "consensual" sexual affair with Monica Lewinsky) cast a pall on his entire presidency. A number of high-profile corporate sexual harassment suits emerged during the 1990s, most notably in the Mitsubishi corporation (see Box 10.6).

The Equal Employment Opportunity Commission (EEOC) (1980) defined sexual harassment as:

> Unwelcome sexual advances, requests for sexual favors and other verbal or physical conduct of a sexual nature when submission to such conduct is made either explicitly or implicitly a term or condition of an individual's employment; submission or rejection of such conduct by an individual is used as the basis for employment decisions affecting the individual; or such conduct has the purpose or effect of unreasonably interfering with an individual's work performance or creating an intimidating, hostile, or offensive working environment. (p. 25024).

For a behavior to be considered sexual harassment, it must meet the following criteria. First, it must be sexual or gender focused. For example, repeated requests for dates are sexual in nature; frequent derogatory comments about women or men are gender focused. Second, it must be unwanted. Conduct is sexually harassing if the person who is the target of the sexual behavior feels uncomfortable, attacked, offended, or intimidated. If the person enjoys or is not bothered by sexual comments, flirting, or requests for romantic attention, then there is no sexual harassment in these behaviors. Third, the conduct must occur in the workplace. In this case, "workplace" is broadly defined. If someone is having a drink at a bar after work and a co-worker approaches him or her with unwanted sexual attention, then we can reasonably assume that the negative impact of this conduct will not just go away when the person returns to work the next day. Although the behavior has not occurred in the physical workplace, it has nonetheless occurred in the workplace.

There are two types of sexual harassment. *Quid pro quo* ("this for that") sexual harassment involves an attempt to gain sexual cooperation through threats of negative job-related consequences and/or promises of positive ones. It is a proposed exchange of influence in return for sex. This category includes *sexual extortion* (e.g., "Have sex with me or I'll fire you."), and *sexual bribery* (e.g., "Have sex with me and I'll give you a raise."). Threats can be implicit or explicit. A supervisor can say, "You'll do well in your career if you know how to 'play ball', if you know what I mean," and this statement can be construed as a kind of offer.

Quid pro quo harassment need happen only once to be chargeable. In fact, sometimes officials can also bring other charges under laws that cover bribery, extortion, or sexual assault. This type of harassment is fairly cut-and-dried—when quid pro quo harassment results in a formal complaint, the dispute usually centers on whether or not the behavior actually occurred, not whether it was harassing.

Hostile environment sexual harassment involves unwelcome and offensive, pervasive and frequent sex-related verbal and/or physical behavior that has the effect of creating discomfort in the working environment. Examples include unwanted touching of a sexual nature, sexually oriented jokes and conversations, asking about sexual experiences, repeated pressure for dates, staring at a person's body, making derogatory gender-related comments, displaying pornographic pictures in the workplace, and a variety of other behaviors.

In contrast to quid pro quo harassment, which needs to happen only once to be chargeable, hostile environment harassment must be severe, persistent, and/or pervasive to be chargeable. In my experience as a sexual harassment prevention trainer, one of the most frequent questions from male employees is, "What if I slip up and say something inappropriate? Will I lose my job and ruin my career?" They seem to have a fear that the "sexual harassment police" will come around the corner and arrest them if they exhibit even a momentary lapse of discretion. Nothing could be further from the truth. The word "environment" within the phrase "hostile environment" means that behavior must have the effect of coloring a person's entire experience within the workplace in order to sustain a legal charge. At the same time, making an inappropriate sexual comment violates the *principle* of workplace respect that underlies sexual harassment policies, and so the person who "slips" would do well to apologize to anyone he or she has offended and make efforts to avoid repeating the behavior.

Legally, sexual harassment law is subsumed under Title VII of the Civil Rights Act of 1964 that forbids discrimination in employment based on sex (and a variety of other characteristics such as race and religion). A campus is a student's workplace, and Title IX of the Education Amendments of 1972 entitles all students to a harassment-free environment. This entitlement extends to protection from the unwanted sexual attention from faculty, administrators, staff, other students, vendors, visitors, and any person who might potentially interfere with the student's learning environment. It also extends to travel away from the campus on school-sanctioned business such as athletic teams' games on other campuses and interns' work on off-campus sites. Schools and employers are legally required to take all reasonable steps to prevent sexual harassment and to provide a swift remedy when given notice of its occurrence. They face legal liability when they knew or should have known that sexual harassment was occurring, yet took inadequate steps to deal with it.

Forty to 60 percent of women (Swisher, 1995) and 15% of men (Foote & Goodman-Delahunty, 2004) report having been sexually harassed at some point during their working lives. Women who work in blue-collar fields that are nontraditional for women (e.g., construction or industrial work) are especially vulnerable (Sandler & Shoop, 1997). Thirty to 50 percent of female college students report having been sexually harassed by male professors or other staff members (Sandler & Shoop, 1997; Fitzgerald, 1993). An Associated Press release reported that 97% of female students at military academies in the United States experienced some form of sexual harassment in 1991 ("Nearly all Women at Academies are Harassed, Study Says," 1994). By 2005, those figures had improved to only 96% at West Point and 93% at the Naval Academy. The Air Force Academy showed a little more progress, with 82% of female cadets reporting unwanted sexual behavior (White, 2005).

The impact of sexual harassment on the victim is enormous—17% of women and nearly 5% of men say they have quit a job because of sexual harassment (Gutek & Nakamura, 1983), 96% have suffered emotional symptoms, and 63% have suffered physical symptoms (Crull, 1982). Many college women report having dropped courses, changed majors, or left school to avoid harassment (Fitzgerald, 1992). In the U.S. federal government alone, sexual harassment is estimated to cost $135 billion annually (Foote & Goodman-Delahunty, 2004). Wagner (1992) estimated that sexual harassment costs an average of $6.7 billion annually for every Fortune 500 company.

In a large-scale study, researchers found that most harassers are male: 95% of female victims and 22% of male victims said that they had been harassed exclusively by males (Tangri, Burt, & Johnson, 1982). The U.S. Supreme Court recently upheld the right of individuals to protection from same-sex harassment (Biskupic, 1998). Men who subscribe to traditional masculine ideologies are more likely to harass than other men (Wade & Brittan-Powell, 2001). Kearney, Rochlen, and King (2004) found that men who report high gender role conflict are also more likely than other men to harass. This study lends support to Pleck's (1981a) hypothesis that violating gender roles leads individuals to overconform to them. Thus the sex difference in perpetrating harassment is tied to various aspects of masculinity.

Sexual harassment depends on whether the target of the behavior experiences the conduct as offensive. This "eye of the beholder" criterion has left many men confused about what they can and cannot do and say in the workplace. It is clear to most people that saying, "Have sex with me or you're fired" to a subordinate constitutes an illegal act, but most sexual harassment is not so blatant. Many men are wondering, at what point does "normal" flirting, sexual discussion, or complimenting cross the line into harassment? Can a man say, "Let's go have a drink after work," "How are things going with your boyfriend?" "You look especially good today," or "I think you have nice legs."

We see a gender role-related problem in the mere understanding of the behavior. Most men are raised with the notion that rules should be clear and unambiguous. Sports, that basic training ground for masculinity, have clear, rigid rules. "Guidelines" like those established by the EEOC, tend to make conventionally gendered men uncomfortable.

More importantly, the "eye of the beholder" definition means that men have to *make judgments about what another person is feeling*. As we have already discussed, many have little experience with this sort of interpersonal orientation. Not surprisingly, men (especially traditionally masculine ones) are much less likely to perceive sexual harassment than women. Fitzgerald (1993) cites 19 studies attesting to a large difference in men's and women's perceptions, however it may be possible to use educational interventions to make men more sensitive to the problem of sexual harassment (Kearney, Rochlen, & King, 2004).

Other aspects of the masculine gender role contribute to a sexual harassment proclivity. The view of women as subservient sexual objects is a primary one. Men who see women as sexual objects first and human beings (or coworkers) second, are at risk for committing harassment. The sense that one has to be dominant in order to be a man is associated with the likelihood of sexual harassment (Pryor, 1987) and generally negative attitudes toward women (Robinson & Schwartz, 2004). Sexual harassment is an abuse of

Box 10.6: Costs of Sexual Harassment:
The Mitsubishi Case

One of the highest profile sexual harassment cases in recent years involved the Mitsubishi Motors plant in Normal, Illinois, where male workers harassed hundreds of women over the course of several years. Spokespersons for the Equal Employment Opportunity Commission (EEOC) reported that male employees "called women employees sluts, whores, and bitches. . .placed drawings of genitals, breasts, and various sexual acts, labeled with female employees names, on car fenders and cardboard signs along the auto assembly line. . .physically threatened women who complained of the treatment. . . In at least one case, a male employee put his air gun between a woman's legs and pulled the trigger" (Grimsley, 1996, p. A1). Male co-workers repeatedly propositioned female workers and made demeaning remarks about women (Grimsley, Swoboda, & Brown, 1996). The EEOC blamed the management at the plant for tolerating these behaviors (Grimsley & Swoboda, 1997a).

When the allegations of widespread sexual harassment at the plant were made public, Mitsubishi officials shut down the plant for a day, rented 59 buses, and transported 2,500 employees on a six-hour bus ride to Chicago to protest at the EEOC building. The costs of the plant shutdown and trip were estimated at $21 million (Grimsley & Brown, 1996). Later, Mitsubishi settled two lawsuits for a total of $43.5 million, a record amount for a sexual harassment suit (Grimsley, 1998; Grimsley & Swoboda, 1997b), and undertook a vigorous corporate program to correct sexual harassment in the workplace (Swoboda, 1996).

People who are sexually harassed suffer a wide variety of negative physical and emotional symptoms. The human toll on their occupational and personal lives is staggering. Besides the human costs, sexual harassment also exacts a high financial price, and not merely from lawsuits. The costs to Mitsubishi far exceeded the estimated $64.5 million cited above. Sexual harassment costs businesses billions annually in lowered productivity, increased absenteeism, use of sick leave and health insurance, time taken to resolve complaints, and employee resignations, which result in significant costs to replace and train new employees. Enlightened businesses are discovering that sexual harassment prevention is not just a nice thing to do for employees; it is good business as well. Maintaining a fully respectful workplace is an important component of maintaining a fully productive workplace.

power, most often perpetrated by people with high status in an organization against subordinates (Basow, 1992). In speaking of verbal harassment on the street (which does not amount to workplace sexual harassment, but has the same kinds of emotional effects), Benard and Schlaffer (1997) described the issue of sexually based harassing behavior and power: "Whether you wear a slit skirt or are covered from head to foot in black chador [(the garb of Muslim and Hindu women who are only allowed to have their eyes uncovered in public)], the message is not that you are attractive enough to make a man lose his self-control but that the public realm belongs to him and you are there by his permission as long as you follow his rules and as long as you remember your place" (p. 396).

The traditional roles of man as sexual initiator and woman as sexual gatekeeper also set the stage for sexual harassment. Men who subscribe to the belief that sexual activity is a matter of power and conquest feel that they must persistently pressure women, and the workplace provides opportunities to do so. Men who hold adversarial sexual beliefs— that sexual relationships are a matter of exploitation and manipulation—are more likely than other men to harass (Pryor, 1987). Foote and Goodman-Delahunty (2004) describe three types of male harassers:

> *Misperceiving harassers* seek sexual relationships and believe that the workplace is an appropriate location for doing so. They misconstrue women's friendliness or dress as invitations for sexual behavior and also tend to hold the belief that relationships between men and women are adversarial and aggressive.

> *Exploitive harassers* associate sexuality with social power and believe that women enjoy being dominated by men. When in positions of organizational power, they use provocative sexual behavior to intimidate women, and they also tend to subscribe to the beliefs that women invite rape by the way they dress or that women like being raped.

> *Misogynistic harassers* hold hostile attitudes toward women and express these attitudes through displays of pornography, derogatory language in reference to women, denigration of women's abilities, and sometimes direct sexual taunting of women.

These characteristics of sexual harassers are not unlike those of acquaintance rapists. Again we find evidence that underlying masculine inadequacy may be related to damaging others and perhaps the self. Sexual harassment is a men's issue, and it is intertwined with other issues involving men's power, emotionality, sexuality, relationships, antifemininity, and gendered self-definition.

As with all gendered victimizing behaviors, sexual harassment takes place within a context of patriarchal male dominance. I was struck by the expectation of male sexual privilege when an older colleague told me the following story. He had just finished graduate school and arrived on campus as a new assistant professor. The college president invited all new faculty members to his house for a welcoming party, and remarked, "Professor, I see that you are a single man. Many of our male faculty members have found their wives from among our student body—I hope you will be as fortunate." Thus, the president not only condoned sexual relationships between people of vastly different power levels on the campus, he encouraged them.

Solutions to the problem of sexual harassment include education, prevention programs, legal and government policy changes, and effective efforts to hold perpetrators responsible for their actions. Organizations must make strong statements that they will not tolerate the behavior, and then follow through with effective institutional policies and strategies. Communicating respect for women in the structures and activities of the organization will be helpful in working against the attitudinal undercurrent of the problem. In the big picture, sexual harassment is an agent of social control of women by men (Fitzgerald, 1993), and thus efforts to end the it also involve social change in the gender and the structure of patriarchy, as well as in the lives of individual men.

MALE-FEMALE RELATIONSHIPS IN DUAL-EARNER HOMES

The continued influx of women into the paid labor force has also changed traditional household arrangements. Women who are equal economic partners usually expect their spouses to become equal domestic partners. A sense of fairness would seem to dictate that a shared breadwinner role means that men's household responsibilities should increase.

Pasick (1990) points out several problems for many men in this area. First, there is sometimes a skill deficit. Many men have little training in cleaning, cooking, and especially child care. Second, gender-typed men resist learning these skills because they consider them unmanly (One of my students reported that her boyfriend was incapable of doing laundry or cooking frozen fish sticks, two skills that could be learned in a matter of minutes.). Third, wives may be reluctant to relinquish control of what has traditionally been women's domain. A man may sometimes feel that he is in a double-bind situation. He feels the demand to contribute, yet he may receive frequent criticism that he is not doing the task "right" or well enough. Finally, many employers do not offer much support to men who are trying to adopt nontraditional roles. For example, a man who leaves work in order to care for a sick child may be subject to much more disapproval than a woman who does the same thing (Schneer & Reitman, 1993).

As a result of these difficulties, women tend to do more housework and child care than men, even when both partners work equally long hours (South & Spitze, 1994). Most people still consider this work to be primarily a woman's responsibility, as evidenced by some men's remarks that they "help out" in their own homes and "babysit" their own children. Only about one-fifth of husbands are fully involved in household chores like cooking and cleaning, compared with virtually all wives (Starrels, 1994).

Traditional men in co-provider families also tend to feel threatened if their wives earn more money than they do. Clearly, subscribing to the belief that money means power and masculinity would cause problems for the man whose wife outearns him. The incredible power of gender roles is illustrated by some men's reactions to their wives' getting a raise—they feel strong resentment and feelings of being unmanly, and they would rather get along with less money than deal with these feelings and their underlying attitudes.

Although the increased entry of women into the paid workforce has complicated the lives of men both at home and at work, the benefits of these changes often outweigh the costs. First, the man can share the breadwinner pressure with his partner. Second, since outcome (earning) can no longer be defined as traditionally masculine, men can pay more attention to process (day-to-day experiences within the workplace) and seek satisfaction from the work itself. Third, egalitarian roles at work and home enhance the appreciation of women as human beings and improves the quality of relationships between women and men. Rather than living in the parallel lives of the 1950s model, partners can claim common ground both at work and at home. Fourth, men may have opportunities to enter new realms of rich experience as they expand the view of themselves beyond that of functional work machines.

In the heterosexual relationship that people have come to view as traditional, the woman experienced success vicariously through the man, who experienced emotions and relationships vicariously through the woman. Now that women are succeeding for themselves, men may have important opportunities to rediscover their emotional lives and reinvolve themselves in the lives of their families and friends.

SUMMARY

1. Work has defined men's identities throughout history, and the masculine socialization process is strongly oriented toward producing workers. The character of work and the sexual division of labor has changed throughout human history.

2. The man-as-breadwinner, woman-as-homemaker arrangement was a temporary transition from agricultural to industrial societies. It does not characterize most of human history, and it is changing. Similar to the transition to single-earner families, the return to co-provider families is a result of economic exigencies. Women's participation as full economic partners is associated with gender egalitarian values. Sex segregation is associated with the oppression of women.

3. As a consequence of industrial demands, most men were effectively removed from their homes and often specialized in some small part of the production process. As a result, they were alienated from both their work and their families, and they had to rely on the financial outcome of work for the validation of masculinity. The provider role requires sacrifice and emotional restrictiveness. These aspects of masculinity continue to live on in many men.

4. The masculine values of task orientation, competition, and independence are conducive to a wide variety of work settings. Boys' sports and play, with their emphasis on outcome and quantification, socialize males toward work.

5. The advantages of this socialization for men are social status, opportunity, and work satisfaction, but many men who lose jobs or do not succeed feel emasculated. Even men who do well at work may encounter difficulties in relating to family and coworkers, maintaining physical and mental health, dealing with the pressures of competition, and coping with gender role strain.

6. Sexual harassment is pervasive in the workplace, and most perpetrators are men. This problem is costly in both human and financial terms, and it is tied to masculine issues of power and sexual privilege. Solutions to the problem involve a wide range of social, legal, organizational, and personal changes.

7. In recent times, economic and social conditions have led to changes in the traditional single-earner family. Men who adhere to gender-typed attitudes may encounter significant problems at work and at home as they find it necessary to adjust to newer, more egalitarian gender roles. Issues around the loss of the masculine breadwinner role, sexual harassment, and the sharing of domestic duties have come to the fore. Although the result is a more complicated life for working men, the benefits may outweigh the costs, as many men are expanding their senses of self beyond their occupational roles.

11

Pleasure and Performance: Male Sexuality

Few areas of human behavior are as fraught with emotion as sexuality. Dealing with one-self as a sexual person can involve a wide array of experiences, including pleasure, mystery, wonder, lust, love, anxiety, guilt, repression, and confusion. During socialization, people receive quite a few messages about sexual feelings, sexual relationships, presumed differences between male and female sexuality, sexual orientation, seduction, intimacy, and sexual communication. Many of these messages are highly value-laden. Some involve misinformation, half-truths, or unhealthy ways of thinking about the self. All of them influence how biological sexual tendencies are shaped into sexual behaviors and feelings, and how the person experiences his or her sexuality within the larger picture of the total self-concept.

Gendered expectations and ideologies pervade virtually every area of experience, and sexuality is no exception. The traditional masculine gender role contains many prescriptions for sexual behavior and experiencing, and these are embedded in the larger context of masculine values and ideologies. Being a "real man" has often included expectations for certain ways of being a sexual man.

In this chapter, I explore the role of sexuality in masculinity, beginning with a discussion of the ways that societies have typically socialized males to think about themselves and behave as sexual people. Then, we turn to a few sexual issues for men: circumcision, sexual orientation, and sexual problems.

SEXUALITY AND PHYSICAL DEVELOPMENT

A boy discovers his penis very early in life. Compared with the girl's vagina and clitoris, the penis is more external and visible. It is easily accessible to the boy's hands, and he finds that touching his penis produces very pleasurable sensations. It is not surprising that boys tend to begin masturbating earlier in life than girls, and that males tend to masturbate more frequently than females throughout life (Strong, DeVault, Sayad, & Yarber, 2005). The stronger social prohibition against sexual expression for females in many cultures may also contribute to this difference.

Since the boy's genitals are so obvious to him and touching them is so pleasurable, there is a tendency in males to focus sexual feelings solely on the penis. In contrast, girls may be more likely to experience their sexuality as more diffuse, internal, and mysterious (Nelson, 1988). The masculine "genitalization" of sex may dissuade males from developing a sensuality—an appreciation of pleasurable sensations in other parts of the body. It is a frequent complaint of adult heterosexual women that their male partners are only interested in the "main event" (sexual intercourse), and that they do not value caressing, intimate conversation, or other forms of sensuality.

When a boy reaches puberty, his genitals increase in size, and he begins to experience very strong sexual feelings. Erections occur frequently and without warning, sometimes at the most inappropriate times. Occasionally, the boy wakes up to find that he has ejaculated in his sleep (a nocturnal emission, or "wet dream"). These events may give the boy a sense that his penis seems to have a "mind of its own." Although he is obviously aware that it is a part of him, he may also experience his penis as somewhat extrinsic to the self. The large number of slang terms for male genitalia may be a cultural reflection of the male sense that a penis has its own identity and personality.

SEXUALITY AND MASCULINITY

Although the physical sex differences described above contribute to the distinct quality of male sexuality, they probably pale in comparison to the social forces that shape sexual expression in the male. Sexuality is central to gender identity, and thus we find prescriptions for sexual experiencing deeply embedded within traditional masculine norms.

Anthropological evidence indicates that there is wide cross-cultural variation in the social rules for handling sexuality. For example, some cultures value marital fidelity, but some peoples in the Arctic consider it etiquette for a man to offer to make his wife sexually available to a male visitor. Kissing is unpopular in some societies. Some cultures encourage sexual experimentation in adolescence, whereas others punish it severely (Rathus, Nevid, & Fichner-Rathus, 2005). And, adolescent boys in some tribes on Papua, New Guinea are expected to perform oral sex on the older men of the tribe as a rite of passage into manhood (Gilmore, 1990).

With regard to mainstream U.S. culture, Brannon's (1985) description of the four themes of traditional masculinity (summarized in Chapter 1) provides a useful framework for understanding masculine sexual demands in the context of general masculine gender role demands:

1. *Antifemininity* ("No Sissy Stuff"): the avoidance of "feminine" behaviors, interests, and personality traits. Mainstream U.S. culture includes a view of women as gentle,

sensual, tender, submissive, passive, relationship-oriented, and sexually desirous toward males. To define the self as masculine, the male may feel pulled toward expressing his sexuality with the opposites of these qualities.

Heterosexual men find themselves in somewhat of a quandary when they try to relate to women sexually. On the one hand, social forces encourage them to be separate from women. On the other hand, they naturally feel drawn toward women. Intimacy is threatening for many men because it involves connecting, being vulnerable, and sharing power, all of which have been labeled feminine. Yet, intimacy would seem to be a human need (Jourard, 1971).

One way that many men deal with the contradiction between naturally occurring desires for intimacy and gender role demands for separation is by learning to equate sex with intimacy. In fact, one euphemism for intercourse is "being intimate with" someone. However, sex and intimacy are not the same thing, and physical intimacy is not the same as psychological intimacy. True intimacy involves letting someone in to some of the most private and vulnerable parts of the self. While some of these parts may be physical, it is certainly possible to be sexual with someone in a very impersonal or detached way. Likewise, it is possible to be intimate without being sexual, through shared communication and experience.

Equating sex with intimacy creates a number of problems for men and women. While women tend to see sex in the context of psychological closeness and affection, many men experience sex in a more isolated way, as a physical release or an adventure (Blumstein & Schwartz, 1983). Women may feel deprived in their intimacy needs and become frustrated with male partners who seem overly focused on the physical aspects of sex.

Some men encounter a different problem: the sense that love and sex are contradictory. Raised to believe that "good girls" do not have sexual feelings, the man may degrade women who express their sexuality. The sexual "double standard" is alive and well. Women who engage in frequent sex with multiple partners are called "sluts" or described with the pejorative term "promiscuous," but men who engage in the same behaviors are "studs," or heroes.

The man who embraces the double standard falls victim to what has been termed the *Madonna/whore complex* (the religious Madonna, not the singer): He cannot love someone if he is sexual with her, and he cannot be sexual with someone if he loves her. Sexual expression is relegated to "one night stands," short-term affairs, or perhaps hiring prostitutes. Most men prefer to have sex and love together (Levine & Barbach, 1983), but some find this to be impossible. They must separate sex from other aspects of relationships in order to define themselves as masculine (Lynch & Kilmartin, 1999; Levant, 1997b). In many studies, researchers have demonstrated that men are much more comfortable than women with viewing sex as a physical activity that is relatively unconnected to relationships (Carroll, Volk, & Hyde, 1985; Blumstein & Schwartz, 1983; Laumann, Gagnon, Michael, & Michaels, 1994).

2. *Status and Achievement* ("The Big Wheel"): the masculine expectation for success and power. This norm is expressed in a set of demands for sexual competence, conquest, and performance. Traditional men view the sexual arena as one in which they can prove their masculinity by being successful competitors.

For many men, "success" is an outcome, not a process. The traditional masculine emphasis has been on getting something *done*, rather than on *the experience* of doing something. Masculine achievements are, by definition, things that have happened in the past that contribute to the sense of masculine identity. They are also *quantifiable*—masculine success means "putting up numbers." Carrying this orientation over into sexual behaviors has often created problems for traditional men and those around them.

Sexual success can be described in a number of ways. First, it can be defined as "scoring"—having sex with as many partners as possible. This goal-oriented attitude toward sex focuses the man on the good feelings that come from having "conquered" someone, and leads to a focus away from enjoying the sexual experience. Some men even want to hurry sex so that they can go and tell their friends about having "scored," and thus gain admiration and status. The sexual partner, however, is a victim of disrespect. She (or he) is dehumanized by being treated as merely an avenue to achievement for the "player."

Another way to succeed is through sexual performance, which is defined as being able to produce erections at will and repeated orgasms in one's partner, as well as having sexual stamina. Of course, "real men" are also described as having huge penises (another quantification). In fact, the penis is sometimes described as "his manhood." The message is that having less of a penis means being less of a man. Worse yet are equations of the penis with personhood: "he put *himself* inside her," or the parental admonition, "don't play with *yourself.*" The masculine norms for performance, size, and stamina are summarized in what Zilbergeld (1992) calls "the fantasy model of sex . . . it's two feet long, hard as steel, always ready, and will knock your socks off" (p. 37).

These masculine demands are impossible to fulfill for most men. Despite reassurances from women and sexuality experts that genital size bears no relationship to sexual pleasure, many a man feels inadequate about the size of his penis (Nelson, 1988). Statements like "it's not the size of the wand, it's the magic in the magician" or "it's not the size of the ship, it's the motion of the ocean" provide little comfort to these men.

Second, penile erection is affected by a variety of factors besides sexual arousal. Among these are hormonal fluctuations, fatigue, anxiety, drug use, distraction, or physiological problems (Crooks & Baur, 2005). There are very few men who have not had at least an occasional transient erectile problem (Zilbergeld, 1992). Because of the social connection between sexual performance and masculinity, these experiences can lead to confusion, anxiety, self-doubt, or depression.

The 1998 introduction of *Viagra* (sildenafil citrate), a drug used to treat erectile dysfunction, was welcomed by many men who saw it as salvation for their masculinity, which they often view as inextricably intertwined with their sexual performances. Later, two similar drugs, *Cialis* (tadalafil) and *Levitra* (vardenifil hci), were introduced into the highly competitive market for pharmaceutical treatment of erectile dysfunction. Commercials for all of these products strongly imply that they improve not only sexual functioning, but men's self-esteem and the quality of their relationships with women. Not surprisingly, no mention is made of gay or bisexual men. Like most drugs, these substances are sometimes linked to a number of side effects, including a possible connection between *Viagra* use and blindness in a small minority of users (Kaufman, 2005). The enormous popularity of these drugs attests to the centrality of sexuality and performance to the sense of masculinity and self-worth in gender-typed men.

Third, men do not "give" women orgasms. Women experience orgasms, sometimes with men's help. If the man takes responsibility for the woman's orgasm, he may be risking his masculine self-esteem on a process over which he has little control. Many men ask "did you come?" and "how many times?" not out of concern for their partners, but to validate their masculinity through success and achievement. Many women report having faked orgasms in order to soothe their male partners' worries about masculinity (Crooks & Baur, 2005).

Fourth, sexual interest wanes on occasion. Men who equate manliness with ubiquitous sexual impulse may feel inadequate at these times. In fact, a surprising number of men report having faked orgasms in order to maintain a facade of perpetual masculine arousal (Levine & Barbach, 1983). The popularly held belief that men have biologically stronger sex drives than women is not supported by any available scientific evidence (Rathus, Nevid, & Fichner-Rathus, 2005). Sexual behaviors, values, and beliefs show wide variations across individuals of both sexes, across cultures, and across historical periods within a culture. In the United States, the Victorian era of the early twentieth century was very sexually repressive, in sharp contrast to the sexually permissive values of the 1960s (Strong, DeVault, Sayad, & Yarber, 2005).

The masculine performance orientation toward sex also downplays the pleasure orientation for the man. Zilbergeld (1992) points out that fictional accounts of heterosexual encounters nearly always emphasize male action and female *feeling*—his performance and her pleasure (which reflects his performance). Zilbergeld notes that, with regard to male characters in erotic novels, "it is rarely clear what he feels and experiences. It's as if his feelings and pleasure are beside the point" (p. 49).

The image that emerges from this view is of the man as a sexual machine with his penis as the main component of that machine. Some slang terms for penis ("tool," "rod") convey this connotation. Of course, the man is supposed to know how to run the machine, and there is a tendency for men to see sex as a set of technical skills rather than as a human connection. Most "sex manuals" reflect the orientation that success involves mastering sexual technique and downplay the relational aspects of sex (Gross, 1978).

3. *Inexpressiveness and Independence* ("The Sturdy Oak"): the maintaining of emotional control and self-reliance. In nearly every arena of conventional masculine behavior, men are expected to know what to do without being told. It is considered un-manly to be unsure of oneself or to ask someone else for help. Many adolescent boys receive relatively little information about sex from parents or the school (Petrie, 1987). Thus, they rely on the peer group, a source notorious for boasting, lying, and transmitting misinformation, for education around this very important topic. To be ac-cepted by his peers, the boy must act like he is "getting it" (from females, of course), and that he knows what to do sexually. In other words, he must display an aura of com-petence and knowledge even if he feels incompetent and ignorant.

The gendered demand for inexpression encourages men to approach sexuality as if it were a job to do rather than a pleasurable encounter. Sexuality would seem to be a highly emotional and self-expressive area of human experience, but men who are oversocialized into their gender role feel compelled to approach it in a machinelike, nonrelational way (Levant, 1997b). Zilbergeld (1992) reports being astonished by frequent reports by men that they do not enjoy sex. A recent study revealed that about one-third of U.S. men have sexual problems of some kind, including lack of desire or high anxiety about sexual performance (Schwartz, 1999).

For many men, sex seems to be the only area of experience where they can express some positive feeling and desire for emotional attachment to another person. When sex and connectedness are compartmentalized together, any feelings of tender emo-tion or attachment become associated with sex. As Nelson (1988) puts it, "if a man feels intense emotion, sex seems called for." (p. 40). But it is clearly possible and also desirable to be emotional and connected to people in nonsexual ways. The asso-ciation between emotion and sexuality, together with the cultural prescription for the sexual objectification of women, makes it very difficult for some men to relate to women as friends or coworkers. These factors are related to a variety of social prob-lems such as sexual assault and harassment (Foote & Goodman-Delahunty, 2004).

The sexualization of feelings of attachment causes considerable consternation when heterosexual men begin to feel close to other men. Because a woman's connectedness tends to not be defined as exclusively sexual, she may feel quite com-fortable in touching, sharing feelings, or even sleeping in the same bed with another woman. Men's relationships with each other, however, are often limited by the ho-mophobic threat of feeling too close. Increasingly, homophobia is being identified as related to a variety of social issues (Kantor, 1998).

4. *Adventurousness and Aggression* ("Give 'em Hell"): the expectation to be daring, fearless, and self-assertive. This masculine norm encourages men to view sexuality as yet another area in which to exercise dominance and control. "Real men" want to get down to the business of intercourse. Fasteau (1974) noted that "for most men,

courting and seduction are nuisances" (p. 32). Gender-typed men consider feelings and communication to be "sissy stuff" (Zilbergeld, 1992). At the extreme, there are implications here for coercive sexuality. The cultural myth, portrayed in movie after movie and novel after novel, is that women are reluctant participants in sex, and that they respond to "forceful" men.

Traditional gender roles dictate that men take every sexual initiative. Farrell (1986) describes the following social message to the male: "be prepared to risk rejection about 150 times between eye contact and sexual contact. Start all 150 over again with each girl." (p. 126). Because men are expected to be tough and strong, rejection is not supposed to hurt. Although the sexual initiator has a kind of power, the ability to reject is also powerful. Neither role in the mainstream culture's sexual script seems very comfortable: she must wait somewhat passively for him to approach, signaling her availability without being "too forward"; he must gather his courage and risk his masculinity despite his anxiety and feelings of inadequacy.

The perceived pressure that one is responsible for all sexual initiative may lead a man into a variety of dysfunctional and harmful behaviors. Treating women as sex objects and inferiors is one way to defend against the pain of rejection. If he reduces her to a less than human status, he can more easily attribute her disinterest to stupidity or deny that, being nothing more than a "piece of ass," she has little power over his feelings. There can also be the tendency to deny the emotional component of sex or to develop anger and resentment toward women in general (Farrell, 1982).

If the man is "successful" at living up to the masculine ideal of promiscuity, then he may be *really* taking risks. The very real threats of AIDS and other sexually transmitted diseases are as serious as ever, and unwanted pregnancies also present as much of a possibility as they ever did. Once again, being a "real man" is hazardous to one's health. "Studs" don't usually spend their time taking precautions to avoid disease or pregnancy, talking to partners about sexual histories and birth control, or turning down sex because it is risky to be promiscuous. Traditional masculine ideology is linked to sexual risk behaviors in adolescent males (Pleck, Sonenstein, & Ku, 1993), and underestimation of the risks involved in sexual behaviors are more common in men, especially those who endorse stereotypical gender beliefs (Courtenay, McCreary, & Merighi, 2002).

In conclusion, sex has traditionally been a major way of demonstrating one's masculinity. Masculine gender role values require the man to be sure of himself sexually, to be perpetually ready to perform, to retain a genital focus and goal orientation, to separate sex from love, and to obtain as many partners as possible. On the one hand, males are encouraged to freely express and enjoy their sexuality. In another sense, however, male sexuality may often be fraught with high anxiety, emotional constriction, and a strong sense of inadequacy.

But we should be careful to avoid the tendency to overstate the issues. Most men want to (and have) loving and intimate relationships with their sexual partners. Moreover, gender role norms may be changing. Levant (1997b) administered a survey in which he asked about these norms to a sample of male college students, who tended to disagree with several stereotypically masculine beliefs, such as that men should always be ready for sex, always take the sexual initiative, never worry about birth control, or only engage in sexual behavior with orgasm as a goal. They agreed that a man should love his sex partner. At the same time, they also endorsed the ideologies of masculine sexual ability and the importance of erectile control. There is a need for more research in this area, using larger and more diverse samples.

It bears repeating that cultural gender demands place pressure on individuals to behave and experience themselves in certain ways, but that individual responses to those pressures vary widely. Men who engage in loving and intimate sexual relationships resist the cultural pressures to seek sex indiscriminately and engage in nonrelational sex.

MALE SEXUAL ISSUES

Circumcision

The cutting and removal of the penile foreskin (prepuce) of the male infant is one of the most common surgeries performed in the United States (Goldman, 1992). In 1989, the American Academy of Pediatrics recommended that parents carefully weigh the risks and benefits of circumcision before deciding whether to subject their newborn boys to it (Rathus, Nevid, & Fichner-Rathus, 2005). Perhaps because of heightened awareness of its risks, circumcision has become much less routine in the United States. In 1975, 93% of newborn boys were circumcised. That figure fell dramatically to 60% by 1996 and currently remains at about that level, although there are significant variations among religious affiliations and regions. For instance, about 20% of Australian and Canadian boys undergo the procedure as infants, and the neonatal circumcision rate in Britain is only one percent (Laumann, 1999). Worldwide, an estimated 85% of male infants are not circumcised (Goldman, 1992).

A century ago, circumcised men were also a small minority in the United States. The rise to the high rate of circumcision in the mid-twentieth century was fueled by beliefs about its value for hygiene, disease avoidance, reduction of cancer risks, and other concerns (Hussey, 1989). Circumcision also has ritual meaning within some religions (Allgeier & Allgeier, 2000). However, complications from circumcision such as hemorrhage, infection, or mutilation, occur in about 4% of cases (Niku, Stock, & Kaplan, 1995), and so the surgery may be more risky than the possible benefits. Following is a description of the circumcision procedure:

> The baby's arms and legs are strapped to a board to prevent movement. The genitals are scrubbed to prepare for surgery. The foreskin is torn from the glans and slit lengthwise to allow for the insertion of the circumcision instrument. Then, the foreskin is cut off. This is usually done without an anesthetic because of the risk to the infant. (National Organization of Circumcision Information Resource Centers (NOCIRC), 1991)

The operation takes between three and ten minutes (Laumann, 1999), and a number of researchers believe that circumcision is quite painful (Goldman, 1992). Sometimes surgeons use a local anesthetic, *lidocaine*. However, the baby is thought to suffer whenever he urinates during the time it takes the wound to heal, 7–10 days (Milos, 1992). Laumann (1999) states that, "no method has been found yet that completely eliminates the discomfort of the surgery." (p. 70).

Why is this seemingly painful and unnecessary surgery performed so routinely? Milos (1992) cites several persistent myths about the value of circumcision:

Myth: A circumcised penis is cleaner than an uncircumcised penis. Although circumcision may reduce the frequency of urinary tract and other kinds of infections (Wiswell & Geschke, 1989), an uncircumcised penis is easy to care for. Infections can easily be avoided by simple hygiene procedures, which most men around the world use routinely. Strong and DeVault (1997) note, "it is no more difficult to wash under one's foreskin than behind one's ears (p. 433).

Myth: Circumcision prevents penile cancer. There are more deaths from circumcision than from penile cancer.

Myth: Babies don't remember the pain. Many experts disagree. There is some evidence that there are lasting effects in babies circumcised without anesthetic (a common practice). In a review of the controversy around circumcision, Laumann (1999) stated that, "even four to six months later, babies circumcised without anesthesia exhibit greater pain reactions to vaccination than uncircumcised boys or babies whose circumcision pain was attenuated by anesthetics" (p. 70).

Myth: A boy needs to look like his father or the other boys in the locker room. This did not appear to be a concern when, from 1870 to 1900, most U.S. boys were circumcised and their fathers were not (Hussey, 1989). Milos (1992) suggests that boys readily accept the explanation that "when I was a boy, they thought circumcision was necessary for health, but now we know better." (p. 15). However, for U. S. parents, the circumcision status of the father is strongly related to the decision of whether to subject the baby boy to the procedure. Ninety percent of sons of circumcised fathers undergo the operation, compared with 23 percent of sons of uncircumcised fathers (Laumann, 1999).

The American Academy of Pediatrics issued a statement in 1999 taking the position that the benefits of circumcision do not outweigh its risks, and that therefore the operation should not be carried out routinely (Rathus, Nevid, & Fichner-Rathus, 2005). The Circumcision Resource Center (2004) claims that "no medical organization in the world recommends routine circumcision of male infants."

Sexual Orientation

Imagine that you are in a movie theater watching a first run feature. The hero of the film is a male detective who cleverly figures out who has committed a murder, outduels the criminal in a gun battle, and returns home triumphantly to his boyfriend.

Imagine parents telling their young son, "Someday you'll meet the right woman or man. You'll settle down and either get married or enter into some kind of domestic partnership, depending on the laws in effect where you live."

Imagine a male presidential candidate proudly accepting his party's nomination and calling for his gay lover to join him on the podium.

Obviously, these three scenes are highly unlikely. Heterosexuality is so ingrained in Western culture that people tend to assume that everyone is attracted exclusively to members of the other sex unless something is wrong with them. Yet a significant portion of the world's population is homosexual or bisexual, and the available evidence suggests that this has been the case throughout human history.

What percentage of the population is homosexual or bisexual? It depends on how these terms are defined. Do we define them with regard to current sexual practices, sexual history, fantasy content, or the identification of the self as being homosexual or bisexual?

Alfred Kinsey and his colleagues (1948; 1953) were the first to recognize that homosexuality and heterosexuality are not neat categories with clearly identifiable boundaries. They proposed a behavioral scale of 0–6 to describe sexual orientation, ranging from an extreme of 0 (exclusively heterosexual) to a midpoint of 3 (equally homosexual and heterosexual) to an extreme of 6 (exclusively homosexual). Sanders, Reinisch, and McWhirter (1990) criticized the Kinsey scale for it's implication that being more homosexual meant that one is less heterosexual and vice versa, in a similar way that Bem (1974) objected to the casting of psychological masculinity and femininity as polar opposites.

Bell and Weinberg (1978) recognized that the content of erotic fantasies was also important in describing the sexual self. It is not unusual for a person with little or no history of homosexual contact to nonetheless be aroused by fantasies involving sexual contact with persons of the same sex. Coleman (1990) expanded the description of sexual orientation to include nine dimensions, including behaviors, fantasies, emotional attachments, idealized sexual orientation, identity, and lifestyle.

Kinsey and his colleagues (1948; 1953) estimated that 4% of males and 2–3% of females were exclusively homosexual as adults. Other estimates range as high as 10–15% (Anctil, 1992). Kinsey, Pomeroy, and Martin (1948) estimated that 37% of adult men had a history of at least one sexual experience with another man that involved orgasm. Basow (1992) reviewed a number of studies and concluded that the best estimates put primarily or exclusively homosexual orientation at 3% to 10% of the population, with another 10% to 25% bisexual. Clearly, sexual behavior and orientation toward same-sex others is not unusual.

Origins of Homosexuality

What causes homosexuality? Even asking this question reveals a heterosexist bias. Rochlin (1982) published a "heterosexual questionnaire" which contained questions like, "What do you think caused your heterosexuality?" and "If you have never slept with a person of the same sex, is it possible that all you need is a good Gay lover?" (p. 1). Obvi-

Box 11.1: *Sexual Conversion "Therapies"*

Can sexual orientation be changed? Should it change? A small group of psychologists and psychiatrists answer both questions in the affirmative (but only with regard to homosexuality). Their efforts to re-orient the sexualities of gay men and lesbians are viewed as remarkably offensive by most gay and lesbian people and their heterosexual allies.

Jack Drescher (2002) notes that there are three prevalent types of theories on the origins of homosexuality. *Normal variant* theories define homosexuality as a minority but naturally occurring orientation, similar to left-handedness. *Pathology* theories define homosexuality as an abnormal condition, and *immaturity* theories regard this orientation as a (perhaps passing) phase. Although the American Psychological Association once endorsed a pathology theory, it changed to a normal variant theory in 1973. Thus, adherents to either of the other two theories are clearly outside the psychology mainstream in the United States.

However, there are obviously many people who continue to believe that homosexuality is an illness, and in recent years, some have sought to change sexual orientation in individuals, mainly because of a perceived contradiction with fundamentalist Christian religious beliefs. Moberly (1983) coined the term "reparative therapy" to describe these efforts. The title obviously implies that something is broken and needs repair, a notion that many find profoundly offensive.

But can "therapy" change one's sexual orientation from homosexual to heterosexual? Even the staunchest advocates of the process claim only moderate conversion rates—35% at maximum—and critics believe that these are overestimates. Moreover, advocates of conversion treatments rarely discuss the risks of this treatment. Schroder and Shidlo (2001) interviewed 150 people who underwent conversion and did not transform their sexual orientations. They often reported that the practitioners told them that gay and lesbian people are fundamentally unhappy, lonely, and mentally ill, and that homosexual relationships are volatile, immature, and characterized by sexual infidelity. They reported numerous ethical violations on the part of the practitioners and also negative mental health effects from the treatment, including depression, anxiety, and feelings of self-hatred. Although advocates of conversion offer glowing testimonials from "successful" clients, they rarely address the considerable risks of undergoing the treatment.

ously, these are questions which would probably never be asked of heterosexuals. Culturally, exclusive heterosexuality is assumed to be normal and natural, and homosexuality is assumed to be some sort of deviation. John Money (1987a), one of the world's foremost experts on sexuality, considers homosexuality to be a *typological dis-*

tinction, not a *syndrome*. He likens the characteristic of same-sex erotic preference to left-handedness—it exists in a minority within the population, but it is not pathological. Many gay and lesbian people enjoy healthy, satisfying lives, and their natural and adopted children are as healthy as those who grow up in families with heterosexual parents (Dingfelder, 2005).

The origins of homosexuality seem to be quite complex. They possibly involve genes (Adler, 1992), brain structure (LeVay, 1991), hormones (Moses & Hawkins, 1982), and environmental factors (Wade & Cirese, 1991). There have been theories that dominant mothers, weak or absent fathers, modeling of homosexual behavior, or "inappropriate" gender role socialization lead a male toward homosexuality, but these theories have not received any scientific support. In fact, homosexuality is not strongly associated with any single origin or family pattern (Money, 1987b).

There is strong evidence that gay and lesbian adults have histories of same-sex erotic arousal and feelings of being different from others, both of which date back to childhood (Bell & Weinberg, 1978). Surprisingly, most homosexual adults are not lacking in heterosexual experience. About one-fifth of gay men have been married, and many are fathers (Raymond, 1992). Contrary to popular belief, gay identification does not usually begin through enjoyable homosexual experience as often as it does from ungratifying heterosexual experience (Bell & Weinberg, 1978). Indeed, many heterosexually identified people have had sexual experiences with people of the same sex as them, even though they report a preference for heterosexuality. Thus, behavioral sexual *experiences* are not the critical determinant of sexual orientation. The *feelings* that precede the behavioral experiences are, and adult homosexuality is a continuation of childhood same-sex erotic arousal. Box 11.1 describes the attempt to change sexual orientation, which has been roundly condemned by the American Psychological Association and other organizations.

SEXUAL PROBLEMS

Sexual problems include difficulties with sexual desire, functioning, or enjoyment. Clinicians often use the terms *sexual dysfunction* or *sexual disorder* to describe these problems. The former term seems to imply that the "equipment" is not working, the latter that there is some pathology. Since male sexuality is not only in the penis, and since sexual difficulties do not necessarily mean that there is something "wrong," the term "problem" seems more appropriate.

Montague (1988) suggests three dimensions for describing male sexual problems. The first is the etiology (source or origin) of the problem, which may be biological, psychological, or mixed. The second is whether the problem is primary (lifelong) or secondary (acquired). The third is whether the problem is global (generalized) or situational (specific to certain times, settings, or partners). These considerations are important with regard to the treatment of the problem. If a condition is longstanding and global, it usually presents a more serious problem than transient or situational difficulties. A problem that is largely biogenic usually points to different interventions than a problem of psychological origin.

The overall incidence of sexual problems is difficult to estimate because sex is usually such a private matter, but it is probably the case that most people have, at sometime in their lives, experienced sexual disinterest, arousal difficulties, and/or sexual performance problems (Laumann, Gagnon, Michael, & Michaels, 1994). Males are also much more likely than females to develop sexual arousal to deviant stimuli such as children, inanimate objects or parts of the body not usually associated with sex, pain and suffering of self and/or partner, exhibitionism, and voyeurism (American Psychiatric Association, 2000). The following discussion centers on problems with arousal and performance.

Inhibited Sexual Desire

Inhibited sexual desire is a lack of interest in sex. It only becomes a problem if it is distressing to the man and/or his partner. The gender prescriptions that a man should always want, need, and be ready for sex may produce negative feelings in the man when he experiences even a normal ebb in his sexual appetite.

Inhibited sexual desire can stem from physiological causes such as fatigue, drug use, or illness, and/or from psychological/interpersonal causes. For example, the man who suffers from the so-called Madonna/whore complex (a felt contradiction between love and lust) may experience low sexual desire for his wife and high desire for other women. Sexual desire might also wane as a consequence of other problems, such as work stress or conflicts in the relationship with the man's sexual partner.

Erectile Problems

Transient or longstanding difficulties in achieving or maintaining erection are relatively common in men, and these problems often produce significant distress. We often see the term *impotent* used to refer to men who experience these difficulties. Literally, this word means "powerless." Clearly, the erection is culturally symbolic of a man's strength. Clinically, these problems are now referred to as *erectile dysfunctions* to more specifically describe the problem and to avoid implicit value judgments about the man's personality (just as the term "frigid" is no longer used to describe a woman with orgasmic difficulty). However, the use of the word "impotence" continues in many circles.

A number of physical and psychological factors are associated with erectile difficulties. Although the exact contributions of physical and psychological causes is not known, the estimate of physical origin has increased in recent years, and some researchers believe that close to half of erectile problems are based more in biology than psychology (Shabsigh, Fishman, & Scott, 1988). Physical causes include illness, disease, high blood pressure, use of some types of prescription and nonprescription drugs, injury, hormonal imbalance, or vascular problems (Allgeier & Allgeier, 2000).

Emotional factors can also play a role in erectile difficulty. Anxiety is probably the most common one (Zilbergeld, 1992). Many men feel a good deal of pressure to perform sexually. Paradoxically, the fear of losing one's erection can result in erectile problems.

Men who think of intercourse as the only mode of sexual expression often think that they must get an erection for sexual pleasure to occur for the self and the partner. Something of a vicious cycle may result: he feels self-induced pressure to get and erection and perform, which leads to anxiety, which leads to erectile difficulty, which results in more pressure, more anxiety, and so on. Nelson (1988) describes the ubiquity of performance anxiety: "[Erectile dysfunction] is a man's threat, always waiting in the wings while he is on stage" (p. 33).

There are several treatments for erectile problems, including the recent pharmacological interventions such as *Viagra*, *Cialis*, and *Levitra*. Men with intractable physiological barriers to erection can opt for penile implants, which produce erections by the pumping of liquid into a cylinder that has been surgically implanted in the penis.

Psychological treatments for erectile problems usually involve turning attention away from penis, intercourse, and performance, and toward sensuality, the partner's pleasure, and sexual communication. Among men whose erectile problems are largely psychogenic, most can achieve erections when the pressure to do so is removed.

Ejaculatory Problems

Many experts believe that premature ejaculation is the most common sexual problem for men (Zilbergeld, 1992). A premature ejaculation is one that occurs very shortly after, or even before, the man's penis enters his partner. It is difficult to define the problem in absolute terms. How soon is too soon? A subjective criterion is probably useful: if the man and/or his partner are unhappy with the man's level of ejaculatory control, some attention may be warranted.

The cause or causes of premature ejaculation are not well understood, but we might guess at some. First, the reproductive function of intercourse requires only that the penis be inside the vagina at ejaculation. Animals are somewhat vulnerable to predators during sexual activity, and so quick ejaculation has some evolutionary utility for survival. Of course, human beings are quite different from other animals in many respects, and so this explanation probably does not tell the whole story.

Another possible explanation is that early male sexual experiences are often rushed. Many times, a pubescent boy might masturbate or have intercourse quickly because his privacy could easily be disturbed in his bedroom or the back seat of a car. However, this explanation does not tell the whole story either, because many men who have had these kinds of boyhood experiences do not experience problems with ejaculatory control (Luria, Friedman, & Rose, 1987).

Although the exact nature of the origins of premature ejaculation is not known, sex therapists have developed reliable treatments for this problem. Pharmacological treatments using low doses of antidepressant drugs have been somewhat successful (Forster & King, 1994; Wise, 1994). Behavioral techniques involve the starting, stopping, and restarting of stimulation at various points of arousal, the squeezing of the base or glans of the penis, and a number of other exercises that the man can do alone or with a partner.

These treatments are also highly effective. Various estimates put their success rates at between 80 and 98 percent (Zilbergeld, 1992).

Some men experience an opposite problem: the inability to ejaculate during a reasonable period of time (or sometimes not at all). This problem is thought to be anxiety based, perhaps related to a fear of impregnating the partner or a discomfort with one's own erotic pleasure. Sex therapists have prescribed a number of techniques for increasing arousal (Zilbergeld, 1992).

Conclusion

Although most men are able to attain personal satisfaction and fulfillment in their sexual lives, the demands of traditional masculinity present a number of characteristic problems and conflicts. Brooks and Levant (1997) have summed up the basic issue: "The fundamental problem is the approach to sexuality that we teach to adolescent boys and young men. Until we reconstruct the traditional standards for male sexual conduct, we will continue to be plagued with men behaving badly." (p. 258). They cite a number of benefits of redefined sexuality for men, including less sexual anxiety, greater appreciation of sexual partners, less possessiveness and jealousy, improved relationships with lovers, and decreased guilt.

Thus we return to where we started in this chapter—with the interconnections among self-concept, biology, gender, body, and relationships. The male sexual self and the masculine self are so intertwined that it would be impossible to change one without changing the other.

SUMMARY

1. The sexual self is obviously shaped by biological forces, but it is also strongly influenced by gender socialization. Males are often encouraged to be promiscuous and perpetually ready for sex, to take sexual risks, to quantify sexual experience as if it were an achievement, to be performance oriented, and to focus sexual feelings in the penis.

2. Masculine socialization can create problems for men and their partners in the areas of sexually transmitted diseases, intimacy, interpersonal exploitation, and sexual satisfaction. The traditional masculine role of sexual initiator is fraught with anxiety and may create resentment toward women.

3. Many men experience at least occasional difficulty with sexual desire, enjoyment, or functioning, including inhibited desire, erectile, or ejaculatory problems. The origins of these difficulties can be physiological, psychological, or mixed. Sometimes, these problems are transient. In other cases, some intervention may be warranted. Sex therapists have developed a number of treatments for various male sexual difficulties.

12

Boys will be Boys:
Men and Violence

In the United States, we hate violence. We think that people who commit violent crimes should go to jail for a long time or even be executed. We shake our heads in disbelief at "senseless" violence like drive-by shootings, pre-teenaged boys who kill their classmates and teachers (as in the school shootings in Jonesboro, Arkansas and Paducah, Kentucky), serial killings, and mass murderers like Timothy McVeigh, who bombed a federal building in Oklahoma City, killing 170 people. The horrific terrorist attacks of September 11, 2001 will remain in people's minds for many years to come.

In the United States, we love violence. We spend large amounts of time and money watching exhibitions like football, boxing, and "professional wrestling" (which is neither professional, nor is it wrestling), in which men inflict pain on other men. We love to see "adventure" film heroes who get the job done with their guns and their fists. We have executed more than 1,000 convicted murderers since the death penalty was reinstated in 1976 (Death Penalty Information Center, 2005). And we are increasingly tolerant of psychological violence on "reality TV" shows in which those in power bully and humiliate the contestants.

There may be no other place in the world where the culture seems to have such a powerful love-hate relationship with aggression. Although we abhor "senseless" violence, we often feel or think that there are times when violence makes a lot of sense. We seem comfortable with destructive acts as long as they are performed for the "right" reasons, against those who "deserve" to be victimized. We glorify those who are willing to "fight the good fight."

It is a well-documented fact that men and boys commit the vast majority of violent acts. While the traditional masculine gender role leads many men to become disturbed, it also leads many to become disturbing. One of the most central issues in the gender-aware study of men is the link between masculinity and violence.

218

I explore this link in this chapter, beginning with a brief description of the extent of male violence, followed by a summary of theories about its origins. Then, I will pay special attention to two specific forms of gender-based violence, domestic violence, and rape, with regard to origin and potential solutions. Finally, I will turn to a discussion of the effects of violence on male victims.

ORIGINS OF MALE VIOLENCE

Although no researcher has documented sex differences in aggressive behavior in infants and toddlers, clear sex differences emerge by preschool age, with males displaying more physical aggression and females displaying more verbal and indirect aggression (Loeber & Stouthamer-Loeber, 1998). Men commit nearly 90% of violent crimes in the United States (United States Department of Justice, 2003). Male partners or ex-partners beat nearly 4 million U.S. women every year (Landes, Squyres, & Quiram, 1997), and males are the virtually exclusive perpetrators of sexual assaults. Although sex comparison research has demonstrated nonexistent or nonsignificant differences between males and females in most areas, violence is a glaring exception.

At the same time, it is important to say that the vast majority of males are not violent. Recall from Chapter 2 the discussion of normal curve overlap between the two sexes and variability among the population of males and among that of females. There is a small difference in violence/aggression at the mean (arithmetic average) of the distribution, but

Although most males are not violent, more violent people are males.

Photo © Bettman / Corbis

this small difference translates to a large difference at the tail (extreme end) of the distribution. In other words, most men are not violent, however most violent people are males.

The search for the connections between masculinity and violence leads us back to the old nature-nurture question. Many people believe that men are biologically predisposed toward aggression. It is certainly also true that gender socialization and cultural support encourage violent behaviors for males more than for females. We probably will never know the relative contributions of nature and nurture to violence, but it is important to consider the roles of each of these types of forces.

The Biological Perspective

Sociobiologists argue that male aggression is tied to reproductive competition. In many different animal species, males engage in violent, confrontational, and sometimes mortal competition for breeding access to females (Daly & Wilson, 1985). Dominant males overcome other males through ritualized violence (such as rams butting horns), and these dominant males mate with more females than their submissive counterparts, who sometimes do not mate at all.

Daly and Wilson (1985) argue that violence among human males can be explained by this evolutionary pattern of ritualized competition. As evidence, they cite a 1958 study in which it was judged that 37% of the cases in which a male murdered another male were precipitated by "trivial" (ritualized) events, such as the killer's "saving face" when another man had insulted him. Daly's and Wilson's contention is that these types of killings are the result of the competition for dominance, and that this competition is most fierce among young, poor men who have little status. Men with higher socioeconomic status, they say, tend to be less violent because they are higher on the dominance hierarchy and thus able to attract suitable mates.

Daly and Wilson are accurate in their description of the population who are most at risk for being involved in violence—young, poor males. And, in fact, they are probably also correct in describing much of this violence as taking place for reasons that most people would consider trivial. However, to say that this kind of behavior is a result of breeding competition seems to be quite a leap of logic. In fact, even in animals, male aggression is not always associated with increased breeding opportunities, nor is it universal (Basow, 1992). Would there be so many angry, aggressive young men if we took better care of their emotional and material needs, ceased to expose them to so many violent models, and stopped holding them to impossible standards of masculinity? As we shall see, other explanations of male violence (and young, poor men's violence) are at least as plausible as the sociobiological one.

Researchers who study biological influences on behavior are often interested in hormonal factors. Because males and females differ greatly both in levels of sex hormones and in levels of violence, it would make sense to look to these hormones for a possible link.

Some researchers speculate that the male sex hormone testosterone may be related to aggression, and there is some evidence in support of this hypothesis. For example, in some animal species, males with high positions in social dominance hierarchies (which are often established by fighting) have higher testosterone levels than lower status males. In fact, rhesus monkey dominance hierarchies have been known to change when low status monkeys are injected with testosterone (Rose, Gordon, & Bernstein, 1972).

Although the above study provides compelling evidence for the role of testosterone in aggression, there are complicating data. First, testosterone levels drop when a monkey falls in the hierarchy. Therefore, although testosterone level may be a cause of aggression (or lack of it), it may also be an effect. Second, the excretion of high levels of testosterone in the urine of the monkey may stimulate other monkeys to aggress toward him, and he must then fight back to protect himself. This evidence comes from a study in which male rats were more likely to attack a castrated male rat after it had been coated with the urine of a dominant male (Pleck, 1981).

The extent to which testosterone is a cause, effect, or simply a marker of aggression is a continuing subject of inquiry. Of course, the degree to which animal studies relate to human behavior is always a matter of debate. In a classic study by Kreuz and Rose (1972), testosterone levels were measured in prison inmates who were labeled as either "fighters" or "nonfighters" on the basis of prison records of aggressive incidents. There were no significant differences in testosterone levels between these two groups of men, casting considerable doubt on the straightforward testosterone-aggression hypothesis. Angier (1996) reported a study in which testosterone replacement therapy actually resulted in an increase in friendliness in men.

Kemper (1990) reviewed the extensive literature on testosterone and concluded that, in animals and in humans, there exists a "socio-bio-social chain" in the effects of testosterone on behavior. When males gain *dominance*, testosterone levels increase, and the male is, in turn, affected by these hormonal surges in various ways. In other words, the social affects the biological, which in turn affects the social. Kemper described a complicated causal chain which included connections between testosterone, dominance, social structure, sexual behavior, and aggression. Mazur's (1983) contention is that dominance, not aggression, is the primary motive, with physical aggression as a frequent avenue for dominance. Therefore, aggression and testosterone may be linked, but only if aggression produces dominance. After thoroughly reviewing the available research on the hormone, Pepler and Slaby (1994) concluded that "The role of testosterone is small and relatively unimportant [in causing violence] compared to psychosocial factors that are experienced during development." (p. 45). Bjorkqvist's (1994) review echoes the conclusion that the testosterone-aggression link is not consistently demonstrated in studies involving human participants.

Endocrinologist Robert Sapolsky (1997) in an essay entitled "The Trouble with Testosterone" echoes some of these findings and summarizes recent research. He asks a crucial question, "Does the action of this hormone tell us anything about *individual* differences in levels of aggression, anything about why some males, some human males, are exceptionally violent? Among an array of males—human or otherwise—are the highest testosterone levels found in the most aggressive individuals?" (p. 151, emphasis original). The answer is no. Changes in testosterone levels over time within an individual do not predict levels of aggression. Although the removal of testosterone in an animal (through castration) drastically lowers aggression, restoring that animal to 20% of the original testosterone level returns aggression to the previous level, and increasing testosterone to 200% of original has no effect (although there is somewhat of an increase at 400%).

Sapolsky's conclusion is that testosterone has a "permissive effect" on aggression—some of the hormone must be present, but the level of the hormone is not a critical factor. Moreover, animal's aggression is not random. Among monkeys, males most often fight with the males who are immediately above and below them in the dominance hierarchy, and so the aggression is instrumental in holding the animal's position within the troop. Sapolsky makes two important conclusions: "testosterone isn't causing aggression, it's *exaggerating* the aggression that's already there." (p. 155, emphasis original), and "the more social experience an individual has prior to castration, the more likely that the behavior persists [after castration]. *Social conditioning can more than make up for the hormone*" (p. 156, emphasis added).

Researchers are also investigating the role of genes in violence. One study of five generations of violent Dutch men found an apparent genetic marker on the X-chromosome (Richardson, 1993). People with close relatives who are antisocial personality disordered are at increased risk for developing the disorder, even when they have no contact with the antisocial relative (Sue, Sue, & Sue, 2003). There is also evidence of brain structural abnormalities in violent people (Stein, 1998).

One more point is very important: male-female differences in aggression are much more pronounced for *physical* aggression (violence) than for other forms of aggression, such as insults or social ostracizing (Pepler & Slaby, 1994), and even these differences do not exist prior to preschool age (Loeber & Stouthamer-Loeber, 1998). Therefore, the major difference is not in the experience of aggression or even the frequency of its expression, but rather in the *mode* of expression. Males and females show relatively large differences in how their aggressive experience is channeled, and it is very likely that the mode of aggressive expression is strongly influenced by gendered forces. Pepler's and Slaby's (1994) conclusion is that "There is a growing recognition that biology is not the primary determinant of gender differences in aggression." (p. 44).

Three other pieces of evidence cast considerable doubt on the hypothesis that biology causes violence in males in a straightforward and universal way. First, as already mentioned, the majority of males are not violent. In one study, six percent of the male population committed about 70% of the violent crimes (Gibbs, 1995). If males' biology causes violence, then social forces have done a pretty good job at inhibiting these "natural" tendencies in the vast majority of the male population. Second, violence is confined to rather narrow settings for many men. The best example of situationally based physical aggression is domestic violence. The most common type of wife batterer is violent only in his own home, so he has little or no problem controlling his aggression elsewhere (Holtzworth-Munroe & Stuart, 1994). Finally, there are considerable cross-cultural variations in the frequency of violence within the male population (Bjorkqvist, 1994; Gilmore, 1990; Lepowsky, 1998). Ideologies of masculinity as antifemininity and unequal social statuses between the sexes are especially strongly associated with male dominance over (Coltrane, 1998) and violence toward (Lepowsky, 1998) women.

Claims about the biological universality of male violence provide a measure of justification for it and leave us with few options for resolving the problem besides punishment and confinement. The view that it is natural and normal to be physically aggressive if you are male is disrespectful to men, most of whom deserve a dignity that goes beyond that of violent animals. But even if there is a biological propensity toward aggression, we should keep in mind that there is also a biological propensity to resist violent impulses—the instincts to protect oneself and empathize with others.

In evaluating the biological bases for male violence, we return to the conclusion of Money (1987a) and many others that biology does not determine behavior, but it appears to set thresholds. Possibly because of temperamentally based higher average activity levels, hormones, neurotransmitters, or some yet undiscovered biological forces, it may take less stimulation to push the average male over the aggression threshold than it does for the average female. We turn now to an examination of how these "pushes" are created through socialization and culture.

Psychosocial Perspectives

A variety of male socialization experiences encourage violence. If we look at masculine norms, we see the seeds of aggression at every turn. Brannon's (1985) description of the structure of traditional masculinity is useful in understanding male violence:

1. *Antifemininity ("No Sissy Stuff")*: the avoidance of stereotypically feminine behaviors. Women are often viewed as caring, nurturing, compassionate, and vulnerable, the very antitheses of aggression. The hallmark of the "sissy" (the feminine man, as traditionally defined) is backing down from a fight. Men may engage in physical aggression, not because they want to dominate, but because they fear being dominated by another male, which is viewed as feminine.

2. *Achievement ("The Big Wheel")*: success and status. Two factors operate here. First, dominance through aggression is one way of rising in status in some male social groups. Second, the male who does not succeed often suffers from doubts about his masculinity, and violence is both a way of proving to himself that he is a "real man" as well as a way of venting his anger at having to live up to masculine norms. Poor and oppressed men tend to be more violent than other men. This is not surprising, given that they feel the pressure to be a "big wheel" while at the same time being prevented from many of the avenues for status attainment that privileged men enjoy.

3. *Self-reliance ("The Sturdy Oak")*: the expectation to be tough and unemotional. In a fight, men try their best. If they are beaten, they "take it like a man." Anger, the emotion that usually precedes aggression, is rarely present by itself. Normally, there are other, more vulnerable feelings associated with it (Lynch & Kilmartin, 1999). Much anger would seem to be a reaction to unacknowledged threat or uncomfortable emotional states. In one study, a team of researchers found that "macho" males respond to a crying baby with less compassion and more anger than other males. Thus, conformity to masculine ideologies is empirically associated with the propensity for converting most emotional experiences into anger (Gold, Burke, Prisco, & Willett, 1992).

We can see the conversion of vulnerability into anger in the world of athletics. Most sports fights seem to be triggered by one athlete's perception that another is trying to hurt him. Because fear is considered unmasculine, especially on the field of play, the player's fear becomes anger, and he expresses it through an act of violence. But it is important to note that this expression takes place within a violence-supportive cultural context. Fighting in many sports (especially professional sports) is condoned and sometimes encouraged by the league and the public. Referees do not intervene in professional ice hockey fights as long as only two players are involved. The punishment for fighting is five minutes in the penalty box (Note that there are very few fights in Olympic hockey, where fighting results in ejection from the game.). In all professional sports, the same assaultive behaviors occurring on the field would meet with legal penalties off the field. Yet, players are prosecuted for their behavior only in the most extreme instances, despite the fact that this violence is often captured on videotape and takes place before thousands of witnesses, including police officers.

4. *Aggression ("Give 'em Hell")*: physical risk taking and violence. Aggression is one of the primary defining features of traditional masculinity. Hockey players with the strongest levels of endorsement of traditional masculine ideologies are more likely to fight than other players. Moreover, teammates and coaches in youth hockey leagues judge players' competence more on their willingness to engage in violence (especially fist fighting) than on their playing and skating skills (Weinstein, Smith, & Wiesenthal, 1995).

Just as there are probably biological forces that work against violence and those that work toward it, there are psychosocial forces that work in both directions. Physical aggression, then, is a behavior that can be either encouraged or inhibited in various ways. We can look at violent men as men who have experienced encouragement and/or a lack of discouragement for aggressive behavior.

Understanding a behavior is not the same as excusing it, and so this approach should not be construed as absolving men from responsibility for their own behavior. As a man matures, he becomes increasingly capable of providing his own inhibitors and of resisting the encouragement to act aggressively. Violent men choose their behavior, and thus they are accountable for it. Still, a look at how gender socialization sets the stage for violence helps us in constructing solutions. Simply put, solutions to male violence involve reducing encouragers and increasing inhibitors. In practice, of course, this is not always easily done.

Violence-Encouraging Factors

1. *Separation*: According to Chodorow (1978), girls' early experiences involve connection and attachment, while boys' experiences involve the construction of a "self in separation." If a person experiences the self as unconnected to others, the he or she can tolerate the other's being hurt. Lepowsky (1998) noted that overt anger and physical aggression are less prevalent in societies that have cultural ideologies of gender egalitarianism and low levels of separation between the sexes.

2. *Objectification*: Male privilege and the masculine mystique encourage men to see other people as objects. It is easier to aggress against someone if he or she is not accorded the status of being a real person. Gender-based violence—rape, domestic violence, and gay bashing—are fueled by this kind of insensitivity, as there is a strong masculine socialization to view women and gay men as less than human.

3. *Externalizing defensive style*: Males are not socialized to "look inside" and think about how they feel. Instead, they are taught to deal with what is "out there" in the world. Therefore, when bad feelings about the self arise, men frequently deal with them in an external way. For example, a man's female partner leaves him, and he feels unlovable and worthless. Experiencing this vulnerability threatens his masculinity, so he projects all of his bad feelings onto the woman and deals with these emotions symbolically by being violent toward her.

4. *Overattention to task*: Men are raised to view the world as competitive and hierarchical (Messner, 1995). They are taught to get the job done regardless of the consequences for others. When tasks become more important than people, violence is sometimes a problem-solving measure. Examples of this mindset are not hard to find: the football player who intentionally hurts the other team's star player to put him out of the game, the gangster who has his rival killed in order to eliminate the competition, the man who rapes his date in order to "score," and the armed services commander who allows many men to be killed in order to secure a strategic position. War is the intentional sacrifice of the lives of human beings in the service of some task. Although the rationale for doing so is often that other lives are being saved, women are more likely than men to want to explore nonviolent solutions to problems (Colburn, 1991).

A college football player who had caused a shoulder separation in the other team's quarterback remarked, "You don't just hit people to tackle them. You tackle them so they don't get up. I say that respectfully." ("Notre Dame Stuns No. 9 Tennessee," 2004, p. E14). Watkins (1997) describes the culture of violence in a (hopefully atypical) college football team's practice sessions:

> [Two days a week], the players ran until they dropped, did exhausting agility drills, and went into 'the Room', a converted locker area that had been stripped bare except for old wrestling mats and a chicken-wire 'ceiling' hanging down from cables four feet off the floor. Surrounded by their teammates and by a battery of assistant coaches, all screaming, two players at a time were required to fight under the chicken wire until one was clearly beaten and lying on the floor. The winner moved on; the loser fought the next player in line, and the next one after that… until he finally won and could crawl out of the cage…. [A player described the scene:] 'I've seen people with blood completely covering their shirts…. You could be standing there puking blood and the coaches would just holler louder, 'Get tough. Get tough.' Everyone was so desperate to win we kicked, slugged, hit each other in the groin, did everything and anything. You could be out there with your best friend, and you'd be trying to kill him. (pp. 85–86)

5. *Reinforcement*: Simply, behaviors that are rewarded tend to increase in frequency. More than one boy has returned home from beating up another boy to receive the glowing approval of his father. Classroom aggression by boys often meets with loud reprimands from the teacher. All of the action in the room stops, and attention (which has a strong social reward quality) focuses on the boy. Girls' aggression is usually reprimanded more quietly (Maccoby, 1988a, 1988b). In some circles, especially sports and war, highly aggressive men reap social and material rewards. Culturally, male violence maintains patriarchal privilege through dominance and intimidation.

6. *Violent models and vicarious reinforcement*: Males may pattern their behavior after violent male role models, who are not hard to find. Sons of aggressive fathers tend to become aggressive themselves. When they grow up, they tend to produce aggressive sons of their own (Holtzworth-Munroe & Stuart, 1994; Huesman, Eron, Lefkowitz, & Walder, 1984), and so imitation is a strong factor in this intergenerational pattern of violence.

One does not have to be a keen social observer to see that a great deal of media idols are violent. In the movies, actors like Arnold Schwartzenegger, Sylvester Stallone, Bruce Willis, Chuck Norris, and Jean-Claude Van Damme have built lucrative careers portraying extremely violent characters. The depiction of male violence in sports, cartoons, Western and war movies, and "cop shows" is a longstanding tradition of the glorification of masculine aggression. Boys who imitate these characters in their play engage in rehearsal for later violence. Toy companies that manufacture toy guns and other play representations of violence also encourage such rehearsal. Nearly 80% of video games include violence; 28% depict women as sex objects, and 21% depict violence directly toward women (Dietz, 1998).

Television and movie violence is rampant, and male characters are much more likely to perpetrate violence than female ones. By the time an average U.S. child finishes elementary school, he or she will have witnessed 8,000 murders and 100,000 other acts of violence on television (Donnerstein, Slaby, & Eron, 1994). Fifty-seven percent of television shows depict violence; one-third of these shows average at least nine acts of violence per program (Seppa, 1996). The movie *Die Hard 2* contained 264 violent deaths; *Robocop* had 81, and *Total Recall* 74 (Donnerstein, Slaby, & Eron, 1994). "Good" characters (attractive role models whom children are likely to imitate) commit 40% of violent television acts. More often than not, characters show no remorse for their violent actions, and rarely do scripts portray the long-term physical, emotional, or financial consequences of violence (Murray, 1998).

Television specifically aimed at child audiences are among the worst offenders. Prime time television shows contain an average of five to six violent acts per hour, but Saturday morning children's programming contains and average of 20 to 25 such acts (Donnerstein, Slaby, & Eron, 1994). Shows like *Mighty Morphin Power Rangers* and *Teenage Mutant Ninja Turtles* are especially pernicious. Not only do they portray violence as an acceptable way to solve problems, and as having no long-term consequences, but they also portray it as being *fun*! Boyatzis, Matillo, and Nesbitt (1995) documented a sevenfold increase in children's violent play immediately after they watched *Mighty Morphin Power Rangers*. In general, mass media depicts violence as masculine and fails to communicate the terrifying and painful aspects of violence, thus rarely encouraging viewers to identify with the suffering of victims or to inhibit their aggression.

Bandura and Walters (1963) demonstrated that behaviors were more likely to be acquired from a model if one observes that the model is rewarded for the behaviors. In movies and television, aggressive men (who engage in what is perceived as "legitimate" violence) obtain the love of women, the admiration of others, and a feeling of self-righteous satisfaction.

In other research by Bandura (1973), girls and boys were compared with regard to their willingness to imitate a physically aggressive model. Boys were more likely to do so. However, when the researchers provided rewards for imitating the model, there were no sex differences. It would not be unreasonable to speculate, then, that the higher incidence of male violence is at least partly the product of the differential reinforcement of physical aggression for males and females. People are also more likely to imitate models who are perceived as being similar to the self (Bandura & Walters, 1963). It is indisputable that there are vastly more violent male models than female ones.

7. *Drug use*: Some drugs have the effect of reducing the inhibition toward violence. The most notable of these is alcohol. Intoxicated people tend to overestimate threats to the self, to choose aggressive solutions when they are frustrated, and to be more sensitive to social pressure to either increase or to decrease aggression (Gustafson, 1986). Drinking is a cultural symbol of masculinity (Lemle & Mishkind, 1989), and male social groups are almost certainly more likely to encourage physical aggression compared with female social groups. However, we must be careful not to imply that alcohol causes violence, as most people who use alcohol are not violent. The relationship between alcohol and violence can be compared to throwing gasoline on a fire. If there is no propensity for aggression, there will be no violence. Rather than causing aggression, alcohol has the effect of exaggerating the pre-existing propensity toward violence.

8. *Social expectations*: We expect males to be aggressive and we communicate these expectations to young males. The phrase, "boys will be boys" captures it well. Sometimes a young boy who is aggressive will elicit the comment, "he's all boy." Classroom teachers expect boys to be rough with one another and intervene in boys' aggressive play less often than they do with girls. Thus, boys' aggression meets with a higher degree of tolerance by the classroom authority figure (Maccoby, 1998). These social-cognitive links between aggression and masculinity carry over into the evaluation of adult men. Miedzian (1991) argues that political leaders are often willing to engage in war in order to affirm masculinity and gain the approval of the populace. The bodies of U.S. servicemen killed during the Persian Gulf and Iraq wars

were quietly buried with little media coverage or government ceremony. As a result, Americans were able to revel in the "glory" of war without experiencing its human tragedy or grieving for loss.

9. *Low masculine self-esteem*: The man who is unsure of his status or identity is prone toward violence as a compensation for feelings of worthlessness (Toch, 1992). The more powerless a man feels, the more likely he is to make attempts to seize power, thus preserving his masculinity through desperate means. This type of violent man is like the stereotypical schoolyard bully who beats up other kids in order to cover his insecurity and vent his anger toward those who will not love him. Peer rejection is strongly correlated with bullying (Coie, Dodge, & Kupersmidt, 1990).

The traditional masculine gender role emphasizes that a man is valued for what he does, not for who he is. Therefore, many men feel that they must prove their masculinity, to themselves and to others, over and over again. The man who is unsuccessful by traditional social standards, the man who succeeds but feels empty inside, and the man who is enraged by a sense that he is not valued, are more likely to be violent. The diminishment of others draws attention away from feelings of a diminished self. The relegation of women, gays, poor men, and men of color to a social underclass serves a precarious sense of defensive masculinity in majority men.

10. *Peer support*: A male peer group usually has powerful influence over its members. Peers can reinforce the ideology that violence is an appropriate way to solve problems, directly encourage a member to fight, and display hateful attitudes that underlie violence. This latter effect is especially in evidence with regard to violence against women.

Violence-Inhibiting Factors

Several social forces may have the effect of preventing violence from occurring. It is therefore important to look at these factors in the context of masculine socialization.

1. *Empathy*: Some of the foremost inhibitors of aggression are the abilities to be sensitive to, identify with, and be concerned about the pain of the potential victim. Girls are often socialized to think about how other people feel and to be connected to others. For example, playing with dolls is a rehearsal for being attuned to another's needs and caring for that person.

Culturally, there seems to be less concern for building these violence-inhibiting qualities in boys. To begin with, boys are socialized away from the emotional life. It would seem to be nearly impossible to understand and experience someone else's emotions when one does not understand one's own. The masculine emphasis on competition and task completion does not emphasize the consideration of others. In team sports, players often feel for and protect their teammates, but it is a byproduct of the task of winning, which is always defined as more important than relationships among teammates.

2. *Modeling*: Just as aggressive models can be imitated, control of aggression can also be imitated. It is vital for fathers to model this control for their sons, and many fathers do. Boys from father-absent families tend to be more aggressive (Hetherington, Cox, & Cox, 1985), perhaps partly because of their decreased exposure to a model of aggression control.

3. *Punishment*: Behaviors that are punished tend to decrease in frequency. Appropriate (nonphysical and nonshaming) and consistent punishment of aggression clearly communicates that this type of behavior is unacceptable. In some social systems, this is done well.

4. *Social and Political Systems*: Increasingly, people are speaking out against the institutional violence of war. Governments are paying more attention to holding perpetrators responsible for domestic violence. Boycotts of violent films and television can be helpful, as can support of women's empowerment and fair treatment for historically marginalized groups.

5. *Therapeutic interventions*: Individual men who have problems with control of violent behaviors can learn how to inhibit explosive urges through a variety of techniques such as anger management and communication skill development (Kivel, 1992).

6. *Reduced access to weapons*: Gun control probably does not reduce the frequency of physical aggression, but there is strong evidence that it reduces the amount of physical injury and mortality. The number of children who were killed by firearms (some by accident or suicide) between 1979 and 1991 was about the same as the number of people who were killed in the Vietnam War (Vobejda, 1994). A person is murdered with a gun about once every 30 minutes in the United States (Colburn & Trafford, 1993), and the risk of homicide is 7.8 times higher if a gun is kept in the home (Cromwell & Burgess, 1996). The handgun homicide rate fell from 14,150 to 9,390 following the enactment of the Brady Law (which imposes background checks and a waiting period for potential gun purchasers) in 1994 ("Pulling the Trigger," 1998). Although we cannot attribute a causal link between the law and the reduction of firearm murders, the evidence is compelling.

7. *Education*: Learning about gender and acquiring alternative means for dealing with frustration and conflict can be powerful tools for reducing violence. Increasingly, educational programs about violence cast the behavior in the context of toxic masculinity (Kilmartin & Berkowitz, 2005).

8. *Withdrawal of male peer support*: When violent behavior or the display of its underlying attitudes meet with disapproval from valued male peers, restraint becomes more likely. Canada's White Ribbon Campaign is a good example of men working to end men's violence against women (see Box 12.1).

The elimination of male violence involves the reduction of the needs and the incentives for this kind of behavior, the increase of disincentives, and the provision of alternative ways for dealing with the feelings that precede the aggression (Toch, 1992). Violence is deeply ingrained in traditional masculinity and in many cultures. Therefore, efforts to-

Box 12.1: The White Ribbon Campaign

For a week in December 1991, tens of thousands of Canadian men wore small white ribbons pinned to their clothing on the anniversary of the 1990 "Montreal Massacre," when Mark Lepine murdered 14 women at L'ecole Polytechnique in Montreal, Canada before committing suicide. The White Ribbon Campaign was an effort to get men to show their support for ending men's violence against women. It was the first large-scale initiative ever developed by men to speak out on a subject usually considered a "women's issue."

Supporters of the campaign distributed the ribbons at schools, churches, shops, and places of employment. The prime minister, several celebrities, and some corporate heads were among the men who participated. Canadian men of conscience also raised money for rape crisis centers, domestic violence shelters, batterer treatment programs, and other organizations that deal directly with the consequences of men's violence against women. As the campaign became highly visible, men's violence against women became a subject for publicity, discussion, and debate. Many men across Canada were talking seriously about the problem for the first time.

One of the goals of the campaign organizers was to break the silence on the issue. In that regard, the effort was an unqualified success. A larger goal is to build a permanent national men's antiviolence organization. That effort is now well underway.

I brought the White Ribbon Campaign to my campus in 1994 (Kilmartin, 1996). Detractors of the campaign voiced the opinion that it is a "feel-good" effort fueled by men's guilt, and that has no positive effect. We were able to answer these critics with two pieces of evidence. First, we raised a significant amount of money for the local rape crisis and domestic violence agencies, a very tangible contribution. Second, we recognized the contention that the White Ribbon Campaign is ineffective as an *empirical* question (one that can only be answered by collecting data). Our research indicated that students' awareness of the problem of men's violence against women and their attitude toward the problem both improved as a direct result of the campaign (Kilmartin, Chirico, & Leemann, 1997).

The White Ribbon Campaign is significant in that it is a grass roots movement by men in the direction of dealing with a central men's social issue. It provides a stimulus for men to begin to understand the impact of gender socialization and sexist culture on their lives (Sluser & Kaufman, 1992).

ward violence reduction must cover a broad range of settings, including parenting practices, education, the legal system, politics, economics, and therapeutic settings. Since violence is so much a part of the masculine gender role, the very fabric of masculinity must change if violence is to be reduced.

DOMESTIC VIOLENCE

It is sad to say that perhaps the most frequent site of men's violence is in the home. Estimates of at least mild physical violence taking place between partners range as high as 60% for married couples (Pagelow, 1984) and 22–28% of people in dating relationships (Thompson, 1990). A review of domestic violence prevalence studies indicates that "between 21% and 34% of women in this country [the United States] will be physically assaulted—slapped, kicked, beaten, choked, or threatened or attacked with a weapon—by an intimate adult partner [during her lifetime]." (Goodman, Koss, Fitzgerald, Russo, & Keita, 1993, p. 1055). In the United States, a male beats a female partner an average of once every 15 seconds (Colburn, 1994). Male partners and ex-partners murder more than 1000 women every year in the United States (United States Department of Justice, 2003). Domestic violence is a serious problem in most parts of the world (Walker, 1999).

Somewhat surprisingly, research indicates that women use physical violence against their partners as much or even more than men (Thompson, 1990; O'Leary, Barling, Arias, Rosenbaum, Malone, & Tyree, 1989; Archer, 2000). However, for many theorists, this finding does not imply gender symmetry in violence in the home. Researchers usually used the Conflict Tactics Scale (CTS; Strauss, 1990) in demonstrating men's and women's similar levels of aggression. The CTS counts acts of violence but does not measure the context or the meaning of each act (Kimmel, 2001). To illustrate, Person A threatens to hit Person B in the head with a baseball bat and rushes toward Person B, who tries to push Person A away as Person A strikes Person B with the bat and causes a severe brain injury which leads to death. Under the CTS, each person's aggression counts as one. Michael Kimmel (2001) uses an even more striking example, "if she punches him to get him to stop beating the children, or pushes him away after he has sexually assaulted her, it would count one for her, none for him." (p. 9). Kimmel goes on to say that ignoring the context of injury is like "observing that death rates have soared for males between 19 and 30 without observing that a country has declared war." (p. 9).

Several researchers have documented gender asymmetry in domestic violence. Women's aggression usually results in less fear (O'Leary & Curley, 1986), and much less physical damage than men's domestic violence (Lardner, 1997). Therefore, although female domestic physical aggression is common and should not be ignored, it is male aggression that engenders the highest levels of terror and danger. Former U.S. Surgeon General C. Everett Koop described domestic violence as the number one health problem for women in the United States, accounting for one-half of all 15-44 year old females' hospital emergency room visits (Cromwell & Burgess, 1996). In 2001, current or former male partners perpetrated about one-fifth of non-fatal violence against females over the age of 12. Female current or former partners account for 3% of violence against males ("2001 Report on Violence Against Women Released," 2003).

Men's violence in the home has a long history. For many years, the exercise of the man's authority over his family via physical abuse was accepted and tolerated (Landes, Squyres, & Quiram, 1997). The patriarchal tradition of woman as property allowed the man to do whatever he wanted with his wife. In 1996, a Maryland judge apologized for sentencing a man who shot and killed his wife when he found her in bed with another man, to time in jail because of mandatory sentencing guidelines (Childress, 1996). His remarks gave the clear impression that this man's homicidal behavior was natural and acceptable.

Research into the characteristics of male batterers reveals that, in general, they tend to be overconforming to the traditional masculine role and the culture of violence (Gondolf, 1988). They have a high need for power and control (Mason & Blankenship, 1987) and tend to blame their partners for their own violent behavior (Cromwell & Burgess, 1996). Thus, they often think that they beat their wives, not because they have trouble controlling their tempers or feel threatened by their partners' independence, but because their wives behaved wrongly or "don't know how to listen." The blaming of the victim allows the man to abdicate responsibility for and downplay the impact of his violent behavior. When a man perceives the source of his problems to be outside of himself, he sees no reason to explore his inner world or change his behavior.

Male batterers also tend to have low self-esteem (Dutton & Golant, 1995) and low social status (Sugarman & Hotaling, 1989). Nearly half of the time when a man murders his female partner, she is either leaving him or threatening to do so (Dutton, 1995). These data support the hypothesis that violence is a compensatory measure for feelings of masculine failure (Gondolf, 1988). It is also true that low socioeconomic status involves higher levels of life stress, fewer resources to cope with that stress, and sometimes a more exaggerated subculture of violence (Sugarman & Hotaling, 1989), although we find men who are violent in their homes in every socioeconomic stratum.

One of the most striking (but not surprising) risk markers of male domestic violence is the presence of a physically aggressive father in the family of origin. Perpetrators are often survivors of some form of childhood abuse and usually witnessed violence within their parents' relationship (Grusznski & Bankovics, 1990). Sugarman & Hotaling (1989) described the following childhood experience of the typical male batterer and its connection to dominance: "Essentially, the individual not only witnessed his father physically aggress against his mother and be reinforced for this behavior (the individual's mother often gave in to the father's demands), but his own violent behavior goes unpunished and is reinforced by his partner's surrendering to his will." (p. 1035).

We should be careful not to forget that domestic violence takes place in a cultural context that supports it. Former football star O.J. Simpson, who pleaded "no contest" to a charge of assaulting his wife, was directed to attend counseling sessions (which he did over the telephone), pay a small fine, and perform some community service. Later, he was charged in the double murder of his wife and a companion (He was acquitted in a criminal trial, however he was found to be responsible for these two deaths in civil court.). Simpson's status as a masculine, powerful former athlete was probably a factor in the leniency of the original sentence and the failure of the legal system to take an interest in rehabilitating him. Football is the quintessential hypermasculine and violent pursuit, and so it is not surprising that a disproportionate number of football players (Brubaker, 1994) and other contact sport athletes are involved in domestic violence and rape (Crosset, Benedict, & McDonald, 1998; Parrot, Cummings, & Marchell, 1994). We should be careful not to characterize all of these athletes as assaultive, as most are not. At the same time, participation in contact sports is associated with the risk of physical violence off the field. Sports ideology is moderately related to negative attitudes toward women, lesbians, and gay men (Harry, 1995).

In summary, male batterers tend to be angry, hypermasculine, and disenfranchised men who often see violence as natural and normal. They are unable to deal with vulnerable emotions and so they convert these feelings into anger. They also have learned that engaging in violence gets them what they want: dominance, power, control, and a vent for their anger. And their behavior takes place within a patriarchal social-cultural context that condones and even encourages it.

Toward Solutions

The reduction of such a widespread problem as domestic violence requires a comprehensive, coordinated effort. The city of Duluth, Minnesota launched such a program in 1982. It involved the establishment of a women's shelter, stricter criminal penalties for spousal assault, and mandatory participation in rehabilitation programs for offenders. Police officers who have probable cause that an assault has taken place are required to make an arrest (Hoffman, 1992). Seminars, trainings, and resource materials are offered for prosecutors, human service providers, community leaders, and educators (Duluth Domestic Abuse Intervention Project, n.d.).

The Duluth project has met with some degree of success, particularly in the city-wide reduction of domestic homicide, and it has been used as a model in many other cities. At the same time, recidivism in offenders is high (about 40%), and even the director of the program doubts that it has a strong deterrent effect on men as they consider engaging in violence (Hoffman, 1992). Holtzworth-Munroe and Stuart (1994) and Gondolf (1988) have noted that a substantial proportion of battering men have antisocial personality tendencies or full blown sociopathic disorders. These men do not respond well to the kind of self-control treatment approaches that batterer programs often use. Unfortunately, many do not respond at all to any psychological interventions, and these men must be controlled through the legal system.

Many male batterers, however, are treatable, and a number of strategies for intervention have emerged in recent years. Among these are social skills training, therapy groups, and educational programs. The goals of these programs are to sensitize men to the personal and interpersonal consequences of their violence, to help them take responsibility for their violence, and to teach them ways of changing their thinking, emotional responses, and behaviors in conflict situations.

RAPE AND OTHER SEXUAL ASSAULT

Rape is sexual penetration without consent. Sexual assault is a broader term; it includes any form of nonconsensual touching of areas of the body that are associated with sexuality (Kilmartin & Allison, 2007). These violent crimes are alarmingly common. In large scale studies researchers have found that rapists have victimized or attempted to victimize as many as 25% of U.S. females at some point in their lives (Russell & Howell, 1983; Koss, 1993). One out of 12 college men has reported that he has forced a woman to have sexual intercourse against her will on at least one occasion (Koss, Gidycz, & Wisniewski, 1985). Sexual assault perpetrators also victimize other males at a much higher rate than is generally believed (See the section below on male victims and survivors.). Very few rapists are ever incarcerated for their crimes (Lisak & Miller, 2002).

The stereotypical rapist is the evil stranger that lurks in the bushes, but in fact, more than three-quarters of rapes occur in cases where the victim knows the attacker (Vobejda, 1995; Parrot & Bechofer, 1991). These *acquaintance rapes* have been the subject of increased research and publicity within the past 30 years. This crime of violence takes place in incredibly high frequency on college campuses. Koss (1990) estimated that sexual assault perpetrators victimize about 50 out of every 1,000 college women in any given year.

One common misconception about rape is that it is primarily motivated by sexuality. For some people, the image of the rapist is one of a lusty, sex-starved man whose frustrated urges get the best of him. However, most experts believe that the primary motivation for rape is not sexual, but aggressive (Groth, 1979; Burt, 1991). It is the use of sex in the expression of power, control, anger, and hate. Groth (1979) referred to rape as a "pseudosexual act." In describing the relationship between rape and sex, we might ask the following question: If I hit you over the head with a frying pan, would you call it cooking?"

Rape and Masculinity

Sexual aggression is part and parcel of the socialization of males. Lisak (1997) cites fourteen recent studies demonstrating that hypermasculine characteristics are strongly connected to sexualized violence. In the search for an understanding of why men rape, it is useful to identify the rape-supporting cultural messages that boys receive as they grow up:

1. *Femiphobia and misogyny*: Males are raised to be separate from women and the feminine in themselves. The result is a fear of femininity. One way of dealing with this fear is to overpower and control the woman. From this perspective, derogatory nicknames, misogynist jokes, and other behaviors that disrespect women create the social atmosphere that encourages rape. Many feminist theorists believe that rape is a symptom of economic and political systems in which women have been rendered relatively powerless by men (Lepowsky, 1998). Mainstream U.S. culture traditionally encourages men to dominate women, and victimizing a woman with something as emotional and intimate as sexuality is extreme domination. Sexual aggression in men is related to stereotyped views of gender roles, among them the belief that women and men are sexual adversaries, and that therefore a heterosexual date is a kind of competition in which the male attempts to obtain sex and the female attempts to obtain affection and/or persuade the male to spend money on her (Hall, 1990).

This belief is an extreme distortion of what is supposedly a pleasurable event in which two people enjoy each other's company, but cultural ideologies like "the battle of the sexes" and linguistic constructions like "the opposite sex," both of which portray men and women as enemies, encourage this kind of distortion.

2. *Emotional denial*: As with any violence, rape is a failure of empathy. The socialized inability to be sensitive to one's own feelings makes it difficult to be sensitive to the feelings of another person. Lisak (1997) summarizes the connection: "…it can be argued that the very fact of being disconnected from emotional experience dramatically increases the likelihood that someone would be able and willing to exploit and abuse the sexuality of another person. Separated from its emotional associations, unlinked from its relationship to human connection, sexuality is more likely to be experienced as simply another physical sensation…the 'other' can be experienced as pure object… ." (p. 163).

3. *Two exceptions of emotional control*: Although men are encouraged to deny and control emotions, the expression of two feelings, anger and lust, is socially condoned. Interestingly, cultural ideologies consider these two emotions to be *completely out of the man's control*. It is not unusual to hear that a "man's gotta do what a man's gotta do" when he gets angry, that a "man's gotta have it" sexually, and that an erect penis "has no conscience."

With anger and lust being the only two culturally permissible emotions, it is not surprising that they can become combined with each other. In fact, probably the most frequently used slang term for sexual intercourse (fuck) is also one of the most frequently used terms for victimization. Violence is sexualized time and time again in movies, television shows, and other media.

Western culture encourages men to *act out* emotion rather than deal with it in other ways (Lynch & Kilmartin, 1999). This may be a partial explanation for the striking difference between East and West in the incidence of rape and other violent crimes (Sue, Bernier, Durran, Feinberg, Pedersen, Smith, & Vasquez-Nattall, 1982).

4. *The "rape myth"*: Some men believe that women secretly want to be raped, say "no" when they mean "yes," and "ask for it" by dressing or acting provocatively, or by putting themselves in risky situations (Burt, 1980; Johnson, 1994). Male undergraduates who viewed films depicting the rape myth were more likely to subscribe to the myth, less likely to identify with the victim, and less likely to agree that the rapist deserves punishment (Briere & Malamuth, 1983; Koss, Leonard, Beezley, & Oros, 1985). One need not see an actual rape depicted in a movie to accept the rape myth. The sexual domination of the woman, followed by her giving in and becoming aroused, conveys the same message in milder form. A typical scene is a leading man who forcefully kisses an unwilling woman, who then "melts into his arms" and falls in love with him. Many romantic comedies portray erotic love as an outcome of conflict between a man and a woman.

Box 12.2: The Question of Pornography

The sale of explicit sexual material in the United States is a $10 billion per year industry, more than double the size of the commercial music industry, and close to the size of the mainstream film industry, which grosses approximately $12.2 billion per year (Stock, 1997). Forty-six percent of men and 16% of women reported having purchased sexually explicit material within a one-year period of the time they were surveyed (Michael, Gagnon, Laumann, & Kolata, 1994). Pornographic images and descriptions are now widely available on the Internet (Kaplan, 1998).

Does pornography cause men to become violent toward women? This question tends to produce strong responses from both sides of the issue. Prior to the 1960s, there were few studies that examined the effects of pornography on behavior (Walsh, 1987). The report of the U.S. Government-sponsored Commission on Obscenity and Pornography (1970) concluded that there was no evidence linking pornography to sex crimes. However, a subsequent government-sponsored commission reached the opposite conclusion (Attorney General's Commission, 1986). Social scientists have challenged the findings of both of these commissions (Walsh, 1987).

One of the difficulties in evaluating the effects of pornography is terminology. When the U.S. Supreme Court first considered legal challenges to explicit erotic material, it had a serious problem with constructing the definition of "obscenity." This difficulty prompted Justice Potter Stewart to say that, "I can't define it, but I know it when I see it." (quoted in Green, 1987, p. 437).

The definition of pornography is a critical factor in research. Explicit photographs and films can depict clothed people in provocative pose and situation, nudity, consensual sexual activity, the dominance of one sex over the other, or the violence and degradation of a person in a sexual situation. In the latter two types of material, it is nearly always women who are depicted as being dominated, objectified, and raped.

Opponents of the pornography-violence hypothesis often cite cross-cultural research that shows a decrease (or lack of increase) in sex crimes for countries, such as Denmark and the former West Germany, following the legalization of sexually explicit material. Still, these are correlational data. Two events occurring together does not mean that one has caused the other. Theorists on this side of the issue also point out that violent pornography and depictions of consensual sex (often referred to as "erotica") produce different effects on viewers (Green, 1987).

On the other side of the argument are theorists like Brownmiller (1975), who argues that pornography is degrading by its very nature and that it creates a social climate for the tolerance of sexual assault. MacKinnon (1985) stated that pornography "eroticizes hierarchy, it sexualizes inequality... institutionalizes the sexuality of male supremacy, fusing the eroticization of dominance and submission with the social construction of male and female." (p. 1). Russo (1998) summarizes several studies demonstrating that a significant number of male pornography consumers use the material to intimidate their wives and girlfriends as well as their female co-workers, neighbors, and social contacts.

Some researchers have focused their investigations of erotic material to that which is overtly aggressive in content, and there is evidence to support the hypothesis that violent pornography may have a link to sexual violence. Male research subjects who viewed sexually violent films became increasingly accepting of sexual violence against women. More specifically, male subjects who viewed scenes depicting the "rape myth" (that the victim becomes sexually aroused during the rape) tend to respond with increased acceptance of this myth, increased self-reported likelihood of raping (Linz & Malamuth, 1993), and increased likelihood of suggesting that rapists should get light prison sentences (Zillmann & Bryant, 1982). Russell (1998) notes many examples of the implication that rape is pleasurable for the female victim in pornographic magazines. Laboratory research by Donnerstein (1983; 1984) demonstrated an increase in men's willingness to aggress against a female after viewing aggressive sexual material.

Thus, the sexualization of violence does seem to have some effect in the direction of producing more callous attitudes toward women's feelings. Donnerstein and Linz (1986) opined

that, "aggressive images are the issue, not sexual images." (p. 601). These same researchers argued that nonpornographic sexualized violence, such as that found in "slasher" films, detective magazines, and many movies, have more of an effect on sexual (and other) violence than does most of the kind of material one would buy in an "adults only" store (Linz & Donnerstein, 1992). However, even if there is no overt aggression, a great deal of pornography contains themes of male dominance, female submission, and indifference to women's pain (Jensen & Dines, 1998). Women who viewed pornographic films tended to react with disgust to scenes that portrayed objectification, dominance, and penis worship much more than they did to explicit sexual depictions (Linz & Malamuth, 1993).

Although nonviolent erotica probably has no direct link to violence against women, there is some evidence that it may have a damaging effect on relationships between men and women. Male research subjects who viewed *Playboy* and *Penthouse* magazine centerfolds tended to give lower ratings of their female partners' attractiveness and individual worth (Malamuth, 1984). Moreover, they reported being less in love with their partners than men who did not view these pictures (Kenrick, Gutierres, & Goldberg, 1989).

"Men's magazines" like these are certainly guilty of the sexual objectification of women. As the above evidence suggests, men who view the physical "perfection" (enhanced with lighting and photograph retouching) of these magazine models seem to make comparisons of centerfolds with other women. The fact that they report being less in love reveals that erotica reinforces the patriarchal notion that relationships between men and women depend on the woman's sexual desirability.

Is pornography harmful? Although, as we have seen, there are some answers, there are probably more questions. The controversy continues, as does the research into this important area.

Sometimes, rape myths are portrayed in subtler forms. A beer commercial aired during the 1990s depicts a woman on a train in the desert by herself. A man is on top of the moving train, and he disconnects her train car from the rest of the train. Her facial expression indicates that she is intrigued, and perhaps sexually aroused, by this stranger's behavior. The implication is that women like to be isolated and overpowered by masculine men whom they do not know. Whether you are male or female, imagine how frightening an experience it would be to be isolated from the rest of the world by someone whom you do not know. Beer commercials are notorious for presenting a number of hypermasculine and misogynistic fantasies (Strate, 1992). There is some evidence that certain kinds of pornography may also encourage violence toward women (see Box 12.2).

5. *Performance and quantification over experience*: Cultural masculinity emphasizes that a man's worth is measured by deeds and results, not by his emotional satisfaction or feelings about himself. We also tend to judge men in quantifiable terms ("More is better."). In the sexual arena, this attitude is played out by the encouragement of men to have intercourse with as many women as possible. "Stud" and "Playboy" are complimentary terms, and the "macho mentality" values the man who "goes after what he wants" and "won't take no for an answer."

6. *Poor sexual communication*: One of the questions that Biernbaum and Weinberg (1991) ask men in their campus rape prevention workshops is, "How do you know when your friend wants to kiss on a date?" Most men respond, "it's in her eyes... she leans toward me and I lean toward her... it's in the air...I just know... Body language" (p. 22). When asked, "Have you ever thought that she wanted to kiss you and been wrong?" most men acknowledge that they have. In most jurisdictions, kissing someone against his or her will is a misdemeanor sexual assault, and so this normative mistake is in fact a crime. In response to Biernbaum and Weinberg's question, few men say, "I ask her," or "I tell her I would like to kiss her and see how she responds."

It is a peculiar part of mainstream U.S. culture that engaging in sex is viewed as acceptable, but talking about it is not. It is probably rare for two people, especially if they are young, to actually discuss sex before engaging in it, thus creating a potential for miscommunication. The man who misreads or ignores the woman's signals may be more likely to commit acquaintance rape. Even if the woman verbally refuses intercourse, the man may rape her if he subscribes to the rape myth, thinking that she really wants to have sex and just needs to be forced a little.

But we should not be fooled into thinking that most rapes are the result of mere misunderstandings between two people. The vast majority of rapes are the result of intentional victimization on the part of male perpetrators, who frequently isolate women and sometimes incapacitate them with alcohol or other drugs as part of planned predatory behavior. In an interview with David Lisak (2005), a rapist describes a methodical sequence in which he identifies a female college student as a potential victim, obtains her trust, reduces her resistance with alcohol, isolates her, and then physically overpowers her. He refers to her as a "target" and as "prey" that he has "staked out." This rapist was never charged with any crime.

7. *Homophobia*: "Scoring" is seen as a way of proving to oneself and others that one is not homosexual. Rape may be a desperate way for the man who is sexually unsuccessful to affirm his heterosexuality.

The behavior of rape requires three conditions: a social-cultural context that supports it, individual pathology, and a personal decision to engage in the harmful act (Kilmartin & Berkowitz, 2005). We turn now to the second set of influences in a discussion of the differences between rapists and normal men.

Rapist Characteristics

Rape encouraging attitudes and socialization experiences are rather common and pervasive, yet it is clear that most men do not rape. Recent research and theory has sought to describe the psychology of the rapist. Although rapists are not all alike, some typical characteristics emerge among perpetrators.

Groth (1979) described three basic patterns in incarcerated rapists. The most common one was *power rape*, in which the major motive of the rapist seems to be to conquer and control the victim. The power rapist's main goal is to possess the person sexually. Intercourse is taken as evidence of conquest, and the rapist uses whatever force he thinks is necessary to subdue the victim.

The power rapist uses sex as a way of "compensating for underlying feelings of inadequacy and serves to express issues of mastery, strength, control, identity, and capability." (Groth, 1979, p. 25). In other words, the rapist makes a desperate attempt to prove his masculinity. He is desperate because his underlying feelings are so painful, and because he has no emotional resources to use in dealing with his pain. About 55% of convicted offenders are judged to be primarily motivated by power.

The second most common pattern is the *anger rape*, which comprises about 40% of imprisoned rapists. The anger rapist's primary objective is to harm the victim. He typically uses more force than he needs to overpower the victim and includes verbal abuse in his attack, as his goal is to make the victim feel as badly as possible, both psychologically and physically. Typically, the anger rapist feels that he has been wronged and hurt by women and rape is his revenge. Any woman is a symbol of the source of his pain.

Like the power rapist, the anger rapist is not usually sexually aroused at the time of the attack, nor does he derive much sexual pleasure from his crime. Often, he does not achieve an erection without masturbating or forcing the victim to stimulate him. Many anger rapists do not have orgasms during the assault, and some even have trouble remembering whether or not they ejaculated.

The least frequent pattern is the *sadistic rape*, in which power and violence are eroticized. For this type (about 5% of incarcerated rapists), sexual gratification comes from hurting another person. The sexual motive is more connected to the assault for the sadistic rapist, unlike the other two patterns. A similarity to the other types is underlying feelings of masculine inadequacy.

Groth's study described men who had been arrested, convicted, and imprisoned as a result of having raped. However, these are a very small minority of rapists, estimated at around only one percent of actual perpetrators (Lisak & Miller, 2002). It remained to be seen whether or not unincarcerated rapists are different from convicted rapists in significant ways.

Lisak and Roth (1988) compared questionnaire responses of college men who reported having engaged in sexually aggressive behavior with those who reported that they had not. Sexually aggressive men were more likely to perceive themselves as having been hurt, betrayed, or dominated by women. They were highly sensitive to being teased or manipulated by women, and they often experienced angry feelings in connection with interactions with women. The conclusion of the researchers was that the motivations for college men's sexual aggression are similar to those of incarcerated rapists.

As we paint the picture of the rapist as an insecure, hypermasculine man, it seems important to search for the origins of masculine inadequacy in the sexual aggressor. Lisak (1991) collected data from psychological measures and conducted in-depth interviews with 15 men who admitted to acquaintance rape and 15 matched control subjects in a college population. Although this was neither a large nor a representative sample of the population of men, this study provides some important clues to the origins of rape within the individual.

Lisak's findings confirm what we have already described. Rapists scored significantly higher than other men on "standardized measures of hostility toward women, underlying anger motivation, dominance as a motive for sexual interactions, underlying power motivation, and on two indices of hypermasculinity." (Lisak, 1991, p. 248). Hypermasculinity has been found to be related to callous sexual attitudes and misogyny in other studies (Mosher & Tomkins, 1988).

In Lisak's (1991) interviews, one striking finding was that the rapists almost invariably expressed bitter feelings and clear disappointments toward their fathers, whom they described as both emotionally and physically distant. Some rapists reported having suffered significant physical violence at the hands of their fathers. Although the other participants in the study also reported having wanted to be closer to their fathers, the underlying bitter feelings were not there, and they made positive statements about their fathers much more often than the rapists. Feelings about mothers were much more variable.

The impression one carries away from these interview data is that many men feel loved and affirmed by their fathers, but that some feel unvalued. These men, who have not been accepted by the most important male figure in their lives, are most likely to lash out against women (although it is important to say that all men with bitter feelings toward their fathers are not rapists).

Without an internal sense of positive masculinity, these men are more likely to be drawn into and contribute to hypermasculine peer groups that are aggressive and misogynist (Koss & Dinero, 1988). They use these groups to protect themselves from their insecurities by identifying with the group and having women as an underclass. The street gang is the most common of these negative male peer cultures. It has also been argued that some fraternities (Sanday, 1990; 1996), and athletic teams (Parrot, Cummings, & Marchell, 1994), especially in contact sports like football, hockey, and basketball (Crosset, 2000) serve this function on college campuses. The sense of some college athletes that they are somehow privileged contributes to the atmosphere of victimization, and male college athletes tend to have more traditional gender role attitudes than nonathletes (Houseworth, Peplow, & Thirer, 1989). The most extreme example of sexual violence in negative cultures of masculinity is the gang rape. Fraternities and athletic teams are disproportionately involved in these crimes (O'Sullivan, 1991).

Boswell and Spade (1996) carried out an interesting study of fraternity male peer culture. Based on surveys of campus women's awareness of sexual assault incidents, they identified four fraternities that were relatively safe places for women (low-risk fraternities) and four that were relatively dangerous (high-risk fraternities). Then, they observed fraternity parties and described differences between these two types of organizations.

Typical parties in low-risk fraternities tended to have a friendly atmosphere and a good deal of social interaction between men and women. Music was not so loud as to make it difficult to have conversation. There was very little cursing, yelling, or jokes and comments that degrade women, and bathrooms provided for women were clean and well supplied. In contrast, parties at high-risk houses were marked by separation of the sexes, heavier drinking, louder music, and fewer conversations between men and women. There was more crude behavior and open hostility toward women, and women's bathrooms were filthy, sometimes with vomit in the sinks and clogged toilets. Men at high-risk houses gathered on porches the morning after parties and shouted derogatory comments to women who were walking home after spending the night there. In contrast to low-risk fraternities, men in high-risk fraternities had few long-term relationships with women, and in fact, the fraternity brothers actively discouraged such relationships.

The findings from this study support the conclusions of anthropological studies by Sanday (1981; 1996) and Lepowsky (1998) that link violence against women to the social separation of the sexes and the lack of gender-egalitarian attitudes. In the high-risk fraternities, men denigrated women and kept them at a distance except for sex. The power distinction between the sexes was very evident, with clear messages that women are subordinate to men, who are in control of the situation, and that respectful relationships with women are a threat to the fraternal brotherhood. Martin and Hummer (1997) conclude that many fraternities "create a sociocultural context in which the use of coercion in sexual relations with women is normative and in which the mechanisms to keep this pattern of behavior in check are minimal at best and absent at worst" (p. 399).

Thus, sexual violence in the context of hypermasculinity is related to patriarchal culture. Whiting (1965) was one of the first to argue that the internal sense of masculinity is only necessary when the culture demands that men be different, more important, and more powerful than women. When the man feels powerless, he denigrates and attacks women in an attempt to affirm this cultural definition of masculinity, an act which Whiting labeled "Masculine Protest." Researchers have found a link between masculine gender role stress and sexual aggression (Malamuth, Linz, Heavey, Barnes, & Acker, 1995).

Thus viewed, rape is an extreme compensatory reaction to the gender role strain created by patriarchy. There would be no motivation to rape if men did not feel the need to prove themselves superior by virtue of being men. Sanday (1981) reports that rape is virtually nonexistent in 44 nonpatriarchal societies, and that only 18% of cultures are "rape prone." She includes mainstream U.S. culture in the latter category.

Toward Solutions

The reduction of rape can involve a variety of strategies, including those that thwart the attempted rapist, prevent the rapist from committing repeated crimes, prevent potential rapists from ever committing the crime, and change the rape-supportive aspects of the culture. These varied interventions can involve legal, educational, economic, family, community, therapeutic, and political systems. To describe all of the possibilities would require several volumes, but we can outline some ideas here.

Preventing a rapist from committing repeated crimes is a critical component of rape prevention, as perpetrators tend to commit multiple rapes as well as other crimes, and only an estimated 1% are ever incarcerated (Lisak & Miller, 2002). These efforts include vigorous legal enforcement and rehabilitative interventions such as facilitating the rapist's acceptance of responsibility for the crime, building the criminal's empathy for the victim, developing social skills, and decreasing sexual arousal to rape. Attempts to thwart the potential rapist have historically taken the forms of rendering environments less conducive to rape, and of educating potential victims. Lighting of dark areas, police patrols, and teaching self-defense skills are strategies in this area. On some college campuses, risk reduction strategies such as escort services, danger avoidance education (i.e., don't walk alone at night, make sure windows and doors are locked, learn what kinds of men are likely to assault), alcohol rules, and fraternity policies are fairly common.

When these kinds of strategies are the sole interventions, there are implicit assumptions that men will rape if given the chance, that there is little we can do to stop them, and that therefore we must deal with the problem largely by helping potential victims to be prepared and making environments less conducive to rape opportunity. Carole Corcoran (1992) described these approaches as "victim control" strategies. She argued that they subtly place the responsibility for rape prevention on women. Alan Berkowitz (Kilmartin & Berkowitz, 2005) strongly suggested that the term *risk reduction* should be used when educating females, and that the term *rape prevention* be reserved for male audiences, to give the clear message that women are not responsible for preventing rape.

Although there is no argument that safety measures can and should be implemented, they are not enough. Broader rape prevention efforts involve changing the behaviors and underlying motivations of men. Rape prevention services for men are a relatively recent development.

The alarming estimates of the incidence of acquaintance rape at colleges and universities have stimulated a number of programmatic efforts to decrease violence against women. Services designed specifically for men include rape awareness programs (Brod, 2005; Stevens & Gebhardt, 1984), experiential workshops (Allison, 2005; Foubert, 2005; Heppner, 2005) sometimes combined with didactic information (Rosenthal, Heesacker, & Neimeyer, 1995), peer education and counseling (Allison, 2005), and specialized workshops for fraternity members (Mahlstedt, 1998; Kilmartin & Ring, 1991) or athletes (Katz, 1995; Stevens, 2005). Other programs offer survivor services, rape education for women and coed groups, alcohol and judicial policies, and faculty and staff training (Parrot, 1991).

Some programs are "one-shot" or annual events, others are ongoing, comprehensive, institutional efforts. Fassinger (quoted in Moses, 1991) noted that the latter are, of course, preferable. Earle's (1992) comparative study showed that the most effective sexual assault prevention programs for men are peer-administered and interactive. A model comprehensive program for men has been in place for several years at Pittsburg State University in Kansas (Allison, 2005).

The goals of all of these rape prevention efforts include: sensitizing men to the negative consequences of sexual violence for the perpetrator, facilitating empathy for victims of sexual assault, and educating men about the rape-encouraging aspects of socialization, culture, and patriarchy. Parrot (1991) pointed out that a major goal is to effect an understanding of the continuum of sexual violence against women. Sexist behavior, objectification, and exploitation of women have the effect of desensitizing men to the seriousness and deep pain of sexual assault.

Recent efforts in sexual assault prevention have emphasized the role of male peer support (Kilmartin & Berkowitz, 2005; Schwartz & DeKeseredy, 1997). When men remain silent or "go along with the joke" when their peers make derogatory comments about women, they contribute to a social atmosphere that makes sexual assault possible. When men learn to confront other men's sexist behavior, they can be effective in undermining the peer cultural support of sexual assault. Doing so requires a good deal of courage and a willingness to be independent enough to resist the cultural pressure to express indifference or hatred toward women when in an all-male group. Both courage and independence are traditionally masculine attributes, yet traditionally masculine men show extreme levels of conformity to sexist behavior.

Preliminary evidence suggests that most men underestimate the degree to which their peers are made uncomfortable by other men's sexism and bragging about sexual conquest (Kilmartin, Green, Heinzen, Kuchler, & Smith, 2004; Berkowitz, 1994; Kilmartin, Conway, Friedberg, McQuoid, Tschan, & Norbet, 1999). Correcting the misconception that men are not bothered by sexist behavior in all-male groups may be useful in helping men to break the silence, as pressure for group conformity is sharply

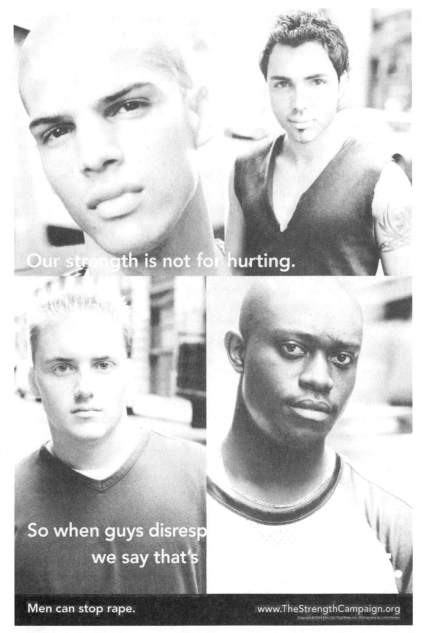

A poster from the "Strength Campaign" of Men Can Stop Rape, a social activist organization in Washington, DC. Public information efforts such as this one are attempts to encourage men's respect for women. Additional information about this organization can be found at http://www.mencanstoprape.org

reduced when a group member perceives that he or she has an ally within the group (Asch, 1965). As many as 75% of college men are uncomfortable with men's sexist behavior. Therefore, the attitude that rape prevention strategists wish to impart already exists in large part, and so increasing the positive influence of this attitude is a matter of leadership (Berkowitz, 1997), another traditionally masculine attribute. Courageous, independent, risk-taking college men must lead their fellow men by speaking out against their peers' sexist behavior.

It is obvious that the rapist causes a great deal of pain for the victim. The awareness that the rapist is also in pain himself needs to be addressed as well. If the pain can be alleviated, or the potential rapist can learn to deal with his pain in a different way, then sexual assault should decrease. In addition to better efforts to hold perpetrators responsible for their behavior, efforts to help men understand themselves as gendered beings, to facilitate the improvement of positive relationship skills, and to support attempts for men to change the destructive aspects of masculinity are positive steps. The overall efforts of men's gender awareness and change should contribute to dealing with the specific problem of sexual assault and the general problem of men's violence.

MALE VICTIMS AND SURVIVORS

The lopsided sex ratio of male to female violence and the incredible frequencies of domestic violence and rape can obscure the fact that males are victims of violence in significant numbers. Males are three times more likely than females to be murdered in the United States. Homicide is the second leading cause of death for males aged 15–24 and the third leading cause for males aged 25–34 (Anderson & Smith, 2005). Males' greater willingness to fight, use firearms, and engage in criminal activity all contribute to a higher risk of being injured or killed by violent means (Courtenay, 1998b). Males comprise 93% of the U.S. federal jail and prison population (The Sentencing Project, 2004), and prison violence is rampant (Toch, 1998).

There is a growing awareness that men are also victims of rape in greater numbers than people would have ever believed. It is estimated that sexual assault perpetrators victimize as many as one in 8 men at some point during his life (Bolton, Morris, & MacEachron, 1989) and the incidence of prison rape is much higher (Lockwood, 1980). Some states do not have gender-neutral rape laws, and thus do not recognize the sexual victimization of adult males (Isely & Gehrenbeck-Shim, 1997). In these states, men who report being raped are actually at risk for being charged with the crime of homosexual sodomy (Scarce, 1997a).

Most male rapes are committed by heterosexual men against homosexual men (King, 1992). Scarce (1997a) considers these types of attacks hate crimes against gay men. Similar to the rape of women, the rape of men is an expression of power, not of sexuality. Funk (1997) describes his chilling victimization at the hands of several men who gang-raped him because of his involvement in feminist causes. Thus we see the use of coercive sexuality to maintain hypermasculine privilege, just as in men's sexual assaults on women.

Male rape survivors experience some similar responses to female survivors. They may suffer from posttraumatic stress disorder and experience various psychological symptoms, including depression, anxiety, anger, shame, relationship difficulties, suicidal thoughts, sexual problems, sleep disturbances, and increased alcohol use, and psychosomatic symptoms (Isely & Gehrenbeck-Shim, 1997). They also experience difficulties that are somewhat unique to male survivors: doubts about their masculinity and sexuality, extreme isolation, and even fewer resources for treatment and support than female victims have available (Scarce, 1997a, 1997b; Isely & Gehrenbeck-Shim, 1997). It is estimated that 90% of male survivors never report the rape to police or hospitals, and 70% never tell anybody at all (VAASA, 1989). Research into the specific effects of sexual assault on men is sorely lacking (P. J. Isely, Busse, & P. Isely, 1998).

Several researchers have made suggestions for dealing with the largely hidden problem of male on male rape. Scarce (1997a; 1997b) recommends lobbying for gender-neutral rape laws where they do not currently exist, providing referrals and information tailored specifically to male survivors, training emergency room and rape crisis workers on the reality and unique character of male victimization, and educating the general public about the extent of the problem. Paul Isely and his colleagues (P. J. Isely, Busse, & P. Isely, 1998) suggest that school counselors and health services professionals be trained to recognize symptoms of sexual victimization and learn how to respond appropriately, as untreated symptoms often develop into chronic behavioral and psychological difficulties.

Traumatic psychological experience also increases the risk that a male survivor will become a perpetrator if he fails to acknowledge his pain. The refusal to deal directly with vulnerable emotions like fear and shame is central to mainstream cultural masculinity. Lisak (1997) noted that men who have been abused in some way as children *and* have accepted masculinity's traditional values are more likely to become violent adults, in comparison to other men who have been abused as children. His contention is that, as children, these men have experienced powerful and painful emotional events. At the same time, they have gotten the social message that expressing vulnerable feelings is taboo for males—the classic "big boys don't cry" dictum. These boys find that they can follow one of two paths: they can reject traditional masculinity and deal with the tragedy of their victimization, or they can accept it and act out their intense rage by becoming abusive themselves and/or by self-abuse, such as risk taking or drug use. Violence to the self and others appears to lie at the confluence of victimization and masculinity.

Many men have experienced varying levels of victimization at the hands of their fathers, other adult men, or peers. Harsh masculine socialization is victimizing in and of itself. When it is combined with hypermasculinity, this inhumane treatment can lead to inhuman behavior (Lynch & Kilmartin, 1999).

The male abuse survivor who seals over his pain cannot feel empathy for his victims because he is so unaware of his own feelings of shame and vulnerability. In other words, it is impossible for a person to feel for others when his own emotional life is impoverished. He has no frame of reference for emotional pain because his defenses against his own pain are so rigid.

David Lisak (1997) suggests that re-humanizing men entails helping them to recover the vulnerable emotionality that accompanied their victimization. He refers to full awareness of one's vulnerable emotions as *empathy for the self* and tells the heart-rending story of a death row inmate who refused to deal with the painful reality of his childhood victimization until, after 10 years in prison, he finally began to acknowledge his pain. One day, during a prison psychotherapy session, he began to cry, perhaps for the first time in his adult life, and sobbed uncontrollably for 45 minutes as he relived the horrors of multiple abuses in his youth. He recovered from this episode and, 15 minutes later, became anguished again as, for the first time, he came to a full emotional awareness of the pain that he had inflicted on his victims. Lisak saw the connection between empathy for the self and empathy for others in this dramatic hour.

Men's violence has biological, historical, economic, social, and cultural roots that interact with the personal histories and ideologies of individual men, and with their decisions to act violently. The cross-cultural variation and striking differences in men's and women's violence lead us to the conclusion that violence is largely centered in the social meanings attached to gender. Solutions to the problems created by men's violence must be broad in scope, encompassing economic, educational, legal, institutional, and social activist strategies.

SUMMARY

1. Men commit the vast majority of violent crimes, which leads researchers to investigate the origins of violence and the connections between aggression and masculinity.

2. Sociobiologists view male aggression as an evolutionary strategy for propagating one's genes, yet aggression is not always associated with an increase in breeding access, even in animals.

3. The hormone testosterone is another possible biological link to male violence. Although testosterone may set the stage for aggression, implicating it as the singular cause of male violence ignores the complexity of human behavior and the powerful influence of psychosocial forces. Cross-cultural variations in the character of violence make singular biological explanations untenable.

4. Socioculturally, aggression is a defining feature of masculinity. A number of factors encourage aggression in men, including the privilege of patriarchy, a socialized external defensive style, unmitigated attention to task, violent modeling, and rewards for aggression. Compared with females, violence-inhibiting factors such as empathy, nonaggressive modeling, and consistent punishment for aggression are less in evidence for males. Male violence is thought by many to be a compensation for the inadequate feelings that sometimes result from masculine gender role strain.

5. Men who are violent in the home often show this compensatory pattern. They have exaggerated needs for power and control as well as the externalizing style of blaming their partners for their own negative feelings and behaviors. Domestic violence

often follows an intergenerational pattern against the backdrop of a patriarchal system that tolerates violence against women and even children. A number of interventions are focused on legal, therapeutic, and educational systems.

6. Research and debate about rape has increased dramatically during the past two decades. Most people are alarmed to hear how commonplace this crime is. Many researchers believe that rape is fueled by aggressive, not sexual motivations. The social construction of masculinity, with its emphasis on misogyny, sexual promiscuity, performance, and homophobia, is both cause and effect of a rape-tolerant social climate.

7. As with other violent behaviors, rape is perpetrated by men who are desperately attempting to compensate for feelings of masculine inadequacy through hypermasculine displays of dominance, anger, and control. For many acquaintance rapists, low masculine self esteem may be related to poor relationships with emotionally and/or physically distant or abusive fathers. Some theorists believe, however, that fathering would not be such a crucial factor if gender roles were more egalitarian and males were not expected to go to such extreme lengths to prove their worth as men.

8. Interventions for decreasing rape include more vigorous law enforcement, rehabilitative efforts, safety measures, and the education of potential victims. However, rape is a men's issue, and men need to address it. Recent interventions have included a focus on potential perpetrators, especially in college populations, where acquaintance rape is rampant. Men who can understand, at a deep level, the negative consequences of rape, the origins of male violence, the pain of victims, and the continuum of violence against women, will be less likely to rape. Positive changes in the masculine gender role and men's willingness to intervene with peers should have a positive impact on rape prevention.

9. Male victimization occurs at alarming levels, especially with regard to murder in the United States. Male-on-male rape is much more common than is generally believed, and male rape survivors face a unique set of negative circumstances in addition to those shared with female survivors. Males with a history of any kind of victimization are at increased risk for becoming perpetrators if they embrace traditional masculine gender role norms.

13

No Man is an Island:
Men in Relationships with
Others

Independence is a central demand of traditional masculinity. Rather, it might be more accurate to say that the *appearance* of independence is demanded. As members of a variety of social systems, men are dependent on others for information, resources, support, and human contact. It is difficult, if not impossible, for a "loner" to be productive or psychologically healthy. The masculine focus on hyperindependence creates relationship conflicts for many men.

From our earliest childhood interactions, we develop styles of relating to others. And, social settings also encourage or discourage certain types of interactions (For example, you might interact with your friends in very different ways than you would with your parents.). There is a large volume of research indicating the social pressures to interact in certain ways differ somewhat between the sexes. We also know that interaction patterns are strongly affected by power relationships between the people involved. Describing the effects of gendered styles on men's relationships with others is the task of this chapter.

MALE SOCIAL DEVELOPMENT

Developmental psychologist Eleanor Maccoby (1998) has described distinct, gender-typed interaction patterns that emerge early in life. Maccoby contends that these are largely a function of children's preferences for same sex interaction. By the age of six and a half, children are spending 90% more of their time with same-sex children than with other-sex ones. Children will play in sex-integrated groups when adults force them to do so, but they will return to sex-segregated groups when adults withdraw. This segregation is not limited to gender-typed activities such as playing with dolls or trucks. It also occurs in gender-neutral activities such as drawing or playing with clay.

Martin and Fabes (2001) found that sex-differentiated behavior is a consequence of the frequency of same-sex play. Often finding themselves in the company of male peers, most boys develop a way of relating to others that is distinctly masculine. This style involves an orientation toward dominance, competition, and rough-and-tumble play (Maccoby, 1998). Boys also tend to play in larger (Levant, 1995), less intimate (Maccoby, 1990), and more publicly visible groups (Thorne & Luria, 1986).

In these all-male groups, we see boys interrupting each other, bragging, telling stories, ridiculing others, and using commands much more frequently than we see these behaviors in girls. Girls' conversation involves more requests rather than demands, expressions of interest in others, and a general communication of a desire to sustain the relationship. Whereas girls' conversations are more of a give-and-take interaction, boys' conversations are more like taking turns, with one boy telling a story, followed by another boy (who often tries to "top" the first boy's story). Maccoby's (1998) view is that, while typical female speech serves the dual purpose of collaboration and self-assertion, typical male conversation is more singularly self-assertive.

These manners of relating to others begin in childhood. By the second grade, female best friends' conversations begin to center around personally significant events, whereas boys' conversations focus on activities. By early adolescence, friendships are somewhat less stereotypical (Golombok & Fivush, 1994). Still, many gender-typed communication patterns continue into adulthood (Tannen, 1990). Because interpersonal interactions serve to form and maintain relationships, men's long-established pattern of communication colors the character of their social ties with women, children, and other men.

ONE OF THE BOYS: MALE-MALE FRIENDSHIPS

Typically, boys and men have more friends than do girls and women. However, the friendships of women are characterized by deeper levels of intimacy (Claes, 1992). Although women often talk about how they feel about their experiences, men's focus is usually on the sharing of activities (Lips, 2005).

It is sometimes said that men have many "buddies," but few true friends. Buddies are people you bond with around an object or activity (sports, work, drinking, etc); friends are people with whom you are intimate. The formation of warm feelings between men is many times the result of an indirect process of spending time in a mutual pursuit or interest (sometimes referred to as "side-by-side" relationships, as opposed to stereotypical women's "face-to-face" relationships), rather than a more direct process of emotional self-disclosure. The expression of closeness between men often takes the form of continuing to spend time with each other and helping each other with tasks, rather than more direct expressions such as touching, or saying "I like you," "I'm glad you're my friend," or "I feel close to you."

Some men lack the more collaborative relationship skills that are helpful in the formation of deeper friendships, yet many have a desire to be emotionally close to other men. Social structures like tasks and rituals enable men to affiliate with one another in cooperative ways. For example, men on athletic teams or men who work together often form close ties with one another (Messner, 1992). Maccoby (1990) argues that males usually need the structure that these settings provide to feel comfortable with others (see Box 13.1 on fraternities). On the other hand, women usually require less structure because they are more readily adaptable to affiliation for its own sake. This social structure hypothesis provides a partial explanation for the almost religious character of athletics in the lives of many men. Being involved as a sports participant or fan serves to give men something to talk about and do together. These activities mitigate the isolation that comes from hiding oneself behind a facade of masculinity. Still, men tend to experience more loneliness than women (Brody & Hall, 2000), probably because they experience lower levels of social support.

Several aspects of the masculine gender role inhibit the formation of intimate relationships between male friends. The orientation toward competition and task completion is one. Males are socialized to believe that other men are their competitors. The establishment of intimacy rests partly on revealing one's weaknesses and vulnerabilities to another (Jourard, 1971). It is not wise to reveal these to a perceived competitor, who might well exploit the weakness. This would be like telling your opponent before a tennis match that your backhand is not very good. Men who feel competitive with other men tend to have friendships that are inhibited by an undercurrent of distrust. Adolescent boys tend to trust their friends less than girls (Berndt, 1992). The gender role demand for self-sufficiency also inhibits self-disclosure. A "real man" is expected to solve his problems on his own. If he is hurt, he must "take it like a man." The expectations for hyperindependence and pain tolerance result in the devaluing of men who reveal weaknesses or ask for help.

Thus, men may face negative social consequences for revealing themselves, yet disclosing oneself to others has demonstrable positive mental health benefits (Pennebaker, 1995). Men who place a high value on traditional masculinity tend to avoid self-disclosure (Winstead, Derlega, & Wong, 1984). When a problem arises, they tend to rely solely on their own resources, even when other people are available and willing to help. The familiar situation where a man who is lost refuses to ask for directions is a good illustration of how some men will solve problems inefficiently in order to protect a fragile sense of masculinity.

As with many areas of investigation, gender is a better predictor of behavior than sex. Androgynous men are as disclosing to their male friends as feminine or androgynous women, thus they achieve a higher level of intimacy with their same-sex friends than gender-typed men. Undifferentiated and masculine women had similar levels of disclosure to men with the same gender characteristics (Wright & Scanlon, 1991). Gay men are more likely than heterosexual men to develop strong emotional intimacy with their male friends, many of whom also tend to be gay (Nardi, 1992).

Homophobia is perhaps the greatest barrier to friendships between men (Reid & Fine, 1992). Because some men have difficulty making a clear distinction between sexual and

Box 13.1: Institutionalized Friendships

Although it has also seen declines in membership in recent years, the college and university social fraternity system continues to constitute a significant presence on many campuses, with an estimated 400,000 college males as members across more than 800 campuses (National Interfraternity Council, 2005). A few of these organizations have abandoned the single-sex tradition, but the vast majority of them have not. The National Interfraternity Council (NIC) website includes this statement:

> Many people argue that because fraternities only recruit men and sororities only recruit women the two institutions are sexist. What these people fail to realize is that federal law has mandated that fraternities and sororities are exempt from Title IX guidelines. Greek chapters are social living organizations and are therefore not required to be coeducational. At the NIC, fraternities and sororities interact on a regular basis. In addition, educational programs and resources regarding sexual harassment, abuse and acquaintance rape are available.

Thus, the Council's position is that practices are only sexist if they fail to comply with the law.

The belief that men and women are fundamentally different seems to be carried as a nonconscious assumption. Public statements by the NIC and by individual fraternities and their chapters are remarkably mute on why most fraternities remain restricted to men only. I could find only one fraternity website that appears to address the question of the single-sex policy continuing to exist in the twenty-first century. However, the question is asked but not really answered:

> Why is Delta Upsilon men only? Since it's founding in 1834, Delta Upsilon's membership has been exclusively men. There are Sororities and Female Fraternities at the University of Manitoba which are comprised of women only. Delta Upsilon continues to uphold its tradition as being a men's International Fraternity. We often have events planned with the sororities and female fraternities on campus. These events include parties, socials, community service work and of course the annual Teeter-Totter-A-Thon with the Alpha Delta Pi Sorority. If you have female friends who are considering Greek Life, please direct them to our links to the websites of the Sororities and Female Fraternities. (Delta Upsilon, 2005)

Phi Mu Alpha Sinfonia is a fraternity for male musicians. The website of the Northwestern University chapter describes the diversity of skills and interests that are welcome: "Sinfonians range from the most serious conservatory musician to the most amateur musician with a lot of room in between. Membership is not dependent on a preference for any particular musical form or genre, any level of proficiency or study. If you are interested in music, learning about it, performing it, or sharing it with others you are a good candidate to be a Sinfonian" (Phi Mu Alpha, 2005). Remarkably, the organization takes the position that a male classical oboist has more in common with a male heavy metal rocker than he does with a female classical oboist.

nonsexual intimacy, getting close to another man may feel similar to being sexual with him. The powerful antifemininity demand of masculinity then rears its ugly head, and near panic sets in. To avoid the discomfort of this anxiety, men often keep other men at arm's length, both physically and psychologically. The friendships of highly homophobic men are significantly less intimate than those of other men (Devlin & Cowan, 1985). Moreover, history reveals that this pattern of male interpersonal distance is a relatively recent phenomenon. In the United States, it seems to have begun at about the time when the label "homosexual" moved from a definition of *behavior* (something one does) to one of *identity* (something one is) (Rotundo, 1993). Greg Lehne (1998) illustrated the role of homophobia in distancing heterosexual men from one another:

> I've asked men to describe their relationships with their best male friends. Many offer descriptions that are ... filled with positive emotions and satisfaction.... However, if I suggest that it sounds as if they are describing a person whom they love, they become flustered.... 'Well, I don't think I would like to call it love, we're just best friends. I can relate to him in ways I can't with anyone else. But, I mean, we're not homosexuals or anything like that.' ...The social stigma of homosexual love denies these close relationships the validity of love in our society. This potential loss of love is a pain of homophobia that many men suffer because it delimits their relationships with other men. (p. 246)

The handshake is symbolic of men's ambivalence around being close to one another. One scholar (Petrie, 1986) asserts that the handshake began as a way of showing the other man that you did not have your hand on a weapon. Young boys whose fathers refuse to kiss, hug, or cuddle them, or tell them that they are loved, deprive their sons of the important human needs for touching and valuing. In addition, these fathers model unaffectionate behavior as a distinctive feature of masculinity. As a result, these boys may well grow up to be distant fathers to their own sons.

According to Thorne and Luria (1986), U.S. boys begin to use homophobic labels such as "queer" or "fag" by the fourth grade. These labels are terms of insult for low-status boys, thus they serve to highlight and maintain a masculine hierarchy (Plummer, 2001). Thorne and Luria theorized about the impact of homophobic labeling on boys' physical contact:

> As 'fag' talk increases, relaxed and cuddling patterns of touch decrease among boys. Kindergarten and first-grade boys touch one another frequently and with ease, with arms around shoulders, hugs, and holding hands. By fifth grade, touch among boys becomes more constrained, gradually shifting to mock violence and the use of poking, shoving, and ritual gestures like 'giving five' (flat hand slaps) to express bonding. (p. 182)

Thus, males appear to have strong desire to maintain interpersonal contact with other males, but (historically and developmentally) the threat of homophobic labeling increasingly forces this contact to become highly ritualized and sometimes aggressive.

It is not only the childhood socialization of individual males that inhibits intimacy, it is also the interpersonal pressures of the social setting. Boys who behave in gender-inconsistent ways are likely to experience disapproval from their friends and lose popularity, and so conforming to peer group norms for communication serves to help the boy avoid social rejection (Burn, 1996).

Social norms constrain behavior in significant ways. Both women and men behave in more gender-stereotypical ways in public than they do in private (Burn, 1996), and males typically express a desire to be more disclosing (Reisman, 1990), suggesting that masculine and feminine styles of friendship are at least partly a function of the social expectations that women and men tend to bring into interactions with others. It may not be unusual for two male friends to both have a desire for greater levels of intimacy with each other, but continue to keep each other at an emotional arm's length because both men overestimate the degree to which the other expects gender-stereotypical behavior. Masculinity inhibits them from talking about their expectations (which would be intimate in itself) and therefore their distorted views of each other's masculinity prevent the friendship from moving in the direction that both friends would like to go. In one study, few men reported the belief that they should take care of their problems by themselves, but they said that they believed that most *other men* had this expectation (Burn, 1996).

There is considerable cross-cultural diversity in the character of men's friendships. In some parts of the world, same-sex best friends go through a ceremony similar to a marriage in order to formalize their commitment to each other. When one of the friends dies, people express more sympathy to his best friend than to family members. In Java and parts of Ghana, and in some native North American tribes, the man turns to his best friend for fulfillment of his primary emotional needs, and husband-wife relationships are marked by less emotional intensity. The romantic ideal of mainstream U.S. culture dictates that a spouse meets all the emotional needs of his or her partner, an ideology that makes deep friendships more difficult (Williams, 1992).

Although there is considerable pressure for contemporary U.S. men to have unemotional and non-disclosing friendships, the desire for true intimate contact with other males sometimes leads men to fight against years of socialization and against the influence of masculine social settings. Although it provides a measure of social support, "male bonding" tends to be a poor substitute for the deeper connections of intimate friendships. Many men experience relationship dissatisfaction even with their best friends (Elkins & Peterson, 1993). It is a difficult task to make a friend when one has a decades-long history of entrenched buddyship patterns. Box 13.2 describes techniques for doing so.

"CROSS-CULTURAL" INTERACTIONS: MEN WITH WOMEN

As we have already discussed, children spend large amounts of time in same-sex groups, and male and female groups tend to have different interpersonal styles and social norms. One could consider all-male and all-female groups to constitute gender cultures. When a person interacts with a person of the other sex, it may be somewhat like meeting a person from another part of the country, another nation, or even a different world. Both men and women often complain that they have difficulty understanding the other sex (Tannen, 1990). This confusion may be due in large part to gender differences in socialization and

Box 13.2: *Guerilla Tactics for Making a Friend*

Letich (1991) makes some excellent, step-by-step suggestions for working on deeper friendships:

1. First, you have to want it: Breaking patterns not only causes anxiety, it is hard work. "You have to remind yourself that there's nothing weird or effeminate about wanting a friend." (p. 87).

2. Identify a possible friend: Seek someone who seems to want to question the values of traditional masculinity.

3. Be sneaky: Get involved in a comfortable, nonpressured activity. Get used to spending time with this man.

4. Invite him to stop for a beer or a cup of coffee: Try to make honest, personal conversation at these times.

5. Call just to get together.

6. Sit down and talk about your friendship.

Letich calls these suggestions "guerilla tactics" because they seem extreme and difficult for traditional men in a culture that discourages male-male intimacy. The last two suggestions are especially antithetical to male gender role norms. Men who try these "tactics" will feel awkward, but as with any skills, they improve and become more comfortable with practice.

Youniss and Haynie (1992) point out that friendships are based on reciprocity, the tendency to respond to a person as he or she has responded to you. Men who bring a different style of relating into their friendships influence other men to also change their behavior.

gendered social environmental characteristics. The effects of these differences may be most salient in mixed-sex interactions.

Male-female Friendships

Friendships between males and females are less common than same-sex friendships. However, they are on the rise. In the late 1970s, only about 18% of people in a U.S. sample reported having a close friend of the other sex. That figure grew to between 25–40% by the mid-1980s (Basow, 1992; Wright & Scanlon, 1991), perhaps reflecting a greater degree of contact between the sexes in the workplace and a greater flexibility in social expectations about gender. In an informal survey, I ask my first-year students to raise their hands if one of their three best friends is a member of the other sex, and I would estimate that 80% of them acknowledge having a cross-sex friendship.

Several factors operate as barriers to male-female friendships. First, we live in a gender-typed culture that emphasizes differences between the sexes despite the fact that men and women are much more similar than they are different. As friendships are often based on having something in common, people are not likely to pursue friendships with those whom they perceive as dissimilar.

Friendships are also based on reciprocity, or mutual influence (Youniss & Haynie, 1992). In the childhood peer culture of males, influence tends to be exerted through direct demands. Girls are more likely to use polite suggestions. Although girls' styles work well with adults, it is not very effective with boys. Therefore, girls may find it quite frustrating and unpleasant to interact with boys who will not respond to their influence attempts (Maccoby, 1998).

While the aversive nature of boys' interaction style keeps girls away from them, the antifemininity norm keeps boys away from girls. The boy who acts like a girl in any way, including being friends with girls, risks losing his place in the male dominance hierarchy. When a boy falls to a low level in this hierarchy, he finds it difficult to exert any influence on his male peers. As a result, his interactions with them may also become aversive.

Thus, the masculine culture does not foster egalitarian relationships with females. Boys are barraged with messages that females are inferior and have value only as sexual objects. It is not surprising, then, that there is a tendency among men to perceive sexual interest in a woman when it is not present. Abbey (1982) demonstrated that men are more likely than women to label a woman "seductive" or "promiscuous." She speculated that this readiness to sexualize behavior may result in men misperceiving friendliness as flirtation, making it difficult to establish nonsexual cross-sex relationships. There may also be a connection between this misperception and sexual harassment in the workplace (see Chapter 10).

Despite the barriers to male-female friendships, some people manage to establish them, and they tend to find them satisfying (Swain, 1992). Although traditional gender roles emphasize sex differences, it is not unlikely that similarity with a person of the other sex would be perceived on occasion. Not surprisingly, androgynous men and women are more likely than gender-typed people to have friends of the other sex (Lavine & Lombardo, 1984).

Both males and females tend to self-disclose more often to female friends, and so a cross-sex friendship frequently offers a man something that may well be lacking in his friendships with other men. Not surprisingly, women have a stronger tendency than men to describe their cross-sex friendships as less satisfactory than their other friendships (Parker & De Vries, 1993), perhaps because it is difficult to establish and maintain relationship equality in the social context of cultural gender inequality (O'Meara, 1989).

The most common developmental period for cross-sex friendships is young adulthood. This is a time of increased cross-sex interaction for many. Later in adulthood, especially after marriage, it is difficult for heterosexuals to establish these types of relationships. Cross-sex friendships among married people are often confined to the context of friendships between couples (Fox, Gibbs, & Auerbach, 1985). As many people suspect a sexual undertone to male-female platonic relationships, it is sometimes difficult for cross-sex friends to convince their romantic partners that their friendship is nonsexual (Swain, 1992).

Romantic Relationships

Most heterosexual males feel a strong urge to approach females beginning at puberty. As they attempt to form close relationships, gender demands exert considerable influence over their behavior. Many men feel caught in a conflict between the masculine values of antifemininity, inexpressiveness, and independence on the one hand, and attraction toward women, natural intimacy needs, and demands for relationship oriented behaviors on the other.

Beginning early in life, cultural demands require boys to put rigid boundaries between themselves and females in order to define themselves as masculine. When they get older, however, they are expected to merge and be intimate with women. Most males have little practice in the skills required for building intimate relationships, including emotional self-disclosure, reciprocity, and empathy for the other person. It is no wonder that they often feel inept in this foreign area, and they may believe that women are the relationship experts. Traditionally masculine expressions of love, such as sexual affection or instrumental helping, are often inadequate when not accompanied by more direct communications of caring (Cancian, 1987).

One interesting research finding is that males tend to "fall in love" faster than females (Huston & Ashmore, 1986), contrary to the popular belief that women are more emotional and love-hungry. We can make some guesses about the origins of this male readiness to fall in love. First, men tend to place more value than women on a partner's physical attractiveness (Deaux & Hanna, 1984). Thus, they may be more likely to report being in love largely on the basis of this attraction, which of course can happen very early in the relationship (or even from across the room). Second, men have not been socialized to understand and manage their emotional lives except through repression. Feelings that are difficult to squelch may be experienced as a "flood" of emotion. Also interesting is the finding that women initiate 80% of breakups in heterosexual couples (Duck, 1991). Thus, men not only fall in love more quickly, they appear to fall out of love more slowly.

Third, the level of intimacy in a romantic relationship is likely to be very different from that of a male's other relationships, which are often centered on activities. This level of intimacy is likely to be less different from the intimacy level of the female's other relationships, which are often focused on feeling and disclosure. The man's hunger for intimacy is greater because he has few or no other places to get this need met. The heterosexual relationship becomes the only safe haven from the masculine demands for independence and inexpressiveness, the only place where he can show the "softer" side of himself. A man might well experience the normal feminine style of reciprocity and consideration as love.

One interesting finding is that married men tend to disclose even less to their male friends than single men do (Tschann, 1988). Perhaps men tend to rely almost solely on their wives for filling their intimacy needs. This is a heavy burden for wives, and males often have difficulty filling these needs if the relationship should break up (Nolen-Hoeksema & Girgus, 1994) (see Chapter 14).

There is a considerable body of evidence indicating that the skills required to make an intimate relationship work and last are traditionally feminine ones. The couples that have the longest lasting and happiest relationships are those in which both partners are either androgynous or feminine (Antill, 1983). This is true for gay and lesbian couples as well as heterosexual ones (Kurdek & Schmitt, 1986). For men, the abilities to be caring and emotionally expressive are strongly related to the longevity of their relationships (Blumstein & Schwartz, 1983).

In contrast, some aspects of traditional masculinity are related to problems in relationships. Women tend to desire high levels of intimacy (McAdams, Lester, Brand, McNamara, & Lensky, 1988), but gender-typed men tend to be emotionally inexpressive and unempathic. James Nelson (1988) believes that, for traditionally masculine men, "there is a deep tension between intimacy and masculinity. He wants both, and each seems to be purchased at the price of the other." (p. 42). Married women often describe their husbands' lack of attention and affection to be a major source of dissatisfaction (Cunningham, Braiker, & Kelley, 1982). Wives tend to report less satisfaction with their marriages when their husbands endorse traditionally masculine ideologies (Bradbury, Campbell, & Fincham, 1995).

The degree to which partners perceive that the relationship is equitable (i.e., that partner's power in the relationship are roughly equal) is also a predictor of marital satisfaction (Aida & Falbo, 1991). A number of factors work against relationship equity. Most notable among these is a cultural climate that confers economic, social status, and other types of power disproportionately to men, and erotic power disproportionately to women. One finding from Pepper Schwartz's (1994) study of egalitarian heterosexual marriages is that the incomes of husband and wife are relatively equal in these relationships. There is also substantial evidence to indicate that most wives do a disproportionate amount of household work, even when they work outside of the home as much as their husbands do (see Chapter 10).

The aforementioned difference in interpersonal styles works against women's power in relationships. Males are often not responsive to the typical feminine influence style of polite suggestion. If this unresponsiveness is common in the context of a relationship, the woman may feel somewhat powerless. Although men may view direct demands as a natural way of negotiating in a relationship, this style may feel aversive and overpowering to women.

The masculine demand for dominance may encourage men to ignore even direct influence attempts by their partners. Women are more likely than men to use unilateral strategies, such as withdrawing by becoming cold or silent, or walking out, in order to influence their partner's behavior. These types of strategies are characteristics of people in all types of relationships who perceive themselves as being at a power disadvantage (Falbo & Peplau, 1980). For example, if one partner is dissatisfied with the relationship and asks the other to accompany him/her to couples counseling but the other partner refuses, the dissatisfied partner may feel that the only option is to offer an ultimatum—"Either we go to couples counseling, or I am going to leave you."

Men are not always the most interpersonally powerful ones in the relationship. In fact, it is the partner who seems to be more attractive or less in love (the one who "needs the relationship least") tends to have the most power (Lips, 2005). However, it is safe to say that when partners view a relationship as an adversarial power competition, it will either not last long, or it will quickly become unsatisfying for one or both partners. Maccoby's (1990) description of successful couples is that "… they develop a relationship that is based on communality rather than exchange bargaining. That is, they have many shared goals and work jointly to achieve them. They do not need to argue over turf because they have the same turf." (p. 518).

Gay couples face some of the same challenges as heterosexual couples, as indicated by their similarities in the factors that most often produce dissatisfaction within the relationship: financial conflict, the intrusion of work into the relationship, lack of time together, and sexual infidelity. But gay couples also display some average differences from heterosexual couples. For instance, they tend to value financial and educational equality more than heterosexual couples (Blumstein & Schwartz, 1983). Like heterosexual couples, gay couples place high value on feelings of attachment (Kurdek & Schmitt, 1986) and the perception that they are true partners, with each holding equal levels of power within the relationship (Aida & Falbo, 1991).

Although heterosexual couples tend to adhere to traditional gender arrangements in many facets of their lives, gay couples are less role-bound (despite many heterosexuals' assumption that one partner in a gay couple takes on a masculine role and the other a feminine one). Gay couples face the stress of cultural prejudice against them, and often of low familial support as well (Basow, 1992). Because gay marriage is not an option in most places, gay men do not have legal ties to each other, and this makes for fewer entanglements should one partner decide to dissolve the relationship (Kurdek & Schmitt, 1986). As with heterosexual couples, gay couples find the higher degrees of satisfaction when at least one partner has emotionally expressive traits, with low levels of satisfaction when one or both partners is masculine or undifferentiated (Cook, 1985).

SONS AND FATHERS

In his gender role workshops with men, John Lee (1991) asks participants to do this simple exercise: close your eyes and get a good mental picture of your father, then pay attention to your feelings as I say these words: "Father… my father …Dad… Daddy… my dad." The emotional responses of men (and perhaps women) to this simple exercise are remarkably powerful. The experience is one of being flooded with feelings: love, anger, disappointment, grief. It is hard to underestimate the role of the father in shaping the personality of the son.

Traditional gender demands emphasize that the father's role is to be the provider and protector, involved in work outside of the home. The mother's role emphasizes being with the children and taking care of the home. As we saw in Chapter 10, these roles are much more variable historically, cross-culturally, and in the ways that individual families have been structured. Most mothers work outside the home (U.S. Department of Labor, 2005), and fathers are more involved in child care than at any time in recent history, albeit still far short of equal participation (Marsiglio & Pleck, 2005). The U.S. Bureau of the

Census recently reported a 25% increase in the number of single-father households over just a three-year period. Between 1970 and 1998, the ratio of single father households increased from one in ten to one in six (Cohn, 1998). Still, the man as breadwinner and woman as caregiver remain the dominant models for parental roles (E. Pleck & J. Pleck, 1997). Some households in which men are reported as single parents may well have a female dating partner, cohabitant, or hired employee who functions as primary caregiver to children.

Fathers' levels of family involvement are difficult to ascertain because of a wide variety of methodological problems (Pleck, 1997). Estimates range from 12 minutes per day (Hochschild & Machung, 1989) to just over two hours (Hossain & Roopnarine, 1993). In every case, however, fathers' time involvement with children pales in comparison to mothers' (Marsiglio & Pleck, 2005). As William Marsiglio (1995) stated, "Clearly, recent increases in mothers' workforce participation have far outstripped fathers' increased involvement in all aspects of child care." (p. 8). It is still not unusual to hear fathers speak of "babysitting" their own children or "helping out" with child care and other household duties. We also see average differences in the ways that fathers and mothers typically spend their interaction time with their children. Mothers are more likely than fathers to be involved in basic child care activities: feeding, dressing, washing clothes, and bathing. Fathers spend more time playing with children (Lips, 2005).

Joseph Pleck (1997) has summarized the factors related to fathers' involvement with their children. Not surprisingly, men's levels of positive fathering are related to characteristics of their own fathers. Those whose childhood experiences were with highly involved fathers are more likely to be actively involved themselves. Men who perceived their fathers as less than positive models, and who display a commitment to doing better, also tend to be highly involved. Men who report having been involved in child care responsibilities as boys or adolescents (and having responded positively to these experiences) are also more involved as fathers. There is some cross-cultural evidence that boys who provide early infant care tend to become involved fathers.

Pleck notes that several studies have demonstrated a connection between psychological androgyny and father involvement, and other characteristics such as high self-esteem, adaptiveness during pregnancy, egalitarian gender beliefs, belief in the importance of the father's role, and a mature understanding of children and of the parent-child relationship are also positively correlated with involved fathering. Other variables known to have a positive effect on paternal involvement are: father's education, mother's education, mother's income, and mother's employment. Father's income and hours spent at work are negatively associated with paternal involvement. The same effect is not seen for mothers (Hofferth & Anderson, 2003).

Hard work and sacrifice are the traditional ways that a man has expressed his love. These are profoundly significant to the family, although as expressions of love, they are somewhat indirect. It is difficult for young children to understand and appreciate that their father disappears in the morning and is gone for most of the day because he loves them. It is much easier to feel loved by someone who feeds you, dresses you, comforts you, and says, "I love you."

In my experience, many men (and women) say two things about their fathers: "I know he loves me, but he rarely shows it," and "I wish I could be closer to my father." Although warm, affectionate feelings for the father predominate for most men, there is also a feeling of deep disappointment for having been deprived of the father's time, affection, and approval (Garfinkel, 1985). This feeling is sometimes referred to as "father hunger" (Bly, 1991) or even as "the wound" (Lee, 1991). It is perhaps the central issue in the lives of many men. Reactions to father hunger include working compulsively at trying to win the father's respect, rebelling against the father by trying hard to be different from him, or acting out the rage at having to earn his love rather than being valued unconditionally.

There are several barriers to fathers' emotional involvement with their children. Sociobiologists would have us believe that it is biologically based—that males have no "maternal instinct" and that they are unmotivated toward attachment to their young. There is a good deal of countervailing evidence to this hypothesis. Joseph Pleck (1981a) reviewed a number of studies that showed that male animals are responsive to the young when exposed to them for a sufficient period of time. When human males are allowed to interact with their children shortly after birth, they react similarly to mothers, showing strong emotional reactions and becoming enthralled with the baby (Parke & Tinsley, 1981). Storey, Walsh, Quinton, and Wynne-Edwards (2000) demonstrated that new and expectant mothers and fathers showed similar physiological reactions to infant-related stimuli. In these early interactions, fathers thus form a paternal "bond" that resembles the mother-child attachment. Although mothers may be more biologically predisposed to respond to children, this sex difference is almost totally erased by males' early and repeated exposure to the young.

Social forces inhibit men from spending time with children and performing care giving behaviors. In industrial and postindustrial society, the sole breadwinner role has been a structural barrier to paternal involvement. This role prescribes that men spend most of their time away from the home and put a greater priority on task and achievement than on relationships (E. Pleck & J. Pleck, 1997). Many men report feeling strong conflicts between work and family roles (O'Neil, Fishman, & Kinsella-Shaw, 1987), and employers have been slow to accommodate employed fathers (and mothers) who wish to participate more fully in family roles (Bowen & Orthner, 1991) through, for example, "flex time" arrangements that will allow a parent to synchronize the workday and school day schedules (Bem, 1993).

Another inhibitor of paternal participation is men's perceived lack of caregiving skill. In contrast to most women, many men have no childhood parent-like experience, such as babysitting or playing with dolls, nor were they taught the psychological skills of nurturing or empathy (Levant, 1990a). They are not likely to approach tasks that are associated with feelings of ineptness (especially considering the role demand to always be competent). Fathers who perceive themselves as skillful in child care are usually more involved with their children (McHale & Huston, 1984). A number of models for training fathers in caregiving have been proposed (see Palm, 1997; Kiselica, 1996; Levant, 1990a; 1988). Recently, researchers have demonstrated that children benefit greatly from warm attachments to their fathers. They tend to form closer relationships with others, and to have lower levels of anxiety and higher levels of self-confidence (Lips, 2005).

Some mothers seem to be reluctant to share the control over child care duties with their husbands. Palkovitz (1984) found that women's negative attitudes toward their husbands' involvement were associated with low levels of paternal involvement. McHale and Huston (1984) suggest that an increase in men's care giving to children is only possible if mothers are willing to relinquish some of their child care duties. Not surprisingly, husbands of less traditional wives tend to be more involved in these duties than husbands of gender-typed wives (Nyquist, Slivken, Spence, & Helmreich, 1985).

At one time, men were usually absent during the births of their children and only peripherally involved during the first few days of the baby's life. The father's presence at this time appears to be critical in the formation of the parent-child bond (Greenberg & Morris, 1974). This is one barrier to paternal involvement that is breaking down in the United States. The proportion of men who attend the births of their children was 80% as of 1985, a nearly threefold increase from 1975 (Lewis, 1986). Clearly, it is also critical for fathers to increase the amount of time they spend with their children during all phases of development. Frequent contact with children facilitates the father's psychological involvement. It is impossible for fathers to have "quality time" with their children unless they have "quantity time," in which they become connected with their children's physical and emotional needs (Lynch & Kilmartin, 1999).

In the United States, current problems associated with inadequate fathering can be traced back to the "separate spheres" ideology that began during the Victorian era (Stearns, 1991). The doctrine that prescribed fathers' role as outside the home and mothers' domestic role was a result of economic exigencies that arose from industrialization. But the economy has changed and it will continue to change, increasingly making the breadwinner-homemaker dichotomy untenable, and giving rise to the different kinds of child care arrangements that we have begun to see during the last three decades. Far from being a biologically ordained necessity, historical and cross-cultural perspectives demonstrate that the protector-provider role (in fact, all of the culturally masculine role) is a historical artifact, driven by ordinary people's needs to make a living and manage families. From this point of view, the current debates over the "natural" roles of women and men in the home (and elsewhere) are the "growing pains" that come with social change.

Scott Coltrane (1995) makes an optimistic of prediction about the future of fatherhood and the household division of labor:

> many American fathers will become more involved in their children's upbringing and begin to share more of the housework.... Some couples will continue to follow conventional sex-segregated divisions of labor, while others will opt for virtual role reversal. Most, however, will fall somewhere in between.... We can predict, however, that the general direction of change will be toward more acceptance of sharing between men and women and more sharing of family work in actual practice. (p. 269)

The general character of masculine demands inhibits many of the kinds of behaviors that make for good parenting. Therefore, better fathering is linked to the process of men breaking out of their rigid roles. Many men become less gender-typed as a result of trying on the nontraditional role of caregiver (Meredith, 1985), and men also feel freer to adopt this role as they reduce their gender-typed views of the world.

SUMMARY

1. Children spend a disproportionate amount of their time in same-sex groups, and distinct, gender-typed, patterns develop at an early age. Boys' orientation is toward dominance and competition, whereas girls tend to value relationship enhancing interactions. The typically masculine communication style and social roles affect the quality and character of men's relationships with other people.

2. Although males tend to have more friends than females, male same-sex friendships are characterized by less intimacy than those of females. Although women share activities and feelings, men are much more likely to share only activities.

3. The skills necessary for building a friendship are sometimes lacking in men, and they often need the social structure of settings like workplaces and sports to affiliate. Masculine demands for competition, task orientation, independence, pain tolerance, and homophobia limit male-male friendships. Many men have a lot of "buddies" but few friends. There is a good deal of historical, individual, and cross-cultural variation in patterns of men's friendships.

4. Gender-typed interaction patterns and gender role demands also make relationships with women difficult for men. Nonsexual friendship between a man and a woman is made difficult by a cultural climate that prescribes nonegalitarian relationships between the sexes. Because of the socialization to view women as sex objects and connect with them only in sexual ways, many men have difficulty in distinguishing friendly behavior from sexual flirtation.

5. In romantic relationships, men feel conflicts between attraction and gender role demands. They often lack the social skills necessary for building and maintaining an intimate relationship, and the traditional masculine behaviors of emotional inexpression and hyperindependence are antithetical to collaborative interactions. Couples' partnerships can become adversarial power struggles, leading to relationship dissatisfaction or dissolution.

6. Feelings toward the father often form a central psychological issue in men's lives. Emotionally and/or physically distant fathers leave sons with feelings of disappointment, neediness, and rage. Fathers are slowly becoming more involved with their children, but at present they must fight social, institutional, and historical forces in order to do so. As economic arrangements change, so will ideologies around fathering ideals. Nontraditional men who have nontraditional partners, and who view themselves as skilled caregivers, are most likely to be actively involved in parenting.

14

Coping in a Difficult World:
Men and Mental Health

A middle-aged man gets so distraught after his wife leaves him that he has to be admitted to a psychiatric hospital. A teenaged boy commits frequent robberies and assaults. A young man cannot resist the urge to expose his genitals to pubescent girls. A senior citizen, despondent from loneliness and the decline of his body, contemplates suicide. An alcoholic experiences significant difficulties with his job, relationships, finances, and the law.

The problems that these men have in living their lives have become unmanageable. All of them are experiencing a good deal of psychological discomfort, although some might be able to hide it. Many of them would have trouble admitting to others, or even to themselves, that they need help, or believing that they could benefit from treatment. Even if they come to an awareness that their problems are out of control, they might be very reluctant to ask for assistance from professionals or even from their closest friends.

Throughout this book, I have described many of the negative psychological effects of uncritically adhering to rigid and unreasonable gender demands. On the other hand, certain aspects of traditional masculinity may also contribute positively to mental health. In this chapter, I explore in more depth the relationships between gender and psychological well-being for men. The chapter is structured in four parts. First, I look at definitions of mental health and their connections with cultural conceptions of gender. Second is a discussion of mental health problems that males experience disproportionately in relation to females and the associations of these disorders with gender role characteristics. Third, I examine life experience factors that either protect men from mental illness or put them at increased risk. Finally, I explore the special issues around men in counseling and psychotherapy.

DEFINING MENTAL HEALTH

Virtually every abnormal psychology textbook begins with a chapter on the definitions of mental health and mental illness. If these were easy concepts to define, it would not take an entire chapter to cover the territory. Setting forth criteria for these concepts turns out to be a rather complicated enterprise. Nearly everyone agrees that a person who hallucinates frequently or cannot remember his or her name is suffering from a mental disturbance. On the other hand, when does "normal" sadness become "abnormal" depression? What if a person is satisfied with a lifestyle that others consider "sick?" How about the person who is a member of an oppressed group—if he or she is suspicious of others' motives, is that "paranoia," or is it "accurate reality testing?" (Sue, Sue, & Sue, 2005).

Some major definitional difficulties lie in the culture-bound character and historical context of definitions of mental health and illness. For instance, suppose that you were visiting the United States without knowing anything about the mainstream culture. You find out that every Saturday and Sunday during autumn, men get together, run as fast as they can, and knock each other down. Some of these men become severely injured and are carried off on stretchers. Others experience a good deal of lingering pain from these frequent violent collisions, and occasionally some even suffer catastrophic spinal cord injuries. Moreover, tens of thousands of people gather to watch these spectacles, and sometimes they even cheer when someone gets hurt.

As an outside observer, you wonder if the term for "war" in the United States is "football," yet you see the players shaking hands afterwards. You might be likely to go back to your native land and describe these "crazy," self-destructive men who engage in these exhibitions and the sadistic people who observe them. If you did, you would be making a judgment about the mental health of these people that few U.S. inhabitants would make.

Even the professional community has difficulty agreeing on criteria for mental illness, and in fact these standards change over time. In 1968, the American Psychiatric Association published the second edition of the *Diagnostic and Statistical Manual of Mental Disorders* (DSM-II), a guide for labeling psychological disturbances. In this version of the manual, homosexuality was defined as a mental disorder. When the next revision (DSM-III) (American Psychiatric Association, 1980) was published, the diagnostic category was called "ego-dystonic homosexuality," which meant that, if you were gay, you had a mental disorder only if you were dissatisfied with being gay and wanted to become heterosexual.

This development prompted psychiatrist Thomas Szasz to describe himself as having "ego-dystonic chronological disorder" because he was older than he wanted to be! His point was well taken. Everybody has some aspects of themselves with which they are dissatisfied. Why have we chosen only sexual orientation to pathologize? Perhaps as a result of convincing arguments by Szasz and others, this diagnostic category disappeared in the next two editions (DSM-III-R; DSM-IV) (American Psychiatric Association, 1987; 1994).

Landrine (1988) pointed out the cultural bias in defining mental health and illness:

Contemporary concepts of normalcy and psychopathology perpetuate the construction of the behavior of minorities and women as pathological along with the view that culture is peripheral to psychopathology.... The term *normal* suggests, among other things, an individual who exhibits abstract and logical thinking, emotional control, independence, delay of gratification, happiness, a concern with developing one's own potential to the fullest, and a sense of self as an autonomous individual who exerts personal control over self and environment… the sense of self described above—from which many other characteristics derive—is not how the poor experience the self … how Blacks experience the self … how Asian Americans experience the self … how women experience the self … or how most people throughout the world experience the self… . This concept of normalcy, held by U.S. public and professionals alike… is largely synonymous with the characteristics of upper income White men in this country … and is firmly rooted in the social meanings shared by middle-class White Americans. (p. 40)

It is clear that gender role definition is a central feature of culture. Because the definition of mental health is culture-bound, it is also strongly tied to gender stereotypes. Children as young as four say that there is something wrong with people who do not conform to gender roles (Stoddart & Turiel, 1985).

Especially since the publication of DSM-III in 1980, some feminist scholars have argued that the mental health establishment pathologizes women for the way that they have been socialized (e.g., to be dependent, emotional, and self-sacrificing). Pantony and Caplan (1991) suggested that a diagnostic category of "Delusional Dominating Personality Disorder" be used to describe people who have an "inability to establish and maintain meaningful interpersonal relationships, an inability to identify and express a range of feeling in oneself and others, and difficulty responding empathically to the feelings and needs of close associates and intimates." (p. 120). This proposed diagnosis is, of course, a description of a hypermasculine interpersonal style. Rather than labeling the behavior as emotionally disturbed, it is more often cast in a language of moral failure. As Prior (1999) stated, there is a tendency to see women as "mad" and men as "bad."

These objections to gender bias in the diagnostic schemata focus on the negative social consequences of being labeled as "disordered," and psychiatry has a rather long history of bias against women that constitutes a serious issue. However, we should not overlook the fact that it is not the purpose of diagnosis to stigmatize and blame people for their problems. Stigmatization is an unfortunate byproduct of diagnosis in a society that is prejudiced against the mentally ill.

The real purpose of diagnosis is to identify problems that require attention. In most cases, the willingness of health insurance providers to pay for treatment hinges on the diagnosability of the person seeking mental health services. Failing to label the hypermasculine behaviors described above as disturbed therefore has at least two consequences. First, it reinforces masculine privilege by tacitly approving the behavior. In other words, it says to the mental health community that it is alright to be emotionally withholding, aggressive, and unempathic. Second, it says that men who behave in such a way merit no attention. There is a denial that such behavior limits the quality of the man's life to a significant enough extent that we should do something for him.

The concepts of gender role conflict and strain (Pleck, 1995) show some promise in the study of gender and men's psychological adjustment. Gender role conflict is a negative psychological state that results from the contradictory and\or unrealistic demands of the gender role (O'Neil, 1990).

The hypothesis of the gender role conflict and strain model is that men who accept traditional gender ideologies, yet do not feel that they fulfill the prescriptions inherent in the role, will experience the highest levels of psychological conflict and negative health consequences. For example, a man thinks that being unemotional means being manly, but he finds it difficult to suppress his emotions. This man would experience more role conflict than either: (a) a man who accepts unemotionality as manly but has no difficulty suppressing his feelings, or (b) an emotional man who does not experience much pressure from the masculine prescription for emotional restrictedness. There is a growing body of evidence linking male gender role conflict with negative psychological states (Cournoyer & Mahalik, 1995; Good, Robertson, O'Neil, Fitzgerald, Stevens, DeBord, Bartels, & Braverman, 1995).

MEN, MASCULINITY, AND MENTAL DISORDERS

There are significant variations in the proportions of men and women who are diagnosed within several categories of mental illnesses. Researchers believe that a number of factors contribute to these sex differences, including gender socialization, which may strongly affect how a person expresses his or her psychological distress. For instance, a gender-typed woman who experiences psychological pain may often become depressed. A gender-typed man might react to the same kind of pain by abusing alcohol. These tendencies may be at least partly fueled by the woman's socialization to "act in" or internalize—to introspect and think about how she feels—and the man's gender-typed encouragement to deny vulnerability and "act out" or externalize—to look to the environment for solutions to his problems. John Lynch and I (Lynch & Kilmartin, 1999) and Terrence Real (1997) maintain that a depressive psychological base underlies many common symptomatologies in men, but that diagnostic criteria reflect a feminine mode of depression (more on this subject later).

A related possibility is that gender socialization sometimes prevents a person from acquiring certain coping skills (O'Neil, 1981b). A highly gender-typed man may not have learned how to deal with emotions and relationships. A highly gender-typed woman may not have learned how to deal with independence. Thus, gender socialization can contribute to behavioral deficits as well as to negative patterns of behavior.

People use psychological *defense mechanisms* to protect themselves from perceived threats to the self (Clark, 1998). Sometimes, their use is very adaptive. For instance, it is quite common for a person who has lost a loved one through death to experience some level of initial *denial* about the death. If the person were to come to a full emotional realization of such a profound loss, he or she would be flooded with anxiety and sadness and become completely incapacitated. The defense mechanism allows the person to protect the self and deal with the loss over time. On the other hand, all defenses involve distortion of reality, and so overusing them results in impaired psychological functioning.

Largely because of early gender socialization, males and females tend to develop somewhat distinct defensive styles. When defensiveness becomes problematic, these gendered styles express themselves in a differential vulnerability to several mental disorders. The masculine-feminine externalizing-internalizing dimension leads men to use the defense of *projection* (attributing one's own conflicts to others) more frequently than women (Clark, 1998). Faced with psychological discomfort such as low self-esteem, a man is more likely than a woman to project his negative feelings on to others and deal with these feelings in a distorted way. As we discussed in Chapter 13, violent behavior is often a projection of unacceptable negative feelings about the self on to another person. Unfortunately, projection leaves the person who is experiencing the conflict with no avenue for dealing with it directly and no process for improving his or her functioning. A person is unlikely to see the need for a change in behavior when that person experiences the problem as external to the self.

As with many areas of investigation, psychological gender characteristics predict defensive behavior better than merely knowing whether the person is male or female. Men who experience high levels of rigid beliefs around masculinity as it relates to success, power, competition, and emotional expression are significantly more likely than other men to use immature defenses—those that are common in 3- to 15-year olds and people who are personality disordered (Mahalik, Cournoyer, DeFranc, Cherry, & Napolitano, 1998). In other words, high levels of gender role conflict and strain tends to result in grown men acting like children.

There is a tendency to think that individuals are predisposed toward certain types of mental disorders only because of the way they were raised. In addition to the contribution of past socialization to current behavior, we should also remember that, in an important sense, men and women live in different gendered cultural worlds. There is a tendency for men and women to experience different stressors and to find themselves in different settings and roles (Cook, 1990). We saw in Chapter 13 that sex-segregated social groups tend to have gender-characteristic interpersonal styles. In the sociocultural context, different behaviors are anticipated, rewarded, and punished on the basis of sex. For example, expressions of sadness and helpless feelings by a woman might be met with sympathy and emotional support. The same behavior in a man might result in social isolation and loss of status.

Researchers have observed the following sex differences in mental illness:

1. Males experience a disproportionate number of most childhood disorders, such as Attention Deficit Hyperactivity Disorder and Conduct Disorder.

2. Women are somewhat more likely to be diagnosed with depression and most anxiety-based disorders, and much more likely than men to have eating disorders. (However, there is a growing awareness of body image disturbances in boys and men (See Box 14.1.).

3. Males constitute a majority of substance abusers, sexual deviates, and people with behavior control problems such as pyromania, compulsive gambling, and intermittent explosive disorder (a pattern of rageful outbursts).

4. There are unequal sex proportions for a variety of personality disorders: more men than women are diagnosed as paranoid, schizoid, schizotypal, narcissistic, obses-

Box 14.1: Body Image Disturbances in Men

The drive for thinness and resultant risk of eating disorders in females is a well-documented phenomenon that is strongly associated with cultural standards of beauty that emphasize body types that are impossible to achieve for most women. As Jackson Katz points out in the documentary film *Tough Guise* (Jhally & Katz, 2000) cultural standards for male body types also appear to be changing, but in the opposite direction—hypermuscularity is more and more evident in media portrayals of men. Katz displays the contrast between the somewhat flabby "professional wrestlers" of the 1960s and today's overdeveloped performers. During approximately the same period of time, the "action figure" (doll) G. I. Joe has changed from having the equivalent of 13 inch biceps (estimated by their proportion to the rest of the body) to 28 inch ones. Former baseball slugger Mark McGwire, a very muscular man, has 20 inch biceps, and so these figurines present a virtually impossible standard of manliness, much as Barbie dolls do with female thinness. *Star Wars* figurines have undergone a similar transformation from commonplace male bodies to hypermuscular ones. Katz believes that this cultural change reflects a crisis of masculinity accompanied by high anxiety in men around their desirability and manliness.

Do changing societal demands for muscular physiques have negative effects on men in similar ways that standards of thinness have on women? Emerging evidence suggests that this is indeed the case. In the same fashion in which eating disordered women are dissatisfied with their bodies and evidence body distortions in which they believe that they are fatter than they actually are, young men often perceive themselves as thinner and less muscular than objective assessments indicate (Raudenbush & Zellner, 1997). The body dissatisfaction and resultant pattern of pathological behaviors has been called *bigorexia* or the *Adonis Complex* (Pope, Phillips, & Olivardia, 2000).

Donald McCreary and Doris Sasse (2000) coined the term *drive for muscularity* and demonstrated negative phenomena associated with this characteristic. Not surprisingly, males are much more motivated to gain weight and muscle than females, and boys with a high drive for muscularity tend to have lower self-esteem and greater levels of depression than other boys. Moreover, they are more likely to binge eat and to use anabolic androgenic steroids, which entails risks to the heart, kidneys, liver, and immune system. Many steroid users also share hypodermic needles, thus risking infection. An estimated 3% of adolescent boys in the United States abuse these substances (Irving, Wall, Neumark-Sztainer, & Story, 2002). Morrison, Morrison, and Hopkins (2003) discovered that high levels of exposure to idealistic images of men's bodies (e.g., in muscle and fitness magazines) and the tendency to compare one's own body with these images were associated with high drive for muscularity. In addition, steroid use is associated with having friends who emphasize muscularity and parents who tease boys about their size (Smolak, Murnen, & Thompson, 2005).

sive-compulsive, and antisocial; more women than men are diagnosed as borderline (Sue et al., 2005).

5. Men are much more likely than women to commit suicide, although women make more incomplete suicide attempts (Stillion & McDowell, 1996) (See Chapter 9 for a discussion of suicide and masculinity.).

MENTAL HEALTH ISSUES FOR MEN

There has been much speculation about the relationships between some aspects of masculinity and the disorders listed above. The following discussion will focus on a few areas of diagnosis (substance abuse, personality disorder, and depression) and mental health issues (the role of marriage in men's mental health, and the psychological effects of parental divorce and father absence on sons).

Substance Abuse

Men are five to six times more likely than women to have difficulty with alcohol abuse or dependence, and twice as likely to abuse other drugs (Sue et al., 2005). Alcoholism is one of the most serious mental health problems in the world. In the United States, nearly 14% of people contract alcohol abuse or dependence disorders at some point during their lives (American Psychiatric Association, 2000). Brooks and Silverstein (1995) report that alcoholics occupy half of all U.S. hospital beds at any given time, that they attempt suicide 75–300% more often than non-abusers, and that as many as one in 10 men become alcoholic (compared with one in 50 women). Alcohol abuse is also strongly related to violence, crime, accidents, work absenteeism, relationship problems, and disease (Lex, 1995).

David Sue and his colleagues (2005) note that there is considerable cultural variation in rates of alcoholism. Although there are possible genetic factors in alcoholism, for example, Native Americans and Asians often have highly sensitive physiological reactions to alcohol (Butcher, Mineka, & Hooley, 2004), the cross-cultural variability in rates of problem drinking suggests that cultural values play an important role in the prevalence of the disorder.

Gender is one of the central organizing principles of mainstream U.S. culture, and we do not have to look far to find social connections between masculinity and alcohol abuse. Following are a few of these connections:

1. *Externalizing defensive style*: As noted earlier, men are encouraged to look outside of themselves for solutions to problems. Being in any kind of psychological pain is considered unmanly, as it implies emotional vulnerability. Drinking can function as "self-medication." Alcohol reduces anxiety and clouds the person's consciousness so that he or she will be both emotionally and physically numb. Men who rely on avoidant forms of coping with negative emotions are more likely to exhibit abusive drinking patterns (Cooper, Russell, Skinner, Frone, & Mudar, 1992).

2. *Toughness and risk-taking*: Some men perceive becoming dead drunk to be a way of proving one's masculinity, since "real men" can hold their liquor (Lemle & Mishkind, 1989). Binge-drinking men have been known to continue drinking *after* throwing up (a body's signal that it has had enough, if ever there were one). Driving and taking other risks while drunk are ways of demonstrating a masculine disregard for safety.

3. *The quantification of experience*: Men are often socialized into the world of sports, where it is important to count things like home runs, touchdowns, and points. Drinking can become a competition whereby the man who drinks the most "wins." Drinking games, where players are forced to drink, bring a masculine sport-like structure into the social arena.

4. Dealing with emotions and relationships indirectly: A friend once told me about an experience he had at a party. He decided to go out on the deck to get some fresh air, and there he found two very masculine men, dead drunk, having an argument about which one of them loved the other one more. Imagine these men having that same conversation when they were sober. Alcohol allows men to lower their masculine inhibitions and behave in affectionate ways with each other (Blazina & Watkins, 1996). Men feel that they can walk down the street with their arms around each other when they are drunk, but not at other times. The next day, they can maintain their interpersonal distance by attributing their affectionate behavior to their drunkenness. Therefore, alcohol abuse enables men to deal with their feelings of attachment while at the same time maintaining a façade of masculine independence (Capraro, 2000).

5. *Modeling and social group factors*: Males are more likely than females to have same-sex peers who are heavy drinkers (Brooks & Silverstein, 1995), and some male social groups actively promote binge drinking. Chiefly among these groups on college campuses are fraternities. Nearly 40% of fraternity members went from being low level drinkers in high school to being high-level drinkers in college (compared with 17% of nonmembers) (Lo & Globetti, 1995). Heavy drinkers tend to seek fraternity membership (Wechsler, Kuh, & Davenport, 1996), and the vast majority of fraternity members are binge drinkers (Smith & Mathews, 1997).

6. *The cultural association of masculinity with alcohol*: Drinking is interconnected with the social meanings attached to being masculine. Male television actors are portrayed drinking significantly more often than females, and alcohol advertisements are largely oriented toward the associating masculine fantasy with alcohol use. Traditional gender attitudes are associated with alcohol-related problems in adult men (McCreary, Newcomb, & Sadava, 1999) and adolescent males (White & Huselid, 1997).

Beer advertisers use male actors twice as often as female actors (Hall & Crum, 1994) and present images of their products as "related to challenge, risk, and mastery over nature, technology, others, and the self." (Fejes, 1992, p. 14). Men in these commercials are usually portrayed in occupational and leisure pursuits, especially in outdoor settings and sometimes with an element of danger. Beer is often presented as a substitute for the overt communication of affection between men, a rite of passage into manhood, and as a reward for hard work. Men are often shown participating in activities that involve speed and coordination, like race-car driving, skiing, and calf-roping, despite the fact that drinking would severely decrease one's performance in these pursuits and increase the risk of injury (Strate, 1992). When women are portrayed, they are often presented as an audience for men (Fejes, 1992), or as a sexual objects (Hall & Crum, 1994). Advertisers often imply that alcohol is a means of sophistication and heterosexual seduction (Barthel, 1992).

In an article titled "Beer Commercials: A Manual on Masculinity," Strate (1992) sums up the impact of this advertising: "…no other industry commercials focus so exclusively and exhaustively on images of the man's man … in reflecting the myth, the commercials also reinforce it." (pp. 78–79). Fejes (1992) adds: "Men who are sensitive, thoughtful, scholarly, gay, or complex are not present in beer commercials." (p.14). Beer commercials also portray a sanitized version of drinking—there is never any smoke in the bar, nobody ever pays for a drink, and nobody ever gets drunk (Strate, 1992).

7. *Gender role conflict and strain*: Men use alcohol to deal with the pressures of social masculinity. Researchers have found that men with high levels of gender role conflict also had higher levels of reported alcohol use (Blazina and Watkins, 1996) and alcohol-related problems (McCreary, Newcomb, & Sadava, 1999) than men with lower levels of gender role conflict.

Williams and Ricardelli (1999) describe two basic gendered dimensions to men's alcohol use. First, alcohol is clearly associated with traditional masculinity. Therefore, drinking is a way to display one's manliness (the *confirmatory* function). Second, drinking can help men to handle the stress and strain of living up to difficult standards of masculinity (the *compensatory* function).

Personality Disorders

Personality is a relatively stable set of behavioral predispositions that characterize a human being's typical functioning (Funder, 2004). In the case of the person who is *personality disordered*, the generalized ways in which he or she approaches the world are marked by an inflexible and self-defeating style that results in poor mental stability (Millon, 1996). The ingrained ways of relating to others that personality disordered individuals use almost always cause them problems in their work and social functioning. They also tend to produce a good deal of personal distress.

The DSM-IV (American Psychiatric Association, 2000) lists 10 of these disorders. Six affect men more often than women and one affects women more often. The remaining three disorders are distributed fairly equally between the sexes. A description of the male-dominated diagnoses follows.

Persons with *Paranoid Personality Disorder* are prone to be overly suspicious and guarded. They tend to view the behavior of others as deceiving or attacking them, and they usually react with hostility on the frequent occasions when these perceptions occur (Millon, 1996). These people are characterized by emotional coldness, no sense of humor, stubbornness, defensiveness, and unwillingness to compromise. They seem especially on guard against losing their independence (American Psychiatric Association, 2000).

Schizoid Personality Disorder is characterized by flat emotionality and interpersonal aloofness. These people seem to lack the capacity to feel and lead dull, joyless, and solitary lives.

Schizotypal Personality Disorder is characterized by peculiarities of thinking and behavior. These oddities of experience and action result in highly impaired interpersonal relationships.

People with *Narcissistic Personality Disorder* display a grandiose sense of self-importance and absorption. They present themselves as exceptionally talented, accomplished, and "special." Narcissists are easily hurt by any kind of criticism and believe that they are entitled to special favors by virtue of being so wonderful. They feel shamed and enraged when others react negatively to them and when they do not receive a steady source of admiration and attention (American Psychiatric Association, 2000). Underneath this grandiose exterior is a fragile sense of self-worth.

Antisocial Personality Disorder is characterized by a long history of behaviors that violate the rights of others, such as lying, stealing, and assaulting. Antisocial people feel little remorse for having mistreated others. They are frequently in legal trouble and fail to sustain any close relationships (American Psychiatric Association, 2000). Many antisocials are dangerous criminals.

People with *Obsessive-compulsive Personality Disorder* are stereotypical perfectionists. They often demand that others conform to their unreasonable standards of order and devotion to details, thus they tend to be interpersonal bullies.

One could characterize many of the traits described in these six disorders as caricatures of negative masculinity. All of these personality types are marked by some mixture of self-absorption, indifference toward others' feelings, and an overemphasis on independence. Narcissistic and antisocial people are interpersonally exploitive, using others to reach their own goals. All of these styles are characterized by extreme difficulty in relationships, another stereotypically masculine characteristic.

There is also pronounced emotional restrictedness in antisocial, paranoid, obsessive-compulsive, and schizoid disorders. Schizoids feel nothing or next to nothing. Antisocials, obsessive-compulsives, and paranoids express little emotion except for anger, which is stereotypically masculine. The combination of hostility and hyperindependence in antisocial and paranoid disorders is an especially volatile one. These people feel that they must protect themselves at all costs, and thus they are prone to violence.

Although mental illnesses are caused by multiple factors, dysfunctional interaction styles in the family of origin are strong influences in the development of personality disorders (Millon, 1996). If we consider hypermasculinity to result from harsh masculine socialization, we could speculate that men who exhibit the above personality disorders may well have received an exaggerated "dose" of overly stern gender socialization in addition to other dysfunctional developmental patterns.

Depression

Depression involves pervasive feelings of hopelessness, helplessness and worthlessness accompanied by a family of behavioral symptoms like social isolation, sleep problems, and loss of interest or pleasure in activities (American Psychiatric Association, 2000). It has been called the "common cold of mental illness" (Seligman, 1990a), affecting approximately one in five people in the United States at some point during their lives. Rates of depression have risen steeply during the twentieth century (Nolen-Hoeksema, 1998), prompting psychologist Martin Seligman (1990b), who has spent his entire professional career studying this mental disorder, to label it an epidemic.

Females are diagnosed with clinical depression twice as often as males in the United States. Susan Nolen-Hoeksema (1995; 1998) believes that women are more depressed than men because of two basic factors: the patriarchal oppression of women, and the tendency for women to be socialized into a *ruminative coping style* in which the depressed person dwells on his or her distress, which tends to make the depression more severe and longer lasting. On the other hand, males are more likely to deal with negative emotions by distracting themselves away from their feelings.

Several theorists believe that the epidemiology of depression in men as a group approaches that of women, but that men tend to have different, gendered styles of expressing their problem. The reported sex difference in depression may be misleading due to a number of factors. First, women may be more likely than men to seek treatment or to report their depression to others (Sue et al., 2005). Males have a tendency to underreport most physical and psychological treatment, as having symptoms implies unmasculine vulnerability (Pollack, 1998). Second, the diagnostic system may be gender biased. Third, males may manifest depression in different ways from females, leading to different diagnoses. For instance, men are more disposed toward heavy drinking, angry outbursts, and aggression in response to sad feelings (Real, 1997; Lynch & Kilmartin, 1999, Cochran & Rabinowitz, 2000; Kilmartin, 2005). Marital conflict is strongly correlated with conventional depression in women and increased use of alcohol in men (Waite, 1995).

Regardless of the debate around the true prevalence rates of depression for men and women, we should avoid being drawn in to a competition between the sexes to claim the title of "most depressed." All depressed people are in need of help. At the same time, the sex differential in diagnosis may provide important clues to the connections between gender demands and mental illness. It might well be that the roots of the illness are different for the average depressed woman and the average depressed man. In other words, it is possible that rigid gendering is a risk factor for depression, but that the character of that gendering may also produce markedly different modes of expression in the two sexes.

Several pieces of evidence lend credence to the hypothesis that depression is underdiagnosed in males. The strongest is that males commit suicide, the ultimate expression of depression, four times more often than females (See Chapter 9). There are also very high rates of psychiatric hospitalization in divorced males compared with divorced females, suggesting that female partners may have a strong role in helping men defend from their underlying depressive senses of self (See the discussion below on the protective function of marriage for men.). And, psychogenic physical diseases, which are related to psychological conflicts, are more common among men (Lynch & Kilmartin, 1999).

Whereas women are prone toward the aforementioned ruminative coping style for dealing with negative emotions, men's externalizing tendencies lead them to gravitate toward distracting themselves and acting out. Alcohol abuse is a major way to hide one's depression, even from the self, and there is ample evidence linking alcohol problems to underlying depression. As Real (1997) stated, "…while the capacity to externalize pain protects some men from *feeling* depressed, it does not stop them from *being* depressed; it just helps them to disconnect further from their own experience." (p. 82, emphasis original).

Masked depression is also in evidence in a number of other typically masculine problems, including violence, overinvolvement in sports or work, narcissism, criminal behavior, and relationship difficulties. Addressing the underlying depressive dynamics of these problems is a key component of effective treatment (Lynch & Kilmartin, 1999; Kilmartin, 2005; Cochran & Rabinowitz, 2000).

The Role of Marriage in Mental Health

A stereotypical scene: A man and a woman have been dating for an extended period of time. The relationship is monogamous and mutually satisfying. They love each other. The woman expresses a desire to marry, and the man shies away. She asks, "Why don't you want to get married?" He doesn't really know. He asks, "Why is getting married so important?" She doesn't really know.

Scenes like this are commonplace. For many men, committing to and being intimate with one woman for the rest of their lives feels very dangerous. He may lose his independence and freedom, and then he would become very unhappy. For many women, committing to and being intimate with one man for the rest of their lives seems like the "thing to do." Remaining unmarried after extended dating feels dangerous. She may feel very unhappy if she does not marry. The cultural myth is that marriage fulfills women and restricts men. Cultural stereotypes reflect this bias—the happy and devoted housewife, the lonely spinster or old maid, the carefree bachelor, and the henpecked husband.

In recent years, social scientists have investigated the accuracy of this bias by examining mental illness rates for married men, single men, married women, and single women. If marriage has damaging or beneficial effects for any of these groups, these effects should be reflected by mental illness rates that are at variance with contrasted groups.

In general, the results of this research cast considerable doubt on the accuracy of the cultural myth. An extensive survey of mental hospital patients revealed that single and divorced men were hospitalized at about three times the rate of married men, and also at a higher rate than single or divorced women. Married women were hospitalized at a higher rate than married men. Married people in general were hospitalized less often than single people, but the size of that difference was much greater for men than for women (Rosenstein, Steadman, McAskill, & Manderschied, 1987). Basow (1992) sums up the findings: "Although males outnumber females as inpatients, a greater percentage of female than male inpatients are married, whereas a greater percentage of male than female patients have never been married." (p. 186). Basow also notes that the same pattern holds for suicide.

Although one can not say from these data that marriage *causes* better mental health in men, there certainly are relationships between being married and staying out of the hospital (Barnett & Baruch, 1987), avoiding mental illness (Walker, Bettes, Kain, & Harvey, 1985), reduction in physical risk-taking (Waite, 1995), and avoiding stress-related physical illnesses (Cleary, 1987). These relationships hold for women, but they are much stronger for men (Denmark, Rabinowitz, & Sechzer, 2000).

If marriage is more protective for men than for women, we should see higher rates of mental illness and hospitalization in divorced and widowed men compared with their female counterparts. This is indeed the case. Divorced men show higher rates of hospitalizations than any of the other groups—nearly eight times the rate for married men (Rosenstein & Milazzo-Sayre, 1981). Men have more long-term psychological difficulties than women in adjusting to divorce and separation. Widowers experience more psychological and physical problems than widows, and men remarry more quickly than women following divorce or the death of a spouse (Helgeson, 2002).

One can make sense of these data by looking at the functions of marriage for men and women. For both partners, marriage would seem to provide opportunities for intimacy and companionship, as well as fulfilling a social obligation—95% of people in the United States get married at some time during their lives (Casteneda & Burns-Glover, 2004).

We have already discussed in Chapter 8 the gender role prohibitions against intimacy and self-disclosure for men. Yet these are human needs, and failing to attend to them has adverse effects on the person. Although marriage does not necessarily involve psychological intimacy, it certainly sets the stage for it. For many men, then, marriage is an opportunity to fill a void that has been created by harsh masculine socialization.

Women need intimacy, too, but they often experience it in relationships with other women (See Chapter 13). In the realm of psychological intimacy, marriage tends to be less novel for women than for men. Men may also tend to be less responsive to women's disclosures. As a result, fewer psychological benefits accrue for women than for men.

The social role aspects of marriage are also worthy of mention. The traditional Christian marriage ceremony begins by asking, "Who gives this woman to be married to this man." It is an exchange of property from father to son-in-law. The celebrant ends by saying, "I now pronounce you man and wife." The man keeps his identity ("man"), and the woman's identity ("wife") seems to become defined by her relationship to the man. As Anthony Porter (Bunch & Porter, 2003) describes it, "She went down the aisle as a piece of property; she came back with a job." The bride relinquishes her last name and sometimes even gives up her first name ("Mrs. John Smith"). Historically, marriage was a legal agreement by which the husband took possession of his wife's property (Herttell, 1839/1992). In fact, the woman herself became her husband's property—rape laws were originally property crimes against a husband or father (Basow, 1992). Clearly, society has historically expected wives to adapt to their husbands and take responsibility for the relationship.

This part of the social role is slowly changing. Some marriage ceremonies have become more egalitarian, with language like, "I now pronounce you *husband* and wife", and "you may now kiss *each other*" rather than "you may now kiss the bride" (as if she had no choice in the matter). We are also seeing many more women retaining their last names, which is emblematic of their having identities apart from their husbands. The social myth that women are incomplete unless they are married is slowly undergoing modification.

Despite their stereotypical resistance to getting married, it appears that considerable benefits are associated with being a husband. The fact that most men eventually marry (despite gender role demands for hyperindependence and promiscuity) is good evidence that men want and need intimacy. Pleck (1985) reported that men usually experience their family roles as more important in their lives than their work roles, and that satisfaction with family roles is strongly associated with psychological well-being.

Divorce and Father Absence

Marital separation and divorce are becoming increasingly prevalent in the United States. Although much research has been done in the context of what Hill (1987) called "Dick and Jane" families (those with a father who works outside of the home, a housewife mother, and two or more children, none of whom are from the parents' previous relationships), these families constitute less than 3% of U.S. households (U.S. Department of Labor Statistics, 2005). One in every two or three U.S. marriages ends in divorce, and the average length of a marriage that ends in divorce is 6.3 years (Coontz, 2005). Social scientists have become interested in how children are affected by parental conflict, divorce, remarriage, and family blending.

The breakup of a marriage is rarely, if ever, easy on any of the people involved. Children of divorce tend to experience psychological difficulties for several years (Hetherington, Stanley-Hagen, & Anderson, 1989). Some researchers have discovered that the process and aftermath of marital dissolution has an especially negative impact on boys.

Researchers Jeanne and Jack Block began to follow a cohort of young children in the late 1960s in a longitudinal study designed to investigate several developmental hypotheses. They collected data on the same youngsters year after year. During that time, some of these children's parents divorced, and together with another colleague, they investigated the effects of parental conflict and divorce on children (Block, Block, & Gjerde, 1986). This study is an especially important one because it is *prospective*, meaning that the researchers were able to gather data on these children prior to the marital breakup, often for several years. They did not have to rely on children's memories of what happened to them and how they felt.

Comparisons of 60 intact families with 41 subsequently divorced or separated families revealed that sons are more vulnerable than daughters to the negative effects of parental conflict. Boys from subsequently divorcing families showed more aggression, more difficulty in controlling impulses, less cooperation, and higher anxiety in novel situations than boys from intact families. These characteristics also stood in contrast to girls from subsequently divorcing families, who showed different and milder symptoms than boys.

Another important finding from this study was that parents were much more likely to engage in marital conflict in the presence of boys than in the presence of girls. If you think about the experience of your mother and father fighting with each other when you were a child, you might recall (or imagine) it to be very frightening indeed. The sex difference in witnessing parental conflict may be a critical factor in explaining the significantly more negative impact of marital difficulties on sons. It is also important to note that these effects are not simply a result of divorce, per se, but from the conflict preceding the divorce. The researchers observed these sex differences in symptomatology for years prior to the marital separation.

The fact that parents in conflict are much more comfortable with expressing their animosity in front of their sons may reflect the beliefs that boys can "take it" and that boys' emotions are nonexistent or less important than those of girls. One can see that childhood gender role strain in interaction with family stress can have pronounced negative effects on the personality development of the boy. Some children carry the wounds of parental conflict well into adulthood (Wallerstein & Blakeslee, 1989).

About 86% of children live with their mothers following divorce (Hetherington & Stanley-Hagen, 1997). Kelly (1988) found that children who live with their same-sex parent after divorce were better off than those living with other-sex parents, as measured by several indices of psychological health. If parental skills and resources are relatively equal (and clearly, this is not always the case), mounting evidence indicates that it is best for boys to live with their fathers. Perhaps this would not be the case if our culture did not imprint antifemininity on males, but we will not know unless and until patriarchy dies its slow death. The reality is that daughters tend to adjust to divorce better than sons (Hetherington, Cox, & Cox 1985), and that boys in their mothers' custody have strong reactions to diminished contact with their fathers (Kelly, 1988).

However, we should not overstate the problem and neglect the wide range of effects in marriage dissolution. Many children of divorced parents adjust very well with a minimum of symptoms, especially when their mothers and fathers cooperate with each other in parenting tasks. Although divorce doubles the risk of emotional and behavioral problems, it raises that risk from about 10% to about 20% (and part of the difficulty can be attributed to relocating and economic stress). Therefore, about 80% of children do well in spite of the unfavorable environment that parental conflict produces (Hetherington & Stanley-Hagen, 1997). Moreover, these risk differences reduce sharply within two to three years following the divorce. Children of divorce who live with a competent single parent are only one-half at risk for problems compared with children living in two-parent conflicted families (Coontz, 1997). The social conservative movement to make divorce more difficult ignores the fact that staying married against one's will perpetuates a conflictual environment that may have adverse effects on children. Although divorce has negative effects on children when it results in the dissolution of a low-conflict marriage, divorce benefits children when it removes them from high-conflict situations (Amato & Booth, 2001; Amato, Loomis, & Booth, 1995).

The effects of father absence on boys are difficult to separate from the effects of parental conflict, economic changes, relocation, and other stressors that accompany marital dissolution. Although parental separation is probably the most prevalent cause of father absence, fathers may also be gone from the home because of death, or due to military service or other work. Additionally, many males have complained about fathers who, although physically present, are psychologically absent because of their emotional unresponsiveness. At the same time, there are physically absent fathers who may be somewhat psychologically present through telephone and email communication, letters, and visits (Way & Stauber, 1996). Father absence may be especially damaging when the father refuses to contribute to his children's economic support, as do an estimated one-quarter of noncustodial fathers (Hetherington & Stanley-Hagen, 1997).

There may well be variant effects of father absence depending on the type of absence (physical, psychological, or both), the circumstances around which the father left the home, the characteristics of the mother or other caretaker, the gender-typing of father and son, and/or other factors. Although there is a widespread societal assumption that father absence is damaging to males (Stevenson, 1991), research on the connections between father absence and mental health has not demonstrated that it is necessary for boys to have same-sex role models in order to develop healthily. On the other hand, it has not been demonstrated that same-sex role models are unnecessary, either (Jones, 1990). A good deal more investigative work in this area remains to be done.

Whatever the effects of father absence on boys are, we can be quite certain that relationships with fathers and feelings about fathers are of profound importance to sons. In an extensive research study of men, Barnett, Marshall, and Pleck (1992) found that the quality of the adult son's relationship with his father was significantly associated with the son's level of mental health, and a later meta-analysis indicates that both sons and daughters are better adjusted when their fathers remain active as parents after a divorce (DeAngelis, 2005). These conclusions support an earlier finding from an equally extensive study by Kamarovsky (1976) that male college seniors with psychological adjustment problems tended to report low levels of satisfaction in their relationships with their fathers. You may also recall from Chapter 12 Lisak's (1991) finding of a connection between negative father-son relationships and the risk of sexual assault perpetration.

In all of these studies, the son's relationship to the father was much more predictive of mental health than his relationship to his mother. This research corroborates a great deal of anecdotal evidence from therapists and men's studies educators that feelings about the father constitute a major psychological issue in men's lives.

COUNSELING AND PSYCHOTHERAPY WITH MEN

Everyone will benefit if we can find ways to alleviate the suffering of people who struggle with mental health problems. The processes for doing include counseling (psychotherapy), education, and social change. The latter two are saved for the final chapter of this book. The following discussion centers on the treatment of individual men in a psychotherapeutic context.

Men as a Special Population

Carl Rogers (1957) first popularized the idea that a counselor's understanding of the client's subjective psychological environment is a critical first step in the therapeutic process. If the therapist is to be helpful, he or she must gain a deep awareness of how the client experiences the self and the world. Rogers was an important early influence in defining the field of *Counseling Psychology*, which is founded on the appreciation and respect of individual differences and perspectives.

One of the important ways in which therapy clients differ is in their identifications with, and memberships in, different sociocultural groups. For example, people of color, physically challenged people, gays, and lesbians have almost always had some different experiences than Caucasians, able-bodied people, and heterosexuals. Some of these experiences have important effects on the person's sense of self and view of the world. When these people see counselors, especially ones who are dissimilar to them, it is important for the counselor to be sensitive to the typical psychological and political issues associated with memberships in various groups.

With this basic assumption in mind, many counselors began to undergo formal and informal training in understanding diversity in the 1960s and 1970s, and this kind of education continues today. One of the basic categories of individual difference is, of course, the sex of the person seeking treatment. In 1979, the American Psychological Association's (APA) Counseling Psychology division published a list entitled "Principles Concerning the Counseling and Therapy of Women." The preamble to these principles begins:

> Although competent counseling/therapy processes are essentially the same for all counselor/therapist interactions, special subgroups require specialized skills, attitudes, and knowledge. Women constitute a special subgroup. (Division 17, 1979, p. 21)

The people who drafted this document believed that it is essential for counselors who treat women to be knowledgeable about biological, psychological and social issues affecting women, to be aware of their own values and biases about women, and to develop skills that are particularly suited to female clients.

Around the same time this document was published, therapists were beginning to realize that men, too, have typical styles and psychological issues that they bring to the therapeutic setting. Therapists also began to recognize and examine their values and biases about men, and some realized that a gender-aware perspective on masculine socialization would be helpful in their treatment of male clients.

A number of excellent books and journal articles have been published in the past 25 years on the subject of men as a special population in psychotherapy. Some of these have integrated men's issues with those of special subpopulations of men such as ethnic, older, divorced, gay, and bisexual men (See Brooks & Good, 2001; Andronico, 1996; Levant & Pollack, 1998.).

Good, Gilbert, and Scher (1990) argued that all counselors should be aware of the impact of gender in the treatments of all clients. They suggested five broad principles of "Gender Aware Therapy":

1. *Regard conceptions of gender as integral aspects of counseling and mental health*: One needs to understand how gender socialization and sexism affect a person's well-being.

2. *Consider problems within their societal context*: "The personal and political cannot be separated for women or men in society. Thus, the availability of quality child care or an employer's policy with regard to paternity or maternity leave would need to be considered in understanding the experience of personal stresses and conflicts" (p. 377).

3. *Actively seek to change gender injustices experienced by men and women*: Counselors should explore nontraditional options and examine gender stereotypes with their clients.

4. *Emphasize development of collaborative therapeutic relationships*: Counseling relationships should de-emphasize power and emphasize cooperation.

5. *Respect clients' freedom to choose despite what is "politically correct," traditional, or nontraditional (p. 377)*. For example, a male client has the right to be emotionally inexpressive. Gender aware therapy does not dictate that this client should change, but rather that he understand the consequences of this option and choose it from an informed perspective.

Counselors are becoming increasingly aware that men constitute a special subgroup of clients. They have identified a number of psychotherapeutic men's issues and developed some specialized treatments for male clients.

MEN'S ISSUES IN COUNSELING AND PSYCHOTHERAPY

Traditional one-to-one psychotherapy is a set of methods that were developed by mostly male therapists to treat mostly female clients. If we look closely at the counseling relationship, we see that very little of traditional masculinity is conducive to requesting treatment, sustaining the therapeutic effort, or performing the activities required of clients.

Help Seeking

People who request psychotherapeutic services have often been stereotyped as "crazy", weak, or out of control. This stigma makes it difficult for almost anyone to come to counseling, but it is especially difficult for men, who often place a special value on being rational, self-sufficient, strong, and in control. The act of telephoning or walking into a counseling center and asking for an appointment may feel like the equivalent of a declaration that, "I am weak, afraid, dependent, and vulnerable. I don't know what is going on with me, even though I should, and I can't handle my problems on my own. I need help."

One would be hard-pressed to find statements that reflect masculine failure more than these. Given the social expectations to "work it out for yourself," "take it like a man," and "control your feelings," it is not surprising that men utilize psychological services considerably less often than women (Addis & Mahalik, 2003). Good, Dell, and Mintz (1989) found that traditional attitudes about masculinity were significantly associated with men's negative attitudes toward help seeking. Clearly, if you cannot ask for directions when you are lost in your car, you will have difficulty asking for help in more emotionally charged areas like mental health counseling.

Since entering counseling is often perceived as a threat to masculine self-esteem, men frequently resist asking for services until they experience a very deep level of psychological pain and until their problems reach crisis proportions. If they begin treatment, they may drop out when their discomfort reaches a barely manageable level. After dropping out their pain may worsen. At that time, it may be even more difficult for them to return and ask for assistance, because they now admit two failures by doing so: the one that brought them to counseling in the first place, and the failure on the first attempt as a therapy client (Kilmartin, 2004b; 2005).

Because of the incompatibility of help seeking with traditional masculinity (as well as other reasons detailed below), the average length of treatment for male clients is about half that for female clients. At college and university counseling centers, many more men than women request short term counseling, despite the fact that counselors judged the therapy needs of the two sexes to be similar (Prosser-Gelwick & Garni, 1988).

Michael Addis and James Mahalik (2003) call for a contextual analysis of help seeking in men across several dimensions including the perceptions of normativeness and ego-centrality. People are more likely to seek help if they think that their problem is shared by others and does not affect the core of their perceptions of self. The National Institute of Mental Health (NIMH) has undertaken an extensive public information campaign called *Real Men, Real Depression* in an effort to re-cast this increasingly common mood disorder as normal for males and not reflective of one's level of masculinity (Rochlen, Whilde, & Hoyer, 2005). The slogan, "It takes courage to ask for help" is an attempt to re-define a positive masculine attribute as reflective of a proscribed behavior.

Counseling Activities

Counseling is an activity in which clients are usually expected to perform certain behaviors thought to be helpful in solving emotional problems. These behaviors often include emotional self-disclosure, exploration of feelings, nondefensive introspection ("looking inside" of oneself), and emphasizing interpersonal material. Men usually have little experience in these areas, which are culturally defined as feminine. Therefore, the counseling setting tends to be a rather poor match of person and environment for men (Bruch, 1980). In other words, asking a man to do these things may make him feel like a fish out of water, and this discomfort may well be another factor that contributes to the high male dropout rate.

Because many counseling activities are uncomfortable for them, men often ask for masculine kinds of help, such as a logical analysis of the problem, an emphasis on thinking over feeling, or help with defending against rather than experiencing the problem. For instance, typically masculine strategies for dealing with the breakup of a romantic relationship might be to find a substitute lover, to use thoughts to master feelings, or to learn how to not think about the former partner (Kilmartin, 2005).

In the above scenario, the counselor might think that it is more important for the man to deal with powerful feelings and go through the process of grieving for the lost lover. This would not fit very well with a client who expects directive, analytical, problem solving. Thus, counselors find themselves in quandaries when these kinds of situations arise. They do not want to reinforce a maladaptive masculine strategy, yet they also do not want their client to terminate treatment. In these cases, counselors should address the client's needs and expectations in the context of feelings about control, independence, and vulnerability. They should also discuss the man's ambivalent feelings about the process of counseling itself. To do so requires sensitivity to men's issues.

Men's skill levels in these emotionally focused activities are another consideration. Many have had their emotional experience systematically removed from their lives. Not only are they uncomfortable with the expression of feeling, they are understandably not very good at it. Asked how he feels, a man might often reply, "about what?" The counselor might then say, "about your girlfriend breaking up with you." The man tells the counselor what he *thinks*, "I feel she shouldn't have done it." He may feel sad, disappointed, angry, and so on, but these emotion-descriptive words are not in his working vocabulary.

It is also vitally important for counselors to introduce the topic of gender very early in the therapeutic relationship. Since masculinity is an important context in which the male client experiences his symptoms and expectations for therapeutic process and outcome, counselors should assess the client's level of gender conformity, educate him about masculinity, and help him find alternative, more adaptive ways of framing his experiences (Kilmartin, 2004b; 2005).

For counselors, it is an extraordinary challenge to reach a man in the context of questions like, "How do you feel?" when the man has been socially manipulated to the point that the question does not even make sense. The good news is that men who can learn emotion-focused coping in the therapeutic setting may gain a skill that will be helpful to them in virtually every area of their lives.

Counselor Sex and Gender

If a man is considering entering therapy, should he choose a male or a female therapist? The answer to this question involves a wide variety of factors. It is usually more important that he choose a competent therapist of either sex who is a good match for him. However, different issues often arise with counselors of different sexes.

With male counselors, typical masculine interaction patterns may often emerge. Men have been socialized to be especially competitive, unemotional, and invulnerable with other men. The male client may feel this pressure and act accordingly making it difficult for the therapeutic work to proceed.

There is a high degree of intimacy in the counseling relationship. Sometimes it is greater than in any other relationship the man has. It is not unusual for clients to feel warm and dependent toward the therapist, and these feelings may stimulate the client's homophobia (Heppner & Gonzales, 1987; Mintz & O'Neil, 1990). Most men feel more comfortable self-disclosing to a female than to a male (Mazur, 1989). Therefore, the male client-male counselor dyad may struggle more than other combinations in this important regard, and male counselors should attempt to encourage emotional self-disclosure on the part of their male clients.

With female counselors, these intimate feelings may also become sexualized, leading to confusion, distraction, or shame. Other feelings may arise in reaction to the power of the female therapist. Having been raised to feel superior to women, the man might try to dominate the counselor and/or exhibit the kind of childlike dependence that men sometimes have with their female partners. In a collaborative relationship, client and counselor can seek to understand and deal with these reactions to address the client's other concerns.

The gender socialization of the therapist is also important. There is an increasing awareness that it is vital for mental health professionals to be aware of their own issues. Counselors are not immune to the influences of the gendered culture, and they have gender biases like anyone else. For instance, in one study, counselors in training tended to react negatively to a male client who chose a nontraditional occupation (Fitzgerald & Cherpas, 1985). Robertson and Fitzgerald (1992) found that the diagnoses of experienced therapists were affected by the sex of the client. They suggested that therapists may also subtly exert pressure on male clients to conform their behavior to masculine standards. Non-conscious gender ideologies may bias counselors' diagnoses (Fernbach, Winstead, & Derlega, 1989) and their attitudes toward male clients (Wisch & Mahalik, 1999).

Counselors must work hard to understand and deal with their own emotional reactions to their clients. Male counselors may find their homophobia stimulated with male clients. Feminist counselors may feel angry toward misogynistic male clients as a part of their general anger toward the oppressive culture of patriarchy. Both male and female therapists may find it harder to empathize with the pain of a male client, a reaction to the social belief that men are to be blamed for their problems and not seen as victims in any sense. Counselors of both sexes may feel uncomfortable when male clients cry or otherwise show vulnerability.

The profession of counseling usually involves deeply personal activities. Counselors who fail to consider the gender issues involved with these activities do a disservice to their clients and perpetuate the negative aspects of gender role socialization.

PSYCHOLOGICAL SERVICES FOR MEN

The specific techniques that a counselor would use with a male client are dependent on the individual's problem and the theoretical orientation of the therapist, among other factors. It is hard to make sweeping generalizations about what techniques work with male clients. At the same time, some writers have identified certain approaches that are helpful in the treatment of many men, and a brief discussion of these approaches is appropriate.

Because the counseling environment is threatening for many men, several theorists have suggested that structured and psychoeducational approaches be considered as alternatives to traditional one-to-one psychotherapy. John Robertson and Louise Fitzgerald (1992) found that college men were more likely to say they would utilize workshops or seminars than personal counseling. Psychoeducational programs that offer self-help and problem-solving approaches allow men to do some psychological work in a masculine context. Men in corporate settings may respond more positively to psychological work if it is called "executive coaching" rather than "therapy." In this approach, the executive's job performance is explored in relationship to his psychological well-being and relationship skills (Hills, Carlstrom, & Evanow, 2001).

As noted in Chapter 13, men often need more structure than women in relationship situations. Several authors have designed workshops on specific, characteristically masculine problems. For example, Moore (1990) developed a structured, 10-week program for increasing emotional expressiveness. Levant (1990b) is involved with teaching fathering skills as well as emotional competencies (Levant, 1997a). Leafgren (1988) described a developmental program for college men around a wide range of men's issues. All of these approaches involve providing an environment that allows men to do what they may rarely do otherwise: share feelings, talk about the inner life, explore personal values, and express the parts of the self that are squelched by traditional masculinity.

In one-to-one counseling, as well as in the approaches described above, it is important to help men understand the effects of their gender training. In therapy, the client's presenting problem can often be viewed in terms of masculine socialization or gender role strain. For example, a man who is feeling very lonely following a breakup could understand his loneliness in the context of the social demands to be independent, nondisclosing, and task-oriented. The mental health practitioner can help the man identify what he believes about masculinity and the sources of these beliefs during this process. Then, the client can start to understand the ways in which he has been restricted by narrow definitions of masculinity and begin the difficult task of freeing himself from gender conformity (Allen & Gordon, 1990). In this way, the counselor lets the man know that his problems are understandable, that he need not feel shamed because he has problems, and that he can work toward feeling better.

In addition to helping male clients learn about the danger of avoiding certain behaviors, therapists can help men understand the value of behaviors that they have not learned. When men become clients, counselors often perform the educative role of helping their clients understand that self-disclosure and other nonsexual intimate behaviors are important for the person's mental health. The therapist communicates to the client that these behaviors are expected of him, but also acknowledges that they are difficult and anxiety provoking.

A major therapeutic task is to reintroduce men to the worlds of emotion and connectedness. At the most elementary level, men often need to incorporate "feeling words" into their working vocabulary. Men who need structure in doing so can keep diaries in which they identify emotional reactions and record the situations in which the feelings occurred. Some men need a checklist of possible emotions because the identification of feeling is such a new task (Levant, 1997a). Some men at the most basic level need to start with the most elementary emotions (mad, sad, glad, afraid), and build their affective vocabulary from there. Importantly, men need to explore the vulnerable emotions underneath their anger (Lynch & Kilmartin, 1999). Ronald Levant's (1997a) structured program for men and emotion was described in Chapter 8.

Therapists can also facilitate men's emotional education by confronting intellectualized interpretations of events, and by communicating the expectation of emotional reaction. This can be done in a very matter-of-fact fashion, by saying in a nonjudgmental way, "I would think you'd have some feelings about"… (whatever is being discussed). Again, because most men need a little structure, the therapist is more successful if he or she talks about feelings in the context of some event, rather than in the abstract (Kilmartin, 2005).

One other strategy for helping men access their feelings is by attending to the physiological sensations that accompany emotions (Rabinowitz & Cochran, 2002). The therapist can ask, "What's going on inside your stomach?" or "Can you feel the tension in your forehead?" A jumpy stomach usually accompanies anxiety; a smile reflects pleasure. When the client is able to understand these connections and become more accepting of his natural emotional life, he may be able to resist the masculine propensity to dissociate the self from feeling. Eventually, he may learn to spontaneously identify his affective responses (Silverberg, 1986).

Therapists can also be helpful to their male clients by tapping into masculine modes of experience. Men who are working on emotional expression can view the development of these skills as a challenging task to accomplish. As most men are familiar with thinking in this kind of mode, this may reduce the threat. A man who has difficulty with learning emotional expression may feel incompetent and thus unmasculine, but if the counselor frames the activity as a skill and connects it to other skills, the client's anxiety could be reduced. For example, the counselor might say to a client, "Remember the first time you swung a golf club or played a scale on the piano? You weren't very good at that, either. But you practiced and got better, and over time, it began to feel like second nature" (Kilmartin, 2004b).

Interestingly, these masculine modes can be useful tools for breaking the client out of his constricted behavior if the therapist is skillful. Wong, Davey, and Conroe (1976) suggested an approach in which the base of positive masculinity is expanded to include other healthful behaviors. For instance, men value independence, and the therapist can help the man view nonconformity to stereotypical masculinity as a kind of independence. Men who value risk taking can learn to take risks with emotional self-disclosure. Men who value assertiveness can see objecting to sexist jokes or telling a male friend that he is valued as assertive communications. Men who are good at goal setting can set goals that are related to family, relationships, or play (Pasick, Gordon, & Meth, 1990).

Group therapy is increasingly popular as an approach to men's issues. Men in groups can experience other men in completely new ways, and the process of intimate connection to other men can have strong therapeutic effects (Lynch & Kilmartin, 1999). Group approaches for men who share a common problem or experience can deal with the interactions between masculine role demands and those experiences. Therapists and educators have recently developed group techniques for working with men of color (See Andronico, 1996), teenage fathers (Kiselica, 1996), survivors of child sexual abuse (Isely, 1992; Harrison & Morris, 1996), and sex offenders (Becker, 1996; Lazur, 1996), to name a few. A number of gender-aware self-help books have also appeared in recent years with focuses on depression (Real, 1997; Lynch & Kilmartin, 1999), sexuality (Brooks, 1995), anger (Lynch, 2004), and grieving for a father who has died (Chethik, 2001).

A gender-aware approach to therapy with men involves giving them permission to be who they are and providing a safe atmosphere in which they can express the socially prohibited parts of the self. The therapy room can become a haven from the harsh demands of masculinity. In his exploration, the male client can discover which of these demands have been internalized and self-imposed, and work toward a less restricted experience of the self. He becomes more prepared to take the changes he has made in counseling and expand them into other parts of his life.

SUMMARY

1. Mental health problems are related to gender from several perspectives. Definitions of mental health are culture bound, and gender stereotypes are a central feature of culture.

2. The proportions of males and females diagnosed in some categories of mental disorder vary significantly. Gender seems to be an important factor in determining how psychological distress finds expression. For adult men, the diagnoses of substance abuse, sexual disorders, behavior control problems, and certain personality disorders are more common than for women.

3. Typically male personality disorders tend to share the masculine characteristics of hyperindependence, emotional restrictedness, self absorption, and interpersonal exploitiveness. Men who exhibit these disorders display the most dysfunctional and destructive aspects of traditional masculinity.

4. Although depression is diagnosed twice as often in women as in men, there is evidence that men's depression is underdiagnosed and misunderstood.

5. Contrary to stereotypical beliefs, marriage seems to have the effect of protecting the mental health of men. The marital relationship may offer the man's only avenue for meeting his intimacy needs. When marriages and other intimate relationships dissolve, men tend to have more psychological difficulties than women.

6. Boys are especially at risk for suffering negative effects from parental conflict and family separation. Sons witness more of their parents' marital conflict than daugh-

ters, and this experience is thought to be a critical factor in the development of psychological distress. Child custody traditions place most sons with their mothers
following divorce, although this practice is contraindicated by the research. Although connections between childhood father absence and mental health problems
have not been convincingly demonstrated, it is clear that sons usually have powerful
psychological issues around their relationships with their fathers.

7. Approaches to treating men in counseling and psychotherapy have recently placed
   an emphasis on the view of men as a special subgroup of clients. Well-trained therapists recognize that men bring characteristic issues to counseling, examine personal
   and societal biases about men and masculinity, and are aware of the impact of gender
   on the therapeutic relationship.

8. One-to-one psychotherapy does not provide a masculine environment. Vulnerability, emotional self-disclosure, and asking for help are connected with the sense that
   one is unmanly. Men are more likely than women to avoid psychological services,
   and to drop out or otherwise shorten therapeutic relationships, even though men's
   need for therapeutic intervention is equal to or greater than that of women. Different
   counseling issues tend to emerge based on differences in therapists' sex and gender.

9. Because the counseling environment is an uncomfortable one for many men, other
   approaches to doing male psychological work have been developed. Workshops,
   seminars, and discussion groups provide for a structured examination of men's issues. Mental health practitioners can help men to understand the effects of gender on
   their lives through these activities, as well as in the traditional therapy setting.

10. Many men have difficulty in dealing with emotions and relationships. In counsel-
    ing, a man can begin to reconnect with his feelings and intimacy needs. As a result,
    he can achieve a fuller experience and expression of the self.

15

Struggles and Changes: New Perspectives on Masculinity

It seems that gender roles as we now know them are becoming archaic because the economic and cultural forces that maintained them are changing, and because they have aspects which limit human potential in modern living. The destructive characteristics of gender-based expectations have negative effects on men, women, and children, and thus the need for transitions in gendered traditions is a quality of life issue for everyone. If we agree that masculinity needs to change (Clearly, many do not agree.), then what aspects should be changed, and how do we go about it? As we shall see, there is a good deal of disagreement around these issues, thus there is no singular, unitary "men's movement."

Anyone who has ever tried to drop a bad habit will tell you that it is a difficult undertaking. Any psychotherapist who has ever tried to help a client change knows what challenge this task entails. And, effecting social reform is always a slow, painstaking process with philosophical controversies and practical problems every step of the way.

Many people think that social problems are a result, not a cause, of changing gender roles—that we would all be better off if we would return to the time when, as fictional character Archie Bunker put it, "girls were girls and men were men." Among those who advocate gender transformation, some believe that men should reclaim "deep masculinity"; some advocate androgyny; some think that gender roles should disappear altogether; some believe that the answers can be found in fundamentalist Christianity; and some just want men to "buck up" and take more responsibility.

When we arrive at the task of creating methods for change, we find that gender is deeply ingrained in individuals, families, social customs, laws, and institutions—indeed in virtually every facet of living. An agenda for change must therefore address multiple levels of intervention. To do so requires time, people, creativity, money, research, education, and other resources.

This may sound pessimistic. It is not intended to be, but we should appreciate the enormity of the tasks of individual and social change. At the same time, changes do happen. It is sometimes said that, "The way to eat an elephant is one bite at a time." Because sexism and patriarchy are ingrained in the culture, and because they have existed for so long, they are rather formidable "elephants."

We can find parallels to these efforts in the more-familiar crusades to end racism. People make individual efforts, and they organize to do what they can collectively. Anti-racism efforts sometimes make progress, and they sometimes suffer setbacks. The people who believe in the value of racial equality continue to fight for it. Racism has not gone away, and so the efforts continue.

It is the same with sexism and patriarchy. The wheels turn slowly, sometimes they seem to be turning backward, and always there are disagreements about the directions in which those wheels should turn. In this final chapter, I examine the history of masculine gender transformation efforts, the philosophies of individuals and organizations interested in these enterprises, and the kinds of activities that address these social issues in individual, social, and political contexts.

VERSIONS OF MEN'S REALITY

Think about how strongly you agree or disagree with the following statements:

1. Modern men are a group of people who are alienated from their "true nature."

2. The innate differences between males and females go well beyond reproductive roles.

3. Men are oppressed, mistreated victims of sexism.

4. Gender roles are a reflection of a natural order in which men are dominant.

5. Men should focus most on discovering and changing themselves.

6. Men should focus most on eliminating sexism and patriarchy in the larger society.

7. Men should focus on eliminating sexism against men.

8. Men should gain a fuller appreciation of their privileged status, work to understand the worlds of people who do not have such status, and strive to help women achieve equality.

9. Fundamental changes in men are not possible.

10. Feminism is men's enemy.

Theorists have taken differing positions on these issues, and thus there are varying perspectives on men's nature and agendas for change or conservation. Kenneth Clatterbaugh (1997) described eight such perspectives:

1. *Conservatives* believe that male dominance and traditional masculinity are natural and desirable. They often see feminism as dangerous. Therefore, they either oppose gender role reforms or see these reforms as impossible.

2. *Profeminists* believe that traditional masculinity is destructive to women and men, in that order. They believe that men ought to work to end patriarchy and men's violence, and to foster equal rights for women, and that men should also deal with the limitations of gender roles in their personal lives.

3. *Men's Rights Advocates* see men as victims of social and legal sexism. They believe that men are more oppressed than women. Their agenda is toward changing divorce, child custody, rape, sexual harassment, and domestic violence laws that they view as favoring women at men's expense. They also complain about "male bashing."

4. *Mythopoetic* types believe that males in modern society have been disconnected from their "deep masculinity." They seek to reclaim this male essence through an agenda of self-development.

5. *Socialist* theorists see masculinity against the backdrop of capitalist oppression. From this perspective, men control women because men control most economic resources. Change in gender only comes from change in economic systems.

6. *Gay male* social movements are responses to the cultural and institutional homophobia that oppresses men who are not exclusively heterosexual.

7. *African-American men's perspectives* emphasize the unique set of problems that face this group of men, who have been victimized by societal oppression for centuries.

8. *The evangelical Christian* men's movement sees the contemporary crisis of masculinity as a product of the diminishing role of Christian religion in men's lives. Advocates of this position want a return to a style of traditional families in which fundamentalist Christianity is at the center of experience.

Various organizations and "movements" have emerged from these differing perspectives of men's social reality. Currently, there appear to be several major foci of men's gender awareness and organized agendas for change: the Mythopoetic Movement, Profeminism, Men's Rights, the Promise Keepers, the gay marriage movement, prison reform, the boys movement, men's health concerns, gender-based violence prevention, international men's movements, and Men's Studies.

One note is important before beginning a discussion of these various efforts. There may be considerable diversity of opinion among individual members of each of these perspectives. The situation is parallel to that of any ideological group. For instance, political conservatives may disagree with each other on certain issues, but the basic approach and view of the world is similar across all group members. Therefore, keep in mind that we are dealing in somewhat stereotypic characterizations of each group.

Profeminism

The profeminist men's movement embraces the philosophical tenets of feminism in its analysis of men's experience. Two major assumptions of this philosophy are, first, that all human beings share a similar need for self-expression, and second, that all human beings are entitled to choose their own behaviors in the service of self- expression. Gender roles are seen as destructive social forces that limit people's choices. Modern feminism has been a reaction against the male-dominated definition of human experience as well as to the social forces that limit the options of women. In the early 1970s, a few men began to write and talk about how gender demands limit men's options and harm women in an application of a feminist perspective to the world of men.

The largest profeminist men's group is the National Organization of Men Against Sexism (NOMAS), which undertakes political activities and has sponsored annual conferences on Men and Masculinity for more than 30 years. Without a doubt, this is the longest organized tradition of gender-aware dialogue about men.

In its statement of principles, NOMAS describes itself as "an activist organization of men and women supporting positive changes for men" and reflecting the value that "working to make this nation's ideal of equality real and substantive is the finest expression of what it means to be a man" (NOMAS, 2005). Its website (www.nomas.org) prominently lists four principles: "pro-feminist, gay-affirmative, anti-racist, and committed to justice" (NOMAS, 2005). Curiously, the latter principle replaced the phrase "dedicated to enhancing men's lives" from an earlier statement of principles (NOMAS, 1992). The efforts of this group involve understanding the effects of masculine privilege, working to end injustices experienced by women, people of color, non-heterosexuals, and other oppressed groups, and challenging the self-destructive aspects of traditional masculinity. NOMAS supports these efforts, not only for individuals, but also in larger social contexts. Over the years, NOMAS has participated in social protest, monitored legislation related to sexism, and filed *amicus* ("friend of the court") opinions in legal cases related to its cause.

The profeminist men's movement has taken a good deal of criticism from the mythopoetic movement, the men's rights movement, social conservatives, and sometimes from women. Because profeminist men reject essentialism and support androgyny, mythopoetic types tend to view them as "soft" males who deny their natural masculine energy—they are "nice guys" but not "real men."

Mythopoetic men and men's rights advocates are often of the opinion that profeminists are overly concerned with women and not focused enough on themselves. Some suggest that their annual conference has an atmosphere of guilt—a sense that men should change mostly for women, and only secondarily for themselves. Mythopoetic men see this attitude as a reflection of a lack of masculine pride. Profeminist Harry Brod (1992) responded, "I learned about male pride in NOMAS."

We see in the mythopoetic-profeminist debate an agreement that men need to change along with disagreements about directions and methods. Both factions seem invested in improving the quality of male-female relationships. The mythopoetic position seems to be that men need to break from their mothers be initiated into manhood by other men (Clatterbaugh, 1997). As a result, they will become more free to express themselves and more psychologically healthy. At that point, they will be better prepared to enter into healthy relationships with others. The profeminist position seems to be that men need to take responsibility for the destructiveness of men as a group and spend time listening to women in a spirit of cooperation.

There is a good deal of common ground between these two approaches. Both reject violent masculinity and embrace introspective psychological development for men. Both affirm the need for men to find new ways to relate to other men that go beyond working and playing along side of one another. Both want to understand how to heal the destructive effects of harsh masculine socialization. The mythopoetics emphasize an individual spiritual path for this process; profeminists emphasize dialogue and political action.

The Men's Rights position is that profeminists do not seem to understand the power of women over men (Williamson, 1985). As we shall see, their view is that men should be seeking to enhance their power rather than that of women. Social conservatives believe that it is impossible and/or undesirable to transform traditional masculinity, and so they disagree fundamentally with nearly every profeminist position. Finally, there are women who view the profeminist movement as paternalistic and as drawing attention away from women. They see profeminists as men who are learning how to act in sensitive ways, but who are not really sincere about it. Williamson (1985) stated that profeminist men:

> have not convinced all feminist women of their sincerity. They have been accused of stealing the women's movement rhetoric in order to gain the limelight, or to trick women into going to bed with them. They have also been accused of adopting a new paternalism toward women by posing as the male protectors of women's liberation. (p. 312)

Women are understandably suspicious of men's groups. After all, the history of many such groups is steeped in the tradition of excluding and oppressing women. It may be difficult for women to believe that men want to change and/or that it is possible for them to do so. However, compared with other activists, profeminists would seem to be most open to participation by and dialogue with feminist women.

The Mythopoetic Movement

In the early 1990s, when people spoke of *the* men's movement, they were almost always referring to the mythopoetic movement. At that time, it was by far the most popular and well-publicized of men's gender-aware activities. This movement leaped into the national spotlight in the early 1990s with two best-selling books: Robert Bly's (1990) *Iron John*, and Sam Keen's (1991) *Fire in the Belly*. Bly is by far the most central figure in this movement. Tens of thousands of men from across the country have attended his seminars and read his books.

The mythopoetic movement has its theoretical roots in Jungian psychology. The philosophical position is that modern men have lost the archetypal masculine essence that was established and passed on from generation to generation since the dawn of human-kind. This "deep masculinity" involves a fierce (but not violent), mysterious, distinctly male energy. Being disconnected from this energy means being alienated from one's na-ture, and this self-alienation is thought to have negative psychological consequences.

The mythopoetic contention is that deep masculinity has been eroded by several forces: the industrial revolution (which banished men from their homes and disconnected them from the land), the loss of male initiation rites, the growing social disrespect of men and masculinity, and the frequent psychological distance between men and their fathers (Bly, 1990, 1991; Kimbrell, 1991). Some mythopoetic types seem to think that feminism has made things worse by devaluing the natural "wild man" quality of males. According to many mythopoetic types, men who buy into the feminist view of the world become "soft," female-dominated, self-alienated "mama's boys."

For mythopoetic men, the agenda for change is mainly a personal one. They must sep-arate from their mothers and be initiated into the world of men through all-male group ac-tivities. Small, somewhat intimate "ritual men's groups" meet regularly (see Liebman, 1991, for a description). "Men's Councils" are larger groups of men who meet on a weekly or monthly basis. A 1991 *Newsweek* article reported that there were at least 160 small groups and men's councils in the Northeast United States alone at that time (Adler, Springen, Glick, & Gordon, 1991).

In the larger context, there are also a variety of men's meetings and "wildman week-end" retreats. In the 1980s and 1990s, Bly sold out medium-sized auditoriums to men who paid considerable sums of money to spend the day with him and several hundred other men. Weekend retreats included a variety of activities in the service of exploring the deep masculine. Schwalbe (1992) estimated that over 100,000 men had attended a mythopoetic gathering during a ten year period.

These meetings involve a variety of activities, including story telling, poetry reading, drumming, face painting, "sweat lodges," and other rituals. The philosophical position of the mythopoetics is that shared male ritual is the major avenue for accessing and reclaim-ing the rich inner experience of being a man. The lack of these rituals in modern society has left individual men disconnected from the larger male community, thus stifling their psychological growth.

A number of criticisms have been leveled against the mythopoetic movement, mostly from feminist perspectives. One of the major controversies concerns the mythopoetic doctrine of *essentialism* (see Chapter 1). The definition of deep masculinity as a guide to experience takes the position that there is a singular, important, innate (essential) mascu-line quality.

Profeminists reject this doctrine. Their view is that gender is more of a social artifact than a "hard-wired" reality. The mythopoetic movement, with its emphasis on masculin-ity as transhistorical, transcultural, and transsituational denies the impact of historical pa-triarchy, misogyny, and power imbalances on the psychologies of men and women. Mythopoetic gatherings, take place in a "ritual space" and allow men the luxury of a decontexualized journey into self. Mythopoetic leaders tend to blame "the system" (Keen, 1991) and the industrial revolution (Bly, 1990), two social forces, for men's self-alienation. However, their solutions are exclusively personal ones, not attempts to transform the societal arrangements that purportedly lie at the root of the problem (Johnson, 1997). In response to this criticism, a more recently formed mythopoetic organization, the ManKind Project, encourages its members to participate in prosocial activities (Burke, Maton, Anderson, Mankowski, & Silvergleid, 2004).

Another criticism is that, because this journey is somewhat expensive, mythopoetic types are most often men who have benefited from the economic advantages of patriarchy, racism, and classism. Brod (1992) characterized these people as men of privilege who "purchase community on the weekend." According to its critics, the mythopoetic movement has excluded large groups of oppressed people: women, people of color, and the poor. Gay, bisexual, and older men can be included if they have the money.

The response of mythopoetic leaders is that they have no intention of excluding men who are not affluent. In fact, small groups and men's councils do not require payment for participation. Even in the larger gatherings, economic support is provided for some who are interested but lack the ability to pay. Critics respond by pointing out that, in fact, very few of these men are interested in joining a group of white, middle-aged, upper-middle-class men who seem to have little in common with them.

The enormous appeal of the mythopoetic movement during the 1990s may well have been due to feelings in so many men that they are disconnected from themselves and other men. Their desire to reconnect is in conflict with homophobia and socialized antifemininity. They sense that it is dangerous to introspect and be intimate with other men, yet they also sense that it is important to do so. Ritual seems to provide a comfortable structure that lowers the anxiety connected with the foreign world of feeling. Although men have plenty of rituals in sports, work, and all-male social activities, mythopoetic assemblies promised to provide new, ostensibly healthier rituals. However, they never provided criteria for ritual goodness nor any evidence beyond the anecdotal that these rituals are effective (Kilmartin, 1997). Critics say that the exclusive and essentialist nature of mythopoetic work serves to reinforce patriarchy, misogyny, and homophobia, because it emphasizes separation from women and because it is a personally focused approach that does not include working toward social change (see Kimmel, 1995). As Schwalbe (1998) stated "...mythopoetic men do not see that, in a male-supremacist society, there can be no innocent celebration of masculinity" (p. 576). Supporters of the mythopoetic movement say that their activities tap a naturally masculine mode for doing important psychological work. Mythopoetic groups have seen a large drop in popularity during the last decade.

The Men's Rights Movement

In 1974, Warren Farrell published *The Liberated Man*, one of the most widely read profeminist books of its time. Farrell gave what some considered an insightful analysis of masculinity and described the psychological benefits that men would accrue for changing in a more androgynous direction. *Why Men Are the Way They Are* was published 12 years later. Farrell also wrote this book, but you will find this fact hard to believe if you read both it and *The Liberated Man*. Rather than extolling the benefits of changing for men, Farrell (1986) was now describing men as victims of "the new sexism," a general lack of respect for men and lack of understanding for their struggles.

Farrell's radical change from a profeminist to a men's rights perspective was a result of what he perceived to be a vilification of men by feminism. Although feminists ostensibly support equal rights for all people, the National Organization for Women (NOW) opposed joint custody legislation in the late 1970s. For Farrell, this was a signal that the most influential feminist group in the United States was not so much a voice for human rights as it was a special interest group for women's rights (Williamson, 1985). He now felt that someone ought to also be looking out for the rights of males. In 2005, Farrell published *Why Men Earn More*, taking the position that men make more money because they deserve it for working longer hours in more dangerous environments than women.

The men's rights movement takes the position that men are the victims of cultural, social, legal, and psychological injustices, and that men's victimization outweighs that of women. This view is clearly anti-feminist, as every feminist analysis begins with the position that women-as-a-group are vastly disadvantaged compared with men-as-a-group (Clatterbaugh, 1997). Baumli (1989) summarizes the view that men's rights is antithetical to feminism: "The men's rights movement does not support feminism because feminism indulges in habitual misandry [man hating] and sexism toward men; but the men's rights movement does support women's liberation [because it] relieves a man of the burden of being a family's main provider" (p. 11).

The men's rights social change strategy is to resist feminist objectives and counterattack with social action that are perceived as advancing the cause of justice for men. The subtext of much men's rights rhetoric seems to be that women and men are political enemies. The historical roots of this movement are in divorce and child custody reform efforts. When divorce began to skyrocket in the 1960s, many men believed that courts unfairly sided with divorcing wives in awarding alimony and child custody, and they founded organizations to combat these perceived inequities. These groups never coalesced into a single national group, but some groups such as Husbands Against Dirty Divorce, Fathers for Equal Rights, and the Joint Custody Association enjoyed widespread support.

In the 1970s, a few men began to feel that men were being unjustly treated, not only by divorce courts, but also by the society at large. The most influential of these men was Herb Goldberg (1977), author of *The Hazards of Being Male*. In this book, Goldberg described similarities between women's and men's issues by drawing parallels between abortion rights and the draft (control over bodies and choices), and between the sexual objectification of women and the work-and-success objectification of men.

Among groups that embraced this thinking, the view that emerged was of men as a victimized and oppressed segment of the population. Their position is that men should not accept women's interpretations of their experience. Feminists complain that men have too much power, yet these individual men do not feel powerful (Recall from Chapter 1 the discussion of the invisibility of privilege). Feminists claim that men are not oppressed, yet these men experience themselves otherwise.

Men's rights advocates have long lists of complaints. Following is a sample (in addition to the major issues already mentioned):

1. Social judgments that are positive for women but negative for men, such as she has "sexual needs," he's an animal; she raises her voice in frustration, he's out of control; she is homeless because society has abused her, he's a lazy bum (Speer, 1990).

2. The social acceptance of "male bashing" (Macchietto, 1991).

3. The demand that men always take the initiative, and therefore risk rejection, in heterosexual relationships (Farrell, 1986).

4. Lack of attention to male victims of spouse abuse, prison rape, war, and false accusations of rape or sexual harassment (Men's Rights, Inc., n.d.).

The men's rights movement is highly controversial and has been the target of criticism and ridicule. Feminists and profeminists tend to see the members of these organizations as men who do not understand or appreciate the cultural privilege of men and the legitimate anger of women. They view men's rights types as working to reinforce a patriarchy that is perceived as eroding. After undertaking in-depth interviews with several Canadian fathers' rights activists, Bertoia and Drakich (1998) concluded that these men seemed much more interested in regaining control of their ex-wives, children, and money than they were in sharing parenting duties.

Men's rights advocates tend to see feminists as man-hating and castrating, and they therefore conclude that feminism is men's enemy. With regard to an agenda for change, this movement takes the position that the emphasis should be on changing the social world's consideration of men. The only part of the traditional gender role they desire to change is the part that "takes it like a man" (silently) when mistreated.

Many feminists and profeminists reject the argument that the oppression of men is worthy of focus, but mythopoetic types seem to accept it. Their difference with men's rights advocates is that they see oppression as an internalized quality that is changed through self-exploration. On the other hand, the men's rights movement sees oppression as a socially pervasive sexism against men, who will continue to be victimized unless something is done about it, and so there is more of an emphasis on political action.

Goldberg (1977), who appears to be somewhat more moderate than the leaders of many men's rights organizations, points out that there is no real contradiction between seeing women as oppressed and men as oppressed at the same time. He concedes that women are more oppressed than men, but maintains that anyone who is being mistreated deserves relief. The amount of relative privilege and abuse received should not be a consideration. Sexism is sexism, regardless of its target. Goldberg's point seems well taken, although one must consider that, when finite resources are being allocated, the amount of mistreatment does of necessity become an important consideration.

It is clear that these three groups have differing versions of male social reality. Some synthesis of these views is possible, although the varying movements seem reluctant to enter into dialogues with one another. It might be quite possible to do individual exploration, work for social justice for women and the same for men, and decry sexism, all at the same time. There may be appropriate settings for all-male (as well as all-female) groups to meet. In other settings, it seems quite important for mixed-sex, gender aware dialogue to take place.

Promise Keepers

In 1990, Bill McCartney and Dave Wardell founded an evangelical Christian men's movement called Promise Keepers. Their aim was to encourage men to recommit themselves to being good fathers and husbands as defined by "biblical principles." The first Promise Keepers conference in 1991 drew 4,200 men. In 1992, 22,500 men came to a football stadium to hear Promise Keepers speakers, and based on this success, organizers began to plan more stadium rallies. 275,000 men attended seven such events in 1994, the year McCartney resigned his position as head football coach at the University of Colorado to devote himself full time to this movement. Thirteen rallies drew over 700,000 in 1995, and over a million men came to 22 rallies in 1996 (Abraham, 1997). In 1997, a huge throng of men flocked to Washington, DC for one of the largest religious gatherings in history (Escobar & Murphy, 1997). The crowd was estimated to be close to 500,000 (Wheeler, 1997). By that time, Promise Keepers had supplanted the mythopoetic movement as the most popular men's movement in the United States.

According to Clatterbaugh (1997), Promise Keepers is based on three major premises. First is the Christian doctrine that men are sinners who must atone and resist temptation to lead moral lives. Promise Keepers strive for "sexual purity," meaning that they condemn extramarital and premarital sex, use of pornography, sexual fantasy, "habitual" masturbation, and homosexuality. Clatterbaugh describes the Promise Keepers view of men's sexuality as the religious conservative parallel to the sociobiological view that men are naturally barbaric, promiscuous, and inclined toward short-term gratification, and that these tendencies must be actively curtailed for the good of society.

The second major premise is that society has become hostile and adversarial to Christians. Thus, Promise Keepers are called to battle the "moral decline" that Satan has wrought in contemporary life. Sexual promiscuity, pornography, single parenthood, homosexuality, divorce, and decreased church attendance are cited as evidence of this decline. There is a good deal of talk about "holy war" in Promise Keepers meetings. In a 1997 rally, McCartney said, "Many of you feel that you have been in a war for a long time, yet the fiercest fighting is just ahead. God has brought us here to prepare us. Let's proceed. It's wartime!" (quoted in Mann, 1997).

The rhetoric of war is accompanied by a view of Jesus Christ as a heroic warrior who leads soldiers into battle. This "muscular Christianity" became popular for a while during the mid-nineteenth century and was revived in the early twentieth century by evangelist Billy Sunday, who described Christ as "no dough-faced, lick-spittle proposition [but rather] the greatest scrapper who ever lived." Contemporary televangelist Jerry Falwell described Christ as "a man with muscles... a he-man." (quoted in Kimmel, 1996, p. 177, 312).

The traditionally masculine theme of men as dominant and aggressive (but for the right reasons) also finds its expression in the frequent reference to sports in Promise Keepers rallies. The ties to athletics are unmistakable. After all, their founder was a football coach and they meet in stadiums. McCartney has referred to the Bible as "God's playbook." I attended the October 1997 Washington, DC rally as an observer and was struck by the number of sports and other masculine themes on tee shirts and baseball caps, such as "Real men follow God," "Live pure, train hard," "cross trainers," "soldiers of the cross," "time to stop looking for heroes and become one," and a shirt that said "Lord's gym" on the top, accompanied by a figure of Jesus on his back with a crown of thorns and a cross across his chest reading "sins of the world." Underneath the drawing, the shirt read, "Bench press this."

The third major premise is the doctrine that men and women are essentially different, with complementary but distinct functions ordained by God. Promise Keepers see men as the natural leaders in the family. They frequently cite New Testament bible verses stating that women were created *for men* and that wives should submit to their husbands, who hold authority in the world. As you can imagine, this rhetoric is especially troubling to feminists and profeminists.

The leaders of Promise Keepers frequently describe their movement as apolitical, and yet some of their main financial supporters are well-known leaders of the Christian conservative political movement: Jerry Falwell, Pat Robertson, and James Dobson (Myers, 1997), and organizations like Focus on the Family and the Family Research Council that are on the extreme political right wing (Equal Partners in Faith, 1997). McCartney has been very involved in anti-gay and other conservative political action. In 1992, he called homosexuality "an abomination against Almighty God" (Abraham, 1997) and supported Colorado's Amendment Two, which called for a ban on making any law that would grant gays civil rights protection, a law that National Organization for Women (NOW) official Rosemary Dempsey called, "in effect, a license for gay bashing" (quoted in Recer, 1995, p. 14). This law passed but was later struck down as unconstitutional by the United States Supreme Court (Conason, Ross, & Cokorinos, 1996). McCartney has also been a featured speaker at meeting of Operation Rescue, a militant anti-abortion group (Myers, 1997). At a 1993 rally, McCartney is quoted as saying, "Whenever the truth is at risk, in the schools or legislatures, we will contend for it." (Ireland, 1997, p. 4). In 1996, he said, "Whoever stands with the Messiah will rule with Him. . . Let's take this nation for Jesus!" (Clarkson, 1997, p. 1).

Whether or not Promise Keepers is a conservative political group, it certainly tends to attract conservative members. A *Washington Post* poll taken at the large 1997 rally revealed that there were three times as many Republicans as Democrats in attendance. About 60% of those polled had unfavorable views of feminists, then-President Bill Clinton, and Hillary Clinton. Sixty-nine percent favored making it harder for married couples with children to divorce, and 94% disapproved of allowing gays to marry and having the same legal rights as heterosexual married couples. Forty-four percent said they would prefer that their wives not work outside of the home (Morin & Wilson, 1997).

As a movement that encourages men to be more involved with their children, faithful to their wives, and helpful in their communities, Promise Keepers has enjoyed widespread support from outside of it's membership, and the testimonials by members of the importance of the organization in their lives are numerous and extremely positive (Abraham, 1997; Escobar & Murphy, 1997; Greene, 1997). Even some of its critics concede that a movement of social responsibility for men cannot be all bad (Goodman, 1997; Minkowitz, 1995; Pharr, 1997a). At the same time, Promise Keepers is the recipient of strong criticism from feminists, liberal Christians, non-Christians, and gay activists.

NOW president Patricia Ireland (1997) referred to this movement as "feel-good male supremacy," and stated that "… this hottest -religious-right marketing tool since televangelism has portrayed women's equality as the source of society's ills." (p. C3). At the root of this criticism is the Promise Keepers ethic of male "leadership," which critics view as a thinly disguised reclamation of men's power over women. In what is perhaps the most frequent quote cited by Promise Keepers critics, Tony Evans (1994), one of the major contributing authors of the group's handbook entitled *The Seven Promises of a Promise Keeper* says:

> The first thing you do is sit down with your wife and say something like this: 'Honey, I've made a terrible mistake. I've given you my role. I gave up leading this family, and I forced you to take my place. Now I must reclaim that role.' Don't misunderstand me. I'm not suggesting that you *ask* for your role back, I'm urging you to *take it back*…. Unfortunately, however, there can be no compromise. If you're going to lead, you must lead. Be sensitive. Listen. Treat the lady gently and lovingly, but *lead*! Having said that, let me direct some carefully chosen words to you ladies who may be reading this: *Give it back!* For the sake of your family and the survival of our culture, let your man be a man if he's willing…. God never meant for you to bear the load you're carrying. (pp. 79–80, emphasis original)

Evans has argued that the decline of the family is a national crisis caused by "the feminization of the American male… a misunderstanding of manhood that has produced a nation of 'sissified' men who abdicate their role as spiritually pure leaders, thus forcing women to fill the vacuum…. In the process, their emotional and physical circuits are being overloaded" (p. 73–74). He describes "feminists of the more aggressive persuasions" as "frustrated women unable to find the proper male leadership" (quoted in Ross & Cokorinos, 1997, p. 6). We see in Evans' rhetoric the same condescending tone and argument that was used as justification for denying women the right to vote (See Kimmel & Mosmiller, 1992).

Ireland (1997) remarked, "The Promise Keepers seem to think women will be so thrilled that men are promising to take 'responsibility' in their families that we will take a back seat in this and every other area of our lives" (p. C3). Mann (1997) characterized the Promise Keepers thus: "They ignore all that we've learned about what happens when men put women on a pedestal and promise to protect them. It was not a good bargain before—for men or for women—and nothing fundamental has changed. Are men going to promise to be good this time?" (p. E13). Equal Partners in Faith (1997), a liberal Christian organization, notes that the Promise Keepers organizational structure mirrors its patriarchal ideologies by restricting women to marginal roles. This organization characterizes Promise Keepers as a sexist, homophobic, religiously bigoted movement that interprets the Bible without reference to historical or cultural context, denigrates people who disagree as not "true" Christians, distorts both the meanings of manliness and godliness, and romanticizes war and conflict.

Few people are lukewarm in their opinions of this movement. The level of passion on both sides seems to reflect the increasing polarization of liberal and conservative politics in the United States. Whatever your opinion about Promise Keepers, there is no denying that their appeal in the late 1990s was tremendous, an indication that masculinity was on the minds of many.

The Promise Keepers movement also waned after a few years, and Kenneth Clatterbaugh (2000) notes that no men's social movement has been able to sustain public attention for very long. Sounding somewhat of a death knell for these efforts, he opines that "All of the men's movements have probably suffered because there are larger social forces at work, and it is with these forces that men and women will make their accommodations with one another" (pp. 891–892). These larger social forces are economics and culture. Later, he went on to say that, "lack of unanimity [in men's movements] should not be surprising. Men are divided by race, class, education, religion, and even different masculinities, and they have no explicit oppressive structures around which to rally" (Clatterbaugh, 2004, p. 531).

One manifestation of this failure to capture the mainstream is in the evolution of the magazine *Men's Health*, which began as an effort to help men learn to take better care of their bodies but quickly morphed into a reinforcement of traditionally gendered attitudes: physical strength, sexual performance, and antifemininity. In 2000, *Men's Health* published a list of the best and worst colleges for men. It described the best colleges as those with good athletic programs and many available women, and the worst as those with strong Women's Studies departments and sexual assault policies, implying that sexual assault was good for men's health. Arran Stibbe (2004) cites numerous examples of the reinforcement of stereotypical masculinity (guns, political conservatism, beer drinking, hypermuscularity, disdain for cats, sexual promiscuity, chivalry, calling women "girls," etc.) and concludes that *Men's Health* is "a lifestyle magazine that gives advice on every aspect of living, from sex to shoes and, [only] incidentally, health" (p. 32).

The magazine *Men's Journal* appears to be a manual for traditional masculinity. On a recent visit to its website (mensjournal.com, 2005), the lead articles were "the 50 best beers in the world," a story about a kayaker who was the first to front-flip a kayak over a waterfall, and the record jump of a freestyle motocross rider. An examination of the website of the more misogynistic *Maxim* magazine (maximonline.com) on the same day included seven sexualized pictures of young women on the homepage, two sports stories, and an article about a contest between two of its editors to drink an entire gallon of milk in one hour.

We can see from these and many other cultural manifestations of masculinity that transformative gender perspectives for men are censored by the marketplace. It is much more profitable to reinforce dominant masculinity than to challenge it. Jackson Katz's contention is that the increase in media portrayals of misogynistic and irresponsible masculinity caters to a significant population of men who feel threatened by gender changes and cannot deal with their anxiety in any other way except to reinforce their aggression and self-absorption (Jhally & Katz, 2000).

Other Gender-Related Movements

It is clear that large-scale cultural efforts to redefine gender for men have stalled in the early twenty-first century. At the same time, we are seeing the emergence of several social change efforts related to the transformation of masculinity. Following is a brief description of the major ones (Some of these movements have been described in earlier chapters.).

Gay marriage emerged as a significant social issue in several parts of the world during the early part of the twenty-first century. Between 2001 and 2005, gay and lesbian couples obtained the right to marry in the Netherlands, Belgium, Spain, and Canada. Other countries (Denmark, Sweden, France, Germany, Finland, Switzerland, and Great Britain) allow "civil unions," arrangements similar to heterosexual marriage. In the United States, the state of Massachusetts granted gays and lesbians the right to marry (Vermont and Connecticut allow civil unions.) (Green, 2005), and the debate continues in many other states, some of which have passed pre-emptive legislation to ban gay marriage despite its never having existed in these jurisdictions (Rauch, 2004). In 2004, The American Psychological Association (APA) adopted a resolution supporting equal legal rights for gay and lesbian people, including the right to marry and adopt (Farberman, 2004), noting that there is no credible research indicating that gay and lesbian marriage and family arrangements are detrimental to anyone. APA also cited a United States General Accounting Office study which identified more than one thousand federal statutory provisions in which marital status is a factor, e.g., in taxes, benefits, federal loans, and other rights and privileges. Therefore, gay marriage is more than a symbolic step; it has a number of tangible and important consequences.

In the United States, there are now more than two million men in federal and state prison or local jails ("Get-Tough Laws Swell Prison Ranks," 2005), a fourfold increase since 1980 (Elsner, 2004). Since males are approximately 93% of the incarcerated population (U.S. Department of Justice, 2004), prison reform is by definition a men's issue. In 2003, Congress unanimously passed the Prison Rape Elimination Act, which provides funding for studying and producing remedies for the very common occurrence of sexual assault behind bars (Tucker, 2003). The Commission on Safety and Abuse in America's Prisons is also attempting to provide solutions to the problems of inadequate physical and mental health care for prisoners (Slevin, 2005).

The risk of criminality and incarceration is certainly one of the most profoundly negative aspects of cultural masculinity, and yet sex and gender are rarely addressed in news stories about prison and crime. The acceptance of toxic gender ideologies, with its emphasis on dominance, control, wealth, and power, is doubtless an important factor in the decision to steal, use illegal drugs, or commit violent acts, especially for marginalized men such as the poor and racial minorities, which are disproportionately represented among the prison population. As James Messerschmidt (1993) put it, "Crime is not simply an extension of the 'male [masculine] sex [gender] role.' Rather crime by men is a form of social practice invoked as a resource, when other resources are unavailable for accomplishing masculinity" (p. 85). Moreover, these men are less likely than others to have adequate legal representation or to be offered plea bargaining that would allow them to avoid incarceration (The Sentencing Project, 2004).

Once they are behind bars, men learn quickly that "Prison is an ultramasculine world where nobody talks about masculinity" (Sabo, Kupers, & London, 2001, p. 1). Sabo (2000) described prison as the penultimate patriarchal institution, marked by hierarchy, sex segregation, and violence. A small but committed group of reformers is trying to make inroads into prison reform, including gender-aware work with male juveniles (Katz, 2001), support groups (Brieman & Bonner, 2001), prison labor reform (Parenti, 2001), mental health services (Kupers, 1999), and efforts to find viable alternatives to incarceration (Kupers, 2004). It would seem that education about toxic masculinity is a key factor in inoculating boys and men against committing criminal acts in the first place or in avoiding recidivism following incarceration.

The late 1990s and early twenty-first century witnessed a good deal of dialogue in the popular culture on the emotional lives of boys. Led by William Pollack's (1998) bestseller, *Real Boys: Rescuing Our Sons from the Myths of Boyhood*, a number of writers began to explore emotional, scholastic, and criminality problems that show a highly imbalanced sex ratio. Laura Bush, wife of the President of the United States, spoke publicly about concerns over boys' problems, thus giving the debate a very high profile (NPR, 2005) as Pollack and others offered solutions to difficulties boys encounter in managing their emotional lives and achieving in a culture that expects stoicism, violence, and hyperindependence (see also Kindlon & Thompson, 1999; Gurian & Stevens, 2005; and Polce-Lynch, 2002).

One of the debates that emerged was whether boys are shortchanged by schools relative to girls, with one author (Sommers, 2001) even claiming that "feminism" is waging a "war" against boys by demanding that boys behave like girls. As evidence, supporters of this position cite statistics indicating that boys achieve lower average grades in school and are a shrinking minority in the college student population (Gurian, 2005). Behind this argument are the assumptions that feminism is males' enemy and that the sexes are adversarial (i.e., attention paid to girls' problems leads boys to be "shortchanged"). On the other hand, males' standardized test scores and working-world achievement are as strong as they ever were (Sadker, 2000), demonstrating that, if there is a war, it is clearly not a very successful one.

One interesting part of the debate is the growing disproportion of male to female college students, with women making up 55% of those who earn bachelor's degrees (Argetsinger, 1999), which at first glance makes it appear that there is a higher education crisis among young men. However, when one looks more closely at the data, a very different picture emerges. Among White students from relatively affluent families, male students are a majority (52%) The sex ratio is roughly equal for middle income Whites, and men are 46% of lower income White college students. The statistics for people of color reveal large discrepancies. For African Americans, males are 32%, 48%, and 41% of college students from lower, middle, and upper income families, respectively, and for Hispanics, 43%, 46%, and 50% (Brownstein, 2000). Therefore, income and race appear to interact strongly with sex.

The debates about how boys are harmed by various social forces will likely continue, but as many scholars (Sadker, 2000; Kimmel, 1999; Pollack, 2000b), have pointed out, we should be careful not to be lulled into playing a game of "boys against the girls." It is clear that both boys and girls face problems that are somewhat specific to their sexes. Addressing the typical male problems of poor school achievement, criminality, bullying, impoverished emotional lives, and suicide need not come at the expense of a focus on girls' struggles.

In recent years, as men's studies scholars have identified a set of health vulnerabilities specific to males, organizations have begun attempts to address the health needs and problems of this population. In the United States, the most visible group is the Men's Health Network (www.menshealthnetwork.org), a nonprofit organization that supports education, research, and political action (such as lobbying Congress to establish an Office of Men's Health) to improve men's wellness. Institutions such as the Mayo Clinic (mayoclinic.com) provide information on health and mental health concerns specific to men. In recognition of the increased risk for negative health outcomes for poor and ethnic minority men, other organizations have attempted to address race and class issues in men's health care (Ro, Casares, Treadwell, & Thomas, 2004; Rich & Ro, 2002). The World Congress on Men's Health (wcmh.info) has a similar mission in the international context.

Men are also becoming more involved in gender equality movements, including efforts to end gender-based violence. I detailed some of these approaches in Chapter 12. Internationally, organizations such as Oxfam and the World Health Organization have taken the lead in supporting these men's movements (Ferguson et al., 2004; Krug et al., 2002; Ruxton, 2004; Chant & Gutmann, 2000). Much remains to be accomplished in the quest to reduce men's violence against women, and men's involvement in this effort, although it is increasing, remains rather sparse.

Men's Studies

During the last 40 years, modern feminist scholars have convincingly demonstrated that gender affects virtually every area of life, including politics, family organization, literature, art, individual psychology, international relations, and views of history. Women's Studies has emerged as a legitimate field of multidisciplinary intellectual inquiry. College and university courses, research programs, and even entire academic departments have been developed to place gender and women's perspectives into the previously male-dominated body of knowledge. As men began to understand that gender has colored their views of the world, it became important to understand the effects of masculinity on the individual and society. The new field of Men's Studies has emerged as an effort in this direction.

Critics have questioned the need for men's studies. The most frequent objection is that nearly all study already *is* men's study, because of the pervasive dominance of men in academia and literature. Kimmel (1987), Brod (1987b), and others have responded to this objection by drawing a distinction between the study of men in the context of specific functions—as scientists, historical figures, artists, and so on—and the study of men as *men*. In the former approach, masculinity is a (usually unarticulated) backdrop of intellectual discourse. The latter approach brings masculinity into the *center* of inquiry. Recall Box 1.5 for an analogy to describe the importance of men's studies.

The field of Men's Studies cuts across traditional academic disciplines. These courses are being taught in a wide variety of academic departments, including psychology, sociology, English, religion, classics, history, education, anthropology, and philosophy. It was conservatively estimated that there were more than 500 such courses being taught in the United States as of the late 1990s (Dobbin, 1997).

The American Psychological Association (APA) is comprised of many divisions (e.g., counseling psychology, abnormal psychology, addictions, and psychology of women), where members are organized around common interests. In 1995, APA recognized the Society for the Psychological Study of Men and Masculinity (SPSSM) as an official division (Brooks & Levant, 1995), giving it legitimate status within mainstream psychology. The following year, the *Washington Post* carried a front-page headline reading "Men's Studies Coming of Age in New Campus Rite of Passage" (Sanchez, 1996). Harry Brod (Laker, Davis, Kellom, & Brod, 2005) cited the publication of two encyclopedias of men's studies as evidence that researchers and theorists in this field have assembled a critical mass of scholarship. It seems that Men's Studies has attained a small but significant and legitimized place in mainstream academe.

Jim Doyle and Sam Femiano (1998) traced the history of two organized men's studies associations. In the early days of NOMAS (then the National Organization for Men), there were several members with an interest in gender research. Led by Harry Brod, Martin Acker, Michael Messner, and others, they formed the Men's Studies Task Group (MSTG, later renamed the Men's Studies Association (MSA)), which began to sponsor sessions during the annual NOMAS conferences. In 1991, several scholars broke from MSA, partly because of the timing of the annual conference, but largely because they rejected the premise that men's studies should be guided exclusively by feminist principles. They formed the American Men's Studies Association (AMSA) and held their first conference in 1993.

Two interdisciplinary journals, *Men and Masculinities* (sponsored by MSA) and the *Journal of Men's Studies* (sponsored by AMSA), are wholly devoted to men's studies scholarship. In addition, SPSSM began publishing its own journal, *Psychology of Men and Masculinity*, in 1999. The journal *Sex Roles* is dedicated to gender scholarship in general, and it also carries many articles that fit within the field of men's studies. Many other journals, such as the *Journal of Marriage and the Family*, the *Journal of Counseling Psychology*, the *Journal of Social Issues*, *Child Development*, and the *Journal of Homosexu-*

ality, to name a few, also carry masculinity articles as they relate to the central focus of the particular journal. This proliferation of masculine gender scholarship into the mainstream attests to the ever-widening acceptance of men's studies.

Following are some examples of broad Men's Studies questions:

1. How have concepts of masculinity changed throughout history (Rotundo, 1993; Kimmel, 1996)?

2. What do images of men in literature, art, and film tell us about masculinity (Craig, 1992)?

3. How do we make sense of the reality of male patriarchal power and its seeming contradiction with the sense of powerlessness in the lives of so many men? (Kimmel, 1992)?

4. What are the connections between masculinity and power, racism, sexism, heterosexism, and social class (Pharr, 1997b)?

5. How has masculinity affected religious institutions and practices (Connell, 2005)?

6. What are the effects of male initiation rites in various cultures, and how are these rites similar or dissimilar? (Herdt, 1992; Gilmore, 1990).

7. How can the various "men's movements" be understood in historical, psychological, and political perspective? (Clatterbaugh, 2000).

8. How does masculinity affect a nation's willingness to enter or avoid war (Connell, 2005)?

9. What kinds of techniques are useful in facilitating men's understanding of the impact of gender on their lives (Gertner & Harris, 1994)?

10. How does masculinity change and evolve in mid-life and old age? (Thompson, 1994).

Most Men's Studies scholars come from profeminist or mythopoetic frames of reference. The general approach is to take seriously the influence of gender on men and articulate its effects. Profeminist-oriented writers are mainly interested in studying the changing character of masculinity and its consequences for individual men and social systems. Mythopoetic writers are mostly involved in writing (or writing about) stories, poems, and rituals that can be used to get closer to the symbolic experience of masculinities. The writing of men's rights advocates seems limited to demonstrating and criticizing perceived sexism against men.

Men's Studies is controversial for many of the same reasons that the various men's movements are controversial. Some feminist scholars point out that the name "Men's Studies" implies a parallel with "Women's Studies." Once these two fields are seen as complementary, there may be pressure to allocate resources more evenly between them. Thus, the existence of Men's Studies can result in fewer academic positions for Women's Studies scholars and a reinforcement of the institutional and economic power of men (Canaan & Griffin, 1990).

There is an implicit goal in much of Women's Studies to remove women's disadvantages and improve the quality of their lives. Many Men's Studies scholars have a similar goal for men. However, it is clear that men have enjoyed far-ranging advantages throughout recorded history by virtue of their status as men. Some of Men's Studies is focused on the disadvantages of masculinity. Brod's (1987a) argument is that men who understand these disadvantages are more likely to discard destructive masculinity and the power that goes with it. This argument is unconvincing to some, who see this focus on disadvantage as drawing attention away from the obvious and more profound disadvantages of women in society, and obscuring the overwhelmingly advantageous and unjust nature of masculine privilege. Having been victimized by men for so long, women are understandably suspicious of these new efforts by men.

Many women seem to want men to change. However, they may doubt whether men really want to (or have the ability to) change. A collection of women's reactions to men's efforts toward change begins with, "Make no mistake about it. Women want a men's movement. We are literally dying for it." (Steinem, 1990, p. v). The rest of the book contains expressions of various writers' doubts about whether this change is a reality, and, if so, whether it is one that will benefit women. At the same time, there is a hopefulness that men will begin to move in a more positive direction.

The belief that men should spend time understanding themselves seems to make a lot of women angry. The feeling is that men need to spend more time listening to and seeking to understand women. One of the assumptions behind gender-aware activity for men is that men's understanding of women is limited by their lack of self-understanding. The processes of individual exploration, challenging traditional stereotypes, productive dialogue between men and women, and working toward social change, can and should take place all at the same time. As scholar Carol Flinders (2002) stated, feminism cannot proceed further without the participation of men.

A Final Word

Cultural constructions of masculinity will continue to change in response to economics, legal changes, shifting ideologies, and various other social forces. And yet there is also strong resistance to change. As one Nicaraguan woman (quoted in de Keizer, 2004), put it "Men are looking for women who don't exist *any more* and women are looking for men who don't exist *yet*." (p. 32, emphasis original). Men in the industrialized world who attempt to apply their fathers' and grandfathers' strategies to reaching life goals will find these approaches increasingly untenable in a modern world where gender is becoming less of an organizing principle in society.

James Nelson (1997) describes a basic dilemma for men in the donning of masculine "armor, which "seems to protect us, but it also prevents us from leaping, dancing, and being seen." What is the future of masculinity? Hopefully, it is a new generation of men who feel less pressure to look, feel, and act like "real men," and more of an urgency to look, feel, and act like the people whom they truly are. It is men who can hear the voices of women, children, other men, Nature, and the self, and who can connect more deeply with all of them. It is men who can retain a vigorous masculine energy and direct it into breaking the cycles of violence and self-destructiveness that have stood in place for centuries. It is a new generation of men who can love, work, and play in different and healthier ways. It is the reconnection of the masculine self with the human self.

SUMMARY

1. There is a good deal of controversy around whether masculinities should change or not. Among those who think that they should change, there are disagreements about the nature and direction these changes should take.

2. As gender is deeply ingrained in all social systems, the alteration of gender roles is a painstaking process. Differing opinions on men's social reality result in differing opinions on the necessity and nature of change.

3. The position of the Mythopoetic Men's Movement is that modern men have gotten out of touch with the spiritual essence of masculinity. This disconnection has resulted in self-alienation and destructive behaviors. The agenda for change, from this perspective, is to restore "deep masculinity" through male initiation rituals. Major criticisms of the Mythopoetic Movement center around its assumption of essential masculinity and its removal of masculinity from its social and political contexts.

4. The Profeminist Men's Movement emphasizes changing the aspects of masculinity that limit freedom of choice for women and men. Profeminists are involved in a variety of individual and social activities concerned with the problems of sexism, racism, heterosexism, and other forms of injustice. Critics of profeminism argue that these men are overly focused on masculine guilt. Some feminists have complained that profeminist men have drawn attention away from women's issues.

5. Men's Rights advocates see men as oppressed victims of sexism. Perceived injustices include unfair divorce and child custody laws, the historical abuse of men in military service, the treatment of men as work and success objects, and "male bashing." Critics of the Men's Rights Movement see these men as ignorant of the privilege of patriarchy and unempathic with those who are truly oppressed.

6. Promise Keepers is an evangelical Christian men's movement focused on encouraging men to recommit themselves to their wives, families, and communities, based on a fundamentalist reading of the Christian Bible. Critics of Promise Keepers characterize it as male-dominant, homophobic, and antifeminist.

7. No men's movement has captured the attention of mainstream cultures for very long. Currently, a number of new social issues have emerged in the public eye, including gay marriage, male criminality and incarceration, social and academic struggles for young boys, men's health, and men's movements to achieve gender equality and end men's violence around the world.

8. There is a growing amount of research and scholarship on men and masculinity from a variety of perspectives. The academic interest in men's studies cuts across traditional disciplines and has established itself as a legitimate area of scholarship. Men's Studies is controversial for many of the same reasons that the various men's movements are. Additionally, some Women's Studies scholars fear that Men's Studies will cut into the already scarce resources that are allocated to them.

9. Cultural constructions of masculinity will continue to change in response to various social forces. With this change comes both discomfort and opportunity.

References

Abbey, A. (1982). Sex differences in attributions for friendly behavior: Do males misperceive females' friendliness? *Journal of Personality and Social Psychology*, *42*, 830–838.

Abraham, K. (1997). *Who are the Promise Keepers? Understanding the Christian men's movement.* New York: Bantam Doubleday Bell.

Adams, H. E., Wright, L. W., & Lohr, B. A. (1996). Is homophobia associated with homosexual arousal? *Journal of Abnormal Psychology*, *105*, 440–445.

Adams, S., Kuebli, J., Boyle, P. A., & Fivush, R. (1995). Gender differences in parent-child conversations about past emotions: A longitudinal investigation. *Sex Roles*, *33*, 309–323.

Addis, M. E. & Mahalik, J. R. (2003). Men, masculinity, and the contexts of help seeking. *American Psychologist, 58 (1)*, 5–14.

Adler, J., Springen, K., Glick, D., & Gordon, J. (1991, June 24). Drums, sweat and tears. *Newsweek*, pp. 46–51.

Adler, L. L. (Ed.) (1993). *International handbook on gender roles.* Westport, CT: Greenwood.

Adler, T. (1992). Study links genes to sexual orientation. *APA Monitor, 23(2)*, 12–13.

Adorno, T., Frenkel-Brunswik, E., Levinson, D., & Sanford, R. N. (1950). *The authoritarian personality.* New York: Harper.

Aida, Y. & Falbo, T. (1991). Relationships between marital satisfaction, resources, and power strategies. *Sex Roles*, *24*, 43–56.

Allen, J. A. & Gordon, S. (1990). Creating a framework for change. In R. L. Meth & R. S. Pasickn (Eds.), *Men in therapy: The challenge of change* (pp.131–151). New York: Guilford.

Allgeier, E. R. & Allgeier, A. R. (2000). *Sexual interactions.* Boston: Houghton Mifflin.

Allison, J. (2005). *Violence response and prevention at Pittsburg State University.* Paper presented in symposium: Sexual assault prevention for men (C. Kilmartin, chair) at the annual convention of the American Psychological Association, Washington, DC.

Alloy, L. B., Jacobson, N. S., & Acocella, J. (1999). *Abnormal psychology: Current perspectives* (8th ed.). Boston: McGraw-Hill.

Amato, P. & Booth, A. (2001). The legacy of parents' marital discord: Consequences for children's marital quality. *Journal of Personality and Social Psychology, 81 (4)*, 627–638.

Amato, P., Loomis, L.S., & Booth, A. (1995). Parental divorce, marital conflict, and offspring well-being during early adulthood. *Social Forces, 73*, 895–915.

American Cancer Society (1994). *Cancer facts and figures: 1994.* Atlanta, GA: Author.

American Cancer Society (2005*). Cancer statistics, 2005.* cancer.org.

American Heart Association (1995). *Heart and stroke facts: 1995 statistical supplement.* Dallas, TX: Author.

American Heart Association (2005). *Annual number of Americans having diagnosed heart attack by age and sex.* Americanheart.org

American Psychiatric Association (1980). *Diagnostic and statistical manual of mental disorders* (3rd ed.) (DSM-III). Washington, DC: American Psychiatric Association.

American Psychiatric Association (1987). *Diagnostic and statistical manual of mental disorders* (3rd ed. - revised) (DSM- III-R). Washington, DC: American Psychiatric Association.

American Psychiatric Association (1994). *Diagnostic and statistical manual of mental disorders* (4th ed.) (DSM-IV). Washington, DC: American Psychiatric Association.

American Psychiatric Association (2000). *Diagnostic and statistical manual of mental disorders* (4th ed., text revision) (DSM-IV-TR). Washington, DC: American Psychiatric Association.

American Psychological Association (2005). Resolution on sexual orientation and marriage and resolution on sexual orientation, parents, and children. *American Psychologist, 60 (5)*, 494–496.

Anctil, J. (1992). Myths about gay men and lesbians. *Mentor, 22*, p. 31.

Anderson, R. N. & Smith, B. L. (2005). Deaths: Leading causes, 2002. *National Vital Statistics Reports, 53 (17)*, 1–90.

Andronico, M. P. (Ed.) (1996). *Men in groups: Insights, interventions, and psychoeducational work.* Washington, DC: American Psychological Association.

Angier, N. (1999a). *The beauty of the beastly: New views on the nature of life.* Boston: Houghton-Mifflin.

Angier, N. (1999b). *Woman: An intimate geography.* Boston: Houghton-Mifflin.

Antill, J. K. (1983). Sex role complementarity vs. similarity in married couples. *Journal of Personality and Social Psychology, 45*, 145–155.

Antill, J. K. (1987). Parents' beliefs and values about sex roles, sex differences, and sexuality: Their sources and implications. In P. Shaver & C. Hendrick (Eds.), *Sex and gender* (pp. 294–328). Newbury Park, CA: Sage.

Archer, J. (1984). Gender roles as developmental pathways. *British Journal of Social Psychology, 23*, 245–256.

Archer, J. (2000). Sex differences in aggression between heterosexual partners: A meta-analytic review. *Psychological Bulletin, 126 (5)*, 651–680.

Argetsinger, A. (1999, November 17). Women outnumber men at many colleges. *The Washington Post*, B5.

Arias, E. (2005). United States life tables 2002. National Vital Statistics Reports, Center for Disease Control, http://www.cdc.gov/nchs/data/nvsr/nvsr53/nvsr53_06.

Aronson, E. (2004). *The social animal* (9th ed.). New York: Worth.

Asch, S. E. (1965). Effects of group pressure upon the modification and distortion of judgments. In H. Proshansky & B. Seidenberg (Eds.), *Basic studies in social psychology.* New York: Holt, Rinehart, and Winston.

Associated Press (2005, July 3). Spanish marriage law to go into effect: Gay couples will be able to wed, adopt. *The Washington Post*, A20.

Astrachan, A. (1992). Men and the new economy. In M. S. Kimmel & M. A. Messner (Eds.), *Men's lives* (2nd ed., pp. 221–225). New York: Macmillan.

Attorney General's Commission on Pornography (1986). *Final report of the Attorney General's Commission on Pornography*. Washington, DC: Government Printing Office.

Avert (international AIDS charity) (2005). HIV and AIDS Statistics. Avert.org.

Baca Zinn, M. (1980). Gender and ethnic identity among Chicanos. *Frontiers, 5,* 18–24.

Baca Zinn, M. (1995). Chicano men and masculinity. In M. S. Kimmel & M. A. Messner (Eds.), *Men's lives* (3rd ed., pp. 33–41). Boston: Allyn and Bacon.

Bagby, R. M., Taylor, G. J., & Ryan, D. (1986). Toronto Alexithymia Scale: Relationship with personality and psychosomatic measures. *Psychotherapy and Psychosomatics, 45,* 207–215.

Balswick, J. (1982). Male inexpressiveness: Psychological and social aspects. In K. Solomon & N. B. Levy (Eds.), *Men in transition: Theory and therapy* (pp. 131–150). New York: Plenum.

Balswick, J. (1988). *The inexpressive male*. Lexington, MA: D.C. Heath.

Bandura, A. (1973). *Aggression: A social learning analysis*. Englewood Cliffs, NJ: Prentice-Hall.

Bandura, A., Ross, D., & Ross, S. (1961). Transmission of aggression through imitation of aggressive models. *Journal of Abnormal and Social Psychology, 63,* 575–582.

Bandura, A., & Walters, R. H. (1963). *Social learning and personality development*. New York: Holt, Rinehart, and Winston.

Barash, D. P. (1982). *Sociobiology and behavior*. New York: Elsevier.

Barash, D. P., & Lipton, J. E. (1997). *Making sense of sex: How genes and gender influence our relationships*. Washington, DC: Island.

Barnett, R. C., & Baruch, G. K. (1987). Social roles, gender, and psychological distress. In R. C. Barnett, L. Biener, and G. K. Baruch (Eds.), *Gender and stress* (pp. 122–143). New York: Macmillan.

Barnett, R. C., Marshall, N. L., & Pleck, J. H. (1992). Adult son-parent relationships and their associations with sons' psychological distress. *Journal of Family Issues, 13,* 505–525.

Barnett, R. C., & Rivers, C. (1996). *She works/he works: How two-income families are happier, healthier, and better-off*. New York: Harper San Francisco/Harper Collins.

Baron, R. A., Byrne, D., & Branscome, N. R. (2006). *Social psychology* (11th ed.). Boston: Allyn & Bacon.

Barr, C. L., & Kleck, R. E. (1995). Self-other perception of the intensity of facial expressions of emotion: Do we know what we show? *Journal of Personality and Social Psychology, 68,* 604–618.

Barthel, D. (1992). When men put on appearances: Advertising and the social construction of masculinity. In S. Craig (Ed.), *Men, masculinity, and the media* (pp. 137–153). Newbury Park, CA: Sage.

Basow, S. (1992). *Gender: Stereotypes and roles* (3rd ed.). Monterey, CA: Brooks/Cole.

Baumli, F. (1989). The men's rights movement and the nurturing agenda versus the toxic triad: Chivalry, machismo, and homophobia. *Transitions, 9(5),* 11–20.

Beach, F. A. (1987). Alternative interpretations of the development of G-I/R. In J. M. Reinish, L. A. Rosenblum, & S. A. Sanders (Eds.), *Masculinity/femininity: Basic perspectives* (pp.29–36). New York: Oxford University Press.

Becker, J. V. (1996). Outpatient treatment of adolescent male sexual offenders. In M. P. Andronico (Ed.), *Men in groups: Insights, interventions, and psychoeducational work* (pp. 377–388). Washington, DC: American Psychological Association.

Beere, C.A. (1990). *Gender roles: A handbook of tests and measures*. New York: Greenwood.

Bell, A. P., & Weinberg, M. S. (1978) *Homosexualities: A study of diversity among men and women*. New York: Simon and Schuster.

Bem, S.L. (1974). The measurement of psychological androgyny. *Journal of Consulting and Clinical Psychology, 42,* 155–162.

Bem, S.L. (1981a). *Bem Sex-Role Inventory: Professional manual.* Palo Alto, CA: Consulting Psychologists Press.

Bem, S. L. (1981b). Gender schema theory: A cognitive account of sex-typing. *Psychological Review, 88,* 354–364.

Bem, S. L. (1985). Androgyny and gender schema theory: A conceptual and empirical integration. In T.B. Sonderegger (Ed.), *Nebraska symposium on motivation, 1984: Psychology of gender, 32,* (pp. 179–236). Lincoln, NE: University of Nebraska Press.

Bem, S. L. (1987). Masculinity and femininity exist only in the mind of the perceiver. In J. M. Reinisch, L. A. Rosenblum, & S. A. Sanders (Eds.), *Masculinity/femininity: Basic perspectives* (pp. 304–314). New York: Oxford University Press.

Bem, S. L. (1993). *The lenses of gender: Transforming the debate on sexual inequality.* New Haven, CT: Yale University Press.

Bem, S. L. (1998). Gender schema theory and its implications for child development: Raising gender-aschematic children in a gender-schematic society. In D. L. Anselmi & A. L. Law (Eds.), *Questions of gender: perspectives and paradoxes* (pp. 262–274). Boston: McGraw-Hill.

Benard, C., & Schlaffer, E. (1997). "The man in the street: Why he harasses." In L. Richardson, V. Taylor, & N. Whittier (Eds.), *Feminist frontiers* IV (pp. 395–398). Boston: McGraw-Hill.

Benson, E. (2003). Hostility is among the best predictors of heart disease in men. *Monitor on Psychology, 34 (1),* 15.

Bergman, S. J. (1995). Men's psychological development: A relational perspective. In R. F. Levant & W. S. Pollack (Eds.), *A new psychology of men* (pp. 68–90). New York: Basic Books.

Berkowitz, A. D. (Ed.) (1994). *Men and rape: Theory, research, and prevention programs in higher education.* San Francisco: Jossey-Bass.

Berkowitz, A. D. (1997). Effective sexual assault prevention programming: Meeting the needs of men and women. Paper presented at the Seventh International Conference on Sexual Assault and Harassment on Campus, Orlando, FL.

Berkowitz, A. D. (1998). Sexual assault prevention: Where have we come and where are we going? Paper presented at the Seventh International Conference on Sexual Assault and Harassment on Campus, Orlando, FL.

Bernard, J. (1981). The good-provider role: Its rise and fall. *American Psychologist, 36,* 1–12.

Berndt, T. J. (1992). Friendship and friends' influence in adolescence. *Current Directions in Psychological Science, 1,* 156–159.

Bertoia, C. E., & Drakich J. (1998). The fathers' rights movement: Contradictions in rhetoric and practice. In M. S. Kimmel & M. A. Messner (Eds.), *Men's lives* (4th ed., pp. 548–564). Needham Heights, MA: Allyn and Bacon.

Best, D. L. , & Williams, J. E. (1993). Cross-cultural viewpoint. In A. E. Beall & R. J. Sternberg (Eds.), *The psychology of gender* (pp. 215–248). New York: Guilford.

Biernbaum, M., & Weinberg, J. (1991). Men unlearning rape. *Changing Men, 22,* 22–24.

Biskupic, J. (1998, March 5). Court says law covers same-sex harassment: Justices unanimous in civil rights case. *The Washington Post,* pp. A1, A8.

Bjorkqvist, K. (1994). Sex differences in physical, verbal, and indirect aggression: A review of recent research. *Sex Roles, 30,* 177–188.

Blazina, C., & Watkins, C. E. (1996). Masculine gender role conflict: Effects on college men's psychological well-being, chemical substance usage, and attitudes toward help-seeking. *Journal of Counseling Psychology, 43,* 461–465.

Bleier, R. (1984). *Science and gender: A critique of biology and its theories on women.* New York: Pergamon.

Block, J. H. (1984). *Sex role identity and ego development.* San Francisco: Jossey-Bass.

Block, J. H., Block, J., & Gjerde, P. F. (1986). The personality of children prior to divorce: A prospective study. *Child Development, 57*, 827–840.

Blumenfeld, W. J. (1992). Squeezed into gender envelopes. In W. J. Blumenfeld (Ed.), *Homophobia: How we all pay the price* (pp. 23–38). Boston: Beacon.

Blumstein, P., & Schwartz, P. (1983). *American couples*. New York: William Morrow.

Bly, R. (1988, May). A day for men. Workshop presentation, Arlington, VA.

Bly, R. (1990). *Iron John*. Reading, MA: Addison Wesley.

Bly, R. (1991). Father hunger in men. In K. Thompson (Ed.), *To be a man: In search of the deep masculine* (pp.189–192). Los Angeles: Tarcher.

Bolton, F. G., Morris, L. A., & MacEachron, A. E. (1989). *Males at risk*. Newbury Park, CA: Sage.

Bonvillain, N. (2001). *Women and men: Cultural constructs of gender* (3rd ed.). Upper Saddle River, NJ: Prentice-Hall.

Boodman, S. (1998, September 15). "Seeds" show effect on early prostate cancer: Study suggests this radioactive treatment may be as good as surgery. *Washington Post Health*, p. 7.

Boswell, A. A., & Spade, J. Z. (1996). Fraternities and collegiate rape culture: Why are some fraternities more dangerous places for women? *Gender and Society, 10(2)*, 133–147.

Bowen, G. L., & Orthner, D. K. (1991). Effects of organizational culture on fatherhood. In F. W. Bozett & S. M. H. Hanson (Eds.), *Fatherhood and families in cultural context* (pp. 187–217). New York: Springer.

Boyatzis, C. J., Matillo, G. M., & Nesbitt, K. M. (1995). Effects of the "Mighty Morphin Power Rangers" on children's aggression with peers. *Child Study Journal, 25*, 45–55.

Bradbury, T. N., Campbell, S. M., & Fincham, F. D. (1995). Longitudinal and behavioral analysis of masculinity and femininity in marriages. *Journal of Personality and Social Psychology, 68*, 328–341.

Brannon, R. (1985). Dimensions of the male sex role in America. In A.G. Sargent, *Beyond sex roles* (2nd ed., pp. 296–316). New York: West.

Bridges, J. S. (1989). Sex differences in occupational values. *Sex Roles, 20*, 205–211.

Bridgewater, D. (1997). Effective coming out: Self-disclosure strategies to reduce sexual identity bias. In J. T. Sears & W. L. Williams (Eds.), *Overcoming heterosexism and homophobia: Strategies that work* (pp. 65–75). New York: Columbia University Press.

Brieman, H. & Bonner, T. P. (2001). Support groups for men in prison: The fellowship of the king of hearts. In D. Sabo, T. A. Kupers, & W. London (Eds.). *Prison masculinities*. Philadelphia: Temple University Press.

Briere, J., & Malamuth, N. M. (1983). Self-reported likelihood of sexually aggressive behavior: Attitudinal versus sexual explanations. *Journal of Research in Personality, 17*, 315–323.

Brod, H. (Ed.) (1987a). *The making of masculinities: The new men's studies*. Boston: Allen and Unwin.

Brod, H. (1987b). A case for men's studies. In M. S. Kimmel (Ed.), *Changing men: New directions in research on men and masculinity* (pp. 263–277). Newbury Park, CA: Sage.

Brod, H. (1992). NOMAS panel: Mythopoetic men - profeminist men: A dialogue. Panel discussion (with W. Liebman, J. Sternbach, & G. Murray) at the 17th National Conference on Men and Masculinity, Chicago, IL.

Brod, H. (2005). Working with men against violence: Strategies for date rape prevention. Annual conference of the Amercian Men's Studies Association, Nashville, TN.

Brody, L. R. (1997). Beyond stereotypes: Gender and emotion. *Journal of Social Issues, 53*, 369–393.

Brody, L. R. (2000). The socialization of gender differences in emotional expression: Display rules, infant temperament, and differentiation. In A. H. Fischer (Ed.), *Gender and emotion: Social psychological perspectives*. Cambridge, UK: Cambridge University Press.

Brody, L. R., & Hall, J. A. (1993). Gender and emotion. In M. Lewis & J. M. Haviland (Eds.), *Handbook of emotions*. New York: Guilford.

Brody, L. R., & Hall, J. A. (2000). Gender and emotion. In M. Lewis & J. M. Haviland (Eds.), *Handbook of emotions* (2nd. ed.). New York: Guilford.

Brody, L. R., Hay, D., & Vandewater, E. (1990). Gender, gender role identity, and children's reported feelings toward the same and opposite sex. *Sex Roles, 3*, 363–387.

Bronstein, P., Briones, M., Brooks, T., & Cowan, B. (1996). Gender and family factors as predictors of late adolescent emotional expressiveness and adjustment: A longitudinal study. *Sex Roles, 34*, 739–765.

Brooks, G. R. (1995). *The centerfold syndrome: How men can overcome objectification and achieve intimacy with women*. San Francisco: Jossey-Bass.

Brooks, G. R. & Good, G. E. (2001). *The new handbook of psychotherapy and counseling with men: A comprehensive guide to settings, problems, and treatment approaches*. San Francisco: Jossey-Bass.

Brooks, G. R., & Levant, R. F. (1995, July). We've done it! SPSSM becomes APA's Division 51. *SPSSM Bulletin*, pp. 1–7.

Brooks, G. R., & Levant, R. F. (1997). Toward the reconstruction of male sexuality: A prescription for the future. In R. F. Levant & G. R. Brooks (Eds.), *Men and sex* (pp. 257–272). New York: Wiley.

Brooks, G. R., & Silverstein, L. B. (1995). Understanding the dark side of masculinity: An interactive systems model. In R. F. Levant & W.S. Pollack (Eds.), *A new psychology of men* (pp. 280–333). New York: Basic Books.

Brownmiller, S. (1975). *Against Our Will: Men, Women, and Rape*. New York: Simon and Schuster.

Brownstein, A. (2000). Are male students in short supply, or is this 'crisis' exaggerated? *The Chronicle of Higher Education, 47 (10)*, A47–48.

Brubaker, B. (1994, November 13). Violence in football extends off field. *The Washington Post*, pp. A1, A24–25.

Bruch, M. A. (1980). Holland's typology applied to client/counselor interactions: Implications for counseling with men. In T. M. Skovholt, P. Schauble, & R. David (Eds.), *Counseling men* (pp.101–119). Monterey, CA: Brooks/Cole.

Bruch, M. A., Berko, E. H., & Haase, R. F. (1998). Shyness, masculine ideology, physical attractiveness, and emotional inexpressiveness: Testing a mediational model of men's interpersonal competence. *Journal of Counseling Psychology, 45*, 84–97.

Brush, S. (1984). *Men: An owner's manual: A comprehensive guide to having a man underfoot*. New York: Simon and Schuster.

Bunch, T. & Porter, A. (2003). Ending domestic violence: A call to men. Presentation at Congreso Nacional Sobre Violencia Domestica Agresion Sexual, Acecho y Violencia en Cita, San Juan, Puerto Rico.

Burke, C. K., Maton, K. I., Anderson, C. A. Mankowski, E., & Silvergleid, C. (2004). The ManKind Project. In M. Kimmel & A. Aronson (Eds.), *Men and masculinities: A social, cultural, and historical encyclopedia*. Santa Barbara, CA: ABC-Clio.

Burn, S. M. (1996). *The social psychology of gender*. Boston: McGraw-Hill.

Burt, M. R. (1991). Rape myths and acquaintance rape. In A. Parrot & L. Bechofer (Eds.), *Acquaintance rape: The hidden crime* (pp. 26–40). New York: Wiley.

Buss, D.M. (1989). Sex differences in human mate preferences: Evolutionary hypotheses tested in 37 countries. *Behavioral and Brain Sciences, 12*, 1–49.

Buss, D. M. (1994). *The evolution of desire*. New York: Basic Books.

Bussey, K., & Bandura, A. (1992). Self-regulatory mechanisms governing gender development. *Child Development, 63,* 1236–1250.

Butcher, J.N. (1987, September 21). The Minnesota report for the Minnesota Multiphasic Personality Inventory. Unpublished individual testing report.

Butcher, J. N., Mineka, S., & Hooley, J. M. (2004). *Abnormal psychology and modern life* (12th ed.). Boston: Allyn & Bacon.

Caldera, Y. M., Huston, A. C., & O'Brien, M. (1989). Social interactions and play patterns of parents and toddlers with feminine, masculine, and neutral toys. *Child development, 60,* 70–76.

Campbell, J. L., & Snow, B. M. (1992). Gender role conflict and family environment as predictors of men's marital satisfaction. *Journal of Family Psychotherapy, 6,* 84–87.

Canaan, J. E., & Griffin, C. (1990). The new men's studies: Part of the problem or part of the solution? In J. Hearn & D. Morgan (Eds.), *Men, masculinities, and social theory* (pp. 206–214). Cambridge, MA: Unwin Hyman.

Cancian, F. M. (1987). *Love in America: Gender and self- development.* Cambridge, England: Cambridge University Press.

Canetto, S. (2000). The paradox of male suicidal behavior. Symposium: Boys, men, depression, and suicide: Cutting-edge research and practice (J. Mahalik & M. Addis, chairs). Annual Convention of the American Psychological Association, Washington, DC.

Capraro, R. L. (2000). Why college men drink: Alcohol, adventure, and the paradox of masculinity. *Journal of American College Health, 48,* 307–315.

Carroll, J. L., Volk, K. D., & Hyde, J. S. (1985). Differences between males and females in motives for engaging in sexual intercourse. *Archives of Sexual Behavior, 14,* 131–139.

Carlson, P. (2004). A hunger for victory: Sonya Thomas is competitive eating's next small thing. *The Washington Post,* January 31, pp. A1, A14.

Casteneda, D. & Burns-Glover, A. (2004). Gender, sexuality, and intimate relationships. In M. A. Paludi (Ed.), *Praeger guide to the psychology of gender.* Westport, CT: Praeger.

Chan, J. (2004). Asian American Men's Studies. In M. Kimmel & A. Aronson (Eds.), *Men and masculinities: A social, cultural, and historical encyclopedia.* Santa Barbara, CA: ABC-Clio.

Chant, S. & Gutmann, M. (2001). Mainstreaming men into gender and development: Debates, reflections, and experiences. Oxford, UK: Oxfam.

Chethik, N. (2001). *FatherLoss: How sons of all ages come to terms with the deaths of their dads.* New York: Hyperion.

Childress, D. M. (1996, May 4). Md. judge cleared of bias in remarks at sentencing: He expressed degree of understanding toward trucker convicted of killing unfaithful wife. *The Washington Post,* p. B3.

Chodorow, N. (1978). *The reproduction of mothering: Psychoanalysis and the sociology of gender.* Berkely, CA: University of California Press.

Chomsky, N. (1957). *Syntactic structures.* The Hague, Netherlands: Mouton.

Circumcision Resource Center (2004). Current position statements of medical societies in English-speaking countries. Self-published.

Claes, M. E. (1992). Friendship and personal adjustment during adolescence. *Journal of Adolescence, 15,* 39–55.

Clark, A. J. (1998). *Defense mechanisms and the counseling process.* Thousand Oaks, CA: Sage.

Clarkson, F. (1997). PK's promise — A Christian nation? *PK Watch,* pp. 1–2.

Clatterbaugh, K. (1997). *Contemporary perspectives on masculinity: Men, women, and politics in modern society* (2nd ed.). Boulder, CO: Westview.

Clatterbaugh, K. (2000). Review essay: Literature of the U. S. men's movements. *Signs: Journal of Women in Culture and Society, 25 (3)*, 883–894.

Clatterbaugh, K. (2004). Men's movements. In M. Kimmel & A. Aronson (Eds.), *Men and masculinities: A social, cultural, and historical encyclopedia*. Santa Barbara, CA: ABC-Clio.

Clay, R. A. (2005). Making working families work: As the number of dual wage-earner families soars, psychologists focus on families' strategies for success. *Monitor on Psychology, 36 (11)*, 54–55.

Cleary, P. D. (1987). Gender differences in stress-related disorders. In R. C. Barnett, L. Biener, & G. K. Baruch (Eds.), *Gender and stress* (pp. 39–72). New York: Macmillan.

Cochran, S. V. & Rabinowitz, F. E. (2000). Men and depression: Clinical and empirical perspectives. San Diego: Academic Press.

Cohen, T. F. (1998). What do fathers provide? Reconsidering the economic and nurturant dimensions of men as parents. In D. L. Anselmi & A. L. Law (Eds.), *Questions of gender: perspectives and paradoxes* (pp. 569–581). Boston: McGraw-Hill.

Cohn, D. (1998, December 11). Single-father households on rise: Census report reveals trends in custody, adoption cases. *The Washington Post*, p. A1.

Cohn, L. D. (1991). Sex differences in the course of personality development. *Psychological Bulletin, 109*, 252–266.

Cohn, N. B., & Strassberg, D. S. (1983). Self-disclosure reciprocity among adolescents. *Personality and Social Psychology Bulletin, 9*, 97–102.

Coie, J. D., Dodge, K. A., & Kupersmidt, J. B. (1990). Peer group behavior and social status. In S. R. Asher & J. D. Coie (Eds.), *Peer rejection in childhood* (pp. 17–59). Cambridge, England: Cambridge University Press.

Colburn, D. (1991, January 29). The way of the warrior: Are men born to fight? *Washington Post Health*, pp. 10–13.

Colburn, D. (1993, October 19). Chewing tobacco: A baseball tradition that can be deadly. *Washington Post Health*, pp. 13–15.

Colburn, D. (1996, January 23). Suicide rate climbs for older Americans. *Washington Post Health*, p. 5.

Colburn, D., & Trafford, A. (1993, October 12). Guns at home: Doctors target growing epidemic. *Washington Post Health*, pp. 12–15.

Coleman, E. (1990). Toward a synthetic understanding of sexual orientation. In D. P. McWhirter, S. A. Sanders, & J. M. Reinisch (Eds.), *Homosexuality/heterosexuality: Concepts of sexual orientation*. New York: Oxford University Press.

Collins, G. (1979, June 1). A new look at life with father. *The New York Times Magazine*, pp. 30–31.

Coltrane, S. (1995). The future of fatherhood: Social, demographic, and economic influences on men's family involvement. In W. Marsiglio (Ed.), *Fatherhood: Contemporary theory, research, and social policy* (pp. 255–274). Thousand Oaks, CA: Sage.

Coltrane, S. (1998). Theorizing masculinities in contemporary social science. In D. L. Anselmi & A. L. Law (Eds.), *Questions of gender: perspectives and paradoxes* (pp. 76–88). Boston: McGraw-Hill.

Comas-Díaz, L. (1993). Hispanic/Latino communities: Psychological implications. In D. R. Atkinson, G. Morten, & D. W. Sue (Eds.), *Counseling American minorities: A cross-cultural perspective* (4th ed., pp. 245–263). Madison, WI: Brown and Benchmark.

Commission on Obscenity and Pornography (1970). *The report of the commission on obscenity and pornography*. New York: Bantam.

Conason, J., Ross, A., & Cokorinos, L. (1996, October 7). The Promise Keepers are coming: The third wave of the religious right. *The Nation*, pp. 11–19.

Connell, R. W. (1995a). *Masculinities*. Berkeley, CA: University of California Press.

Connell, R. W. (2005). *Masculinities* (2nd ed.). Berkeley, CA: University of California Press.

Cook, E. P. (1985). *Psychological Androgyny*. New York: Pergamon.

Cook, E. P. (1987). Psychological androgyny: A review of the research. *The Counseling Psychologist, 15*, 471–513.

Cook, E. P. (1990). Gender and psychological distress. *Journal of Counseling and Development, 68*, 371–375.

Coontz, S. (1997). *The way we really are: Coming to terms with America's changing families.* New York: Basic Books.

Coontz, S. (2005). *Marriage, a history: From obedience to intimacy, or how love conquered marriage*. New York: Viking.

Cooper, D. E., & Holmstrom, R. W. (1984). Relationship between alexithymia and somatic complaints in a normal sample. *Psychotherapy and Psychosomatics, 41*, 20–24.

Cooper, M. L., Russell, M., Skinner, J. B., Frone, M. R., & Mudar, P. (1992). Stress and alcohol use: Moderating effects of gender, coping, and alcohol expectancies. *Journal of Abnormal Psychology, 101*, 139–152.

Corcoran, C. B. (1992). From victim control to social change: A feminist perspective on campus rape prevention programs. in J. Chrisler & D. Howard (Eds.), *New directions in feminist psychology* (pp. 130–140). New York: Springer.

Cournoyer, R. J., & Mahalik, J. R. (1995). Cross-sectional study of gender role conflict examining college-aged and middle-aged men. *Journal of Counseling Psychology, 42*, 11–19.

Courtenay, W. H. (2000a). Constructions of masculinity and their influence on men's well-being: A theory of gender and health. *Social Science and Medicine, 50 (10)*, 1385–1401.

Courtenay, W. H. (2000b). Behavioral factors associated with disease, injury, and death among men: Evidence and implications for prevention. *Journal of Men's Studies, 9 (1)*, 81–142.

Courtenay, W. H., McCreary, D. R., & Merighi, J. R. (2002). Gender and ethnic differences in health beliefs and behaviors. *Journal of Health Psychology, 7 (3)*, 219–231.

Cozby, P. C. (1973). Self-disclosure: A literature review. *Psychological Bulletin, 79*, 73–91.

Craig, S. (Ed.), *Men, masculinity, and the media*. Newbury Park, CA: Sage.

Crites, J. O., & Fitzgerald, L. F. (1978). The competent male. *The Counseling Psychologist, 7*, 10–14.

Cromwell, N. A., & Burgess, A. W. (Eds., 1996). *Understanding violence against women*. Washington, DC: National Academy Press.

Crooks, R. & Baur, K. (2005). *Our sexuality* (9th ed.). Belmont, CA: Thomson Wadsworth.

Crosset, T. W. (2000). Athletic affiliations and violence against women: Toward a structural prevention project. In J. McKay, M. A. Messner, & D. F. Sabo (Eds.), *Masculinities, gender relations, and sport*. Thousand Oaks, CA: Sage.

Crosset, T. W., Benedict, J. R., & McDonald, M. A. (1998). Male student-athletes reported for sexual assault: A survey of campus police departments and judicial affairs offices. In M. S. Kimmel & M. A. Messner (Eds.), *Men's lives* (4th ed., pp. 194–204). Needham Heights, MA: Allyn and Bacon.

Crull, P. (1982). Stress effects of sexual harassment on the job: Implications for counseling. *American Journal of Orthopsychiatry, 52*, 539–544.

Culp, R. E., Cook, A. S., & Housely, P. C. (1983). A comparison of observed and reported adult-infant interactions: Effects of perceived sex. *Sex Roles, 9,* 475–479.

Cunningham, J. D., Braiker, H., & Kelley, H. H. (1982). Marital-status and sex differences in problems reported by married and cohabiting couples. *Psychology of Women Quarterly, 6,* 415–427.

Daly, M. & Wilson, M. (1983). *Sex, evolution, and behavior* (2nd ed.). Boston: Willard Grant.

Daly, M., & Wilson, M. (1985). Competitiveness, risk taking, and violence: The young male syndrome. *Ethology and Sociobiology,* 6, 59–73.

Daly, M., Wilson, M, & Weghorst, S.J. (1982). Male sexual jealousy. *Ethology and Sociobiology, 3,* 11–27.

Damasio, A. R. (1994). *Descartes' error: Emotion, reason, and the human brain.* New York: Avon.

Darwin, C. (1871). *The descent of man, and selection in relation to sex.* New York: Appleton & Co.

Davidson, B. J., Balswick, J., & Halverson, C. (1983). Affective self-disclosure and marital adjustment: A test of equity theory. *Journal of Marriage and the Family, 45,* 93–102.

DeAngelis, T. (2005). Stepfamily success depends on ingredients. *Monitor on Psychology,* 36 *(11),* 58–61.

Death Penalty Information Center (2005). Executions in the United States. http://www.deathpenaltyinfo.org.

Deaux, K. (1985). Sex and gender. *Annual Review of Psychology, 36,* 49–81.

Deaux, K. (2000). Gender and emotion: Notes from a grateful tourist. In A. H. Fischer (Ed.), *Gender and emotion: Social psychological perspectives.* Cambridge, UK: Cambridge University Press.

Deaux, K., & Hanna, R. (1984). Courtship in the personals column: The influence of gender and sexual orientation. *Sex Roles, 11,* 363–375.

de Keizer, B. (2004). Masculinities: Resistance and change. In S. Ruxton, (Ed.). *Gender equality and men: Learning from practice.* Oxford, UK: Oxfam.

Delta Upsilon (2005). Join Delta Upsilon Fraternity. Deltau.mb.ca.

Denmark, F., Rabinowitz, V., & Sechzer, J. (2000). *Engendering psychology.* Boston: Allyn & Bacon.

Derlega, V.J., Winstead, B.A., & Jones, W.H. (1991). *Personality: Contemporary theory and research.* Chicago: Nelson-Hall.

Devlin, P. K., & Cowan, G. A. (1985). Homophobia, perceived fathering, and male intimate relationships. *Journal of Personality Assessment, 49,* 467–473.

de Waal, F. B. M. (1997, June 27). Bonobos are from Venus. *The Chronicle of Higher Education,* 43, B8–B9.

de Waal, F. B. M. (2005). Our inner ape: What primate behavior tells us about human nature. Paper presented at the Annual Convention of the American Psychological Association, Washington, DC.

Diener, E., Larsen, R. J., Levine, S., & Emmons, R. A. (1985). Intensity and frequency: Dimensions underlying positive and negative affect. *Journal of Personality and Social Psychology, 48,* 1253–1265.

Dietz, T. L. (1998). An examination of violence and gender role portrayals in video games: Implications for gender socialization and aggressive behavior. *Sex Roles, 38,* 425–442.

Dingfelder, S. F. (2005). The kids are all right: Research shows that families headed by gay and lesbian parents are as healthy as traditional families, but misperceptions linger. *Monitor on Psychology, 36 (11),* 66–68.

Division 17, American Psychological Association (1979). Principles concerning the counseling and therapy of women. *The Counseling Psychologist, 8*, 21.

Dobbin, B. (1997, July 20). Men will be men. . .maybe: University hopes courses will dispel myths of manhood. *Richmond Times-Dispatch*, p. C1.

Dolnick, E. (1991, August 13). Why do women outlive men? *Washington Post Health*, pp. 10–13.

Donnerstein, E. (1983). Erotica and human aggression. In R. Green & E. Donnerstein (Eds.), *Aggression: Theoretical and empirical reviews*. New York: Academic Press.

Donnerstein, E. (1984). Pornography: Its effects on violence against women. In N. M. Malamuth & E. Donnerstein (Eds.), *Pornography and sexual aggression* (pp. 53–81). Orlando, FL: Academic Press.

Donnerstein, E., Slaby, R. G., & Eron, L. D. (1994). The mass media and youth aggression. In L. D. Eron, J. H. Gentry, & P. Schlegel (Eds.), *Reason to hope: A psychosocial perspective on violence and youth* (pp. 219–250). Washington, DC: American Psychological Association.

Dosser, Jr., D. A. (1982). Male inexpressiveness: Behavioral intervention. In K. Solomon & N. B. Levy (Eds.), *Men in transition: Theory and therapy* (pp. 343–437). New York: Plenum.

Downey, K. (2002, November 19). Women rising in corporate ranks, report says. *The Washington Post*, E1, E4.

Doyle, J., and Femiano, S. (1998). Reflections on the early history of the American Men's Studies Association and the evolution of the field. *Men's Studies News, 7(1)*, 8–11.

Drescher, J. (2002). Sexual conversion ("reparative") therapies: History and update. In B. E. Jones & M. J. Hill (Eds.), *Mental health issues in lesbian, gay, bisexual, and transgender communities*. Washington, DC: American Psychiatric Publishing.

Duck, S. (1991). *Understanding relationships*. New York: Guilford.

Duluth Domestic Abuse Intervention Project (n.d.). *Creating a public response to private violence*. Duluth, MN: self.

Duneier, M. (1992). *Slim's table*. Chicago: University of Chicago Press.

Dutton, D. G., & Golant, S. K. (1995). *The batterer: A psychological profile*. New York: Basic.

Eagly, A. H. (1987). *Sex differences in social behavior: A social-role interpretation*. Hillsdale, NJ: Erlbaum.

Earle, J. P. (1992). Acquaintance rape workshops: Their effectiveness in changing the attitudes of first year college men. Unpublished doctoral dissertation, University of Connecticut.

"Eating Champ Downs 44 Lobsters in Win" (2005). *The Washington Post*, B3.

Edwards, R. (1996). Can sexual orientation change with therapy? APA ponders its stance on a therapy designed to convert gay men and lesbians into heterosexuals. *APA Monitor, 27(9)*, 49.

Ehrenberg, M. (2005). The role of women in human evolution. In C. B. Brettel & C. F. Sargent (Eds.), *Gender in cross-cultural perspective* (4th ed.). Upper Saddle River, NJ: Pearson/Prentice-Hall.

Ehrenreich, B. (1983). *The hearts of men: American dreams and the flight from commitment*. Garden City, NY: Anchor.

Eichenfield, G. A. (1996). University-based group therapy for faculty, students, and staff. In M. P. Andronico (Ed.), *Men in groups: Insights, interventions, and psychoeducational work* (pp. 81–96). Washington, DC: American Psychological Association.

Eisenstock, B. (1984). Sex-role differences in children's identification with counterstereotypical televised portrayals. *Sex Roles, 10*, 417–430.

Eisler, R. M. (1995). The relationship between masculine gender role stress and men's health risk: The validation of a construct. In R. F. Levant & W.S. Pollack (Eds.), *A new psychology of men* (pp. 207–225). New York: Basic Books.

Eisler, R. M., & Blalock, J. A. (1991). Masculine gender role stress: Implications for the assessment of men. *Clinical Psychology Review, 11*, 45–60.

Eisler, R. M., Skidmore, J. R., & Ward, C. H. (1988). Masculine gender role stress: Predictor of anger, anxiety, and health-risk behaviors. *Journal of Personality Assessment, 52 (1)*, 133–141.

Elkins, L. E., & Peterson, C. (1993). Gender differences in best friendships. *Sex Roles, 29*, 497–508.

Elsner, A. (2004). America's prison habit. *The Washington Post*, A19.

Equal Employment Opportunity Commission (EEOC) (1980). Discrimination because of sex under Title VII of the Civil Rights Act 1964, as amended; adoption of interim interpretive guidelines. *Federal Register, 45*, 25024–25025.

Escobar, G., & Murphy, C. (1997, October 5). Promise Keepers answer the call: Christian men flock to the Mall for rally massive and moving. *The Washington Post*, pp. A1, A18.

Espiritu, Y. L. (1997). *Asian American men and women: Labor, laws, and love*. Thousand Oaks, CA: Sage.

Espiritu, Y. L. (2001). All men are *not* created equal: Asian American men in U.S. history. In M. S. Kimmel & M. A. & Messner (Eds.), *Men's lives* (5th ed). Boston: Allyn and Bacon.

ESPN (1994, October 23). *Outside the Lines* (television documentary).

Equal Partners in Faith (1997). Promise Keepers information. New York: self-published.

Evans, T. (1994). Spiritual purity. In *Seven promises of a promise keeper* (pp.73–81). Colorado Springs, CO: Focus on the Family.

Fagot, B. I., & Hagan, R. (1985). Aggression in toddlers: Responses to the assertive acts of boys and girls. *Sex Roles, 12*, 341–351.

Falbo, T., & Peplau, L. A. (1980). Power strategies in intimate relationships. *Journal of Personality and Social Psychology, 38*, 618–628.

Falicov, C. J. (1996). Mexican families. In M. McGoldrick, J. Giordano, & J. K. Pearce (Eds.), *Ethnicity and family therapy* (2nd ed., pp. 169–182). New York: Guilford.

Farberman, R. (2004). Council actions include gay-marriage resolution. *Monitor on Psychology*, 36 (9), p. 24.

Farrell, W. (1974). *The liberated man*. New York: Bantam.

Farrell, W. (1986). *Why men are the way they are: The male-female dynamic*. New York: McGraw-Hill.

Farrell, W. (1990). We should embrace traditional masculinity. In K. Thompson (Ed.), *To be a man: In search of the deep masculine* (pp. 10–16). Los Angeles: Tarcher.

Farrell, W. (1991). Men as success objects. *Utne Reader*, May/June, 81–84.

Farrell, W. (2005). *Why men earn more: The startling truth behind the pay gap, and what women can do about it*. New York: AMACOM.

Fassinger, R. E. (1998). Lesbian, gay, and bisexual identity and student development theory. In R. L. Sanlo (Ed.), *Working with lesbian, gay, bisexual, and transgender college students: A handbook for faculty and administrators* (pp. 13–22). Westport, CT: Greenwood.

Fasteau, M. F. (1974). *The male machine*. New York: McGraw-Hill.

Fausto-Sterling, A. (1992). *Myths of gender: Biological theories about women and men* (3rd ed.). New York: Basic Books.

Fausto-Sterling, A. (1996). The five sexes: Why male and female are not enough. In K. E. Rosenblum & T. C. Travis (Eds.), *The meaning of difference: American constructions of race, sex and gender, social class, and sexual orientation* (pp. 68–73). Boston: McGraw-Hill.

Fausto-Sterling, A. (2000). *Sexing the body: Gender politics and the construction of sexuality*. New York: Basic Books.

Fazio, R. H. & Olson, M. A. (2003). Implicit measures in social cognition research: Their meaning and use. *Annual Review of Psychology, 54,* 297–327.

Federal Bureau of Investigation (2005). Uniform Crime Reports: Crime in the United States, 2003: Murder victims by race and sex. http://www.fbi.gov/ucr/cius_03/xl/03tbl2–3.xls.

Fejes, F. J. (1992). Masculinity as fact: A review of empirical mass communication research on masculinity. In S. Craig (Ed.), *Men, masculinity, and the media* (pp. 9–22). Newbury Park, CA: Sage.

Feldman, S. S., Biringen, Z. C., & Nash, S. C. (1981). Fluctuations of sex-related self-attributions as a function of stage in the family life cycle. *Developmental Psychology, 17,* 24–35.

Ferguson, H., Hearn, J., Holter, O. G., Jalmert, L., Kimmel, M., Lang, J., & Morell, R. (2004). *Ending gender based violence: A call for global action to involve men.* Sweden: SIDA Productions.

Fernbach, B. E., Winstead, B. A., & Derlega, V. J. (1989). Sex differences in diagnosis and treatment recommendations for antisocial personality and somatization disorders. *Journal of Social and Clinical Psychology, 8,* 238–255.

Fine, R. (1987). *The forgotten man: Understanding the male psyche.* New York: Haworth.

Fiske, S. T., & Taylor, S. E. (1991). *Social cognition* (2nd ed.). New York: McGraw-Hill.

Fitzgerald, L. F. (1992). *Sexual harassment in higher education: Concepts and issues.* Washington, DC: National Education Association.

Fitzgerald, L. F. (1993). Sexual harassment: Violence against women in the workplace. *American Psychologist, 48,* 1070–1076.

Fitzgerald, L. F., & Cherpas, C. C. (1985). On the reciprocal relationship between gender and occupation: Rethinking the assumptions concerning masculine career development. *Journal of Vocational Behavior, 27,* 109–122.

Flinders (2002). The values of belonging. Workshop presented at the Satayana Institute on Gender Reconciliation, Boulder, CO.

Fogel, R., & Paludi, M. A. (1984). Fear of success and failure, or norms for achievement? *Sex Roles, 10,* 431–443.

Fong-Torres, B. (1992). Why are there no male Asian anchor*men* on TV? In M. S. Kimmel & M. A. Messner (Eds.), *Men's lives* (2nd ed.). New York: Macmillan.

Foote, W. E. & Goodman-Delahunty, J. (2004). *Evaluating sexual harassment.* Washington, DC: American Psychological Association.

Forster, P., & King, J. (1994). Fluoxetine for premature ejaculation. *American Journal of Psychiatry, 151,* 1523.

Foubert, J. (2005). *The men's program: A peer education guide to rape prevention* (3rd ed.). New York: Routledge.

Fox, M., Gibbs, M., & Auerbach, D. (1985). Age and gender dimensions of friendship. *Psychology of Women Quarterly, 9,* 489–502.

Francis, R. C. (2004). *Why men won't ask for directions: The seductions of sociobiology.* Princeton, NJ: Princeton University Press.

Frankl, V. (1960). *The doctor and the soul.* New York: Knopf.

Franklin, C. W. (1984). *The changing definition of masculinity.* New York: Plenum.

Freiberg, P. (1991). Black men may act cool to advertise masculinity. *APA Monitor, 22 (3),* 30.

French, K. & Poska, A. (2006). *Women and gender in the Western past.* Boston: Houghton-Mifflin.

"Freshman Profile" (2005). National statistics on the incoming first year class. *The Chronicle of Higher Education, 51 (22),* p. A33.

Freud, S. (1905/1963). *Dora: An analysis of a case of hysteria*. New York: Collier.

Freud, S. (1910/1989). Leonardo da Vinci and a memory of his childhood. In P. Gay (Ed.), *The Freud reader* (pp. 443–481). New York: Norton.

Freud, S. (1915/1989). Three essays on the theory of sexuality. In P. Gay (Ed.), *The Freud reader* (pp. 239–293). New York: Norton.

Freud, S. (1924/1989). The dissolution of the Oedipus complex. In P. Gay (Ed.), *The Freud reader* (pp. 661–669). New York: Norton

Freund, K., Nagler, E., Langevin, R., Zajac, A., & Steiner, B. (1974). Measuring feminine gender identity in homosexual males. *Archives of Sexual Behavior*, *3*, 249–260.

Funder, D. C. (1997). *The personality puzzle*. New York: Norton.

Funder, D. C. (2004). *The personality puzzle* (3rd ed.). New York: Norton.

Funk, R. E. (1997). Men who are raped: A profeminist perspective. In M. Scarce, *Male on male rape: The hidden toll of stigma and shame* (pp. 221–231). New York: Plenum.

Garcia, A. M. (1991). The development of Chicana feminist discourse. In J. Lorber & S. A. Farrell (Eds.), *The social construction of gender* (pp. 269–287). Newbury Park, CA: Sage.

Garnets, L., & Pleck, J. H. (1979). Sex role identity, androgyny, and sex role transcendence: A sex role strain analysis. *Psychology of Women Quarterly*, *3*, 270–283.

Garfinkel, P. (1985). *In a man's world: Father, son, brother, friend, and other roles men play*. New York: New American Library.

Gastil, J. (1990). Generic pronouns and sexist language: The oxymoronic character of masculine generics. *Sex Roles*, *23*, 629–643.

Gay, P. (Ed., 1989). *The Freud reader*. New York: Norton.

Gelles, R. J. (1997). *Intimate violence in families* (3rd ed.). Thousand Oaks, CA: Sage.

Gentry, W.D. (1984). Behavioral medicine: A new research paradigm. In W.D. Gentry (Ed.), *Handbook of behavioral medicine* (pp. 1–12). New York: Guilford.

Gertner, D. M., & Harris, J. E. (1994). *Experiencing masculinities: Exercises, activities, and resources for teaching and learning about men*. Denver: Everyman.

"Get-Tough Laws Swell Prison Ranks" (2005, April 25). *The Washington Post*, A5.

Gibbs, J. T. (1992). Young Black males in America: Endangered, embittered, and embattled. In M. S. Kimmel & M. A. Messner (Eds.), *Men's lives* (2nd ed., pp. 50–66). New York: Macmillan.

Gibbs, J. T. (1994). Anger in young black males: Victims or Victimizers? In R. G. Majors & J. U. Gordon (Eds.), *The American Black male: His present status and his future* (pp. 127–143). Chicago: Nelson-Hall.

Gibbs, W. W. (1995, March). Seeking the criminal element. *Scientific American*, pp. 100–107.

Gilder, G. (1986). *Men and marriage*. London: Pelican.

Gilmore, D. D. (1990). *Manhood in the making: Cultural concepts of masculinity*. New Haven, CT: Yale University Press.

Giordano, J., & McGoldrick, M. (1996). Italian families. In M. McGoldrick, J. Giordano, & J. K. Pearce (Eds.), *Ethnicity and family therapy* (2nd ed., pp. 567–582). New York: Guilford.

Glick, P. (2005). Ambivalent gender ideologies and perceptions of the legitimacy and stability of gender hierarchy. Paper presented in Symposium: New weave sexism research – Tangled webs of feminism, romance, and inequality (S. T. Fiske, Chair). Annual Convention of the American Psychological Association, Washington, DC.

Glick, P. & Fiske, S. T. (2001). An ambivalent alliance: Hostile and benevolent sexism as complementary justifications for gender inequality. *American Psychologist*. *56*(2), 109–118.

Goffman, E. (1963). *Stigma*. Englewood Cliffs, NJ: Prentice-Hall.

Gold, S. R., Burke, C. H., Prisco, A. G., & Willett, J. A. (1992). Vicarious emotional responses of macho college males. *Journal of Interpersonal Violence*, *7*, 165–174.

Goldberg, H. (1977). *The hazards of being male*. New York: New American Library.

Goldfoot, D. A. & Neff, D. A. (1987). Assessment of behavioral sex differences in social contexts: Perspectives from primatology. In J. M. Reinisch, L. A. Rosenbaum, & S. A. Sanders (Eds.), *Masculinity/femininity: Basic perspectives* (pp. 179–195). New York: Oxford University Press.

Goldman, R. F. (1992). Questioning circumcision: A growing movement. *Wingspan, 6 (2)*, 12–13.

Golombok, S., & Fivush, R. (1994). *Gender development*. New York: Cambridge University Press.

Gondolf, E.W. (1988). Who are those guys? Toward a behavioral typology of batterers. *Violence and Victims, 3*, 187–203.

Good, G. E., Dell, D. M., & Mintz, L. B. (1989). Male role and gender role conflict: Relations to help seeking in men. *Journal of Counseling Psychology, 36*, 295–300.

Good, G. E., Gilbert, L. A., & Scher, M. (1990). Gender aware therapy: A synthesis of feminist therapy and knowledge about gender. *Journal of Counseling Psychology, 68*, 376–380.

Good, G. E. & Mintz, L. B. (1990). Gender role conflict and depression in college men: Evidence for compounded risk. Journal of Counseling and Development, *69*, 17–21.

Good, G. E., Robertson, J. M., O'Neil, J. M., Fitzgerald, L. F., Stevens, M., DeBord, K. A., Bartels, K. M., & Braverman, D. G. (1995). Male gender role conflict: Psychometric issues and relations to psychological distress. *Journal of Counseling Psychology, 42*, 3–10.

Goodman, E. (1997, October 4). The two sides of Promise Keepers. *The Washington Post*, p. A21.

Goodman, L. A., Koss, M. P., Fitzgerald, L. F., Russo, N. F. & Keita, G. P. (1993). Male violence against women: Current research and future directions. *American Psychologist, 48*, 1054–1058.

Gordon, B., & Allen, J. A. (1990). Helping men in couple relationships. In R. L. Meth & R. S. Pasick, *Men in therapy: The challenge of change* (pp. 224–233). New York: Guilford.

Gordon, D. F. & Cerami, T. (2000). Cancers common in men. In R. M. Eisler & M. Herson (Eds.), *Handbook of gender, culture, and health* (pp. 179–195). Mahwah, NJ: Erlbaum.

Gough, H. G. (1957). *Manual for the California Psychological Inventory*. Palo Alto, CA: Consulting Psychologists Press.

Gould, R. E. (1974). Measuring masculinity by the size of a paycheck. In J.H. Pleck & J. Sawyer (Eds.), *Men and masculinity* (pp. 96–100). Englewood Cliffs, NJ: Prentice-Hall.

Gould, S. J. (1981). *The mismeasure of man*. New York: W. W. Norton.

Gould, S. J. (1987). *An urchin in the storm*. New York: W. W. Norton

Greely, A. M. (1981). *The Irish Americans*. New York: Harper & Row.

Green, J. (2005, July 1). Spain legalizes same-sex marriage: Prime Minister's unexpected support helps pass law termed "unjust" by Church. *The Washington Post,* A14.

Green, R. (1987). Exposure to explicit sexual materials and sexual assault: A review of behavioral and social science research. In M. R. Walsh (Ed.), *The psychology of women: Ongoing debates* (pp. 430–440). New Haven, CT: Yale University Press.

Greenberg, M., & Morris, N. (1974). Engrossment: The newborn's impact upon the father. *American Journal of Orthopsychiatry, 44*, 520–531.

Greene, M. S. (1997, October 5). At assembly, a call to bring the races together. *The Washington Post*, p. A16.

Gregersen, E. (1982). *Sexual practices: The story of human sexuality*. New York: Franklin Watts.

Greif, E. B. (1976). Sex-role playing in preschool children. In J. S. Bruner, A. Jolly, & K. Sylva (Eds.), *Play*. Harmondsworth, England: Penguin.

Grimm, L., & Yarnold, P. R. (1985). Sex typing and the coronary-prone behavior pattern. *Sex Roles, 12*, 171–178.

Grimsley, K. D. (1996, April 10). EEOC says hundreds of women harassed at auto plant. *The Washington Post*, p. A1.

Grimsley, K. D. (1997, December 13). Avon calling. . . on a man: Board bypasses staff, names former Duracell chief next CEO. *The Washington Post*, p. G1.

Grimsley, K. D. (1998, June 12). Mitsubishi settles for $34 million: Amount is record in harassment suits. *The Washington Post*, p. A1.

Grimsley, K. D., & Brown, W. (1996, April 23). Mitsubishi workers march on EEOC: UAW alleges, company denies "pressure" to protest suit. *The Washington Post*, p. A1.

Grimsley, K. D., & Swoboda, F. (1997a, September 16). Mitsubishi managers blamed for environment at plant: EEOC says supervisors created, tolerated a "sexually hostile and abusive situation." *The Washington Post*, p. C1.

Grimsley, K. D., & Swoboda, F. (1997b August 30). Mitsubishi settlement said to total $9.5 million: Company still faces larger suit filed by EEOC. *The Washington Post*, pp. F1, F3.

Grimsley, K. D., Swoboda, F., & Brown, W. (1996, April 29). Fear on the line at Mitsubishi: Women recount allegations of sexual harassment at auto plant. *The Washington Post*, p. A1.

Gross, A. E. (1992). The male role and heterosexual behavior. In M. A. Kimmel & M. S. Messner (Eds.), *Men's lives* (2nd ed., pp. 424–432). New York: Macmillan.

Grossman, D. (1995). *On killing: The psychological cost of learning to kill in war and society.* Boston: Little, Brown.

Groth, A. N. (1979). *Men who rape: The psychology of the offender*. New York: Plenum.

Groth-Marnat, G. (2003). *Handbook of psychological assessment* (4th ed.). New York: Wiley.

Grusznski R. & Bankovics, G. (1990). Treating men who batter: A group approach. In D. Moore & F. Leafgren (Eds.), *Men in conflict* (pp. 201–212). Alexandria, VA: American Association for Counseling and Development.

Gugliotta, G. (1994, May 16). Institute finds that a number that adds up, has meaning on the streets. *The Washington Post*, p. A3.

Gugliotta, G. (2003, October 11). Concussions, impact studied by the NFL. *The Washington Post*, p. D3.

Gurian, M. (2005). Where have the men gone? No place good. *The Washington Post,* p. B1.

Gurian, M. & Stevens, K. (2005). *The minds of boys: Saving our sons from falling behind in school and life*. San Francisco: Jossey-Bass.

Gustafson, R. (1986). Threat as a determinant of alcohol-related aggression. *Psychological Reports, 58*, 287–297.

Gutek, B. A., & Nakamura, C. Y. (1983). Gender roles and sexuality in the world of work. In E. R. Allgeier & N. B. McCormick (Eds.), *Changing boundaries: Gender roles and sexual behavior* (pp. 182–201). Palo Alto, CA: Mayfield.

Gutierrez, F. J. (1990). Exploring the macho mystique: Counseling Latino men. In D. Moore & F. Leafgren (Eds.), *Men in conflict* (pp. 139–151). Alexandria, VA: American Association for Counseling and Development.

Gutmann, D. (1977). The cross-cultural perspective: Notes toward a comparative psychology of aging. In J. E. Birren & K. W. Schaie (Eds.), *Handbook of the psychology of aging* (pp.302–326). New York: Van Nostrand Reinhold.

Gutmann, D. (1987). *Reclaimed powers*. New York: Basic Books.

Hackett, T. P.; Rosenbaum, J. F. & Cassen, N. H. (1985). Cardiovascular disorders. In H. I. Kaplan & B. J. Saddock (Eds.), *Comprehensive textbook of psychiatry/IV* (pp. 1148–1159). Baltimore: Williams and Wilkins.

Hall, C. C., & Crum, M. J. (1994). Women and "body-isms" in television beer commercials. *Sex Roles, 31*, 329–337.

Hall, C. S., Lindzey, G., & Campbell, J. B. (1998). *Theories of personality* (4th ed.). New York: Wiley.

Hamilton, J. B., Hamilton, R. S., & Mestler, G. E. (1969). Duration of life and causes of death in domestic cats: Influence of sex, gonadectomy, and inbreeding. *Journal of Gerontology, 24*, 427–437.

Hamilton, J. B. & Mestler, G. E. (1969). Mortality and survival: Comparison of eunuchs with intact men and women in a mentally retarded population. *Journal of Gerontology, 24*, 395–411.

Hamilton, M. C. (1991). Masculine bias in the attribution of personhood: People = male, male = people. *Psychology of Women Quarterly, 15*, 393–402.

Haney, C., Banks, C., & Zimbardo, P. (1973). Interpersonal dynamics in a simulated prison. *International Journal of Criminology and Penology, 1*, 69–97.

Haney, D. Q. (1996, July 4). Steroids make muscles, not rage, study finds. *The Washington Post*, p. A3.

Hansen, J. E., and Schuldt, W. J. (1984). Marital self-disclosure and marital satisfaction. *Journal of Marriage and the Family, 46*, 923–926.

Hare-Mustin, R. T., & Maracek, J. (1990). Gender and the meaning of difference: Postmodernism and psychology. In R. T. Hare-Mustin & J. Maracek (Eds.), *Making a difference: Psychology and the construction of gender* (pp. 22–64). New Haven, CT: Yale University Press.

Harris, I. (1992). Media myths and the reality of men's work. In M. S. Kimmel & M. A. Messner (Eds.), *Men's lives* (2nd ed., pp. 225–231). New York: Macmillan.

Harris, I. M. (1995). *Messages men hear: Constructing masculinities*. London: Taylor and Francis.

Harrison, J.; Chin, J., & Ficarotto, T. (1995). Warning: Masculinity may be dangerous to your health. In M. S. Kimmel & M. A. Messner (Eds.), *Men's lives* (3rd ed., pp. 237–249). Boston: Allyn and Bacon.

Harrison, J. B. (1978). Warning: The male sex role may be dangerous to your health. *Journal of Social Issues, 34*, 65–86.

Harrison, J. B., & Morris, L. A. (1996). Group therapy for adult male survivors of child sexual abuse. In M. P. Andronico (Ed.), *Men in groups: Insights, interventions, and psychoeducational work* (pp. 339–356). Washington, DC: American Psychological Association.

Harry, J. (1995). Sports ideology, attitudes toward women, and anti-homosexual attitudes. *Sex Roles, 32*, 109–116.

Hartley, R. E. (1959). Sex role pressures and the socialization of the male child. *Psychological Reports, 5*, 457–468.

Hathaway, C. R. & McKinley, J. C. (1951). *Minnesota Multiphasic Personality Inventory*. New York: Psychological Corporation.

Haviland, M. G., Shaw, D. G., Cummings, M. A., & MacMurray, J. P. (1988). The relationship between alexithymia and depressive symptoms in a sample of newly abstinent alcoholic inpatients. *Psychotherapy and Psychosomatics, 50*, 81–87.

Hawke, C. C. (1950). Castration and sex crimes. *Journal of Mental Deficiency, 55*, 220–226.

Helgeson, V. S. (1990). The role of masculinity in a prognostic predictor of heart attack severity. *Sex Roles, 22*, 755–774.

Helgeson, V. S. (1995). Masculinity, men's roles, and coronary heart disease. In D. Sabo & D. F. Gordon (Eds.), *Men's health and illness: Gender, power, and the body* (pp.68–104). Thousand Oaks, CA: Sage.

Helgeson, V. S. (2002). *The psychology of gender*. Upper Saddle River, NJ: Prentice-Hall.

Hendryx, M. S., Haviland, M. G., & Shaw, D. G. (1991). Dimensions of alexithymia and their relationships to anxiety and depression. *Journal of Personality Assessment, 56*, 227–237.

Heppner, M. (2005). *Theoretically driven rape prevention programming for men*. Paper presented in symposium: Sexual assault prevention for men (C. Kilmartin, chair) at the annual convention of the American Psychological Association, Washington, DC.

Heppner, P. P., & Gonzales, D. S. (1987). Men counseling men. In M. Scher, M. Stevens, G. E. Good, & G. A. Eichenfield (Eds.), *Handbook of counseling and psychotherapy with men* (pp. 30–38). Newbury Park, CA: Sage.

Herdt, G. (1982). *Rituals of manhood*. Berkeley, CA: University of California Press.

Herdt, G., & Boxer, A. (1991). Introduction: Culture, history, and life course of gay men. In G. Herdt (Ed.), *Gay culture in America: Essays from the field* (pp. 1–28). Boston: Beacon.

Herek, G. M. (1985). On doing, being, and not being: Prejudice and the social construction of sexuality. *Journal of Homosexuality, 12*, 135–151.

Herek, G. M. (1986). On heterosexual masculinity: Some psychical consequences of the social construction of gender and sexuality. *American Behavioral Scientist, 29*, 563–577.

Herek, G. M. (1991). Stigma, prejudice, and violence against lesbians and gay men. In J. C. Consiorek & J. D. Weinrich (Eds.), *Homosexuality: Research implications for public policy* (pp. 60–80). Newbury Park, CA: Sage.

Herek, G. M. (1994). Assessing heterosexuals' attitudes toward lesbians and gay men. In B. Greene & G. M. Herek (Eds.), *Lesbian and gay psychology: Theory, research, and clinical applications*. Thousand Oaks, CA: Sage.

Herek, G. M. (1998). Psychological heterosexism and anti-gay violence: The social psychology of bigotry and bashing. In M. S. Kimmel and M. A. Messner (Eds.), *Men's lives* (4th ed., pp. 254–266). Needham Heights, MA: Allyn and Bacon.

Herttell, T. (1839/1992). The right of married woman to hold and control property. (pp. 76–78). In M. S. Kimmel & T. E. Mosmiller, *Against the tide: Pro-feminist men in the United States, 1776–1990*. Boston: Beacon.

Herzog, A. R., Bachman, J. G., & Johnson, L. D. (1983). Paid work, child care, and housework: A national survey of high school seniors' preferences for sharing responsibilities between husband and wife. *Sex Roles, 9*, 109–135.

Hetherington, E. M., Cox, M., & Cox, R. (1985). Long term effects of divorce and remarriage on the adjustment of children. *Journal of the American Academy of Child Psychiatry, 24*, 518–530.

Hetherington, E. M., & Stanley-Hagen, M. M. (1997). The effects of divorce on fathers and their children. In M. Lamb (Ed.), *The role of the father in child development* (3rd ed., pp. 191–211). New York: Wiley.

Hetherington, E. M., Stanley-Hagen, M., & Anderson, E. R. (1989). Marital transitions: A child's perspective. *American Psychologist, 44*, 303–312.

Hetrick, E. S., & Martin, A. D. (1988). The stigmatization of the gay and lesbian adolescent. *Journal of Homosexuality, 51*, 163–183.

Hewlett, B. S. (2005). The cultural nexus of Aka father-infant bonding. In C. B. Brettell and C. F. Sargent (Eds.), *Gender in cross-cultural perspective* (4th ed.). Upper Saddle River, NJ: Prentice-Hall.

Heyl, B. S. (1996). Homosexuality: A social phenomenon. In K. E. Rosenblum & T. C. Travis (Eds.), *The meaning of difference: American constructions of race, sex and gender, social class, and sexual orientation* (pp. 120–129). New York: McGraw-Hill.

Hoffman, J. (1992, February 16). When men hit women. *The New York Times Magazine*, pp. 23–27, 64–66, 72.

Hill, J. P. (1987). Research on adolescents and their families: Past and prospect. *New Directions for Child Development, 37*, 13–31.

Hills, H. I., Carlstrom, A., & Evanow, M. (2001). Consulting with men in business and industry. In G. R. Brooks & G. E. Good (Eds.). The new handbook of psychotherapy and counseling with men: A comprehensive guide to settings, problems, and treatment approaches. San Francisco: Jossey-Bass.

Hines, P. M., & Boyd-Franklin, N. (1996). African American families. In M. McGoldrick, J. Pearce & J. Giordano (Eds.), *Ethnicity and family therapy* (pp. 66–84). New York: Guilford.

Hochschild, A., & Machung, A. (1989). The second shift. New York: Avon.

Hofferth, S. L. & Anderson, K. G. (2003). Are all dads equal? Biology versus marriage as a basis for paternal investment. *Journal of Marriage and the Family, 65 (1)*, 213–232.

Holtzworth-Munroe, A., & Stuart, G. L. (1994). Typologies of male batterers: Three subtypes and the differences among them. *Psychological Bulletin, 116*, 476–497.

Horne, A. M., Jolliff, D. L., & Roth, E. W. (1996). Men mentoring men in groups. In M. P. Andronico (Ed.), *Men in groups: Insights, interventions, and psychoeducational work* (pp. 97–112). Washington, DC: American Psychological Association.

Horney, K. (1932). The dread of women: Observations on a specific difference in the dread felt by men and women respectively for the opposite sex. *International Journal of Psychoanalysis, 13*, 348–360.

Hossain, Z., & Roopnarine, J. L. (1993). Division of household labor and child care in dual-earner African-American families with infants. *Sex Roles, 29*, 571–583.

Houseworth, S., Peplow, K., & Thirer, J. (1989). Influence of sport participation upon sex role orientation of Caucasian males and their attitudes toward women. *Sex Roles, 20*, 317–325.

Hubbard, R. (1998). The political nature of "human nature." In In D. L. Anselmi & A. L. Law (Eds.), *Questions of gender: perspectives and paradoxes* (pp. 146–153). Boston: McGraw-Hill.

Huesman, L. R., Eron, L. D., Lefkowitz, M. M., & Walder, L. O. (1984). *The stability of aggression over time and generations*. Victoria, BC, Canada: International Society for Research on Aggression.

Hussey, A. (1989). Neonatal circumcision: A uniquely American ritual. *Transitions, 9 (4)*, 18–22.

Huston, T. L., & Ashmore, R. D. (1986). Women and men in personal relationship. In R. D. Ashmore & R. K. Del Boca (Eds.), *The social psychology of female-male relations* (pp. 167–210). New York: Academic Press.

Huyck, M. (1992). Evaluating the parental imperative in Parkville. Paper presented at the Annual Meeting of the American Gerontological Society, Washington, DC.

Hyde, J. S., (1984). Children's understanding of sexist language. *Developmental Psychology, 20*, 697–706.

Hyde, J. S., & Plant, E. A. (1995). Magnitude of psychological gender differences: Another side to the story. *American Psychologist, 50*, 159–161.

"In light of Gay Days festival, Robertson warns of storms" (1998, June 11). Associated Press.

Ireland, P. (1997, September 7). Beware of "feel-good male supremacy." *The Washington Post*, p. C3.

Irving, L., Wall, M., Neumark-Sztainer, D., & Story, M. (2002). Steroid use among adolescents: Findings from Project EAT. Journal of Adolescent Health, 30, 243–252.

Isely, P. J. (1992). A time-limited group therapy model for men sexually abused as children. *Group, 16,* 233–246.

Isely, P. J., Busse, W., & Isely, P. (1998). Sexual assault in males in late adolescence: A hidden phenomenon. *Professional School Counseling, 2,* 153–160.

Isely, P. J., & Gehrenbeck-Shim, D. (1997). Sexual assault of men in the community. *Journal of Community Psychology, 25,* 159–166.

Jacobs, N. R., Siegal, M. A., & Quiram, J. (Eds.) (1997). *Prisons and jails: A deterrent to crime?* Wylie, TX: Information Plus.

James, S. (1984). *A dictionary of sexist quotations.* Totowa, NJ: Barnes and Noble.

Jansz, J. (2000). Masculine identity and restrictive emotionality. In A. H. Fischer (Ed.), *Gender and emotion: Social psychological perspectives.* Cambridge, UK: Cambridge University Press.

Jaschik-Herman, M. L., & Fisk, A. (1995). Women's perceptions and labeling of sexual harassment in academia before and after the Hill-Thomas hearings. *Sex Roles, 33,* 439–446.

Jenkins, S. (2005). The age-old question: How young is too young? *The Washington Post,* July 6, pp. E1, E7.

Jensen, R., & Dines, G. (1998). The content of mass-marketed pornography. In G. Dines, R. Jensen, & A. Russo, *Pornography: The production and consumption of inequality* (pp. 65–100). New York: Routledge.

Jhally, S. & Katz, J. (2000). T*ough guise: Violence, media, and the crisis in masculinity* (documentary film). Northampton, MA: Media Education Foundation.

Johnson, A. G. (1997). *The gender knot: Unraveling our patriarchal legacy.* Philadelphia: Temple University Press.

Johnson, J. D. (1994). The effect of rape type and information admissibility on perceptions of rape victims. *Sex Roles, 30,* 781–792.

Joint, M. (1995). Road rage. The Automobile Association Group Public Policy Road Safety Unit, online at aaafoundation.org/resources.

Jones, G. P. (1990). The boy is father to the man: A men's studies exploration of intergenerational interaction. *Men's Studies Review, 7 (1),* 9–13.

Jourard, S. M. (1971). *The transparent self.* New York: Van Nostrand.

Joyce, A. (2005, June 6). Workplace improves for gay, transgender employees, rights group says. *The Washington Post,* A5.

Judd, C. M., Park, B., Ryan, C. S., Brauer, M., & Kraus, S. (1995). Stereotypes and ethnocentrism: Diverging interethnic perceptions of African American and White American youth. *Journal of Personality and Social Psychology, 69,* 460–481.

Jung, C. G. (1959/1989). Concerning the archetypes with special reference to the anima concept. In C. G. Jung, R. F. C. Hull (Translator) & J. Beebe (Ed.), *Aspects of the masculine* (pp. 115–122). Princeton, NJ: Princeton University Press.

Kagan, J. (1964). Acquisition and significance of sex typing and sex role identity. In M. L. Hoffman & L. W. Hoffman (Eds.), *Review of child research* (Vol. 1, pp. 137–169). New York: Russell Sage.

Kamarovsky, M. (1940/1971). *The unemployed man and his family: The effect of unemployment upon the status of the man in fifty-nine families.* New York: Dryden Press/Arno Press.

Kamarovsky, M. (1976). *Dilemmas of masculinity: A study of college youth.* New York: Norton.

Kantor, M. (1998). *Homophobia: Description, development, and dynamics of gay bashing.* Westport, CT: Praeger.

Kaplan, D. (1998). Internet pornography should be censored. In C. Wekesser (Ed.), *Pornography: Opposing viewpoints,* San Diego, CA: Greenhaven.

Katz, J. (1995). Reconstructing masculinity in the locker room: The Mentors in Violence Prevention Project. *Harvard Educational Review, 65(2)*, 163–174.

Katz, J. (2001). Boys are not men: Notes on working with adolescent males in juvenile detention. In D. Sabo, T. A. Kupers, & W. London (Eds.). *Prison masculinities*. Philadelphia: Temple University Press.

Kaufman, Mark (2005, July 1). FDA was told of Viagra, blindness link months ago: Senator criticizes delay in alerting consumers after safety officer warned agency about drug. *The Washington Post*, A2.

Kaufman, Michael (1994). Men, feminism, and men's contradictory experiences of power. In H. Brod and Michael Kaufman (Eds.), *Theorizing masculinities* (pp. 142–163). Thousand Oaks, CA: Sage.

Kawakami, K., Dovidio, J. F., Moll, J., Hermsen, S., & Russin, A. (2000). Just say no (to stereotyping): Effects of training in the negation of stereotypic associations on stereotype activation. *Journal of Personality and Social Psychology, 78 (5)*, 871–888.

Kay, S. A. & Meikle, D. B. (1984). Political ideology, sociobiology, and the U.S. women's rights movement. In M.W. Watts (Ed.), *Biopolitics and gender* (pp. 67–96). New York: Haworth.

Kearney, L. K., Rochlen, A. B., & King, E. B. (2004). Male gender role conflict, sexual harassment tolerance, and the efficacy of a psychoeducative training program. *Psychology of Men and Masculinity, 5 (1)*, 72–82.

Keen, M. (1984). Chivalry. New Haven, CT: Yale University Press.

Keen, S. (1991). *Fire in the belly: On being a man*. New York: Bantam.

Kelly, J. B. (1988). Longer-term adjustment in children of divorce: Converging findings and implications for practice. *Journal of Family Psychology, 2*, 119–140.

Kemper, T. D. (1990). *Social structure and testosterone*. New Brunswick, NJ: Rutgers University Press.

Kenrick, D. T. (1987). Gender, genes and the social environment: A biosocial interactionist perspective. In P. Shaver & C. Hendrick (Eds.), *Sex and gender* (pp. 14–43). Newbury Park, CA: Sage.

Kenrick, D. T., Gutierres, S. E., & Goldberg, L. L. (1989). Influence of popular erotica on judgments of strangers and mates. *Journal of Experimental Social Psychology, 25*, 159–167.

Kenrick, D. T., Neuberg, S. L., & Cialdini, R. B. (2005). *Social psychology: Unraveling the mystery* (3rd ed.) Boston: Pearson.

Kerns, J. G., & Fine, M. A. (1994). The relation between gender and negative attitudes toward gay men and lesbians: Do gender role attitudes mediate this relation? *Sex Roles, 31*, 297–307.

Kilmartin, C. T. (1988). Interpersonal influence strategies: Gender differences in response to nurturant behavior. Unpublished doctoral dissertation, Virginia Commonwealth University.

Kilmartin, C. T. (1996). The White Ribbon Campaign: Men working to end men's violence against women. *Journal of College Student Development, 37 (3)*, 347–348.

Kilmartin, C. T. (1997). Book review: Men in groups: Insights, interventions, and psychoeducational work. *Group Dynamics: Theory, Research, and Practice, 1*, 267–271.

Kilmartin, C. T. (2004a). "Midlife crisis". In M. Kimmel & A. Aronson (Eds.), *Men and masculinities: A social, cultural, and historical encyclopedia*. Santa Barbara, CA: ABC-Clio.

Kilmartin, C. T. (2004b). Masculinity as a cultural variable in psychotherapy. Paper presented in Symposium: Men and mental health: New directions in marketing and treatment *(M. E. Addis & J. M. Lane, Chairs). Annual Convention of the American Psychological Association, Honolulu, HI*.

Kilmartin, C. T. (2005). Depression in men: communication, diagnosis, and therapy. *Journal of Men's Health and Gender, 2 (1)*, 95–99.

Kilmartin, C. T., & Allison, J. (2007). *Men's violence against women: Integrating theory, research, and practice*. Mahwah, NJ: Erlbaum.

Kilmartin, C. T., & Berkowitz, A .D. (2005). *Sexual assault in context: Teaching men about gender*. Mahwah, NJ: Erlbaum.

Kilmartin, C. T., Chirico, B., & Leemann, M. *The White Ribbon Campaign: Evidence for Social Change on a College Campus*. Paper presented at the Spring Convention of the Virginia Psychological Association, Roanoke, VA.

Kilmartin, C. T., Conway, A., Friedberg, A., McQuoid, T., Tschan, T., & Norbet, T. (1999, April). Using the social norms model to encourage male college students to challenge rape-supportive attitudes in male peers. Paper presented at the Virginia Psychological Association Spring Conference, Virginia Beach, VA.

Kilmartin, C., Green, A., Heinzen, H., Kuchler, M., & Smith, T. (2004). *Sexual assault in context: Teaching college men about gender*. Poster presentation at the Annual Convention of the American Psychological Association, Honolulu, HI.

Kilmartin, C. T., & Ring, T .E. (1991). Understanding and preventing acquaintance rape on college campuses: Services for men. Paper presented at the annual meeting of the Maryland College Personnel Association, College Park, MD.

Kim, E. (1990). "Such opposite creatures": Men and women in Asian American literature. *Michigan Quarterly Review, 29*, 68–93.

Kimbrell, A. (1991, May/June). A time for men to pull together. *Utne Reader*, pp. 66–74.

Kimmel, M. S. (1987). Rethinking masculinity: New directions in research. In M. S. Kimmel (Ed.), *Changing men: New directions in research on men and masculinity* (pp. 9–24). Newbury Park, CA: Sage.

Kimmel, M. S. (1992, July). Accountability in men's studies scholarship: The academic is political. Paper presented at the 17th National Conference on Men and Masculinity, Chicago.

Kimmel, M. S. (1994). Masculinity as homophobia: Fear, shame, and silence in the construction of gender identity. In H. Brod and Michael Kaufman (Eds.), *Theorizing masculinities* (pp. 119 -141). Thousand Oaks, CA: Sage.

Kimmel, M. S. (Ed.) (1995). *The politics of manhood: Profeminist men respond to the mythopoetic men's movement (and the mythopoetic leaders answer)*. Philadelphia: Temple University Press.

Kimmel, M. S. (1996). *Manhood in America: A cultural history*. New York: Free Press.

Kimmel, M. S. (1999). "What about the boys?" What the current debates tell us – and don't tell us – about boys in school. *Michigan Feminist Studies, 14*, 1–28.

Kimmel, M. S. (2001). Male victims of domestic violence: A substantive and methodological research review. Report to the Equality Committee of the Department of Education and Science.

Kimmel, M. S. & Levine, M. P. (1992). Men and AIDS. In M. S. Kimmel & M. A. Messner (Eds.), *Men's lives* (2nd ed., pp. 318–329). New York: Macmillan.

Kimmel, M. S., & Mosmiller, T. E. (1992). *Against the tide: Pro-feminist men in the United States, 1776–1990*. Boston: Beacon.

Kindlon, D., & Thompson, M. (1999). *Raising Cain: Protecting the emotional lives of boys*. New York: Ballantine.

King, J. L. (2004). *On the down low: A journey into the lives of "straight" black men who sleep with men*. New York: Broadway.

King, M. B. (1992). Male sexual assault in the community. In G. C. Mezey & M. B. King (Eds.), *Male victims of sexual assault* (pp. 3–12). New York: Oxford University Press.

Kinsey, A. C., Pomeroy, W. B., & Martin, C. E. (1948). *Sexual behavior in the human male*. Philadelphia: W. B. Saunders.

Kinsey, A. C., Pomeroy, W. B., Martin, C. E., & Gebhard, P. H. (1953). *Sexual behavior in the human female*. Philadelphia: W. B. Saunders.

Kiselica, M. S. (1996). Parenting skills training with teenage fathers. In M. P. Andronico (Ed.), *Men in groups: Insights, interventions, and psychoeducational work* (pp. 283–300). Washington DC: American Psychological Association.

Kiselica, M. S. (2005). Personal communication.

Klein, A. M. (1995). Life's too short to die small: Steroid use among male bodybuilders. In D. Sabo & D. F. Gordon (Eds.), *Men's health and illness: Gender, power, and the body* (pp. 105–120). Thousand Oaks, CA: Sage.

Knight, A. (1998, January 14). NCAA changes wrestling rules. *The Washington Post*, p. D1.

Kochanek, K. D., Murphy, S. L., Anderson, R. N., & Scott, C. (2004). Deaths: Final data for 2002. National Vital Statistics Reports, 53 (5), http://www.cdc.gov/nchs/data/nvsr/nvsr53/ nvsr53_05acc.pdf

Komiya, N., Good, G. E., & Sherrod, N. (2000). Emotional openness as a contributing factor to reluctance to seek counseling among college students. *Journal of Counseling Psychology, 47*, 138–143.

Kopper, B. A., & Epperson, D. L. (1996). The experience and expression of anger: Relationships with gender, gender role socialization, depression, and mental health functioning. *Journal of Counseling Psychology*, 43, 158–165.

Koss, M. P. (1983). The scope of rape: Implications for the clinical treatment of victims. *The Clinical Psychologist, 36*, 88–91.

Koss, M. P. (1990, August 29). Testimony before the United States Senate Judiciary Panel.

Koss, M. P. (1993). Detecting the scope of rape: A review of prevalence research methods. *Journal of Interpersonal Violence, 8*, 98–122.

Krishnamurthy, K. (1998, June 17). No pomp, but honor student gets diploma. *The Free-Lance Star*, p. C1.

Kruckoff, C. (1993, August 17). Men, women, and exercise: Sexes differ in approach to activity. *Washington Post Health*, p. 16.

Krug, E. G., Dahlberg, L. L., Mercy, J. A., Zwi, A. B., & Lozano, R. (Eds., 2004). *World report on violence and health*. Geneva: World Health Organization.

Kupers, T. A. (1993). *Revisioning men's lives: Gender, intimacy, and power*. New York: Guilford.

Kupers, T. A. (1999). *Prison madness: The mental health crisis behind bars and what we must do about it*. San Francisco: Jossey-Bass.

Kupers, T. A. (2004). Prisons. In M. Kimmel & A. Aronson (Eds.), *Men and masculinities: A social, cultural, and historical encyclopedia*. Santa Barbara, CA: ABC-Clio.

Kurdek, L. A. (1988). Correlates of negative attitudes toward homosexuals in heterosexual college students. *Sex Roles, 18*, 727–738.

Kurdek, L. A., & Schmitt, J. P. (1986). Interaction of sex role self-concept with relationship quality and relationship beliefs in married, heterosexual cohabiting, gay, and lesbian couples. *Journal of Personality and Social Psychology, 51*, 365–370.

L'Abate, L. (1980). Inexpressive males or overexpressive females? A reply to Balswick. *Family Relations, 29*, 229–230.

Laker, J., Davis, T., Kellom, G., & Brod, H. (2005). (EN)Gendering men on campus: A state of field discussion on college men. Panel discussion: American Men's Studies Association 13th Annual Conference, Nashville, TN.

Lakoff, R. T. (1990). *Talking power: The politics of language*. New York: Basic Books.

Lambert, W., & Simon, S. (1991, July 30). Military discharges gay veterans of gulf. *The Wall Street Journal*, p. B8.

Landes, A. B., Squyres, S. & Quiram, J. (Eds.) (1997). *Violent relationships: Battering and abuse among adults*. Wylie, TX: Information Plus.

Landrine, H. (1988). Revising the framework of abnormal psychology. In P. Bronstein and K. Quina (Eds.), *Teaching a psychology of people: Resources for gender and sociocultural awareness* (pp. 37–44). Washington, DC: American Psychological Association.

Lange, A. J., & Jackubowski, P. (1976). *Responsible assertive behavior: Cognitive/behavioral procedures for trainers*. New York: Research Press.

Lardner, G. (1997, August 25). Violent injuries far surpass estimates, study finds. *The Washington Post*, p. A6.

Lash, S. J., Eisler, R. M., & Southard, D. R. (1995). Sex differences in cardiovascular as a function of the appraised gender relevance of the stressor. *Behavioral Medicine, 21*, 86–94.

Laumann, E. O. (1999). The circumcision dilemma: Physicians in the U. S. are at odds over neonatal circumcision. Is it preventive medicine, cosmetic surgery, or inhumane mutilation? *Scientific American Presents, 10 (2)*, 68–72.

Laumann, E. O., Gagnon, J., Michael, R. T., & Michaels, S. (1994). *The social organization of sexuality*. Chicago: University of Chicago Press.

Lavine, L. O., & Lombardo, J. P. (1984). Self-disclosure: Intimate and nonintimate disclosures to parents and best friends as a function of Bem sex-role category. *Sex Roles, 11*, 760–768.

Lazur, R. F. (1996). Managing boundaries: Group therapy with incarcerated adult male sexual offenders. In M. P. Andronico (Ed.), *Men in groups: Insights, interventions, and psychoeducational work* (pp. 389–410). Washington, DC: American Psychological Association.

Leafgren, F. (1990). Men on a journey. In D. Moore & F. Leafgren (Eds.), *Men in conflict* (pp. 3–10). Alexandria, VA: American Association for Counseling and Development.

Lee, C. C. (1990). Black male development: Counseling the "native son." In D. Moore & F. Leafgren (Eds.), *Men in conflict* (pp. 125–137). Alexandria, VA: American Association for Counseling and Development.

Lee, J. (1991). *At my father's wedding: Reclaiming our true masculinity*. New York: Bantam.

Lehne, G. (1998). Homophobia among men: Supporting and defining the male role. In M. S. Kimmel and M. A. Messner (Eds.), *Men's lives* (4th ed., pp. 237–249). Needham Heights, MA: Allyn and Bacon.

Lemann, N. (1991). *The promised land*. New York: Knopf.

Lemle, R., & Mishkind, M. E. (1989). Alcohol and masculinity. *Journal of Substance Abuse Treatment, 6*, 213–222.

Lepowsky, M. (1998). Women, men, and aggression in an egalitarian society. In D. L. Anselmi & A. L. Law (Eds.), *Questions of gender: perspectives and paradoxes* (pp. 171–178). Boston: McGraw-Hill.

Lerner, G. (1986). *The creation of patriarchy*. New York: Oxford University Press.

Lester, D. (1997). Suicide in an international perspective. In A. A. Leenaars, R. W. Maris, & Y. Tadahashi (Eds.), *Suicide: Individual, cultural, international perspectives* (pp. 104–111). New York: Guilford.

Letich, L. (1991, May/June). Do you know who your friends are? *Utne Reader*, pp. 85–87.

Levant, R. F. (1988). Education for fatherhood. In P. Bronstein & C. P. Cowan (Eds.), *Fatherhood today: Men's changing role in the family* (pp. 253–275). New York: Wiley.

Levant, R. F. (1990a). Coping with the new father role. In D. Moore & F. Leafgren (Eds.), *Men in conflict* (pp. 81–94). Alexandria, VA: American Association for Counseling and Development.

Levant, R. F. (1990b). Psychological services designed for men: A   psychoeducational approach. *Psychotherapy, 27*, 309–315.

Levant, R. F. (1995). *Masculinity reconstructed: Changing the rules of manhood — at work, in relationships, and in family life*. New York: Dutton.

Levant, R. F. (1997). Nonrelational sex. In R. F. Levant & G. R. Brooks (Eds.), *Men and sex* (pp. 9–27). New York: Wiley.

Levant, R. F. (1997). Men and emotions: A psychoeducational approach. New York: Newbridge Professional Programs.

Levant, R. F. (1998). Desperately seeking language: Understanding, assessing, and treating normative male alexithymia. In W.S. Pollack & R. F. Levant (Eds.), *New psychotherapy for men* (pp. 35–56). New York: Wiley.

Levant, R. F. (2003). Treating male alexithymia.. In L.B. Silverstein & T. J. Goodrich (Eds). *Feminist family therapy: Empowerment in social context* (pp. 177–188). Washington, DC: American Psychological Association.

Levant, R. F., & Pollack, W. S. (1995). Introduction. In R. F. Levant & W. S. Pollack (Eds.), *A new psychology of men* (pp. 1–8). New York: Basic Books.

Levant, R. F., Richmond, K., Majors, R. G., Inclan, J. E., Rossello, J. M., Heesacker, M., Rowan, G. T., & Sellers, A. (2003). A multicultural investigation of masculinity ideology and alexithymia. *Psychology of Men and Masculinity, 4 (2)*, 91–99.

LeVay, S. (1991). A difference in hypothalmic structure between heterosexual and homosexual men. *Science, 253*, 1034–1037.

Levenson, R., Carstensen, L., & Gottman, J. (1994). The influence of age and gender on affect, physiology, and their interrelations: A study of long-term marriages. *Journal of Personality and Social Psychology, 67*, 56–68.

Levinson, D. J., Darrow, C. N., Klein, E. B., Levinson, M. H., & McKee, B. (1978). *The seasons of a man's life*. New York: Knopf.

Levine, L., & Barbach, L. (1983). *The intimate male: Candid discussions about women, sex, and relationships*. Garden City, NY: Anchor.

Levine, H. J., & Evans, N. J. (1996). The development of gay, lesbian, and bisexual identities. In K. E. Rosenblum & T. C. Travis (Eds.), *The meaning of difference: American constructions of race, sex and gender, social class, and sexual orientation* (pp. 130–136). New York: McGraw-Hill.

Levine, M. P. (1991). The life and death of the gay clone. In G. Herdt (Ed.), *Gay culture in America: Essays from the field* (pp. 68–86). Boston: Beacon.

Levine, M. P. (1998). *Gay macho: The life and death of the homosexual clone*. New York: New York University Press.

Levy, C. J. (1992). ARVN as faggots: Inverted warfare in Vietnam. In M. S. Kimmel & M. A. Messner (Eds.), *Men's lives* (2nd ed., pp. 183–197). New York: Macmillan.

Lewin, T. (1998, December 6). U.S. colleges begin to ask, where have all the men gone? *The New York Times*, pp. 1, 38.

Lewis, M. (1987). Early sex role behavior and school age adjustment. In J. M. Reinisch, L. A. Rosenblum, & S. A. Sanders (Eds.), *Masculinity/femininity: Basic perspectives* (pp. 202–226). New York: Oxford University Press.

Lewis, R. A. (1986). Men's changing roles in marriage and the family. In R. A. Lewis (Ed.), *Men's changing roles in the family* (pp. 1–10). New York: Haworth.

Lewis, E. T., & McCarthy, P. R. (1988). Perceptions of self-disclosure as a function of gender-linked variables. *Sex Roles, 19*, 47–56.

Lex, B. W. (1995). Alcohol and other psychoactive substance dependence in women and men. In M. V. Seeman (Ed.), *Gender and psychopathology* (pp. 358). Washington, DC: American Psychiatric Press.

Liebow, E. (1967). *Talley's corner*. Boston: Little, Brown.

Liebman, W. (1991). *Tending the fire: The ritual men's group*. St. Paul, MN: Ally Press.

Linz, D., & Donnerstein, E. (1992). Research can help us explain violence and pornography. *Chronicle of Higher Education, 39(6)*, pp. B3–B4.

Linz, D., & Malamuth, M. (1993). *Pornography*. Newbury Park, CA: Sage.

Lippa, R. A., Martin, L. R., & Friedman, H. S. (2000). Gender-related individual differences and mortality in the Terman longitudinal study: Is masculinity hazardous to your health? *Personality and Social Psychology Bulletin, 12*, 1560–1570.

Lips, H. (2005). *Sex and gender: An introduction* (5th ed.). Boston: McGraw-Hill.

Lisak, D. (1991). Sexual aggression, masculinity, and fathers. *Signs, 16*, 238–262.

Lisak, D. (1993, November). Sexual assault: Perpetrator characteristics and solutions. Invited address, Mary Washington College.

Lisak, D. (1997). Male gender socialization and the perpetration of sexual abuse. In R. F. Levant & G. R. Brooks (Eds.), *Men and sex* (pp. 156–177). New York: Wiley.

Lisak, D. (2005). The undetected rapist. Videotaped re-enactment of an interview with a sexual assault perpetrator. Available from legal momentum.org.

Lisak, D. & Miller, P. M. (2002). Repeat rape and multiple offending among undetected rapists. *Violence and Victims, 17 (1)*, 73–84.

Lisak, D., & Roth, S. (1988). Motivational factors in nonincarcerated sexually aggressive men. *Journal of Personality and Social Psychology, 55*, 795–802.

Liu, W. M. (2002). Exploring the lives of Asian American men: Racial identity, male role norms, gender role conflict, and prejudicial attitudes. *Psychology of Men and Masculinity, 3 (2)*, 107–118.

Lo, C. C., & Globetti, G. (1995). The facilitating and enhancing roles Greek associations play in college drinking. *International Journal of the Addictions, 30*, 1311–1322.

Lockwood, D. (1980). *Prison sexual violence*. New York: Elsevier.

Loeber, R., & Stouthamer-Loeber, M. (1998). Development of juvenile aggression and violence: Some common misconceptions and controversies. *American Psychologist, 53*, 242–249.

Long, D. (1987). Working with men who batter. In M. Scher, M. Stevens, G. Good, & G. A. Eichenfield (Eds.). Handbook of counseling and psychotherapy with men. Newbury Park, CA: Sage.

Lorber, J. (1986). Dismantling Noah's ark. *Sex Roles, 14*, 567–580.

Lorber, J. (1994). *Paradoxes of gender*. New Haven, CT: Yale University Press.

Loughery, J. (1998). The other side of silence: Men's lives and gay identities: A twentieth century history. New York: Henry Holt.

Luria, Z., Friedman, S., & Rose, M. D. (1987). *Human sexuality*. New York: Wiley.

Lynch, J. (1998). Personal communication.

Lynch, J. (2004). *When anger scares you: How to overcome your fear of conflict and express your anger in healthy ways*. Oakland, CA: New Harbinger.

Lynch, J., & Kilmartin, C. T. (1999). *The pain behind the mask. Overcoming masculine depression*. Binghamton, NY: Haworth.

Lynn, D. B. (1959). A note on sex differences in the development of masculine and feminine identification. *Psychological Review, 66*, 126–135.

Lynn, D. B. (1966). The process of learning parental and sex-role identification. *Journal of Marriage and the Family, 28*, 466–477.

Lynn, D. B. (1969). *Parental and sex role identification: A theoretical formulation*. Berkeley, CA: McCutchan.

Lytton, H., & Romney, D.M. (1991). Parents' differential socialization of boys and girls: A meta-analysis. *Psychological Bulletin, 109*, 267–296.

Macchietto, J. (1991). Editor's comment: Hallmark learns about male-bashing: A slow but productive task. *Transitions, 11 (5)*, p. 2.

Maccoby, E. E. (1987). The varied meanings of "masculine" and "feminine." In J.M. Reinisch, L.A. Rosenblum, & S.A. Sanders (Eds.), *Masculinity/femininity: Basic perspectives* (pp. 227–239). New York: Oxford University Press.

Maccoby, E. E. (1988a). Gender as a social category. *Developmental Psychology, 24*, 755–765.

Maccoby, E. E. (1988b). Gender as a social construct. Paper presented at the Annual Meeting of the Eastern Psychological Association, Buffalo, NY.

Maccoby, E. E. (1990). Gender and relationships: A developmental account. *American Psychologist, 45*, 513–520.

Maccoby, E. E. (1998). *The two sexes: Growing up apart, coming together*. Cambridge, MA: Harvard University Press.

Maccoby, E. E. & Jacklin, C. N. (1974). *The psychology of sex differences*. Stanford, CA: Stanford University Press.

MacKinnon, C.A. (1985). Pornography, civil rights, and speech. *Harvard Civil Rights-Civil Liberties Law Review, 20*, 1–70.

Maddi, S. R. (2001). *Personality theories: A comparative analysis* (6th ed.). Prospect Heights, IL: Waveland.

Mahalik, J. R., Cournoyer, R. J., DeFranc, W., Cherry, M., & Napolitano, J. M. (1998). Men's gender role conflict and use of psychological defenses. *Journal of Counseling Psychology, 45*, 247–255.

Mahalik, J. R., Locke, B. D., Ludlow, L. H., Diemer, M. A., Scott, R. P. J., Gottfried, M., & Freitas, G. (2003). Development of the Conformity to Masculine Norms Inventory. *Psychology of Men and Masculinity, 4 (1)*, 3–25.

Mahlstedt, D. (1998). Getting started: A dating violence peer education program for men. West Chester, PA: self-published.

Majors, R., & Billson, J. M. (1992). *Cool pose: The dilemmas of black manhood in America*. New York: Lexington.

Malamuth, N. M., Linz, D., Heavey, C. L., Barnes, G., & Acker, M. (1995). Using the confluence model of sexual aggression to predict men's conflict with women: A 10–year follow-up study. *Journal of Personality and Social Psychology, 69*, 353–369.

Mann, J. (1997, October 1). Promise Keepers marching backward. *The Washington Post*, p. E13.

"Many concussions go undetected, unreported." (2004, June 16). *The Washington Post*, p. D2.

Marsh, H.W., Antill, J.K., & Cunningham, J.D. (1989). Masculinity and femininity: A bipolar construct and independent constructs. *Journal of Personality, 57*, 625–663.

Marsiglio, W. (1993). Attitudes toward homosexual activity and gays as friends: A national survey of heterosexual 15– to 19–year-old males. *Journal of Sex Research, 30*, 12–17.

Marsiglio, W. & Pleck, J. H. (2005). Fatherhood and masculinities. In M. S. Kimmel, J. Hearn, & R. W. Connell (Eds.), *Handbook of studies on men and masculinities*. Thousand Oaks, CA: Sage.

Martin, C. L. (1990). Attitudes and expectations about children with nontraditional and traditional gender roles. *Sex Roles, 22*, 151–165.

Martin, C. L. (1995). Stereotypes about children with traditional and nontraditional gender roles. *Sex Roles, 33*, 727–751.

Martin, C. L. & Fabes, R. A. (2001). The stability and consequences of young children's same-sex peer interactions. *Developmental Psychology, 3*, 431–446.

Martin, E. (1991). The egg and the sperm: How science has constructed a romance based on stereotypical male-female roles. *Signs*, *16*, 485–501.

Martin, P. Y., & Hummer, R. A. (1997). Fraternities and rape on campus. In L Richardson, V. Taylor, & N. Whittier (Eds.), *Feminist frontiers* IV (pp. 398–409). Boston: McGraw-Hill.

Mason, A., & Blankenship, V. (1987). Power and affiliation motivation, stress, and abuse in intimate relationships. *Journal of Personality and Social Psychology*, *52*, 203–210.

May, R. (1958). Contributions of existential psychotherapy. In R. May, E. Angel, & H. F. Ellenberger (Eds.), *Existence: A new dimension in psychiatry and psychology*. New York: Basic Books.

May, R. J. (1986). Concerning a psychoanalytic view of maleness. *The Psychoanalytic Review*, *73*, 579–597.

May, R. J. (1988). The developmental journey of the male college student. In R. J. May & M. Scher (Eds.), *Changing roles of men on campus* (pp. 5–18). San Francisco: Jossey-Bass.

Mazur, E. (1989). Predicting gender differences in same-sex friendships from affiliation motive and value. *Psychology of Women Quarterly*, *13*, 277–292.

McAdams, D. P., Lester, R. M., Brand, P. A., McNamara, W. J., & Lensky, D. B. (1988). Sex and the TAT: Are women more intimate than men? Do men fear intimacy? *Journal of Personality Assessment*, *52*, 397–409.

McAllister, B. (1996, March 13). Harassment case took five years to resolve: Many say lengthy proceedings show difficulty of proving charges in federal bureaucracy. *The Washington Post*, p. A19.

McCreary, D. R. (1994). The male role and avoiding femininity. *Sex Roles*, 31, 517–531.

McCreary, D. R., Newcomb, M. D., & Sadava, S. W. (1999). The male role, alcohol use, and alcohol problems: A structural modeling examination in adult women and men. *Journal of Counseling Psychology*, *46*, 109–124.

McCreary, D. M. & Sasse, D. K. (2000). An exploration of the drive for muscularity in adolescent boys and girls. *Journal of American College Health*, *48*, 297–304.

McHale, S. M., & Huston, T. L. (1984). Men and women as parents: Sex role orientations, employment, and parental roles with infants. *Child Development*, *55*, 1349–1361.

Mead, M. (1935). *Sex and temperament in three primitive societies*. New York: Morrow.

Mead, M. (1949). *Male and female: A study of the sexes in a changing world*. New York: Morrow.

Men's Rights, Inc. (n.d.). MR I.Q. Test (advertising brochure).

Meredith, D. (1985, June). Dad and the kids. *Psychology Today*, 63–67.

Merriam-Webster Dictionary (on line, 2005). .

Messerschmidt, J. W. (1993). *Masculinities and crime: Critique and reconceptualization of theory*. Lanham, MD: Rowman & Littlefield.

Messner, M. A. (1992). Like family: Power, intimacy, and sexuality in athletes' friendships. In P. M. Nardi (Ed.), *Men's friendships* (pp. 215–237). Newbury Park, CA: Sage.

Messner, M. A. (1995). Boyhood, organized sports, and the construction of masculinity. In M. A. Kimmel & M. S. Messner (Eds.), *Men's lives* (3rd ed., pp. 102–114). Boston: Allyn and Bacon.

Michael, R. T., Gagnon, J. H., Laumann, E. O., & Kolata, G. (1994). *Sex in America: A definitive survey*. Boston: Little, Brown.

Miedzian, M. (1991). *Boys will be boys: Breaking the link between masculinity and violence*. New York: Doubleday.

Mihoces, G. (2002, January 18). Two big guys are key to success. *USA Today*, 1A.

Milgram, S. (1963). Behavioral study of obedience. *Journal of Abnormal and Social Psychology*, *67*, 371–378.

Miller, A. (1949). *Death of a salesman*. New York: Viking.

Miller, T. Q., Smith, T. W., Turner, C. W., Guijarro, M. L., & Hallet, A. J. (1996). A meta-analytic review of research on hostility and physical health. *Psychological Bulletin*, *119*, 322–348.

Millon, T. (1996). *Disorders of personality: DSM-IV and beyond* (2nd ed.). New York: Wiley.

Milos, M. F. (1992). Circumcision: Don't be conned by the pros. Journeymen, 14–16.

Minkowitz, D. (1995). In the name of the father. Ms., *6(3)*, 64–71.

Mintz, L. B., & O'Neil, J. M. (1990). Gender roles, sex, and the process of psychotherapy: Many questions and a few answers. *Journal of Counseling and Development*, *68*, 381–387.

Moberly, E. (1983). *Homosexuality: A new Christian ethic*. Cambridge, UK: Clarke.

Moitoza, E. (1982). Portuguese families. In M. McGoldrick, J. .Pearce & J. Giordano (Eds.), *Ethnicity and family therapy* (pp. 412–437). New York: Guilford.

Money, J. (1987a). Propaedeutics of diecious G-I/R: Theoretical foundations for understanding dimorphic gender-identity/role. In J. M. Reinisch, L. A. Rosenblum, & S. A. Sanders (Eds.), *Masculinity/femininity: Basic perspectives* (pp. 13–28). New York: Oxford University Press.

Money, J. (1987b). Sin, sickness, or status? Homosexual gender identity and psychological neuroendocrinology. *American Psychologist*, *42*, 384–399.

Montague, D.K. (1988). *Disorders of male sexual function*. Chicago: Year Book Medical.

Moore, D. (1990). Helping men become more emotionally expressive: A ten-week program. In D. Moore & F. Leafgren (Eds.), *Men in conflict* (pp. 183–200). Alexandria, VA: American Association for Counseling and Development.

Moore, D., & Haverkamp, B. E. (1989). Measured increases in male emotional expressiveness following a structured group intervention. *Journal of Counseling and Development*, *67*, 513–517.

Morawski, J.G. (1985). The measurement of masculinity and femininity: Engendering categorical realities. *Journal of Personality*, *53*, 196–223.

Morin, R., & Wilson, S. (1997, October 5). Men were driven to "confess their sins": In survey, rally attendees also voice concerns about roles of women, politics. *The Washington Post*, pp. A1, A19.

Morrison, T. G., Morrison, M. A., & Hopkins, C. (2003). Striving for bodily perfection? An exploration of the drive for muscularity in Canadian men. *Psychology of Men and Masculinity, 4 (2)*, 111–120.

Moses, A. E., & Hawkins, R. O. (1982). *Counseling lesbian women and gay men: A life-issues approach*. St. Louis: Mosby.

Moses, S. (1991, March). Rape prevention 'must involve men'. *APA Monitor*, pp. 35–36.

Moses-Zirkes, S. (1993). Colo. psychologists involved in anti-gay amendment case. *APA Monitor*, *24 (8)*, 50.

Mosher, D. L., & Tomkins, S. S. (1988). Scripting the macho man: Hypermasculine socialization and enculturation. *Journal of Sex Research*, *25*, 60–84.

Mueller, F. O. & Cantu, R. C. (2005). National Center for Catastrophic Sports injury research data tables: Annual survey of catastrophic football injuries, 1977–2004. http://www.unc.edu/depts/nccsi/CataFootballData.htm.

Murray, B. (1995). Gender gap in math scores is closing. *APA Monitor*, *26 (11)*, 43.

Murray, B. (1998). Study says TV violence still seen as heroic, glamorous: Psychologists call on television executives to embed antiviolence messages in programming. *APA Monitor*, *29 (6)*, p. 16.

Myers, B. (1997). NOW promises "No surrender" to right-wing Promise Keepers. *National NOW Times, 29(4)*, pp. 1, 16.

Myers, D. G. (2005). *Social psychology*. Boston: McGraw-Hill.

Naifeh, S., & Smith, G. (1984). *Why can't men open up? Overcoming men's fear of intimacy*. New York: Clarkson N. Potter.

Nardi, P. M. (1992). Sex, friendship, and gender roles among gay men. In P. M. Nardi (Ed.), *Men's friendships* (pp. 173–185). Newbury Park, CA: Sage.

Nathan, S. (1981). Cross-cultural perspectives on penis envy. *Psychiatry, 44*, 39–44.

National Center for Health Statistics (2004). Health, United States 2004 with chartbook on trends in the health of Americans. Hyattsville, MD: Center for Disease Control.

National Gay and Lesbian Task Force (NGLTF) (1993). *NGLTF policy institute leadership council report*. Letter to members.

National Interfraternity Council (2005). Fraternity myths revealed. Fraternityinfo.com.

National Organization of Circumcision Information Resource Centers (NOCIRC) (1991). *Circumcision: Why? (brochure)*.

National Safety Council (1996). *Accident facts* (1996 ed.). Itasca, IL: self.

National Safety Council (1997). *Accident facts* (1997 ed.). Itasca, IL: self.

National Spinal Cord Injury Association (2005). More about spinal cord injury (fact sheet). www.spinalcord.org.

"Nearly all Women at Academies are Harassed, Study Says", (1994). *The Washington Post*, p. D3.

Nelson, J.B. (1985). Male sexuality and masculine spirituality. *Siecus Reports, 13*, 1–4.

Nelson, J.B. (1988). *The intimate connection: Male sexuality, masculine spirituality*. Philadelphia: Westminster.

Nelson, J.B. (1997). Male sexuality, masculine spirituality. Keynote address, 22nd Conference on Men and Masculinity, Collegeville, MN.

Nemiah, J. C., Fryberger, H., & Sifneos, P. E. (1976). Alexithymia: A view of the psychosomatic process. In O.W. Hill (Ed.), *Modern trends in psychosomatic medicine*, Vol. 3. London: Butterworths, 430–439.

Newfield, J. (2001, November 12). The shame of boxing. The Nation, pp. 13–22.

Niku, S. D., Stock, J. A., & Kaplan, G. W. (1995). Neonatal circumcision. *Common Problems in Pediatric Urology, 21*, 57–65.

Nolen-Hoeksema, S. (1998). Gender differences in coping with depression across the lifespan. *Depression, 3*, 81–90.

Nolen-Hoeksema, S., & Girgus, J. S. (1994). The emergence of gender differences in depression during adolescence. *Psychological Bulletin, 115*, 424–443.

NOMAS (National Organization for Men Against Sexism) (1992). Statement of principles. Published in conference schedule for "Coming Home to New Families: The 17th National Conference on Men and Masculinity". Chicago.

NOMAS (National Organization for Men Against Sexism) (2005). NOMAS Statement of Principles. www.nomas.org.

Notarius, C., and Johnson, J. (1982). Emotional expression in husbands and wives. *Journal of Marriage and the Family, 44*, 483–489.

"Notre Dame Stuns No. 9 Tennessee" (2004, November 7). *The Washington Post,* E14.

NPR (National Public Radio) (2005, February 9). Laura Bush: Putting boys into the spotlight. Radio interview.

Nyquist, L., Slivken, K., Spence, J. T., & Helmreich, R. L. (1985). Household responsibilities in middle-class couples: The contribution of demographic and personality variables. *Sex Roles, 12*, 15–34.

Ochberg, R. (1988). Ambition and impersonality in men's careers. *Men's Studies Review*, *1*, 10–13.

O'Donovan, D. (1988). Femiphobia: Unseen enemy of intellectual freedom. *Men's Studies Review*, *5*, 14–16.

O'Leary, K. D., Barling, J., Arias, I., Rosenbaum, A., Malone, J., & Tyree, A. (1989) Prevalence and stability of physical aggression between spouses: A longitudinal analysis. *Journal of Consulting and Clinical Psychology*, *57*, 263–268.

O'Leary, K. D., & Curley, A. D. (1986). Assertion and family violence: Correlates of spouse abuse. *Journal of Marital and Family Therapy*, *12*, 281–290.

O'Meara, J. D. (1989). Cross-sex friendship: Four basic challenges of an ignored relationship. *Sex Roles*, *21*, 525–543.

O'Neil, J.M. (1981a). Patterns of gender role conflict and strain: Sexism and fear of femininity in men's lives. *Personnel and Guidance Journal*, *60*, 203–210.

O'Neil, J.M. (1981b). Male sex role conflicts, sexism, and masculinity: Psychological implications for men, women, and the counseling psychologist. *Journal of Counseling Psychology*, *9*, 61–80.

O'Neil, J.M. (1982). Gender role conflict and strain in men's lives. In K. Solomon & N. Levy (Eds.), *Men in transition: Theory and therapy* (pp. 5–43). New York: Plenum.

O'Neil, J. M. (1990). Assessing men's gender role conflict. In D. Moore & F. Leafgren (Eds.), *Men in conflict* (pp. 23–38). Alexandria, VA: American Association for Counseling and Development.

O'Neil, J. M. (1996). The Gender Role Journey Workshop: Exploring sexism and gender role conflict in a coeducational setting. In M. P. Andronico (Ed.), *Men in groups: Insights, interventions, and psychoeducational work* (pp. 193–213). Washington, DC: American Psychological Association.

O'Neil, J.M., Egan, J., Owen, S.V., & Murry, V. M. (1993). The Gender Role Journey Measure: Scale development and psychometric evaluation. *Sex Roles*, *28*, 167–185.

O'Neil, J. M., Fishman, D. M., & Kinsella-Shaw, M. (1987). Dual-career couples transitions and normative dilemmas: A preliminary assessment model. *The Counseling Psychologist*, *15*, 50–96.

O'Neil, J.M., Helms, B.J., Gable, R.K., David, L., & Wrightsman,L.S. (1986). Gender-Role Conflict Scale: College men's fear of femininity. *Sex Roles*, *14*, 335–350.

O'Rand, A. M. (1987). Gender. In G. L. Maddox (Ed.), *The Encyclopedia of Aging* (p. 271). New York: Springer.

Orlofsky, J.L., Ramsden, M. W., & Cohen, R. S. (1982). Development of the revised Sex-Role Behavior Scale. *Journal of Personality Assessment*, *46*, 632–638.

O'Sullivan, C. S. (1991). Acquaintance gang rape on campus. In A. Parrot & l. Bechofer (Eds.), *Acquaintance rape: The hidden crime* (pp. 140–156). New York: Wiley.

Pagelow, M. D. (1984). *Family violence*. New York: Praeger.

Palkovitz, R. (1984). Parental attitudes and fathers' interactions with their 5–month old infants. *Developmental Psychology*, *20*, 1054–1060.

Palm, G. F. (1997). Promoting generative fathering through parent and family education. In A. J. Hawkins & D. C. Dollahite (Eds.), *Generative fathering: Beyond deficit perspectives* (pp. 167–182). Thousand Oaks, CA: Sage.

Pantony, K. L., & Caplan, P. J. (1991). Delusional dominating personality disorder: A modest proposal for identifying some consequences of rigid masculine socialization. *Canadian Psychology*, *32*, 120–135.

Parenti, C. (2001). Rehabilitating prison labor: The uses of imprisoned masculinity. In D. Sabo, T. A. Kupers, & W. London (Eds.). *Prison masculinities*. Philadelphia: Temple University Press.

Parke, R. D., & Tinsley, B. R. (1981). The father's role in infancy: Determinants of involvement in caregiving and play. In M. Lamb (Ed.), *The role of the father in child development* (2nd ed., pp. 429–457). New York: Wiley.

Parker, S., & De Vries, B. (1993). Patterns of friendship for women and men in same- and cross-sex relationships. *Journal of Social and Personal Relationships, 10,* 617–626.

Parnes, H. S., & Nestel, G. (1981). The retirement experience. In H. S. Parnes (Ed.), *Work and retirement* (pp. 155–197). Cambridge, MA: MIT Press.

Parrot, A. (1991). Recommendations for college policies and procedures to deal with acquaintance rape. In A. Parrot & L. Bechofer (Eds.), *Acquaintance rape: The hidden crime* (pp. 368–380). New York: Wiley.

Parrot, A., & Bechofer, L. (1991). *Acquaintance rape: The hidden crime.* New York: Wiley.

Parrot, A., Cummings, N., & Marchell, T. (1994). *Rape 101: Sexual assault prevention for college athletes.* Holmes Beach, FL: Learning Publications.

Pasick, R. S. (1990). Raised to work. In R. L. Meth & R. S. Pasick, *Men in therapy: The challenge of change* (pp. 35–53). New York: Guilford.

Pasick, R. S., Gordon, S., & Meth, R. L. (1990). Helping men understand themselves. In R. L. Meth & R. S. Pasick (Eds.), *Men in therapy: The challenge of change* (pp. 152–180). New York: Guilford.

Patrick, M. S., Colvin, J. R., Fulop, M., Calfas, K., & Lavato, C. (1997). Health risk behaviors among California college students. *Journal of American College Health, 45,* 265–272.

Patterson, G. R., Reid, J., & Dishion, T. (1992). *Antisocial boys.* Eugene, OR: Castalia.

Paul, W., Weinrich, J., Gonsiorek, J., & Hotvedt, M. (Eds.) (1982). *Homosexuality: Social, psychological, and biological issues.* Beverly Hills, CA: Sage.

Pennebaker, J. W. (1995). Emotion, disclosure, and health: An overview. In J. W. Pennebaker (Ed.), *Emotion, disclosure, and health.* Washington, DC: American Psychological Association.

Penwell, L. W. (1992). Personal communication.

Pepler, D. J., & Slaby, R. G. (1994). Theoretical and developmental perspectives on youth and violence. In L. D. Eron, J. H. Gentry, & P. Schlegel (Eds.), *Reason to hope: A psychosocial perspective on violence and youth* (pp. 27–58). Washington, DC: American Psychological Association.

Perry, D. G., & Bussey, K. (1979). The social learning theory of sex differences: Imitation is alive and well. *Journal of Personality and Social Psychology, 37,* 1699–1712.

Peskin, H. (1992). Shifts in uses of the past in the Intergenerational Longitudinal Studies. Paper presented at the Annual Meeting of the Gerontological Society of America, Washington, DC.

Petrie, R. (1986). Personal communication.

Pharr, S. (1997a, July 19). Our search for liberation in the time of the Right. Paper presented at the 22nd National Conference on Men and Masculinity, Collegeville, MN.

Pharr, S. (1997b). *Homophobia: A weapon of sexism.* (Expanded Edition). Little Rock, AR: Chardon.

Phi Mu Alpha (2005). Phi Mu Alpha Sinfonia, Iota Chapter. Iota.sinfonia.net.

Pinker, S. (1994). *The language instinct: How the mind creates language.* New York: Morrow.

Pleck, J. H. (1975). Masculinity-femininity: Current and alternative paradigms. *Sex Roles, 1,* 161–178.

Pleck, J. H. (1978). The work family role system. *Social Problems, 24,* 417–427.

Pleck, J. H. (1981a). *The myth of masculinity.* Cambridge, MA: MIT Press.

Pleck, J. H. (1981b, September). Prisoners of manliness. *Psychology today,* 24–27.

Pleck, J. H. (1987). The theory of male sex-role identity: Its rise and fall, 1936 to the present. In H. Brod (Ed.), *The making of masculinities: The new men's studies* (pp. 21–38). New York: Routledge.

Pleck, J.H. (1988), Letter to the Editor, *APA Monitor, 18*(11), 2.

Pleck, J. H. (1994, July). Men's studies institute award presentation speech. Paper presented at the 19th National Conference on Men and Masculinity, Providence, Rhode Island.

Pleck, J. H. (1995). The gender role strain paradigm: An update. In R. F. Levant & W. S. Pollack (Eds.), *A new psychology of men* (pp. 11–32). New York: Basic Books.

Pleck, J. H. (1997). Paternal involvement: Levels, sources, and consequences. In M. E. Lamb (Ed.), *The role of the father in child development* (3rd ed., pp. 66–103). New York: Wiley.

Pleck, E. H., & Pleck, J. H. (1997). Fatherhood ideals in the United States: Historical Dimensions. In M. E. Lamb (Ed.), *The role of the father in child development* (3rd ed., pp. 33–48). New York: Wiley.

Pleck, J. H., Sonenstein, F. L., & Ku, L. C. (1993). Masculinity ideology: Its impact on adolescent males' heterosexual relationships. *Journal of Social Issues, 49 (3)*, 11–29.

Plummer, D. C. (2001). The quest for modern manhood: Masculine stereotypes, peer culture, and the social significance of homophobia. *Journal of Adolescence, 24 (1)*, 15–23.

Polce-Lynch, M. (2002). *Boy talk: How you can help your son express his emotions*. Oakland, CA: New Harbinger.

Polce-Lynch, M.; Myers, B. J.; Kilmartin, C. T.; & Forssmann-Falk, R. (1998). The development of body image, emotional expression, and self-esteem: A qualitative analysis of gender and age patterns. *Sex Roles, 38*, 1025–1048.

Pollack, W. (1998). *Real boys: Rescuing our sons from the myths of boyhood*. New York: Random House.

Pollack, W. (2000). Sacrifice of Isaac: Identifying and preventing suicide in male youth. Symposium: Boys, men, depression, and suicide: Cutting-edge research and practice (J. Mahalik & M. Addis, chairs). Annual Convention of the American Psychological Association, Washington, DC.

Pollack, W. (2000b). Real boys' voices. Paper presented at the Annual Convention of the American Psychological Association, San Francisco, CA.

Pollack, W. S. & Levant, R. F. (Eds., 1998). *New psychotherapy for men*. New York: Wiley.

Pomerleau, A., Bolduc, D., Malcuit, G., & Cossette, L. (1990). Pink or blue: Environmental stereotypes in the first two years of life. *Sex Roles, 22*, 359–367.

Pope, H. G., Phillips, K. A. & Olivardia, R. (2000). *The Adonis complex: The secret crisis of male body obsession*. New York: Free Press.

Poppen, P. J. (1995). Gender and patterns of sexual risk taking in college students. *Sex Roles, 32*, 545–555.

Prior, P. M. (1999). *Gender and mental health*. New York: New York University Press.

Prosser-Gelwick, B., & Garni, K. F. (1988). Counseling and psychotherapy with college men. In R.J. May & M. Scher (Eds.), *Changing roles for men on campus* (pp. 67–77). San Francisco: Jossey-Bass.

Pryor, J. B. (1987). Sexual harassment proclivities in men. *Sex Roles, 17*, 269–290.

"Pulling the Trigger" (1998, April 4). *The Washington Post*, p. A18.

Rabinowitz, F. E. & Cochran, S. V. (2002). *Deepening psychotherapy with men*. Washington, DC: American Psychological Association.

Ramsey, L. R. (2005). Personal communication.

Raphael, R. (1988). *The men from the boys: Rites of passage in male America*. Lincoln, NB: University of Nebraska Press.

Rappaport, B. M. (1981). Helping men ask for help. *Public Welfare*, 22–27.

Rathus, S. A., Nevid, J. S., & Fichner-Rathus, L. (2005). *Human sexuality in a world of diversity* (6th ed.). Boston: Pearson.

Rauch, J. (2004, June 13). Virginia's new Jim Crow. *The Washington Post*, B7.

Raudenbush, B. & Zellner, D. A. (1997). Nobody's satisfied: Effects of abnormal eating behaviors and actual and perceived weight status on body image satisfaction in males and females. *Journal of Social and Clinical Psychology, 16*, 95–110.

Raymond, D. (1992). "In the best interests of the child": Thoughts on homophobia and parenting. In W. J. Blumenfeld (Ed.), *Homophobia: How we all pay the price* (pp. 114–130). Boston: Beacon Press.

Real, T. (1997). *I don't want to talk about it: Overcoming the secret legacy of male depression.* New York: Scribner.

Recer, J. (1995). Whose promise are they keeping? *National NOW Times, 27(5)*, p. 14.

Reid, B. (2002, October 29). A mouth guard for the brain? *The Washington Post*, F3.

Reid, H. M., & Fine, G. A. (1992). Self-disclosure in men's friendships. In P. M. Nardi (Ed.), *Men's friendships* (pp. 132–152). Newbury Park, CA: Sage.

Reisman, J. M. (1990). Intimacy in same-sex friendships. *Sex Roles, 23*, 65–82.

Renaissance Education Association (1987, October). Reasons for male-to-female crossdressing. Background paper no. 2.

Rich, J. A. & Ro, M. (2002). *A poor man's plight: Uncovering the disparity in men's health.* Battle Creek, MI: W. K. Kellogg Foundation.

Richardson, L. R. (1981). *The dynamics of sex and gender: A sociological perspective* (2nd ed.). Boston: Houghton-Mifflin.

Richardson, L. (1997). Gender stereotyping in the English language. In L Richardson, V. Taylor, & N. Whittier (Eds.), *Feminist frontiers* IV (pp. 115–122). Boston: McGraw-Hill.

Richardson, S. (1993). A violence in the blood: Five generations of aggressive men in a Dutch family have led researchers to a gene that seems to lie at the root of violence. *Discover, 14(10)*, 30–31.

Rime, B., Mesquita, B., Philippot, P., & Boca, S. (1991). Beyond the emotional event: Six studies on the social sharing of emotion. *Cognition and Emotion, 5*, 435–465.

Ring, T. E., & Kilmartin, C. T. (1991). Man to man about rape: A rape prevention program for men. *Journal of College Student Development, 33*, 82–84.

Ro, M. J., Casares, C., Treadwell, H. M., & Thomas, S. (2004). *A man's dilemma: Heathcare of men across America: A disparities report.* Atlanta, GA: The National Center for Primary Care at the Morehouse School of Medicine.

Roberts, T. (1991). Gender and the influence of evaluations on self-assessments in achievment settings. Psychological Bulletin, *109*, 297–308.

Robertson, J. M., & Fitzgerald, L. F. (1992). Overcoming the masculine mystique: Preferences for alternative forms of assistance among men who avoid counseling. *Journal of Counseling Psychology, 39*, 240–246.

Robinson, D. T., & Schwartz, J. P. (2004). Relationship between gender role conflict and attitudes toward women and African Americans. *Psychology of Men and Masculinity, 5 (1)*, 65–71.

Rochlen, A. B., Whilde, M. R., & Hoyer, W. D. (2005). The Real Men, Real Depression Campaign: Overview, theoretical implications, and research considerations. *Psychology of Men and Masculinity, 6 (3)*, 186–194).

Rochlin, C. (1982). The heterosexual questionnaire. *Changing Men, 13*, 1.

Rodin, J., & Ickovics, J. R. (1990). Women's health: Review and research agenda as we approach the 21st century. *American Psychologist, 45*, 1018–1034.

Rogers, C. R. (1957). The necessary and sufficient conditions of therapeutic personality change. *Journal of Consulting Psychology, 21*, 95–103.

Rogers, C. R. (1959). A theory of therapy, personality, and interpersonal relationships, as developed in the client-centered framework. In S. Koch (Ed.), *Psychology: A study of a science:*

Volume 3: Formulations of the person and the social context (pp. 184–256). New York: McGraw-Hill.

Rogers, C. R. (1961). *On becoming a person.* Boston: Houghton-Mifflin.

Rogers, C. R. (1980). *A way of being.* Boston: Houghton Mifflin.

Rose, R. M., Gordon, T. P., & Bernstein, I. S. (1972). Sexual and social influences on testosterone secretion in the rhesus. *Psychosomatic Medicine, 34,* 473.

Rosenblum, K. E. & Travis, T. C. (2003). Framework essay: experiencing difference. In K. E. Rosenblum, & T. C. Travis (Eds.), *The meaning of difference: American constructions of race, sex and gender, social class, and sexual orientation* (3rd ed., pp. 182–202). Boston: McGraw-Hill.

Rosenblum, L. A. (1987). The study of masculinity/femininity from a comparative developmental perspective. In J. M. Reinisch, L. A. Rosenblum, & S. A. Sanders (Eds.), *Masculinity/femininity: Basic perspectives.* New York: Oxford University Press.

Rosenstein, M., & Milazzo-Sayre, L.J. (1981). *Characteristics of admissions to selected mental health facilities, 1975: An annotated book of charts and tables.* Washington, DC: U.S. Government Printing Office.

Rosenstein, M. J., Steadman, H. J., McAskill, R. L., & Manderschied, R. W. (1987). *Characteristics of admissions to Veterans Administration medical center psychiatric inpatient services, United States, 1980* (Mental Health Statistical Note No. 184). Rockville, MD: Department of Health and Human Services.

Rosenthal, E. H., Heesacker, M., & Neimeyer, G. J. (1995). Changing the rape-supportive attitudes of traditional and nontraditional male and female college students. *Journal of Counseling Psychology, 42,* 171–177.

Rosin, H. (1998, August 15). Battle over homosexuality. *The Washington Post,* p. C9.

Rosin, H., & Edsall, T. B. (1998, July 15). Religious right targets homosexuality: Ad, fund-raising drive coordinated. *The Washington Post,* pp. A1, A13.

Ross, A., & Cokorinos, L. (1997). Promise Keepers: A real challenge from the right. *National NOW Times, 29(3),* 1, 6.

Rotter, J.B. (1954). *Social learning and clinical psychology.* Englewood Cliffs, NJ: Prentice-Hall.

Rotundo, E. A. (1993). *American manhood: Transformations in masculinity from the Revolution to the modern era.* New York: Basic Books.

Royner, S. (1992, February 4). What men won't tell. *Washington Post Health,* p. 10.

Ruble, T. L. (1983). Sex stereotypes: Issues of change in the 1970's. *Sex Roles, 9,* 397–402.

Rudman, L. A. & Glick, P. (2001). Prescriptive gender stereotypes and backlash toward agentic women. *Journal of Social Issues, 57 (4),* 743–762.

Russell, D., & Howell, N. (1983). The prevalence of rape in the United States revisited. *Signs, 8,* 688–695.

Russell, D. E. H. (1998). *Dangerous relationships: Pornography, misogyny, and rape.* Thousand Oaks, CA: Sage.

Russo, A. (1998). Feminists confront pornography's subordinating practices: Politics and strategies for change. In G. Dines, R. Jensen, & A. Russo, *Pornography: The production and consumption of inequality* (pp. 9–35). New York: Routledge.

Ruxton, S. (Ed., 2004). *Gender equality and men: Learning from practice.* Oxford, UK: Oxfam.

Rybarczyk, B. (1994). Diversity among American men: The impact of aging, ethnicity and race. In C. T. Kilmartin, *The masculine self.* New York: Macmillan.

Sabo, D. (1998). Masculinities and men's health: Moving toward post-Superman era prevention. In M. S. Kimmel and M. A. Messner (Eds.), *Men's lives* (4th ed., pp. 347–361). Needham Heights, MA: Allyn and Bacon.

Sabo, D. (2000). Men in prison. Paper presented at the annual conference of the American Men's Studies Association, Nashville, TN.

Sabo, D. (2005). The study of masculinities and men's health. In M. S. Kimmel, J. Hearn, & R. W. Connell (Eds.), *Handbook of studies on men and masculinities*. Thousand Oaks, CA: Sage.

Sabo, D., Kupers, T. A., & London, W. (Eds., 2001). *Prison masculinities*. Philadelphia: Temple University Press.

Sadker, D. (2000, July 31). Gender games. *The Washington Post*, A19.

Sadker, M., & Sadker, D. (1985). Sexism in the classroom of the '80s. *Psychology Today*, *3*, 54–57.

Sanchez, R. (1996, November 17). Men's studies coming of age in new campus rite of passage: Female attendance attests: It's not just a guy thing. *The Washington Post*, pp. A1, A11.

Sanday, P. R. (1981). The socio-cultural context of rape: A cross-cultural study. *Journal of Social Issues*, *37*, 5–27.

Sanday, P. R. (1990). *Fraternity gang rape: Sex, brotherhood, and privilege on campus*. New York: New York University Press.

Sanday, P. R. (1996). *A woman scorned: Acquaintance rape on trial*. New York: Doubleday.

Sanders, S. A., Reinisch, J. M., & McWhirter, D. P. (1990). Homosexuality/heterosexuality: An overview. In D. P. McWhirter, S. A. Sanders, & J. M. Reinisch (Eds.), *Homosexuality/heterosexuality: Concepts of sexual orientation*. New York: Oxford University Press.

Sandler, B. R. & Shoop, R. J. (1997). What is sexual harassment? In B. R. Sandler & R. J. Shoop (Eds.), *Sexual harassment on campus: A guide for administrators, faculty, and students*. New York: Allyn & Bacon.

Sapolsky, R. M. (1997). The trouble with testosterone: Will boys just be boys? In R. M. Sapolsky, *The trouble with testosterone and other essays on the biology of the human predicament* (pp. 147–159). New York: Touchstone.

Sattel, J. (1976). The inexpressive male: Tragedy or sexual politics? *Social Problems*, *23*, 469–477.

Sattel, J. (1998). Men, inexpressiveness, and power. In B. M. Clinchy & J. K. Norem (Eds.), *The gender and psychology reader* (pp. 498–504). New York: New York University Press.

Saurer, M. K., & Eisler, R. M. (1990). The role of masculine gender role stress in expressivity and social support network factors. *Sex Roles*, *23*, 261–271.

Scarce, M. (1997a). *Male on male rape: The hidden toll of stigma and shame*. New York: Plenum.

Scarce, M. (1997b). Same-sex rape of male college students. *Jounal of American College Health*, *45*, 171–173.

Schein, V. E. (2001). A global look at psychological barriers to women's progress in management. *Journal of Social Issues, 57 (4)*, 675–688.

Schneer, J. A., & Reitman, F. (1993). Effects of alternate family structures on managerial career paths. *Academy of Management Journal*, *36*, 830–843.

Schroder, M. & Shidlo, A. (2001). Ethical issues in sexual orientation conversion therapies: An empirical study of consumers. *Journal of Gay and Lesbian Psychotherapy, 5*, 133–168.

Schumm, W. R., Barnes, H. L., Bollman, S. R., Jurich, A. P., & Bregaighis, M. A. (1986). Self-disclosure and marital satisfaction revisited. *Family Relations*, *34*, 241–247.

Schwalbe, M. (1992, July). The mythopoetic men's movement and male-female relations. Paper presented at the 17th National Conference on Men and Masculinity, Chicago.

Schwalbe, M. (1998). Mythopoetic men's work as a search for *Communitas*. In M. S. Kimmel and M. A. Messner (Eds.), *Men's lives* (4th ed., pp. 565–577). Needham Heights, MA: Allyn and Bacon.

Schwartz, J. (1999, February 10). Study uncovers high rates of bedroom blues. *The Washington Post*, pp. A1, A9.

Schwartz, M. D., & DeKeseredy, W. S. (1997). Sexual assault on the college campus: The role of male peer support. Thousand Oaks, CA: Sage.

Schwartz, P. (1994). *Love between equals: How peer marriage really works*. New York: Free Press.

Sears, J. T., & Williams, W. L. (Eds.) (1997). *Overcoming heterosexism and homophobia: Strategies that work*. New York: Columbia University Press.

Seligman, M. E. P. (1990a, March). Attributional style and depression. Paper presented at the annual meeting of the Eastern Psychological Association, Philadelphia, PA.

Seligman, M. E. P. (1990b). *Learned optimism: How to change your mind and your life*. New York: Simon & Schuster.

The Sentencing Project (2004). Facts about prisons and prisoners. Available on line: http://www.sentencingproject.org/pdfs/1035.pdf.

Seppa, N. (1996). TV displays violence without the mess. *APA Monitor, 26(4)*, p. 8).

Serbin, L. A., Zelkowitz, P., Doyle, A., Gold, D., & Wheaton, B. (1990). The socialization of sex-differentiated skills and academic performance: A mediational model. *Sex Roles, 23*, 613–628.

Shabsigh, R., Fishman, I, & Scott, F. (1988). Evaluation of erectile impotence. *Urology, 32*, 83–90.

Shapiro, L. (2001, August 2). NFL's fluid situation: Over time, teams changed course on water. *The Washington Post*, D10.

Sharpe, M. J., & Heppner, P. P. (1991). Gender role, gender role conflict, and psychological well-being in men. *Journal of Counseling Psychology, 38*, 323–330.

Shea, C. (1995, January 13). Disengaged freshmen: Interest in politics among first-year students is at a 29–year low, survey finds. *The Chronicle of Higher Education, 41*, A29–A31.

Sheehy, G. (1976). *Passages*. New York: Dutton.

Sherif, C. W. (1982). Needed concepts in the study of gender identity. *Psychology of Women Quarterly, 6*, 375–398.

Shields, S. A. (2000). Thinking about gender, thinking about theory: Gender and the emotional experience. In A. H. Fischer (Ed.), *Gender and emotion: Social psychological perspectives*. Cambridge, UK: Cambridge University Press.

Siegel, J. M., & Kuykendall, D. H. (1990). Loss, widowhood, and psychological distress among the elderly. *Journal of Consulting and Clinical Psychology, 58*, 519–524.

Sifneos, P. E. (1972). *Short-term psychotherapy and emotional crisis*. Cambridge, MA: Harvard University Press.

Signorielli, N., & Lears, M. (1992). Children, television, and conceptions about chores: Attitudes and behaviors. *Sex Roles, 27*, 157–170.

Silverberg, R. A. (1986). *Psychotherapy for men: Transcending the masculine mystique*. Springfield, IL: Charles C. Thomas.

Simons, J. (1997, March 24). Improbable dreams. *U. S. News and World Report*, 46–57.

Skinner, B. F. (1974). *About behaviorism*. New York: Alfred A. Knopf.

Skovholt, T. M. (1990). Career themes in counseling and psychotherapy with men. In D. Moore & F. Leafgren (Eds.), *Men in conflict* (pp. 39–53). Alexandria, VA: American Association for Counseling and Development.

Skovholt, T. M., & Hansen, A. (1980). Men's development: A perspective and some themes. In T. M. Skovholt, P. Schauble, & R. David (Eds.), *Counseling men* (pp. 1–39). Monterey, CA: Brooks/Cole.

Slevin, P. (2005, July 26). Prison experts see opportunity for improvement. *The Washington Post*, A3.

Sluser, R., & Kaufman, Michael (1992, July). The White Ribbon Campaign: Mobilizing men to take action. Paper presented at the 17th National Conference on Men and Masculinity, Chicago, IL.

Smiler, A. P. (2004). Thirty years after the discovery of gender: Psychological concepts and measures of masculinity. *Sex Roles*, 50, 15–26.

Smith, D. (2003). Angry thoughts, at risk hearts. *Monitor on Psychology, 34 (3)*, 46–48.

Smith, K. (1971). Homophobia: A tentative personality profile. *Psychological Reports*, 29, 1091–1094.

Smith, L., & Mathews, J. (1997, December 7). In Va., a sobering lesson doesn't sink in: Binge drinking remains common on college campuses, despite recent tragedies. *The Washington Post*, pp. B1, B7.

Smolak, L., Murnen, S. K., & Thompson, J. K. (2005). Sociocultural influences and muscle building in adolescent boys. *Psychology of Men and Masculinity, 6 (4)*, 227–239.

Snell, Jr., W. E. (1989). Development and validation of the Masculine Behavior Scale: A measure of behaviors stereotypically attributed to males vs. females. *Sex Roles*, 21, 749–767.

Snow, M. E., Jacklin, C. N., & Maccoby, E. E. (1981). Birth- order differences in peer sociability at thirty-three months. *Child Development*, 52, 589–595.

Sodomylaws.org (2005). Sodomy laws around the world. http://www.sodomylaws.org/index.htm.

Solomon, K. (1982). The older man. In K. Solomon & N. B. Levy (Eds.), *Men in transition: Theory and therapy* (pp. 205–240). New York: Plenum.

Sommers, C. H. (2001). *The war against boys: How misguided feminism is harming our young men*. New York: Simon & Schuster.

South, S. J., & Spitze, G. (1994). Housework in marital and non-marital households. *American Sociological Review*, 59, 327–347.

Speer, J. (1990). Office politics and men's liberation. *Transitions, 10 (1)*, 18–19.

Spence, J. T., Helmreich, R. L., & Stapp, J. (1974). The Personal Attributes Questionnaire: A measure of sex role stereotypes and masculinity-femininity. *JSAS Catalog of Selected Documents in Psychology*, 4, 43 (MS no. 617).

Stangor, C., & Schaller, M. (1996). Stereotypes as individual and collective representations. In C. N. Macrae, C. Stangor, & M. Hewstone (Eds.), *Stereotypes and stereotyping* (pp. 3–37). New York: Guilford.

Stanistreet, D., Bambra, C., & Scott-Samuel, A. (2005). Is patriarchy the source of men's higher mortality? *Journal of Epidemiological Community Health, 59*, 873–876.

Stapely, J. C., & Haviland, J. M. (1989). Beyond depression: Gender differences in normal adolescents' emotional experiences. *Sex Roles*, 20, 295–308.

Starrels, M. E. (1994). Husbands' involvement in female gender-typed household chores. *Sex Roles*, 31, 473–491.

Stearns, P. N. (1990). *Be a man! Males in modern society*. New York: Holmes and Meier.

Stearns, P. N. (1991). Fatherhood in historical perspective: The role of social change. In F. W. Bozett & S. M. H. Hanson (Eds.), *Fatherhood and families in cultural context* (pp. 28–52). New York: Springer.

Stein, R. (2005, June 20). Report shows drop in baby boys. *The Washington Post*, p. A5.

Steinem, G. (1992). Foreword. In K. L. Hagan (Ed.), *Women respond to the men's movement* (pp. v-ix). San Francisco: Harper Collins.

Stepp, L. S. (1992, July 17). Anti-gay bias OK by Vatican. *The News Journal*, p. A2.

Stevens, M. (2005). *Scoring without consent: Rape prevention workshops for male college athletes*. Paper presented in symposium: Sexual assault prevention for men (C. Kilmartin, chair) at the annual convention of the American Psychological Association, Washington, DC.

Stevens, M., & Gebhardt, R. (1984). *Rape education for men: Curriculum guide*. Columbus, OH: Ohio State University.

Stevenson, M. R. (1991). Myth, reality, and father absence. *Men's Studies Review, 8(1)*, 3–8.

Stibbe, A. (2004). Health and the social construction of masculinity in Men's Health magazines. *Men and Masculinities, 7*, 31–51.

Stillion, J. M. (1995). Premature death among males. In D. Sabo & D. F. Gordon (Eds.), *Men's health and illness: Gender, power, and the body* (pp. 46–67). Thousand Oaks, CA: Sage.

Stillion, J. M., & McDowell, E. E. (1996). *Suicide across the life span* (2nd ed.). Washington, DC: Taylor and Francis.

Stillion, J. M., McDowell, E. E., & May, J. H. (1989). *Suicide across the life span: Premature exits*. New York: Hemisphere.

Stillson, R. W., O'Neil, J. M., & Owen, S. V. (1991). Predictors of adult men's gender-role conflict: Race, class, unemployment,age, instrumentality-expressiveness, and personal strain, *Journal of Counseling Psychology, 38*, 458–464.

Stock, W. E. (1997). Sex as commodity: Men and the sex industry. In R. F. Levant & G. R. Brooks (Eds.), *Men and sex* (pp. 100–132). New York: Wiley.

Stoddart, T., & Turiel, E. (1985). Children's concepts of cross-gender activities. *Child Development, 56*, 1241–1252.

Strate, L. (1992). Beer commercials: A manual on masculinity. In S. Craig (Ed.), *Men, masculinity, and the media* (pp. 78–92). Newbury Park, CA: Sage.

Straus, M. A. (1990). *Physical violence in American families: Risk factors and adaptations to violence in 8,145 families*. New Brunswick, NJ: Transaction.

Street, S., Kimmel, E. B., & Kromrey, J. D. (1995). Revisiting university student gender role perceptions. *Sex Roles, 33*, 183–201.

Storey, A. E., Walsh, C. J., Quinton, R. L., & Wynne-Edwards, K. E. (2000). Hormonal correlates of paternal responsiveness in new and expectant fathers. *Evolution and human behavior, 21 (2)*, 79–95.

Strong, B., DeVault, C., Sayad, B. W., & Yarber, W. L. (2005). *Human sexuality: Diversity in contemporary America* (5th ed.). Boston: McGraw-Hill.

Strong, S. R. (1986). Interpersonal influence theory and therapeutic interactions. In F.J. Dorn (Ed.), *Social influence processes in counseling and psychotherapy*. Springfield, IL: Thomas.

Sue, David, Sue, Derald, and Sue, S. (2005). *Essentials of Understanding abnormal behavior* (7th ed.) Boston: Houghton-Mifflin.

Sugarman, D. B., & Hotaling, G. T. (1989). Violent men in intimate relationships: An analysis of risk markers. *Journal of Applied Social Psychology, 19*, 1034–1048.

Swain, S. O. (1992). Men's friendships with women: Intimacy, sexual boundaries, and the informant role. In P. M. Nardi (Ed.), *Men's friendships* (pp. 153–171). Newbury Park, CA: Sage.

Swim, J., Borgida, E., Maruyama, G, & Myers, D. G. (1989). Joan McKay versus John McKay: Do gender stereotypes bias evaluations? *Psychological Bulletin, 105*, 409–429.

Swisher, K. L. (1995). Businesses should clearly define sexual harassment. In K. L. Swisher (Ed.), *What is sexual harassment?* (pp. 28–31). San Diego, CA: Greenhaven.

Symons, D. (1987). An evolutionary approach. In J. H. Geer & W. T. O'Donahue (Eds.), *Theories of human sexuality* (pp. 91–125). New York: Plenum.

Tangri, S., Burt, M. R., & Johnson, L. B. (1982). Sexual harassment at work: Three explanatory models. *Journal of Social Issues, 38*, 33–54.

Tannen, D. (1990). *You just don't understand: Women and men in conversation.* New York: Morrow.

Tavris, C. (1989). *Anger: The misunderstood emotion* (rev. ed.). New York: Touchstone.

Tavris, C. (1992). *The mismeasure of woman.* New York: Simon and Schuster.

Tavris, C., & Wade, C. (2001). Psychology in perspective (3rd ed.). Upper Saddle River, NJ: Prentice-Hall.

Taylor, G. J. (1984). Alexithymia: Concept, measurement, and implications for treatment. *American Journal of Psychiatry, 141,* 725–732.

Taylor, P. (1995, September 8). His home — the Capitol — was his castle. *The Washington Post,* pp. A1, A17.

Tennenbaum, H. R. & Leaper, C. (2002). Are parents' gender schemas related to their children's gender related cognitions? A meta-analysis. Developmental Psychology, 38 (4), 615–630.

Terman, L. M., & Miles, C. C. (1936). *Sex and personality: Studies in masculinity and femininity.* New York: McGraw-Hill.

Thompson, Jr., E. H. (1990). Courtship violence and the male role. *Men's Studies Review, 7(3),* 1; 4–13.

Thompson, Jr., E. H. (Ed.) (1994). *Older men's lives.* Newbury Park, CA: Sage.

Thompson, Jr., E. H., & Pleck, J. H. (1995). Masculinity ideologies: a review of research instrumentation on men and masculinities. In R. F. Levant & W. S. Pollack (Eds.), *A new psychology of men* (pp. 129–163). New York: Basic Books.

Thompson, T. (1998, August 2). ". . . And morally straight": Gay men v. the Boy Scouts. *The Washington Post Magazine,* pp. 6–26.

Thorndike, E. L. (1898). Animal intelligence: An experimental study of the associative processes in animals. *Psychological Review Monograph Supplement, 2* (Whole no. 8).

Thorne, B. (1993). *Gender play: Girls and boys in school.* New Brunswick, NJ: Rutgers University Press.

Thorne, B. (1995). Girls and boys together . . . but mostly apart: Gender arrangements in elementary schools. In M. S. Kimmel & M. A. Messner (Eds.), *Men's lives* (3rd ed., pp. 61–73). Boston: Allyn and Bacon.

Thornhill, R. & Palmer, C. T. (2000). *A natural history of rape: Biological bases of sexual coercion.* Cambridge, MA: MIT Press.

Tiger, L. (1969). *Men in groups.* New York: Random House.

Tillich, P. (1952). *The courage to be.* New Haven, CT: Yale University Press.

Timmers, M., Fischer, A., & Manstead, A. (1998). Gender differences in motives for regulating closeness. *Personality and Social Psychology Bulletin, 24,* 974–985.

Tobin, J. (1991, December 15). In modern politics, big boys really do cry. *The News Journal,* p. A2.

Toby, J. (1966). Violence and the masculine mystique: Some qualitative data. *Annals of the American Academy of Political and Social Science, 36,* 19–27.

Toch, H. (1992). *Violent men: An inquiry into the psychology of violence.* Washington, DC: American Psychological Association.

Toch, H. (1998). Hypermasculinity and prison violence. In L. H. Bowker (Ed.), *Masculinities and violence* (pp. 168–178). Thousand Oaks, CA: Sage.

Tolman, D. L., Spencer, R., Rosen-Reynoso, M., & Porsche, M. V. (2003). Sowing the seeds of violence in heterosexual relationships: Early adolescents narrate compulsory heterosexuality. Journal of Social Issues, 59, 159–178.

Trafford, A. (1996, February 20). Boxing's biggest risk. *Washington Post Health,* p. 14.

Tschann, J. (1988). Self-disclosure in adult friendship: Gender and marital status differences. *Journal of Social and Personal Relationships*, *5*, 65–81.

Tucker, N. (2003, July 26). Reform plan targets prison rape: Congress unanimously approves study, efforts to stop assaults. *The Washington Post*, A10.

"2001 Report on Violence Against Women Released" (2003, February 24). *The Washington Post*, A22.

Tyson, P. (1986). Male gender identity: Early developmental roots. *The Psychoanalytic Review*, *73*, 405–426.

Unger, R. K. (1979). Toward a redefinition of sex and gender. *American Psychologist*, *34*, 1085–1094.

United States Bureau of the Census (USBC) (2003), *Tables of income by detailed socioeconomic characteristics.*

United States Department of Justice (2004). Bureau of Justice Statistics Bulletin: Prison and jail inmates at midyear 2003.

United States Department of Justice (2003). Criminal victimization in the United States, 2002 statistical tables. http://www.ojp.usdoj.gov/bjs/pub/pdf/cvus0202.pdf

United States Department of Labor, Bureau of Labor Statistics (2005). Families with own children: Employment status of parents by age of youngest child and family type, 2003–04 annual averages. www.bls.gov.

United States General Accounting Office (2004). Defense of Marriage Act: Update to prior report [GAO-04–353R]. www.gao.gov.

USA Today (2005, November 29). Vatican publishes, defends gay priest document. usatoday.com/news/world/2005–11–29–vatican-priests_x.htm?csp=1

Vaillant, G. E. (1977). *Adaptation to life*. Boston: Little, Brown.

Valdés, L. F., Baron, A. Jr., & Ponce, F. Q. (1987). Counseling Hispanic men. In M. Scher, M. Stevens, G. Good, & G. A. Eichenfield (Eds.), *Handbook of counseling and psychotherapy with men* (pp. 203–217). Newbury Park, CA: Sage.

van Hertum, A. (1992, January 17). WHO removes homosexuality from its list of disorders. *The Washington Blade*, 23 (3), pp. 1, 12.

Vasta, R., Haith, M. M., & Miller, S. A. (1992). *Child psychology: The modern science*. New York: Wiley.

Virginians Allied Against Sexual Assault (VAASA) (1989). *Volunteer manual*. Richmond, VA: self-published.

Vobejda, B. (1994, January 21). Children's defense fund cites gun violence. *The Washington Post*, p. A3.

Vobejda, B. (1995, August 17). Survey finds familiar face on sex crime: Four out of five victims report they knew assailant. *The Washington Post*, p. A6.

Vobejda, B., & Perlstein, L. (1998, June 17). Girls close gender gap in ways welcome and worrying. *The Washington Post*, pp. A1, A9.

Wade, C., & Cirese, S. (1992). *Human Sexuality*. San Diego: Harcourt Brace Jovanovich.

Wade, J. C. & Brittan-Powell, C. (2001). Men's attitudes toward race and gender equity: The importance of masculinity ideology, gender-related traits, and reference group identity dependence. *Psychology of Men and Masculinity, 1*, 98–108.

Waite, L. J. (1995). Does marriage matter? Demography, *32*, 483–507.

Wagner, E. J. (1992). *Sexual harassment in the workplace: How to prevent, investigate, and resolve problems in your organization*. New York: AMACOM.

Waldron, I. (1976). Why do women live longer than men? *Journal of Human Stress*, *2*, 1–13.

Waldron, I. (1995). Contributions of changing gender differences in behavior and social roles to changing gender differences in mortality. In D. Sabo & D. F. Gordon (Eds.), *Men's health and illness: Gender, power, and the body* (pp. 22–45). Thousand Oaks, CA: Sage.

Walker, E., Bettes, B. A., Kain, E. L., & Harvey, P. (1985). Relationship of gender and marital status with symptomatology in psychotic patients. *Journal of Abnormal Psychology*, *94*, 42–50.

Walker, L. E. (1999). Psychology and domestic violence around the world. *American Psychologist*, *54*, 21–29.

Wallerstein, J. S., & Blakeslee, S. (1989). *Second chances: Men, women, and children a decade after divorce*. New York: Ticknor and Fields.

Walsh, M. R. (1987). Is pornography harmful to women? In M. R. Walsh (Ed.), *The psychology of women: Ongoing debates* (pp. 427–429). New Haven, CT: Yale University Press.

Watkins, S. (1997). *The black O: Racism and redemption in an American corporate empire.* Athens, GA: University of Georgia Press.

Way, N. & Stauber, H. (1996). Are "absent fathers" really absent? Urban adolescent girls speak out about their fathers. In B. J. R. Leadbeater & N. Way (Eds.), Urban girls: Resisting stereotypes, creating identities (pp. 132–148). New York: NYU Press.

Wechsler, H., Kuh, G., & Davenport, A. E. (1996). Fraternities, sororities, and binge drinking: Results from a national study of American colleges. *National Association of Student Personnel Administrators, 33*, 831–847.

Weinstein, M. D., Smith, M. D., & Wiesenthal, D. L. (1995). Masculinity and hockey violence. *Sex Roles, 33*, 831–847.

Weiss, R. (1997, July 22). Your personality may be killing you: Psychologists look at how social factors affect longevity. *Washington Post Health*, pp. 18–22.

Weiss, R. S. (1990). *Staying the course: The emotional and social lives of men who do well at work*. New York: Macmillan.

Wheeler, L. (1997, October 5). Unofficial estimates point to crowded day on the Mall. *The Washington Post*, p. A17.

White, H. R., & Huselid, R. F. (1997). Gender differences in alcohol use during adolescence. In R. W. Wilsnack & S. C. Wilsnack (Eds.), *Gender and alcohol: Individual and social perspectives* (pp. 176–198). New Brunswick, NJ: Rutgers Center of Alcohol Studies.

White, J. (2005, December 23). Air Force Academy shows improvement: Rigorous training credited for decrease in reported cases of sexual misconduct. *The Washington Post*, A2.

Whitely, B. E., & Kite, M. E. (1995). Sex differences in attitudes toward homosexuality: A comment on Oliver & Hyde (1993). *Psychological Bulletin, 117*, 146–154.

Whiting, B. (1965). Sex identity conflict and physical violence: A comparative study. In L. Nader (Ed.), *The ethnography of law* (pp.123–140). Menasha, WI: American Anthropological Association.

Whiting, B. B., & Edwards, C. P. (1988). *Children of different worlds: The formation of social behavior*. Cambridge, MA: Harvard University Press.

Wilkie, J. R. (1991). The decline in men's labor force participation and income and the changing structure of family economic support. *Journal of Marriage and the Family, 53*, 111–122.

Williams, C. L. (2001). The glass escalator: Hidden advantages for men in the "female" professions. In M. S. Kimmel and M. A. Messner (Eds.), *Men's lives* (5th ed.). Boston: Allyn and Bacon.

Williams, J. E., & Best, D. L. (1990). *Measuring sex stereotypes: A multination study*. Newbury Park, CA: Sage.

Williams, J. E., Nieto, J., Sanford, C. P., Couper, D. J., & Tyroler, H. A. (2002). The association between trait anger and incident stroke risk: The atherosclerosis risk in communities (ARIC) study. *Stroke, 33 (13)*, 13–20.

Williams, R. B., Jr., Baufort, J. C., & Shekelle, R. B. (1985). The health consequences of hostility. In M. Chesney & R. Rosenman (Eds.), *Anger and hostility in cardiovascular and behavioral disorders*. Washington, DC: Hemisphere.

Williams, R. J. & Ricciardelli, L. A. (1999). *Gender congruence in confirmatory and compensatory drinking. Journal of Psychology, 133*, 323–331.

Williams, W. L. (1992). The relationship between male-male friendship and male-female marriage. In P. M. Nardi (Ed.), *Men's friendships* (pp. 186–200). Newbury Park, CA: Sage.

Williams, W. L. (1996). The berdache tradition. In K. E. Rosenblum & T. C. Travis (Eds.), *The meaning of difference: American constructions of race, sex and gender, social class, and sexual orientation* (pp. 73–81). Boston: McGraw-Hill.

Williamson, T. (1985). A history of the men's movement. In F. Baumli (Ed.), *Men freeing men: Exploding the myth of the traditional male* (pp. 308–324). Jersey City, NJ: New Atlantis Press.

Wilson, E. O. (1975). *Sociobiology: The new synthesis*. Cambridge, MA: Harvard University Press.

Wilson, E. O. (1979). *On human nature*. New York: Bantam.

Wilson, M. H., Baker, S. P., Teret, S. P. & Garbarino, J (1991). *Saving children: A guide to injury prevention*. New York: Oxford University Press.

Wilson, W. J. (1987). *The truly disadvantaged*. Chicago, IL: University of Chicago Press.

Wilson-Schaef, A., & Fassel, D. (1988). *The addictive organization*. New York: Harper Religious Books.

Winawer, H., & Wetzel, N. A. (1996). German families. In M. McGoldrick, J. Giordano, & J. K. Pearce (Eds.), *Ethnicity and family therapy* (2nd ed., pp. 496–516). New York: Guilford.

Winstead, B. A., Derlega, V. J., & Wong, P. T. P. (1984). Effects of sex-role orientation on behavioral self-disclosure. *Journal of Research in Personality, 38*, 541–553.

Wisch, A. F., & Mahalik, J. R. (1999). Male therapists' clinical bias: Influence of client gender roles and therapist gender role conflict. *Journal of Counseling Psychology, 46*, 51–60.

Wise, T. N. (1994). Sertraline as a treatment for premature ejaculation. *Journal of Clinical Psychiatry, 55*, 417.

Wiswell, T. E., & Geschke, D. W. (1989). Risks from circumcision during the first month of life compared with those for uncircumcised boys. *Pediatrics, 83*, 1001–1005.

Wright, P. H., & Scanlon, M. B. (1991). Gender role orientations and friendship: Some attenuation, but gender differences abound. *Sex Roles, 24*, 551–566.

Youniss, J., & Haynie, D. L. (1992). Friendship in adolescence. *Developmental and Behavioral Pediatrics, 13*, 59–66.

Ziff, B. (1990). (Letter to Ann Landers). *The Washington Post*, p. D10.

Zilbergeld, B. (1992). *The new male sexuality*. New York: Bantam.

Zillmann, D., & Bryant, J. (1982). Pornography, sexual callousness, and the trivialization of rape. *Journal of Communication, 32*, 10–21.

Zuk, M. (2005). Animal models and gender. In C. B. Brettell and C. F. Sargent (Eds.), *Gender in cross-cultural perspective* (4th ed.). Upper Saddle River, NJ: Prentice-Hall.

Zuo, J. (1997). The effect of men's breadwinner status on their changing gender beliefs. *Sex Roles, 37*, 799–816.

Subject Index

Name Index